The Praeger Handbook
of Media Literacy

Credits

Advisory Board

Frank Baker
Renee Hobbs
Elizabeth Thoman
Kathleen Tyner

Contributing Editors

Project Manager: Lisa Marcus
Threads:
Media Literacy Organizations: Shirley Brinker
Notable National Media Literacy Figures: Alex Detrick
International Media Literacy Programs: Kit Jenkins and Kathleen Marie
    Straubinger
Media Literacy Resources: Debra Finkel and Caitlin Leahy
Editing: Angela Sherman
Entries: Kim William Gordon and Lisa Marcus
Research: Donald Miller, Devin Hurst, Andrew Smith, Jessica Bellomo,
    LeeAnn Tapscott, Robert Armbrister, and Patrick Hughes

The Praeger Handbook of Media Literacy

VOLUME 2

Art Silverblatt, Editor

 PRAEGER

AN IMPRINT OF ABC-CLIO, LLC
Santa Barbara, California • Denver, Colorado • Oxford, England

Copyright 2014 by ABC-CLIO, LLC

Library of Congress Cataloging-in-Publication Data

The Praeger handbook of media literacy / Art Silverblatt, editor.
     volumes cm
  Includes bibliographical references and index.
  ISBN 978-0-313-39281-8 (hardcopy : alk. paper) — ISBN 978-0-313-39282-5 (ebook)
1. Media literacy—United States.   2. Mass media in education—United States.   3. Media literacy.   I. Silverblatt, Art, editor of compilation.
  P96.M42U5846   2014
  302.23—dc23   2013022536

ISBN: 978-0-313-39281-8
EISBN: 978-0-313-39282-5

18 17 16 15 14   1 2 3 4 5

This book is also available on the World Wide Web as an eBook.
Visit www.abc-clio.com for details.

Praeger
An Imprint of ABC-CLIO, LLC

ABC-CLIO, LLC
130 Cremona Drive, P.O. Box 1911
Santa Barbara, California 93116-1911

This book is printed on acid-free paper ∞
Manufactured in the United States of America

Contents

VOLUME 2

THREAD 2

Monographs by Media Literacy Scholars

Thread 2 consists of a series of scholarly articles that expand on an aspect of a media literacy issue, concept, or approach presented in Thread 1 (Media Literacy Concepts, Approaches, and Education).

1. On the Genesis of Media Literacy in the United States, as Seen through the Lens of a Wisconsin Participant

Marieli Rowe

A Beginning

The National Telemedia Council (NTC) is the oldest ongoing national media literacy organization in the United States, having been formed in the mid-1930s in Madison, Wisconsin, and incorporated as a national membership organization in 1953. The NTC has its origins in a rich environment of inspired Wisconsin pioneers who forged what has come to be widely known as the *Wisconsin Idea*. Rooted in principles and goals that date back to the mid-1800s, the Wisconsin Idea proudly proclaimed that "the boundaries of the University should extend to the boundaries of the State," meaning that the university—and education—should serve all the people of the state and improve their lives beyond the university classroom. Add to this concept the pioneering development by university engineers of "9XM," the University of Wisconsin (UW) radio station and the Wisconsin State Radio Network known today as WHA/WERN (on the air continuously since 1916 and thus the "Oldest Station in the Nation"), and a new vehicle for the Wisconsin Idea was launched.

The Wisconsin Idea is alive and well today. With time, it grew beyond its original sights, inspired by visionaries and willing participants. Today, the borders of the university have expanded to the borders of the nation, the world, and beyond. That small campus radio station has seen the rise of what is today's digital world in cyberspace, spanning the globe and its many cultures. The two parallels and the potential for a symbiotic relationship and mutual support are today self-evident.

It is easy to imagine, in that dynamic environment of the early 1930s, the small group of young Madison women, all college graduates in the local chapter of the American Association of University Women (AAUW), interested in and concerned about the role of this new electronic box in their midst. The group's president was Mrs. Ralph McCanse, English teacher, wife of a UW professor, and daughter of a former president of the University of Missouri. Jessie Hill McCanse managed to juggle her life as a mother of two, faculty wife, and active educator by teaching English via the UW's Outreach Extension courses, an early version of what we today know as distance education. She led her AAUW group to respond to the concern about radio by establishing a "study committee" and appointed as its chair Dr. Leslie Spence.

Dr. Spence (or "Leslie" as she preferred to be called) had a PhD in English from UW and extensive experience. She taught high school English in Madison rather than on the college level at the university because . . . she was a woman. Her intellect, vision, and passion, however, empowered her to bypass the traditional academic road and create a major early effort toward qualitative evaluation, critical thought, active participation, study, and definition.

Leslie also sought out collaboration and advice from others, and by a fortunate coincidence found that her next-door neighbor was one of the pioneering leaders in the early years of public broadcasting. Harold B. McCarty, affectionately known as "H. B." or "Mac," was a major figure at the University of Wisconsin's radio station, WHA, since 1929 and its director from 1931 until his retirement in 1967; he was also a key leader in the development of the statewide FM radio network as well as the WHA-TV television station. He had directed both since their inception.

H. B. McCarty's influence was a succession of "firsts" in developing the statewide network reach, programming, people and involvement, and in searching for a philosophy of principles that underlie educational goals for communicators and educators; indeed, his ideas helped shape the philosophy of our council. Mac's and Leslie's conversations were a reciprocal process. He claimed that he gained as much as he offered. The AAUW study committee's choice not to set itself up as an authority on what's good and what's bad on the radio suited his vision as a broadcaster and educator. There were many discussions about principles for evaluation and the need to teach "how" to think rather than "what" to think. "I was seeking guiding principles also, for a course I taught on Classroom Use of Radio. I wanted to help teachers develop guidelines for the use of radio in schools."

Among the more visible, exciting outcomes was an on-air program, a first of its kind series, called *Broadcast on Broadcasts* that began about 1941. Hosted by Leslie Spence at first and later by Jessie McCanse, the weekly program used interviews and discussed promising programs, reports, and research—"how-to" guides on evaluating and participating, generating interest, media awareness, and new knowledge. Guided by our ongoing philosophy of a nonjudgmental, although aware, positive, and deeply reflective approach, the popular program continued for more than a quarter of a century.

The Early Years of the 1930s and 1940s

Leslie's AAUW Radio committee worked diligently to better understand how to utilize the new medium, seek out its best potential, figure out how to evaluate programs, and publicize these ideas. The committee met regularly to discuss, evaluate, and recommend radio programs of interest, which were published in a weekly column of the local newspaper. Also, as early as 1935, the group published a monthly brochure, *Good Listening*, that listed these programs but soon began adding additional comments. Here's one—"Let's Know Our Commentators" in the November 1942 brochure:

> H.V. Kaltenborn spent his boyhood in Merrill, Wisconsin; distinguished himself at Harvard in writing and speaking; traveled extensively. He learned several European languages. He met important people among them Hitler, Mussolini, and Chamberlain. He was broadcasting as early as 1923. During the critical days of Munich, he gave 85 broadcasts in 18 days, sleeping in the studio between times. (Kaltenborn 1942)

The *Good Listening* brochures also tell us more. Their logo heading contained the title "Radio, Everyone's Responsibility, A Monthly List of Some Good Radio Programs, prepared by American Association of University Women." And "Recommended by (a new coalition gathered together) the Wisconsin Joint Committee for Better Radio Listening" (*Better Broadcasts News,* 1983 Nov/Dec).

Word spread rapidly, and as a variety of other local organizations came to join in to form *Good Listening* study committees, the group graduated from a "committee" of the Madison AAUW, to the "Wisconsin Joint Committee for Better Radio Listening," and then to the "Wisconsin Association for Better Radio Listening." The list included both local and statewide chapters of organizations such as Women's Clubs, PTAs, business and professional women groups, church groups, and the American Legion Auxiliary. By the early 1950s, it had become the Wisconsin Association for Better Radio and Television, a statewide organization. Television had come upon the scene, and people soon turned their major attention to the newest medium.

These early years were a period of rich growth. Visionary broadcasters set the bar high with such innovations as President FDR's "Fireside Chats," legendary news journalists of those tumultuous times that included World War II, the amazing experience of Arturo Toscanini conducting a Symphony Orchestra sponsored by NBC, or the Metropolitan Opera Live on Saturday afternoons—still alive and well today in its 80th year. Meanwhile, back in Wisconsin, word spread about the new Wisconsin Association for Better Radio and Television. A visible structure began to emerge. The group scheduled regular, well-attended "Institutes" for the exchange of their teaching experiences; made *Good Listening* available to teachers, students, and parents; evolved the annual "Look Listen" project; and began producing publications. The early years produced big ideas and pioneering activities garnered from across the land.

In a decade that was marked by economic recovery from the Great Depression followed by the devastation of World War II, the emergence of radio and later television played a growing role. Although war shortages temporarily curtailed some printing activities such as the newspaper columns, the Wisconsin group never stopped its work. Indeed, one could consider that the war years, 1941 to 1945, provided a theater in which the quality of journalism via the "new medium" was tested and demonstrated front and center, producing some of the legendary voices of that time.

Not surprisingly, we find in those years a remarkably rich intellectual interest led by visionaries such as McLuhan in Canada, the BBC and others in England, and in the United States a diverse coming together from among academics, pioneering teachers in the field, communications innovators in public and commercial broadcasting, federal government, and inspired, educated citizens. As the leader and first president of the Wisconsin group, itself guided by teachers of English, literacy, and habits of deeper thinking, Leslie Spence sought out and ignited the interest and participation of these pioneers. The ideas of Louis Forsdale at Columbia Teachers College, Keith Tyler and Edgar Dale at Ohio State University, and H. B. McCarty in Madison, among others, can be seen in the Wisconsin brochures and early newsletters. They contributed to the discourse on policy, pedagogy, and philosophy. They participated as conference speakers, chaired key committees, and served as board members.

It is interesting to note a 1942 report titled "Criteria for Children's Radio Programs" (Rowland, Tyler, & Woelfel, 1942). The 42-page booklet was published by the Federal Radio Education Committee, a diversified body comprising national leaders that represented commercial, educational, and government agencies: the U.S. Commissioner of Education; the National Education Association; the Columbia Broadcasting System (CBS); National Broadcasting Company (NBC); a college president; the National Association of Broadcasters (NAB); and the National Association of Educational Broadcasters (NAEB), represented by H. B. McCarty. Among the three authors of the report was Professor Keith Tyler of Ohio State University and future board member of the Madison-born organization.

Following up on this early publication, there appeared a progression of postwar pamphlets, edited, coordinated, and authored by Leslie Spence in her role as chair of the Committee on Education. All were published by Wisconsin's Joint Committee for Better Radio Listening, and it successors:

- By 1946, along with its monthly *Good Listening* notes, the group had published *Radio Listening*, a 66-page "Aid to Evaluating Radio Programs" (Spence, 1946).
- *Can Radio Listening Be Taught?* (Spence, 1950) is a series of first-person teacher accounts on how they taught students to listen effectively to radio.
- *Let's Learn to Look and Listen* and *Enjoying Radio and Television* (Spence, 1952a, 1952b) added the television dimension and the subtitles "Radio-TV, Everyone's Responsibility" and "Better Listening-Better World."

These brochures are a joy to read. They offer a firsthand record of the amazing pioneering Wisconsin teachers who developed courses on radio listening. The depth of evaluative skills explored by these teachers went well beyond mere content analysis often attributed to the "early days" of media awareness and education.

1953, a National Organization Is Born—The American Council for Better Broadcasts

"On June 24, 1953, in Minneapolis, the American Council for Better Broadcasts [ACBB] was formed. Representatives from 18 national organizations, 18 state groups and many local organizations attended the formative meetings. Delegates were from 93 cities in 34 states"; so announces the first issue of the new ACBB newsletter, *Better Broadcasts News*, in October 1953 (Spence, 1953). ACBB was launched as "a non-profit, coordinating organization to correlate the efforts of scattered groups and individuals for better radio-TV programming."

The move was a landmark event. Earlier attempts to form a national organization of people and groups concerned about the new media of radio and television had failed because of basic differences over negative versus positive philosophies and over often heated debates about the value of media education versus media reform and media effects. As had been its founding approach, the new ACBB chose education, a positive philosophy, and a constructive, nonjudgmental agenda. The ACBB's goal was to be dedicated to working toward an American culture of excellence through education, observation, evaluation, and active participation.

The new organization quickly set out to build its structure:

- It would maintain its founding base and headquarters in Madison, supported by the Wisconsin group, now renamed the Wisconsin Association of the American Council for Better Broadcasts.
- The Board of Directors would extend across the country to include the pioneering educators, university scholars, community leaders, collaborating organization representatives and volunteers nationwide—but significantly, not members of the broadcast industry. (Although it was to welcome and work positively with broadcast professionals, they would not be in policy-making roles.)
- In all its endeavors, the ACBB would strive to maintain enduring philosophy and policy, the basic principles of which could stand the test of time, could do so while embracing innovation, and yet could remain truthful in the changing ecology of our 21st century human culture.
- The agenda for carrying out the mission of the ACBB would include the following:
  1. **An annual national ACBB project** that would involve everyone and would clearly identify the organizations purpose. The Look-Listen Opinion Poll was to be this project, a qualitative evaluation of programs that could serve teachers, families, community groups, and collaborating organizations. As the first qualitative versus quantitative poll, Look-Listen was a highly effective participatory project that reached across the nation and in its best years included more than 10,000 participants in 32 states, ranging from schoolchildren to seniors, from parent–teacher groups to university students and faculty—and any others who wanted to contribute their critical thinking skills to the voice of the project.

     For many teachers, it started a habit of teaching media literacy skills across the curriculum. The annual Look-Listen Opinion Poll continued for nearly four decades (1953–1991). As new technologies dramatically changed and fractionated the viewing experience, they changed and proliferated the tools for addressing it.

  2. **The annual conferences of ACBB,** building on the earlier practice of the Wisconsin Institutes, were convened each year, at first under the wing of the Institute for Education by Radio and Television (IERT) later the National Association of Educational Broadcasters (NAEB) beginning in Columbus, Ohio, later in other cities where ACBB's groups served as hosts. The conferences bore titles that focused on media education topics: "Teaching Evaluation of Radio-TV" and

"Expectations from the Classroom-Some Criteria." In 1979 in Chicago, "Toward a Media Wise Society" featured FCC commissioner Abbott Washburn, NBC president Robert Mulholland, and former Apollo Mission astronaut and then U.S. senator, Harrison Schmitt. The landmark 1981 conference in Washington, DC, titled "Telecommunications in Our Everyday Lives: Kids-to-Kids Meet across Space" was another first as children from our Sun Prairie, Wisconsin KIDS-4 Children's cable channel conducted a live, hands-on, hour-long exchange via satellite with a Brisbane, Australia, group of children. The demonstration was covered in the United States by the brand-new cable channel C-SPAN. And a surprised, young Ted Turner accepted ACBB's special recognition award for his pioneering idea and newly launched All-News, Cable-News network, CNN.

3. **A regular newsletter,** beginning with the first issue, October 1953, which announced the formation of the new organization, ACBB. In *Better Broadcast News* (published five times a year as a small four-page publication to the membership and available at a $1.00 annual subscription), editor Leslie Spence gathered both reports and results from ACBB's active participants, began the regular "Teacher Idea Exchange" column, and provided information about upcoming programs, events, the media, and contributions from the scholars and pioneers in the media literacy movement. Among these, in an early 1955 issue, is a call for "helping our students gain necessary multimedia literacy." Was its author, Professor Louis Forsdale, the first to use the term *media literacy*?

Through the decades, from the growth of television's early broadcasting days to the advent of cable and satellite communications, the excitement of new ways for the public were on the horizon. While laying a growing foundation with its established activities, the ACBB and its collaborative groups pushed ahead full steam in inventing and innovating: in Cleveland, they sponsored "lunch with a broadcaster" events; in Louisiana, they started a vibrant new ACBB state chapter guided by Louisiana State University English professor Dr. Clinton Bradford and developed strong classroom practices in teaching evaluation through the Look-Listen project; from Columbus, Ohio, Freda Koch took the helm as president of ACBB, started a chapter, and made it her mission to "spread the word, far and wide." In Wisconsin, the state group and ACBB had separate agendas but worked to mutually support each other. In the early 1960s, in response to the need for quality children's programming, the local Madison group organized yearly children's film festivals complete with evaluators young and old. When the promise of cable TV awakened ideas of what the new technology could do for children, the Sun Prairie KIDS-4 Children's cable channel, "TV by and for Kids" was born, dreamed up, supported and launched under ACBB's wing. Unique in the country at the time, it was still going strong in 2011 and is a community treasure.

Meanwhile, wearing her ACBB hat, Jessie McCanse carried on the pioneering weekly radio program, "Broadcast on Broadcasts," whose listeners spanned the state and beyond—the Wisconsin Idea in action! Leslie Spence, in addition to masterminding the affairs of the new national organization from her small one-room apartment in the historic center of downtown Madison, relentlessly pursued her mission to extend the borders of ACBB's purpose again. With her background as an English teacher, she sought to carry the message to her colleagues, especially to the National Council of Teachers of English (NCTE). The NCTE, steeped in the long tradition of championing print, appeared unimpressed. With diplomacy and understanding, she forged the important bonds that led to an NCTE media education policy statement and reciprocal membership in the 1970s and beyond. The indefatigable Dr. Spence approached people and resources where she saw an opportunity: FCC commissioners Kenneth Cox and Abbott Washburn responded with esteem and support for her and ACBB's work; they spoke at our conferences, included the topic of critical viewing skills in FCC inquiries, and contributed their best advice.

Another unique glimpse into who Leslie Spence was took place in the summer of 1955 as the organization was just two years old. She set out, driving by herself on a two-month-long journey crisscrossing the United States, making connections to promote her media education mission. We know all of this from her meticulously kept notebook recording the names of the people she met with, along with places, dates, and notes—some 52 years ago.

These are but brief, selected snapshots of a few of the many activities undertaken by this passionate group of individuals during the initial decades of the national organization. ACBB's years leading to the 1980s were rich in building a groundwork of awareness, guidelines, and experience, channeling the "concern about media" toward a mindful response through education. What the story does not dwell on is the struggle to be heard and to bring about the positive educational change. The latter decades leading into the 21st century were a difficult time in the United States in which the voices for media literacy were often drowned out by louder, more popular calls for dramatic methods and were more likely to be "voices in the wilderness" as a divided society and the American infrastructure of education itself struggled with finding and redefining its role in the new media world. Nevertheless, they were also important debates, for they forced us to examine the rigor of our projects and the authenticity of the basic concepts. The pioneers in academic studies from Great Britain, Canada, and other places helped us.

In this period of monumental change, new advances in technology rapidly outpaced the society they promised to serve. Along with hope and excitement came struggle, misunderstandings, and confusion about the deeper nature of these changes, the role of media in society, and in particular, how to best serve our children. For ACBB, this meant a redoubled effort to clarify and advocate the teaching of media literacy skills, to embrace the new technologies as opportunities for education and also for ourselves and our organization.

1983, the Evolution Continues—Another New Name

As we explored new ground with such initiatives as the KIDS-4 Children's cable channel, the international satellite interconnect, the new desktop computer in our office, the spectre of 100-channel TV sets, and other future "telemedia," the time had come to recognize that our very name was now obsolete. At the 30th Annual Conference, November 20, 1983, with Wisconsin's governor Lee Sherman Dreyfus giving the keynote address, ACBB acquired a new name to reflect this monumental shift. We became The National Telemedia Council: Look-Listen-Learn-Respond. Governor Dreyfus's (1983) message is worth noting:

> As you change your name today to the National Telemedia Council, I tell you, you are on the verge of changing an entire organization to adapt to the "chip."

And he predicted,

> The last thirty years of explosive telecommunications growth may have been a "garden hose" compared to the potential Niagara Falls of the next thirty years' telecommunications. The public's defense against inundation rests in the citadel of the individual mind, in education, and in selective attention to the media. (Dreyfus, 1983)

Working now on a truly new platform of innovation in fresh territory, the NTC leadership once again relied on the tenets of the Wisconsin Idea and searched for its role in the new millennium. It would not be in isolation; it would embrace innovation; it would enter a world with an entirely different vocabulary and a vision that, although still "working toward a media-wise global society," would do so within an entirely new "ecology."

To this end, we would streamline our vision, shedding projects we could no longer support, and remain focused and flexible for those to be undertaken. So the big annual Look-Listen project ended in 1991; the Sponsor-Recognition Awards that honored major examples of excellence were phased out. Instead, inspired by Lee Dreyfus's colorful eloquence, we reemphasized NTC's mission to focus on that "citadel of the individual mind" for the journey into the 21st century.

The name change was more than symbolic. It moved us into the Age of Cyberspace and digital technologies. We turned up our focus on those visionary, pioneering teachers who, with little (or no) access to sophisticated new teaching aids or institutional support—indeed often opposition—were turning otherwise discouraged students into passionate learners—all through "active, learning-by-doing," relevant media literacy activities.

An example of these came from long-time Madison high school teacher Mary Moen who annually contacted the ACBB/NTC office for her classes to participate in the Look-Listen Evaluation Project, relevant because "it was real, not just a classroom exercise." She combined the evaluation skills of the Look-Listen Project with actual public service production experience using simple audio equipment and tape recordings. These were made real and relevant through in-class interaction with willing, visiting local broadcast professionals who chose to air the best on their local stations.

Mary was an outstanding example and a role model for these innovative teachers who discovered and created such essential experiences in media education. To recognize and honor the passionate, often courageous pioneers in education reform, NTC established the Jessie Hill McCanse Award for Individual Contribution to Media Literacy, awarded to those whose contributions spanned a long time. Honored on her 90th birthday with the award in her name, Mrs. McCanse was herself one of these visionary teachers. The list of recipients to date is a distinguished testimonial to the groundbreaking work done by these pioneers. They recognized and understood that a paradigm shift has come to pass in what it means to be an educated person today and into the future. Included are British, Canadian, Swiss, and U.S. scholars and educators to whom we are deeply indebted for their insights and clarity of thought and for their generous efforts in sharing these important pedagogies with us. They helped build the academically valid and rigorous underpinnings for media literacy education in the United States; they responded enthusiastically and continue to this day, providing guidance and ideas, participating in conferences and workshops, and contributing important articles to our *Journal of Media Literacy*

Over the past three decades, our journal has been a major goal of the National Telemedia Council. We deemed essential the growth of our publication (first renamed *Telemedium*, then *The Journal of Media Literacy*), to inform, enrich, and share, on a new level of excellence. Passed through the crucible of our editorial board's rigorous examination, each issue is focused on a chosen topic that is deemed worthy and valuable in opening new vistas, making important connections, and clarifying needed pedagogy. A few examples of past issues are the following:

- "Media Literacy and the Arts" (2003; *49/50* [1]): a 100-page issue edited by Dr. Martin Rayala, built a previously unrecognized and unsung bridge between media literacy and the arts.
- "Challenges and Opportunities: Integrating English Literacy into the English Classroom" (2006, *53* [2]): edited by NTC president Karen Ambrosh and Marieli Rowe, this issue builds a strong pedagogy for teaching media literacy in the English classroom.
- "Cultural Diversity: Issues of Diversity in Media Education" (2008, *55* [1–2]): edited by Dr. David Considine, this double-issue features articles regarding diversity in media education.

A few additional titles of note from the 57 years of the journal are "Video Game Culture: Seizing the Chance for Good Learning" (2005); "The New Literacy Renaissance: Media Convergence and the Collective Community" (2007); "School 2.0: Transforming 21st Century Education through New Media Literacies" (2009); and "School 2.0: A Global Perspective" (2010).

Our success has been made possible by the freely given contributions of inspiring and passionate authors and the outstanding editorial board that included these international visionaries in media, education, and literacy. *The Journal of Media Literacy* has today become a major contributor to the field. It reflects the philosophy of the organization that takes a positive, nonjudgmental approach to media literacy education as an essential life skill for the 21st century.

Also, through the 1980s, 1990s, and into the new millennium, the important annual conferences continued to center on aspects of media literacy education. They aimed to inspire, inform and, taking a cue from the old Wisconsin Idea, "to expand these horizons to the borders of" . . . anywhere in the world! They broadened insights into philosophies and pedagogies from visionaries that would move the hope for media literacy onto a whole new level of effective teaching and reaching. In more recent years, the NTC conferences have no longer been held on an annual basis but rather for specific reasons. They have become laboratories of innovation as well, such as the five-site international forum that spanned Seattle, Madison, Toronto, New York, and London on NTC's 50th anniversary, as well as several exciting events built on the idea of "media literacy cafés" that created informal interactive encounters with other worlds, other cultures, and new friends.

It is beyond the scope of this chapter to detail all that constitutes the more than 75-year history of the Wisconsin-born media literacy organization or to mention the many others across the nation that deserve recognition. Rather, this chapter is a snapshot, especially of the beginnings but also recent ways in which we have navigated our ship, "working toward a media wise society" in the tumultuous past decades—decades that have shaken up cultures, even long-entrenched governments, and certainly education.

Left out are many worthwhile parts of the story, including some that failed such as our attempted experiment with an early version of a "Media Literacy Clearinghouse" that was to be a computerized, searchable site, a living library housed in what we envisioned as a Madison-based physical, structured "Centre for Media Literacy." First proposed in 1978, it was too early and too ambitious for its time and our abilities, even though it was "created" as it was with the enthusiastic participation of the UW Journalism School researchers and experts. After a two-year effort, it simply fell through the cracks. (Interestingly, the problem was not strictly technical but also faltered in the validity of content evaluation.)

Left for another time as well is the extensive story of NTC's all-volunteer infrastructure, with the remarkable leaders who served on our board of directors and editorial board, visionaries all, who have forged the ongoing, forward-looking policy of embracing the future. Too numerous to name individually in this chapter, they came from varied professions—from business, the community; they were the parents, college professors, academic scholars, and the passionate teachers of the past three, and more, decades. It has been a privilege for me to take on the role of executive director and journal editor during this exciting era. They have been years of immense inspiration both from these visionary leaders and from the passionate youth. They have seen the changing face of the learning *process* in the Cyber Age. The opportunity to participate in this amazing voyage toward a new culture of global media literacy is a source of enduring, never-ending rewards.

Concluding Thoughts

Reflecting on the genesis of media literacy as seen from a Wisconsin perspective and those who began it all, little could they have known the extent to which media technology would make possible today's world of personal interactivity, social presence, the instant global impact of the smallest whisper, and new pedagogies that would revolutionize education. But they would not be surprised at

- the ongoing media pervasiveness;
- the graphic, indeed cataclysmic examples of the Internet changing the world; and
- the crucial role of media literacy as an indispensible and fundamental imperative for life.

In the New Media Age, the basic principles prevail although the "ecology" has changed. We are simply "writing" with yet another new pencil.

Since the earliest days of Better Radio Listening and the American Council for Better Broadcasts, the practice of evaluation, participation, respect for others' opinions, and mindful thinking have been the hallmarks that informed the genesis of our organization in setting its goal toward a media-literate society. The wishes fulfilled are many—a rich heritage on a sound foundation; an ongoing mission with passionate educators who continue the work; and the wisdom, willingness, and ability to adapt to change.

Of the many dreams yet to achieve, the most urgent, I am convinced, is a willingness to change a decades-old atmosphere of confrontation, politics, and competitive negativism to a culture of inclusiveness and collegiality, mutual respect, and collaboration devoid of personal agendas in which ideas and education in a new century can thrive.

As for achieving the goal of a multimedia-wise and reflective society, the quest goes on. Remembering always that learning to be literate in all media is a personal journey, the challenge is to be global in scope while remaining relevant at home; to expand the vision to tomorrow while remaining grounded today; to strive for a positive, nonjudgmental, and passionate spirit of listening to diverse voices of individuals and cultures; and to know that achieving the goal in a world that has become a global village is not static but involves living mindfully with change. NTC works toward this goal—it is still the Wisconsin Idea!

References

Better Broadcasts News. (1983, November/December). *30* (2), 1.

Dreyfus, L. S. (1983, November 20). *"Change": The Challenge for the Next 30 Years*. Address to the 30th Anniversary Conference of the American Council for Better Broadcasts. *Better Broadcasts News 30* (1).

Kaltenborn, H. V. (1942, November). "Let's Know Our Commentators." *Good Listening*. Madison: Wisconsin Joint Committee for Better Radio Listening.

Rowland, H., Tyler, I. K., & Woelfel, N. (1942). *Criteria for Children's Radio Programs*. Washington, DC: The Federal Radio Education Committee, U.S. Office of Education and Federal Security Agency.

Spence, L. (Ed.). (1946). *Radio Listening. An Aid to Evaluating Radio Programs*. Madison: Wisconsin Joint Committee for Better Radio Listening.

Spence, L. (Ed.). (ca. 1950). *Can Radio Listening Be Taught?* Madison: Wisconsin Association for Better Radio and Television.

Spence, L. (Ed.). (1952a). *Enjoying Radio and Television*. (rev. ed. of *Radio Listening*). Madison: Wisconsin Association for Better Radio and Television.

Spence, L. (Ed.). (1952b). *Let's Learn to Look and Listen*. (rev. ed. of *Let's Learn to Listen*). Madison: Wisconsin Association for Better Radio and Television.

Spence, L. (Ed.). (1953, October 1). "A Chance to Work for Better Radio-TV—ACBB Is Born." *Better Broadcasts Newsletter*, 1.

Young, P., & Koehl, M. J. (1983). "A Conversation with Harold B. McCarty—ACBB History Special." *Better Broadcasts News*. Supplement to Sept/Oct issue.

2. Digital Media Literacy: A Plan of Action

Renee Hobbs

Integrate digital and media literacy as critical elements for education at all levels through collaboration among federal, state and local education officials.

Recommendation 6, *Informing Communities: Sustaining Democracy in the Digital Age*

The Knight Commission Recommendation

Children and young people are growing up in a world with more choices for information and entertainment than at any point in human history. Most Americans now live in "constantly connected" homes with broadband Internet access, 500+ channels of TV, on-demand movies, and mobile phones offering on-screen interactive activities with the touch of a fingertip. Global media companies from Google to Viacom to News Corporation dominate the media landscape, despite the rapid growth of user-generated content. As entertainment and news aggregators replace editorial gatekeepers, people now have access to the widest variety of content—the good, the bad, and the ugly—in the history of the world.

But in addition to mass media and popular culture leisure activities, many people are discovering the pleasures of participating in digital media culture, being able to stay connected to friends and family, share photos, learn about virtually anything, and exercise their creativity by contributing user-generated content on topics from cooking to politics to health, science, relationships, the arts, and more. It used to be expensive and difficult to create and distribute videos and print publications, but now anyone can publish his or her ideas on a blog or upload a video to YouTube.

The rapid rate of change we are experiencing in the development of new communications technologies and the flow of information is likely to continue. Consequently, people need to engage actively in lifelong learning starting as early as preschool and running well into old age to use evolving tools and resources that can help them accomplish personal, social, cultural, and civic activities. At the same time, people are increasingly aware of the negative aspects of life in a media- and information-saturated society. Contemporary media culture includes ultraviolent and sexually explicit movies, pornography, gossip-mongering blogs, public relations masquerading as news, widespread sales promotion of unhealthy products, hate sites that promote prejudice, sexism, racism and terrorism, cyberbullying, cyberterrorism, and unethical online marketing practices. Stalking, online bullying, and cellphone harassment may affect physical and psychological safety. Intellectual property and reputation are also vitally important issues in a time when we are experiencing rapidly shifting notions of ownership, authorship, privacy, and social appropriateness.

Such ubiquitous and easy access to so many information and entertainment choices requires that people acquire new knowledge and skills in order to make wise and responsible decisions. For people to achieve the personal, professional, and social benefits of thriving in a digital age, these skills are not just optional or desirable—they are the essential elements of *digital citizenship*.

The Knight Commission's (2009) report, *Information Communities: Sustaining Democracy in the Digital Age*, recognized that people need news and information to take advantage of life's opportunities for themselves and their families. To be effective participants in contemporary society, people need to be engaged in the public life of the community, the nation, and the world. They need access to relevant and credible information that helps them make decisions. This necessarily involves strengthening the capacity of individuals to participate as both producers and consumers in public conversations about events and issues that matter. Media and digital literacy education is now fundamentally implicated in the practice of citizenship.

To address these needs of digital citizenship, the Knight Commission (2009) made three recommendations that directly address the issue of digital and media literacy education in the context of formal and informal public education sectors:

Recommendation 6: Integrate digital and media literacy as critical elements for education at all levels through collaboration among federal, state, and local education officials.

Recommendation 7: Fund and support public libraries and other community institutions as centers of digital and media training, especially for adults.

Recommendation 12: Engage young people in developing the digital information and communication capacities of local communities.

The Heritage of Digital and Media Literacy

When people think of the term *literacy*, what generally springs to mind is reading and writing, speaking, and listening. These are indeed foundational elements of literacy. But because today people use so many types of expression and communication in daily life, the concept of literacy is beginning to be defined as the ability to share meaning through symbol systems to fully participate in society. Similarly, the term *text* is beginning to be understood as any form of expression or communication in fixed and tangible form that uses symbol systems, including language, still and moving images, graphic design, sound, music, and interactivity.

New types of texts and new types of literacies have been emerging over a period of more than 50 years. Many closely interrelated terms describe the new set of competencies required for success in contemporary society. These include terms such as *information literacy*, *media literacy*, *media education*, *visual literacy*, *news literacy*, *health media literacy*, and *digital literacy*, among others. Each term is associated with a particular body of scholarship, practice, and intellectual heritage, with some ideas stretching back to the middle of the 20th century and other ideas emerging in the past couple of years. These terms reflect both the disciplinary backgrounds of the stakeholders and the wide scope of the knowledge and skills involved.

These concepts must not be treated as competitors. Referencing philosopher Ludwig Wittgenstein's concept of family resemblance, one scholar identifies the shared heritage among these new literacies and argues, "The boundaries between the various members of this family overlap, but they should be seen as a closely-knit family" (Horton, 2007: 15).

We can consider different types of literacy to be part of the same family. For example, information literacy has typically been associated with research skills. Media literacy typically has been associated with critical analysis of news, advertising, and mass media entertainment. Health media literacy has been associated with exploring media's impact on making positive choices related to nutrition, exercise, body image, violence, and substance abuse prevention. Digital literacy is associated with the ability to use computers, social media, and the Internet.

Although they reflect distinct and important theoretical ideas and values from different disciplinary traditions and historical contexts, effective programs in all of the "new media literacies" reveal many similarities. The recommendations in this report draw on the broad similarities that unite this work, which comes from many fields and disciplines including education, reading and literacy, public health, literature and the humanities, sociology, human development and psychology, cultural studies, library and information science, journalism, communication, and new media studies.

In this report, the term *digital and media literacy* is used to encompass the full range of cognitive, emotional, and social competencies that includes the use of texts, tools, and technologies; the skills of critical thinking and analysis; the practice of message composition and creativity; the ability to engage in reflection and ethical thinking; as well as active participation through teamwork and collaboration. When people have digital and media literacy competencies, they recognize personal, corporate, and political agendas and are empowered to speak out on behalf of the missing voices and omitted perspectives in our communities. By identifying and attempting to solve problems, people use their powerful voices and their rights under the law to improve the world around them.

For all aspects of daily life, people today need a constellation of well-developed communication and problem-solving skills that include five competencies. These five competencies work together in a spiral of empowerment, supporting people's active participation in lifelong learning through the processes of both consuming and creating messages. This approach is consistent with constructivist education, which, as Brazilian education scholar Paolo Freire described, adopts "a concept of women and men as conscious beings . . . and with the posing of the problems of human beings in their relations with the world" (1968, p. 51).

The five digital and media literacy competencies described in the next section represent a synthesis of the full complement of scholarship and thinking about "new literacies." These ideas have been acknowledged by major groups and professional associations including the International Reading Association (IRA), the National Council of Teachers of English (NCTE), and the National Council for Accreditation of Teacher Education (NCATE), just to name a few.

As the Common Core State Standards Initiative (2010) points out,

To be ready for college, workforce training, and life in a technological society, students need the ability to gather, comprehend, evaluate, synthesize, report on, and create a high volume and extensive range of print and nonprint texts in media forms old and new. The need to research and to consume and produce media is embedded into every element of today's curriculum.

Teacher education programs recognize the importance of preparing future teachers to be skilled in digital and media literacy. The Professional Standards for the Accreditation of Teacher Preparation Institutions states:

Teachers understand media's influence on culture and people's actions and communication; as a result, teachers use a variety of approaches for teaching students how to construct meaning from media and nonprint texts and how to compose and respond to film, video, graphic, photographic, audio, and multimedia texts. (NCATE Standards, 2007: 57)

The NCTE adopted a resolution encouraging "preservice, inservice, and staff development programs that will focus on new literacies, multimedia composition, and a broadened concept of literacy" (NCTE, 2003). The National Communication Association (NCA, 1998) states that media-literate communicators should be able to do the following:

- Understand how people use media in their personal and public lives
- Recognize the complex relationships among audiences and media content
- Appreciate that media content is produced within social and cultural contexts
- Understand the commercial nature of media
- Use media to communicate to specific audiences

But genuine educational change in K–12 and higher education does not come about simply by generating documents or developing written standards.

Essential Competencies of Digital and Media Literacy

1. **ACCESS.** Finding and using media and technology tools skillfully and sharing appropriate and relevant information with others
2. **ANALYZE & EVALUATE.** Comprehending messages and using critical thinking to analyze message quality, veracity, credibility, and point of view, while considering potential effects or consequences of messages
3. **CREATE.** Composing or generating content using creativity and confidence in self-expression, with awareness of purpose, audience, and composition techniques
4. **REFLECT.** Applying social responsibility and ethical principles to one's own identity and lived experience, communication behavior, and conduct

5. **ACT.** Working individually and collaboratively to share knowledge and solve problems in the family, the workplace, and the community, and participating as a member of a community at local, regional, national, and international levels helping teachers acquire the knowledge and skills they need to bring these practices to their students

What is needed now is a clear and compelling vision of the instructional practices that can best support the development of these new competencies among all Americans. In this chapter, a plan of concrete action is offered to help these practices to become standard in the context of home, school, and workplace.

Meeting the Needs of All

In a country with more than 300 million residents, there is no "one-size-fits-all" program. Many different types of programs will be necessary to help build a community education movement for digital and media literacy. Both formal and informal learning environments can support the development of people's digital and media literacy competencies. These skills can be developed in the home and through programs in K–12 schools, libraries, museums, summer and afterschool programs, local cable access centers, colleges and universities, and nonprofit organizations.

It is important to maximize effectiveness by developing community-based informal or formal learning programs that reach specific subgroups or targeted populations. For example, K–12 programs reach children and teens, university programs reach young adults, and libraries and cable access programs reach working and nonworking adults. But many groups of American citizens go without access to resources or programs that support digital and media literacy education. There are some underserved audiences that will benefit from special opportunities to develop digital and media literacy competencies.

Minority Children, Youth and Families. A recent report by the Kaiser Family Foundation showed that African American and Hispanic children aged 8 to 18 spent more than 12 hours daily in some form of mediated experience, which is nearly 2 hours more than white children (Kaiser Family Foundation, 2010). Meanwhile, all parents are faced with many decisions about parenting in a technology-saturated society, as children may watch videos in the car, play video games on cell phones as early as age 3, have their own cell phones by age 7 or 8, and create their own Facebook pages before reaching their teen years.

Special Education Students. Students enrolled in special education programs may be more vulnerable to media influence because of limitations in skills, including comprehension, inference making, and using social or environmental cues. They may not recognize the difference between informative and persuasive messages, for example, or may be quick to click on a link based on purely visual cues. Yet these young people also need the ability to use the media in all its forms, including new and emerging forms of technology that may be helpful in supporting their learning.

Juvenile Offenders. Young people who experience the juvenile justice system may be among the most vulnerable to negative messages in the media because of the lack of supportive adults and other resiliency factors. But when exposed to digital and media literacy education, they can receive valuable benefits from using the power of media and technology for reflection and expression, building self-esteem, advocacy, and critical thinking skills.

New Immigrants. These individuals are highly motivated to acquire the knowledge and skills they need to be successful in their new homeland. Many use communication devices and media to stay connected with family and their countries of origin. But they also may use media and technology as a "window on the world" to develop language skills and to understand American culture and values without appreciating the unique characteristics of the American commercial media system, which differs in fundamental ways from those of many other countries.

Senior Citizens. Older people are heavy consumers of television and may be particularly vulnerable to certain persuasive messages, (e.g., advertisements for prescription medicine, over-the-counter drugs, and nutritional supplements). Improving their digital and media literacy would not only help them better evaluate this information, it would also offer them the benefits of information sharing and the social connectedness available through social media. In the United Kingdom, the Silver Surfers Program provides one-on-one assistance for seniors who need support as they master basic computer skills, including using the mouse, keyboarding, and file management. SeniorNet has been doing the same in the United States since 1986.

Sadly, there are too few programs in the United States that help bring digital and media literacy to special education students, parents of young children, those in juvenile justice programs, new immigrants, people with disabilities, and senior citizens. To meet the needs of all the members of our communities, it will be important to support the development of customized, replicable and scalable digital and media literacy programs to reach these underserved groups. It is necessary to do so in the environments where learning already occurs.

Where Learning Occurs

Strategic partnerships between families, schools, nongovernmental organizations, and libraries can help build a community education movement for digital and media literacy education. Consider where learning occurs.

In the Home. Digital and media literacy competencies can be learned in the home, where most people watch television and movies, surf the Internet, listen to music, read newspapers and magazines, and play video games. With appropriate levels of parental engagement, many digital and media literacy competencies can be learned at home, provided parents have high levels of interest and motivation and the drive to gain knowledge and skills. Organizations such as Common Sense Media provide parents with tools to help them start conversations with their children about the responsibilities of media and technology use.

K–12 Education. Programs in elementary and secondary schools can help students develop access, analysis/evaluation, and creative competencies in relation to the academic subjects of math, language arts, social studies, science, and health education. For example, these programs may help children and teens use online databases to find information related to school subjects like science or health, create multimedia slide presentations, engage in group problem solving, or work collaboratively on a video project related to school subjects in history or literature.

Library Programs. Libraries provide the general public with access to computers and the Internet and may offer programs to help people use technology tools. One third of Americans age 14 and older (about 77 million people) accessed the Internet at a public library in the past year (Becker et al., 2010). Libraries generally offer one-on-one support to patrons, helping them find information on the Internet or demonstrating how to use e-mail and other software applications, library databases, or search engines. This is the most personalized and effective form of education. Librarians connect people to jobs, news, education, services, health information, friends, and family—as well as community engagement and civic participation. Librarians often model critical thinking skills in finding and evaluating information.

Youth Media Programs. Hundreds of small programs that serve teens provide them with opportunities to critically analyze and create multimedia messages using traditional and interactive media. These programs can help young people see themselves as active participants in their communities, helping to solve problems through the power of effective communication and social advocacy.

Local Access. In those communities where there is a cable public access system, members of the public can learn to use video and digital media and can create programs that reflect their special interests, issues, and hobbies. These programs help people use video cameras to collect and edit footage and produce an in-studio talk show, "how-to" program, or documentary.

Higher Education. Programs offered through colleges and universities may emphasize competencies that focus on critical analysis and advocacy. For example, these programs may involve groups of people analyzing local press coverage of a particular event or topic of local concern or creating a public information campaign about an important issue to increase community awareness.

Learning and Teaching: What Works

Today, educators use a variety of engaging texts, including those from mass media, popular culture, and digital media, to support the development of digital and media literacy competencies across K–12 and higher education. With support from creative teachers, students use books, movies, Web sites, newspapers, blogs, wikis, and games for learning. They also use instructional practices that enable students to take personal responsibility for their own learning.

Instructional Practices of Digital and Media Literacy Education

Record-keeping activities help people keep track of media choices and reflect on decisions about sharing and participation, deepening awareness of personal habits.

Finding, evaluating, and sharing content from a variety of sources helps people explore diverse sources of information. Using search strategies appropriate to one's needs helps people make discriminating choices about quality and relevance.

Active interpretation of texts helps people acquire new ideas, perspectives, and knowledge and make sense of them in relation to lived experience. Dialogue and sharing help deepen understanding and appreciation.

Careful examination of the constructed nature of particular texts encourages people to use critical questioning to examine the author's intent and issues of representation.

Comparing and contrasting two texts that address the same topic help people develop critical thinking skills. By examining genre, purpose, form and content, and point of view, people recognize how media shape message content.

Playful activities promote imagination, creativity, and decision-making skills, supporting people's reflective thinking about choices and consequences.

Message composition using a combination of language, images, sound, music, special effects, and interactivity provides real-world experience addressing a particular audience in a specific context to accomplish a stated goal. Teamwork, collaboration, and knowledge sharing enhance creativity and deepen respect for the diverse talents of individuals.

Keeping a media-use diary
Using information search and evaluation strategies
Reading, viewing, listening and discussing
Close analysis
Cross-media comparison
Gaming, simulation and role-playing
Multimedia composition

Notice that none of these instructional practices are dependent on using a particular set of texts, tools, or technologies. This is why digital and media literacy education can be applied to a variety of technologies and with entertaining, persuasive, and informational content. These instructional practices can be used across all grade levels and subject areas, including social studies, science, literature, health, mathematics, the arts, and the vocational and professional fields, in both formal and informal educational settings.

It is also important to recognize that many of these instructional practices are already standard in some fields of study. They do not necessarily require either expensive equipment or time-consuming hours of instruction to develop. They *do* require the presence of educators who have the skills and experience necessary to use these practices in productive ways to support genuine learning. In this report, we see teachers and learners (not technology) as the vital resources at the heart of the vision for how digital and media literacy competencies are best acquired.

The successful application of these instructional practices depends on creating a respectful learning environment where students' lived experience is valued and multiple points of view are encouraged. Digital and media literacy education activates independent thinking, authentic dialogue, collaboration, reflection, creativity, and social responsibility as applied to the practices of responding to, creating and sharing messages (NAMLE, 2007; Partnership for 21st Century Skills, 2010). Fortunately, this definition of digital and media literacy education resonates with diverse stakeholders in the education, media, technology, museum, nonprofit, social service, and library communities.

A comprehensive plan of action is needed to build a community education movement for digital and media literacy education. Many diverse stakeholders are already moving toward this goal. Groups like the Partnership for 21st Century Skills have done a commendable job in helping school leaders and policy makers understand the "big picture" scope of the challenge. The federal government, through the Commerce Department's National Telecommunications and Information Administration (NTIA) is providing $4 billion through the Broadband Technology Opportunities Program (BTOP), which will help bring broadband infrastructure to local communities along with supporting public computing centers and providing training opportunities. With support from the John D. and Catherine T. MacArthur Foundation, the Digital Youth Network and the YOUmedia program at the Chicago Public Library have enabled young people to collaborate and create using digital media. Still, much work is needed to make digital and media literacy a fundamental part of K–12, higher education, and lifelong learning, in and out of school.

Issues to Consider When Implementing Digital and Media Literacy Programs

In developing a plan of action, there are five challenges that educators and community leaders must consider in implementing programs in digital and media literacy: (a) moving beyond a tool-oriented focus that conflates having access to technology with the skillful use of it, (b) addressing risks associated with media and digital technology, (c) expanding the concept of literacy, (d) strengthening people's capacity to assess message credibility and quality, and (e) bringing news and current events into K–12 education.

Moving Beyond a Tool-Oriented Focus That Conflates Having Access to Media and Technology with the Skillful Use of It. Generally, neither children nor adults acquire critical thinking skills about mass media, popular culture, or digital media just by using technology tools themselves. Educators frequently complain about a generation of children who cannot distinguish between standard English grammar and spelling and the discourse of text messaging. Many teens lack the ability to identify appropriate key words for an online search activity, and many young adults cannot identify the author of a Web page. These same children and young people often are convinced they are expert researchers because they can find information "on Google." However, some of these same youth produce and upload their own dance videos for their favorite songs, collaborate to solve problems in video games, use mobile phones to show up for impromptu local events, and make their own fictional newspapers about their favorite fantasy-novel characters.

The larger concern is whether people will be able to transfer their self-developed digital skills beyond their affinity groups, fan communities, or local social cliques. Although young people are using digital media, we should not assume they are digitally literate in the sense that we are discussing it here (Vaidhyanathan, 2008). People who play Farmville on Facebook may (or may not) have the skills they need to search for information about jobs, education, and health care. For young people today, it is vital that formal education begin to offer a bridge from the often insular and entertainment-focused digital culture of the home to a wider, broader range of cultural and civic experiences that support their intellectual, cultural, social, and emotional development.

In many schools, despite significant investment in technology, teachers are not making effective use of the engaging instructional practices of digital and media literacy. The reasons for this vary. Some teachers do not know how to use technology tools. Some mistake the mere transfer of classroom materials from paper to a computer screen as effective use. Others do not have the time to spare on media production projects because they are busy preparing children for high-stakes testing.

One thing is certain: Simply buying computers for schools does not necessarily lead to digital and media literacy education. Schools have a long way to go on this front. Access to broadband is a substantial issue as diffusion is uneven across American cities and towns (Levin, 2010). Mandatory Internet filtering in schools means that many important types of social media are not available to teachers or students. And although there are computers with Internet access in most classrooms, fewer than half of American teachers can display a Web site because they do not have a data projector available to them. When computers are used, most American students use them to prepare written documents, drill-and-practice on basic skills, or to make PowerPoint presentations (U.S. Department of Education).

Sadly, some people equate the amount of money that school districts spend on technology or the numbers of students enrolled in online learning programs as a proxy for digital and media literacy education. Some of the hype surrounding "digital natives" and the transformative potential of technology in education is promoted uncritically by fans of social media or subsidized by those who stand to benefit from selling data systems, interactive whiteboards, games, or cell phones.

Many American parents mistakenly believe that simply providing children and young people with access to digital technology will automatically enhance learning. These days, across a wide range of socioeconomic strata, the "soccer mom" has been replaced by the "technology mom" who purchases a Leapfrog electronic toy for her baby; lap-surfs with her toddler; buys a Wii, an Xbox, or a Playstation for the kids and their friends; puts the spare TV set in the child's bedroom; sets her child down for hours at a time to use social media like Webkinz and Club Penguin; and buys a laptop for her preteen so she will not have to share her own computer with the child.

In many American homes, the computer is primarily an entertainment device, extending the legacy of the television, which is still viewed for more than 3 hours per day by children aged 8 to 18, who spend 10 to 12 hours every day with some form of media (Kaiser Family Foundation, 2010). The computer is used for downloading music, watching videos, playing games, and interacting on social networks.

Although some may assume that the computer is used as a research tool for exploring the world, keeping up with current events, and learning new things, research has shown that many people lack the knowledge and skills to use the computer for these purposes (Hargittai & Walejko, 2008). Parents' behavior and attitudes toward technology are a critical factor in predicting a child's experience and approaches toward media (Pew Internet and American Life Project, 2009). Research shows that students who have at least one parent with a graduate degree are significantly more likely to create content, either online or offline, than others. "While it may be that digital media are leveling the playing field when it comes to exposure to content, engaging in creative pursuits remains unequally distributed by social background" (Hargittai & Walejko, 2008: 256).

For these reasons, educators must not just teach *with* digital technologies, tools, or games. To develop digital and media literacy competencies, it is necessary to teach *about* media and technology, making active use of the practices of dialogue and Socratic questioning to promote critical thinking about the choices people make when consuming, creating, and sharing messages. As Buckingham (2007, p. 113) explains, "Rather than seeing the web as a neutral source of 'information,' students need to be asking questions about the sources of that information, the interests of its producers and how it represents the world."

One example of a program that works to develop these competencies in children and teens is Kids Voting USA, which provides civic education and preparation for voting with news reading and media analysis activities. Students are also encouraged to analyze political advertisements, news stories, and candidate debates (McDevitt & Chaffee, 2000). Similarly, research conducted in Maine as part of the middle-school laptop initiative shows that when science teachers use engaging digital and media literacy projects as part of a science lesson, students retain information longer, and when digital and media literacy instructional practices are used in teaching middle-school students, their ability to analyze the content and quality of informational Web sites improves (Berry & Wintle, 2009; Pinkham, Wintle, & Silvernail, 2008).

The inherently engaging and immersive environment of games may make it difficult for young people to recognize the constructed nature of the digital environment and how it shapes personal and social action. But when children and young people become game-makers, they develop important skills while building an understanding of games as an interactive message system. The World Wide Workshop Foundation's Globaloria project is an example of a program that uses game design to develop important digital and media literacy skills through its emphasis on participation and critical thinking. By becoming authors, game programmers, and designers, students deepen their awareness of the choices involved in the structure and function of technology tools themselves.

Learners need opportunities to interact with audiences beyond their family and like-minded friends. The competencies promoted by digital and media literacy are fundamentally tied to true participation in a community, where engaging with people different from ourselves helps us clarify our own ideas, look at the world for different viewpoints, and, in the process, deepen our own learning and develop a sense of connectedness to the people around us.

Using Game Design in Education: Globaloria

Produced and launched by the World Wide Workshop Foundation in 2006, Globaloria is an innovative social learning network for designing and programming Web games that uses social media technology and computational tools for project-based learning.

Participants create educational games for their own personal and professional development, and for the social and economic benefit of their communities. The program, although aimed at youth aged 12 years and older, is suitable for students at all levels and does not require any previous Web design or programming experience.

Instead of separate silos for vocational and technical education, academic subjects, and college preparation, Globaloria combines them all into a yearlong project of approximately 150 hours, similar to computer gaming and software industry workplace practices. The scalable learning network includes programmable wikis and blogs, game programming tutorials, game content resources, and a customizable self-paced curriculum with model implementations and alignments to a state's curriculum standards.

The largest Globaloria pilot is in West Virginia, where educators in 41 middle schools, high schools, community colleges, and universities work with students, individually and collectively, to develop games and create original content. Globaloria West Virginia is used as a vehicle for teaching core subjects such as biology, English, and civics, where educators customize and align the curriculum with the West Virginia Department of Education's Content Standards and Objectives and 21st-Century Skills (Global21).

East Austin College Prep Academy (EACPA) in Austin, Texas, is the first charter school to integrate Globaloria curriculum schoolwide. During the 2010–2011 school year, sixth- and seventh-grade students at EACPA are taking a daily, 90-minute Globaloria class, where they develop original math and science games in addition to tracking social issues affecting the community they live in. The program reaches out to students' families as well, to extend learning into the home. The Globaloria EACPA curriculum is aligned with the Texas Content Standards for Mathematics (TEKs), English Language Acquisition (ELA), and Technology Learning. Support for Globaloria at EACPA is provided by AMD, Southwest Key, the Caperton Fund, and the World Wide Workshop Foundation.

What makes Globaloria successful, according to Dr. Idit Harel Caperton, president and founder of the World Wide Workshop Foundation, are three things. First, the participatory structure at the center of the program's design. Students and teachers learn by doing. Second, the strong partnerships the program has forged with government officials, education departments, private and public foundations, local business, industry, and institutes of higher education. Third, the culture of transparency and collaboration that Globaloria brings into schools.

Addressing Risks Associated with Media and Digital Technology. Digital and media literacy competencies are not only needed to strengthen people's capacity for engaging with information but also for addressing potential risks associated with mass media and digital media. For example, concerns about identity theft are emerging as the Federal Trade Commission reports that 10 million Americans were victimized last year by willingly giving personal information to robbers, often because "they couldn't distinguish an email from their bank from an email from a predator" (Rothkopf, 2009: 5). This example is just the tip of the iceberg, of course. Although many people actively support prosocial goals by contributing to a social network, there are others who exploit digital technology for harmful ends.

In the United States and many Western countries, the risk–benefit pendulum swings back and forth over time, through periods of increased (or decreased) concern about the negative aspects of media and technology. Comprehensive research from the European Union (Staksrud, Livingstone, Haddon, & Ólafsson, 2009) identifies three types of risk associated with the use of mass media, popular culture, and digital media:

1. **Content risks.** This includes exposure to potentially offensive or harmful content, including violent, sexual, sexist, racist, or hate material.
2. **Contact risks.** This includes practices in which people engage in harassment, cyberbullying, and cyberstalking; talk with strangers; or violate privacy.
3. **Conduct risks.** This includes lying or intentionally misinforming people, giving out personal information, illegal downloading, gambling, hacking, and more.

Some people are determined to flatly ignore, dismiss, or trivialize any risks associated with digital media, mass media, and popular culture. In the United States, the discourse about risks and opportunities continues to swing back and forth from fear, to anxiety, to optimism, reflecting ideas about the need to both protect and empower children and youth in relation to media and technology. In recent years, we have seen fear-inducing headlines about suicides brought on by online harassment give way to anxieties about Internet predators, then give way again to optimism about social networking, including the possibility that children are developing social learning skills by updating their Facebook pages or playing World of Warcraft (Ito et al., 2008).

But most people recognize that the stances of protection and empowerment are not examples of "either–or" thinking because these two positions are not in opposition—they are two sides of the same coin. Both empowerment and protection are needed to address the transformative social potential of the Internet in the context of child and adolescent development.

For example, when it comes to sexuality, both empowerment and protection are essential for children, young people, and their families. Young people can use the Internet and mobile-phone texting services to ask difficult questions about sexuality, get accurate information about sexual health, and participate in online communities. The Internet also enables and extends forms of sexual expression and experimentation, often in new forms, including webcams and live chat. Pornography is a multibillion-dollar industry in the United States. In a country with the highest teenage pregnancy rate of all Western industrialized countries in the world, a recent report from the Witherspoon Institute (2010) offers compelling evidence that the prevalence of pornography in the lives of many children and adolescents is far more significant than most adults realize, that pornography may be deforming the healthy sexual development of young people, and that it can be used to exploit children and adolescents. Teens have many reasons to keep secret their exposure to pornography, and many are unlikely to tell researchers about their activities. But about 15 percent of teens aged 12 to 17 do report that they have received sexually explicit images on their cell phones from people they knew personally (Pew Internet and American Life Project, 2009).

A 2008 Centers for Disease Control and Prevention report notes that 9 percent to 35 percent of children and young people also say they have been victims of electronic aggression (Centers for Disease Control and Prevention, 2008). Sexting and cyberbullying are examples of how human needs for power, intimacy, trust, and respect intersect with the ethical challenges embedded in social participation in a digital environment. That is why empowerment and protection are so deeply linked.

Digital and media literacy will not be a panacea for American social problems, and it will not let media companies and producers off the hook when it comes to their own social responsibility. As Jenkins et al. (2006, p. 19) point out, one key goal of media literacy education is to "encourage young people to become more reflective about the ethical choices they make as participants and communicators and the impact they have on others."

Expanding the Concept of Literacy. Make no mistake about it: Digital and media literacy does not replace or supplant print literacy. At a time when the word *text* now means any form of symbolic expression in any format that conveys meaning, the concept of literacy is simply expanding. *Literacy is beginning to be understood as the ability to share meaning through symbol systems in order to fully participate in society.* Print is now one of an interrelated set of symbol systems for sharing meaning. Because it takes years of practice to master print literacy, effective instruction in reading and writing is becoming more important than ever before. To read well, people need to acquire decoding and comprehension skills plus a base of knowledge from which they can interpret new ideas. To write, it is important to understand how words come together to form ideas, claims, and arguments and how to design messages to accomplish the goals of informing, entertaining, or persuading.

Some literacy educators recognize the value of digital media simply for its ability to get kids engaged in learning, to help them pay attention in school.

Although educators know that motivation and engagement are enhanced when mass media, popular culture, and digital media and technology are incorporated into learning, this is not (and should not be) the sole rationale for implementing digital and media literacy into the curriculum. When used well, news media, mass media, and digital media texts can support the acquisition of literacy competencies including comprehension, inference making, analysis, and prediction. Concepts such as audience, purpose, and point of view must be applied to messages from digital media and popular culture as well as printed texts. Participating in digital and media literacy activities also promotes writing, public speaking, and advocacy, empowering children and young people by offering opportunities to express themselves using language, images, sound, and interactivity (Alvermann, 2004; Hobbs, 2008; Gainer & Lapp, 2010).

Reading online is now a fundamental dimension of digital and media literacy that requires many interrelated practices, including using a search engine, reading search engine results, and quickly reading a Web page to locate the best link to the information that is required. Many people lack these skills (Coiro, 2007). When observing individuals using a search engine, it is not uncommon to see inefficient practices such as clicking down the list of links in a "click and look" strategy without looking for clues to determine the relevance of the Web sites to the purpose and goal.

Digital and media literacy education requires and supports the practices of reading comprehension and writing. Large-scale empirical research evidence shows that student participation in media literacy education programs in high school can strengthen reading comprehension, writing, and print-media analysis skills (Hobbs, 2007). That is because digital and media literacy educational practices cultivate an active approach to the process of meaning making in ways that help knowledge and skills to transfer from school to home and back.

To promote reading and writing skills, adolescent literacy experts have long urged teachers to make literacy experiences more relevant to students' interests, everyday life, and important current events, recommending, "Look for opportunities to bridge the activities outside and inside the classroom. Tune into the lives of students to find out what they think is relevant and why, and then use this information to design instruction and learning opportunities that will be more relevant" (U.S. Department of Education, 2008: 28).

But although people do develop many skills informally through their use of digital media with peers in online communities and social groups, without routine practice in making connections between print literacy and digital and media literacy competencies, those skills are unlikely to transfer to new contexts (Salomon & Perkins, 1989). Digital and media literacy education can provide a bridge to transfer print literacy skills from informal to formal, familiar to new, and narrow to broad contexts.

Strengthening People's Capacity to Access Message Credibility and Quality. Librarians and researchers tell us that, when looking for information online, many people give up before they find what they need. People use a small number of search strategies in a repetitive way even when they do not get the information they are seeking. They do not take the time to digest and evaluate what they encounter. In many cases, "students typically use information that finds them, rather than deciding what information *they* need" (Cheney, 2010: 1).

In addition, many people also use superficial criteria for assessing the quality of a message. Likeability, attractiveness, trustworthiness, and expertise all affect our decisions about the credibility of people, information, and ideas. We can easily understand that younger children may be more susceptible to digital misinformation and less able to discern credible sources. But actually, few people verify the information they find online—both adults and children tend to uncritically trust information they find, from whatever source. "Digital media allow for the uncoupling of credibility and authority in a way never before possible," notes Miriam Metzger (2009), a researcher at the University of California, Santa Barbara. In addition, family, coworkers, and friends have always influenced our decisions about what to trust. Today, judgments about what is credible can be shaped by participation in online communities. Our ideas about credibility and reliability are also shifting in relation to networked environments and services like collectively created encyclopedias, reviews, and ratings services (Metzger, 2009).

So how do we expand our capacity to use reasoning in deciding who and what to believe? With so many sources of information available, assessing credibility is difficult, even for adults. Many people simply use cues like graphic design to evaluate the credibility of a source. According to this view, if it "looks right," it is credible. The Internet blurs the lines between amateur and professional, between entertainment and marketing, between information and persuasion. We experience a "context deficit," where information about authorship is often unavailable, masked, or entirely missing. For example, Web sites that aggregate information may display materials from multiple sources on one Web page, which may itself be inaccurately perceived as the source. Hyperlinking may make it even more difficult for users to follow and evaluate multiple sources (Harris, 2008; Metzger, 2007).

At a broader level, the immediacy and immersive social characteristics of digital media may also discourage reflective, analytic thinking about sources, content, and credibility. It is just so simple: point, click, and wow, you're on to something new.

To judge the credibility of information, it is important to begin by answering these three basic questions: Who's the author? What's the purpose of this message? How was this message constructed? These simple but powerful questions enable people to assess the relative credibility of a media message.

In fact, for the savvy user, skillful use of digital information can enhance the process of fact checking and source comparison.

People who pay attention to the quality of media messages also need to be self-aware, possessing a general understanding of human perceptual and cognitive processes. Among these, include our natural tendencies to value sources as credible only when they reinforce our existing beliefs and attitudes. It is part of human nature: People tend to trust the sources that match our existing opinions and distrust information that challenges our beliefs. Awareness of this tendency, which is emphasized by those who teach news media literacy, can help people become more open and receptive to diverse sources and points of view. These insights can be useful in addressing the problem of political polarization, where extreme and often simplistic positions come to dominate and overpower more moderate, nuanced points of view.

People also need increased awareness of the practice of "source stripping," where almost immediately as we process information, we detach the content from the source, forgetting where we learned it (Eysenbach & Kohler, 2002). Digital and media literacy education can offer people an increased knowledge of human information processing, self-awareness, and self-reflexivity, which can help counteract these tendencies. Research and assessment tools are needed to better understand which instructional "best practices" support the development of people's ability to evaluate the quality of information they receive from print, television, movies, advertising, and digital media sources.

Bringing News and Current Events into K–12 Education. American adults can probably remember the practice of cutting out a newspaper article about a "current event" and bringing it into social studies class. But civics-oriented education, with its use of everyday journalistic resources, has been declining as a component of the American educational curriculum for more than 50 years. In 1947, more than half of American high schools offered a course called Problems in Democracy that emphasized reading of news magazines (Hobbs, 1998). Times have changed.

Today, young people tell us that the news is a significant source of stress because it reminds them of the peril the world is in and makes them feel unsafe and threatened. Although teens read the news only incidentally; when they do, they prefer news about music, entertainment, celebrities, and sports (Vahlberg, Peer, & Nesbit, 2008). Some child development professionals believe it is not good for children or young people to read or watch the news (American Academy of Child and Adolescent Psychiatry, 2002). Research has shown that violent news content actually induces more fear reactions than violent fiction, creating persistent worrisome thoughts in some children and young people (Kaiser Family Foundation, 2003). Almost 4 in 10 parents report that their children have been frightened or upset by something they have seen in the news and have concern that it can happen to them or their family (Cantor & Nathanson, 1996).

Using news and current events in the classroom can also be controversial. When President Obama's televised back-to-school speech to the nation's schoolchildren was blasted by conservative critics who accused the president of trying to spread propaganda, it illustrated perhaps the biggest challenge teachers face in bringing news and current events into the classroom. In addition, in an era of competition for and fragmentation within the news audience, no simplistic assumptions can be made about the nature of what information sources count as trustworthy and authoritative. Many teachers are reluctant to use news and current events in an increasingly polarized political climate (Hobbs, 2001; Hobbs et al., 2010). But as Mihailidis has observed, "Making the connections between media literacy, freedom of expression, and civic engagement can reposition media literacy as the core of new civic education" (2009, p. 9).

In the United Kingdom and Western Europe news and information programming for children and teens is provided as a public service initiative, but in the United States, it is almost purely a commercial enterprise. At the secondary level, *Channel One News* provides television news and advertising to 6 million teens. Research has shown that teens gain current events knowledge from viewing this program only when teachers support students' learning by asking questions and promoting reflective dialogue (Johnston, Brzezinski, & Anderman, 1994). At the elementary level, *Time for Kids* and Scholastic both offer magazines and online content specifically for children; however, these programs generally have a limited focus on news and current events, often favor articles of topical or seasonal interest, and are less likely to reach students in low-income schools.

Newspaper industry programs such as Newspapers in Education (NIE) provide newspapers to schools through advertising sponsorship and other donation programs. However, NIE programs have faced substantial cutbacks as newspaper revenues continue to decline. With NIE staff assuming responsibility for fundraising, sales, and marketing, there is less time to focus on curriculum and instruction (Arnold, 2010). Access to quality journalism has been an additional expense for school districts in communities that are often strapped to manage even basic expenses. In both the United States and the United Kingdom, "[i]t has proved difficult to support, develop and sustain teaching about broadcast news because of the ephemerality of the subject matter and the effort involved in bringing current TV, radio or Internet news into the classroom" (Bazalgette, Harland, & James, 2008: 81).

Whether we like it or not, the use of news media in the K–12 classroom is not sufficiently on the radar screen in American public education. Still, there are efforts under way to explore the development of curriculum and resources to engage students as active participants in the process of creating journalism. Although these efforts are more developed at the university level, programs are springing up at the high school level and even younger. One example is Palo Alto High School in Palo Alto, California, where the media program is the fastest-growing program in the school. The program's director has reported that more than 500 students out of a student body of 1,900 have elected to take journalism on one platform or another (Wojcicki, 2010).

We have good evidence from studies of high school journalism, which show that participating student journalists enhance their own civic engagement skills by exercising a public voice (Levine, 2008). But much less is known about how regular reading, viewing, and discussion of news and current events affects the development of students' knowledge and skills. Regular engagement with news and current events may support the development of learners' background knowledge. It may help build connections between the classroom and the culture. It may help learners see how news and current events are constructed by those with economic, political, and cultural interests at stake. It may help them appreciate how audiences understand and interpret messages differently based on their life experiences, prior knowledge, and attitudes.

Careful video documentation of instructional practices in digital and media literacy education, especially in relation to the use of news and current events in the context of formal and informal education, is needed. This will help build a base of research evidence to help scholars and educators determine which approaches to using news and current events in the classroom are most likely to empower students in a way that supports their development as citizens.

A Plan of Action: 10 Recommendations

To support the development of digital and media literacy competencies for all Americans, we need a comprehensive community education movement.

Local, regional, state, and national initiatives are essential. It will take time to build the infrastructure capacity and human resources necessary to bring digital and media literacy education to all citizens.

There are some key audiences and locations where this work must occur, including children and youth, new immigrants, special education students, juvenile offenders, and senior citizens, in K–12 schools, universities, and colleges.

A Look Inside One Program: Seattle's Common Language Project

Nearly every city in America has at least one program in digital and media literacy. In Seattle, the Common Language Project at the University of Washington offers media literacy and production workshops in a variety of educational settings. Jessica Partnow, a Seattle media literacy educator, wants her students to more deeply understand how news values are culturally inflected.

Working in local schools, she began one lesson by asking students to compare and contrast the English-language news monthly *Egypt Today* with *Newsweek*. Both magazines had featured articles on the Israeli-Lebanese conflict in 2006. *Egypt Today* ran a several-page spread of full color photos depicting desperate people searching for friends and family in the dusty rubble of a freshly bombed apartment complex; another photo showed a dead body before it had been covered with a sheet. In contrast, *Newsweek* used an infographic as its main illustration: stick figures in red and blue to indicate the numbers of injuries and deaths on either side of the conflict.

As Partnow (2010) explains, students "respond to the idea that our media are sanitizing our information for us. They enjoy a rebellious, typical teenage reaction to being told what to think. Others pick up on the emotional manipulation inherent in printing pictures of extreme suffering—or in choosing not to print them." These discussions help students think about how—and who— is processing their information for them. And perhaps even more importantly, the lessons "foster a love for what she calls the 'mind-boggler,' or questions that do not have one simple answer—where wrestling with every side of the issue is what is most important" (p. 1). This program also provides an interactive portal where students can not only read, listen to, and view stories but also interact with journalists and fellow students in the United States and in Nairobi, Kenya, created in partnership with the Pulitzer Center on Crisis Reporting.

Portraits of Success (found in the appendix) offers a list of other noteworthy organizations and programs where pioneering stakeholders have shown a common interest in strengthening students' digital and media literacy competencies. These programs are enabling communities to acquire the knowledge and expertise that is needed to develop and implement effective programs at the local, state, and national levels.

To achieve the buy-in necessary for success, initiatives must capitalize on existing local programs and resources and enroll new stakeholders, including educational leaders, members of the business community, and members of professional associations who are motivated to develop and sustain programs.

Community Initiatives

1. Map existing community resources in digital and media literacy and offer small grants to promote community partnerships to integrate digital and media literacy competencies into existing programs.

City and community leaders often have little awareness of programs and services in digital and media literacy education. Increased awareness and better coordination would help develop leadership, promote partnerships, and build organizational capacity to support the expansion of work in the community. Community-focused foundations, media, or technology companies should support the work of community leadership panels to map existing community resources in digital and media literacy. For example, the Comcast Foundation, through its partnership with Digital Connectors, could support digital and media literacy mapping projects in the communities where Comcast provides service.

In each participating community, the sponsoring entity would charge an experienced local group with mapping a community's existing programs in digital and media literacy. Mapping resources, training, and services along the essential dimensions of digital and media literacy education will make it possible to identify the assets that already exist in the community as well as the core values and priorities each program offers. It can also identify underserved populations. This will help identify gaps in programs and services.

The foundation or corporate sponsor could offer small annual grants of between $25,000 and $75,000, targeted to develop pilot programs to bring digital and media literacy education to specific populations with greatest need in the community. The foundation and its partners could host an annual community event to showcase programs and projects and promote networking and leadership development at the community level.

One example of a local group with the capacity to map a community's digital and media literacy resources is the Gateway Media Literacy Partners, a confederation of community leaders with experience in developing media literacy programs in St. Louis, Missouri. This group is established as a regional caucus of the NAMLE.

2. Support a national network of summer learning programs to integrate digital and media literacy into public charter schools.

Schools should leverage their in-school summer programs to fully realize the transformative potential of digital and media literacy education, especially for children in low-income communities. More than 75 percent of American children receive no summer learning experience during the months of summer vacation. Much of the achievement gap between lower- and higher-income youth can be explained by the summer learning loss that disproportionately affects low-income children (Finn, 2010). Taking advantage of the ability to blend fun and education and keeping kids involved in learning activities during the summer, a national network of summer learning programs in digital and media literacy for urban youth should be formed. One example of such a program is Powerful Voices for Kids, a university-school program that brings digital and media literacy education to children aged 5 to 15 through a summer learning program. The program is staffed by recent college graduates and includes a professional development program for teachers, in-school and after-school mentoring, and a research and assessment program. It receives support from the Wyncote Foundation, Verizon Foundation, and the Brook J. Lenfest Foundation.

Community Partnerships: The Digital Connectors Program

The Digital Connectors Program was launched by One Economy in 2001 in Washington, DC. The program identifies young people from diverse backgrounds between the ages of 14 to 21 and immerses them in certified technology training. The training helps these young *digital connectors* build leadership skills and prepares them to enter the 21st-century workplace. Participants give back to their community by training family members and residents on how to use technology effectively.

In addition to hands-on learning, digital connectors also learn about career opportunities through site visits to technology companies, job-shadowing experiences, and campus tours. Many participating youth receive stipends through their city's employment program or new computers as compensation for their efforts.

Programs are run in housing developments, community centers, libraries, and schools. To date, more than 3,500 young people from diverse, low-income backgrounds have been trained as *digital connectors*. These young people have contributed more than 77,000 hours of service to their communities spreading digital literacy.

In late 2010, with federal funding from the American Recovery and Reinvestment Act (ARRA) and corporate matches, One Economy and the

Broadband Opportunity Coalition, a leading civil rights organization, will expand Digital Connector programs substantially. The expanded program will train 2,500 to 3,000 youth through the launch of 167 Digital Connector programs in 19 major cities throughout the country.

Charter schools in low-income communities are receptive to innovation and ready to implement in-school summer learning programs. More than 1 million children in 3,500 schools are enrolled in public charter schools (Berends et al., 2009). In-school summer programs can also help inspire teachers to introduce the instructional practices of digital and media literacy during the academic year. By engaging students in enrichment activities that capitalize on their interests in mass media, popular culture, and digital media, the program enables children to build positive relationships with peers and adults, use digital media and technology for learning, and develop critical thinking and communication skills. Recent college graduates and media professionals can serve as program staff for the four- to six-week summer learning program, providing a powerful service learning opportunity that builds civic awareness. In coordination with the National Alliance for Public Charter Schools, this program could be supported in the same manner as the National Writing Project, with direct federal funding to build, sustain, and expand the national network. Federal investment could be matched one-to-one by university, local, state, and private dollars. Congress should pass the Healthy Media for Youth Act (H.R. 4925) because this competitive grant program could also support summer programs that support media literacy programs for children and youth.

3. Support a Digital and Media Literacy (DML) Youth Corps to bring digital and media literacy to underserved communities and special populations via public libraries, museums, and other community centers.

There are many American adults who are not using broadband connections and services. They cite factors such as access, relevance, lack of digital literacy skills, and cost among the reasons they have not become adopters of high-speed Internet and digital media. They may see media as "just entertainment" and have declared themselves "not computer people." They may be intimidated by technology and unsure of where to start or how to use it. By opting out, they are missing out on the opportunity to use digital media to enhance daily life. To accommodate often busy lives, adults need flexible, short-term, and drop-in programs, catered to their needs, where they can explore and learn, supported by knowledgeable and supportive assistants who offer just-in-time learning strategies. Most people learn new digital skills from a combination of trial-and-error strategies along with an "elbow-to-elbow" friend who offers appropriate help and support when needed.

Congress should dedicate 10 percent of Americorps funding for the development of a DML Youth Corps. The DML Youth Corps would be a service outreach program that offers training and professional development in digital and media literacy to a group of recent college graduates and places them in teams, to work in public libraries, school libraries and technology centers, local public access centers, and other community nonprofit organizations.

Three to five partnership programs from different regions of the United States could be tapped to recruit, train, and support DML corps members. Existing programs, such as the recently launched Public Media Corps, or a National Digital Literacy Corps as proposed in the National Broadband Plan, could be engaged or serve as models. Corps members would be responsible for offering informal digital media learning programs to adults in coordination with the hosting organization. Participants might be introduced to innovative Web sites such as Finding Dulcinea, which helps Internet users quickly and easily find the best, most credible Web sites. In coordination with the American Library Association, some members of this team could be responsible for hosting a "Silver Surfers Week" based on the model developed in the United Kingdom, which is a library-based program designed to support the development of digital and media literacy competencies among people ages 55+. Corps members could receive a small stipend for their 12-month service.

Partnerships for Teacher Education

4. Support interdisciplinary bridge building in higher education to integrate core principles of digital and media literacy education into teacher preparation programs.

Digital and media literacy education cannot come into the classroom without teachers who have the knowledge and skills to teach it. At present, many K–12 educators are not familiar with the instructional practices of digital and media literacy education, creating a leadership gap in schools. A parallel gap exists at most colleges and universities because the silos between disciplines mean there is little interface between faculty in the schools of education and communication. Most schools of education lag behind in bringing innovative digital and media literacy education to their students because faculty do not make active use of digital media themselves. Most faculty in schools of communication specialize in professional digital media training but have little expertise in developing non-specialist programs that address the needs of children, youth, and other underserved populations. Teacher education programs must give their students rich digital and media literacy learning experiences if they hope to inspire them to include this pedagogy in their own teaching.

Future teachers would be well served if colleges and universities invested in the building of interdisciplinary bridges that bring faculty and students together for co-learning opportunities. Programs at the University of Minnesota, the University of New York at Buffalo and Stony Brook, the University of Southern California, Temple University, Syracuse University, Webster University in St. Louis, Sacred Heart University in Connecticut, and other schools have begun such initiatives, bringing together faculty in schools of communication and education for community-based learning initiatives.

State departments of education should make available a competitive pool of monies exclusively for university and college partnerships to support cross-disciplinary teacher education programs in digital and media literacy education that enable intensive collaboration between faculty and students in education and communication/media studies programs to support community-based digital and media literacy learning. These colleges and universities should develop certification programs in digital and media literacy so that school districts can hire teachers with this specific set of knowledge and skills.

5. Create district-level initiatives that support digital and media literacy across K–12 via community and media partnerships.

To integrate digital and media literacy education into the curriculum, teachers already in service must receive meaningful staff development. The average American teacher is 50 years old and will be working for another 10 to 15 years (Ingersoll, 2009). School districts should dedicate funding to support a fast-track, 12-month coordinated staff development program in digital and media literacy at the district level. This could be staffed by teams that include technology specialists, library/media educators, education and communication faculty, and community partners, including those from professional media organizations. Training should make use of the instructional practices of digital and media literacy education. School districts could offer opportunities to "catalyst teachers" who would participate in 10 full days of professional development in partnership with a college or university over the course of an academic year. Some of this training can be offered online. On completion of the program, educators will receive a certificate that enables them to offer professional development to others in their district. A rigorous evaluation component should assess program impact on both teachers' classroom practices and their students' knowledge and skills. States should make available matching funds for school districts that invest in teacher education programs in digital and media literacy. Foundations should support research on district-level initiatives to help develop a base of scholarship to support the field.

6. Partner with media and technology companies to bring local and national news media more fully into education programs in ways that promote civic engagement.

News media resources can be powerful tools to support citizenship education and strengthen digital and media literacy competencies. Whereas in the past, access to print news required a subscription, and TV news content was available only by viewing at a specific time, now it is at our fingertips on a 24/7 basis. New services are emerging online to help people use, analyze, and share news content. As the Knight Commission (2009) report noted, technology companies can make an enormous contribution to the public interest by volunteering their expertise and resources.

There are a host of innovative online news tools already on the market that could better enable teachers and students to use and analyze print, online, and television news as part of general education. For example, the Know the News project from Link TV enables students to remix broadcast news, discovering how choices in language, image, and editing shape the meaning-making process. *The New York Times* Learning Network has more than 3,000 lesson plans and activities that help teachers and students easily and meaningfully connect current events to perennial classroom topics and enable students to comment on the news. Video news aggregation services like Red Lasso (www.redlasso.com) make it possible for people to select, edit, and circulate excerpts of local TV news content for private or public purposes, selecting and embedding clips of local news from more than 150 media markets. News Trust (www.newstrust.com) uses a news ratings system to enable people to see how others evaluate the quality of informational content of print-news media reports. NBC Learn has launched I-Cue (www.icue.com), a social networking Web site where NBC video clips and related news stories are fashioned into virtual trading cards.

At present, however, few educators are taking advantage of these new tools. To help develop a cadre of teacher leaders to spread the word about the value of using existing online news tools, modest grants from media and technology companies could be used to support partnerships between the developers of these new tools and key educational groups. School districts, community colleges, museums, libraries, colleges, and universities could be invited to apply for these funds, which would support teacher education and outreach activities. This would empower educators and their students to discover fresh ways to engage with local news using new online resources. Well-publicized examples of effective instructional strategies for using these tools, generated by educators and students themselves, could also support the growth of digital and media literacy education across the disciplines and content areas.

Research and Assessment

7. Develop online measures of media and digital literacy to assess learning progression and develop online video documentation of digital and media literacy instructional strategies to build expertise in teacher education.

It is important to make a case for the importance of digital and media literacy—and offering compelling evidence of need is a vital first step. Many people who have well-developed digital and media literacy competencies wrongly assume that others have the same levels of knowledge and skills they possess. Those who lack these skills may be unaware of the utility or value of these competencies. Compelling test results are essential to help establish the importance of—and need for—digital and media literacy education.

Two key action items are proposed here that reflect the need for both top-down and bottom-up assessment strategies: (a) online measures of students' learning progression and (b) video documentation of instructional practices to support best-practices research that will enhance teacher education.

Online Measures to Assess Students' Learning Progression. Measures of digital and media literacy are desperately needed to assess learning progression. There are so many dimensions of media and digital literacy that it will take many years to develop truly comprehensive measures that support the needs of students, educators, policy makers, and other stakeholders. Although "technological literacy" was part of the 2012 National Assessment of Educational Progress (NAEP), this framework will *not* include digital and media literacy competencies (Cavanaugh, 2009). Therefore, an online test dedicated to digital and media literacy is needed. First, three to five benchmarks for assessment need to be developed, targeted to children and young people aged 9, 14, and 19. This could be used to both establish the need for new programs and to measure program effectiveness. The U.S. Department of Education should initiate funding to support a simple online test requiring no more than 30 minutes to complete that could measure the ability to (a) use digital tools including basic and more advanced skills, (b) analyze and evaluate the author's purpose and point of view, (c) identify ethical issues in message production and reception, (d) make judgments of the credibility of information sources, and (e) compose messages using language, image, and sound.

Video Documentation of Instructional Practices. Like most professionals, teachers learn new skills best when they have the opportunity to observe and analyze the practices of their peers and colleagues. An online database of video excerpts of digital and media literacy learning is needed as a resource for teacher education programs locally, districtwide, and statewide, nationally, and around the world. These video excerpts should be accompanied with teacher-created lesson plans, samples of student work and other materials, including opportunities for users to comment, review, and critique. Such a resource should also be used to develop research evidence to identify "best practices" by determining which approaches to digital and media literacy education are most effective. It could also be used as the basis upon which to develop a meaningful test for new teachers to measure their ability to implement digital and media literacy instructional practices into the curriculum.

At the present, few states require new teachers to demonstrate competence in digital and media literacy education. Texas does include measures of digital and media literacy education competencies as 15 percent of the test for new English teachers in grades 8 through 12 (Texas Education Agency, 2006), but the methodology of brief written vignettes with multiple-choice options limits its effectiveness. The online video documentation tool should be coordinated by NAMLE. Members should be able to upload clips of their own teaching practices and download clips for use in teacher education. Such a database should be supported by a major philanthropy or charitable foundation in order to dramatically improve our knowledge of effective practices in teacher education for digital and media literacy education.

Parent Outreach, National Visibility, and Stakeholder Engagement

8. Engage the entertainment industry's creative community in an entertainment-education initiative to raise visibility and create shared social norms regarding ethical behaviors in using online and social media.

As participation in digital culture spreads, we are seeing the development of social norms for how people interact with technology. Right now, there are few culturally normative practices that truly support the growth of digital and media literacy. For example, most people do not know exactly what it means to "ask critical questions" about mass media, digital media, or popular culture. Parents may not be aware of the importance of sitting with their children and learning along with them about online social media. Others may think of the television and the computer as devices for diversion or entertainment only. To strengthen people's capacity for engaging with information, it is important to envision what digital and media literacy practices actually look like in the context of ordinary life in the family, workplace, and community.

To raise the level of visibility of the concept of digital and media literacy in the home, an education-entertainment initiative, similar to the one developed for the "designated driver" campaign, is needed. In the classic case, Jay Winsten of the Harvard School of Public Health met with Hollywood producers and writers to explore possibilities for integrating the topic of the designated driver into popular television programs. Because "entertainment not only mirrors social reality, but also helps shape it by depicting what constitutes popular opinion," the program was effective because it used short messages, embedded within dialogue, that were casually presented by characters who serve as role models within a dramatic context (Winsten, 2010). With support from the Writers Guild of America West, over a four-year period, more than 160 prime-time programs incorporated subplots, scenes, and dialogue on the subject, including frequent references to the use of designated drivers. Most important, alcohol-related traffic fatalities declined by 30 percent over this time period.

We propose targeting a specific dimension of digital and media literacy, perhaps an ethically problematic but common online behavior (such as spying, harassment, intolerance, cyberbullying, or sexting). A Web site that archives and offers examples of this programming could help parents and educators use these TV clips to extend learning and discussion opportunities in both the home and the classroom.

Working with the Writer's Guild of America West, the Creative Coalition, and potentially other partners, including Viacom, Comcast, Time Warner, and Disney, entertainment programs for children, teens, and adults could address the problem and identify appropriate solutions, helping to establish and reinforce social norms about responsibilities and behavior in online communication. With a modest investment in an entertainment-education campaign, social norms and ethical practices regarding the use of online social media could become part of our cultural vocabulary.

9. Host a statewide youth-produced PSA competition to increase visibility for digital and media literacy education.

Youth media programs involve students in video, print, and online media production. There are a number of youth media initiatives across the United States despite the extremely limited funding opportunities available to them. The optimistic spirit of "youth voice" is inspiring to those who work in cities and communities. Now the field is well developed enough to support a journal, *Youth Media Reporter*, which offers a place for youth media advocates and professionals to share ideas about what works and why. A community education movement for digital and media literacy must include a prominent role for youth media advocates. Local or national celebrities also have a role to play in bringing attention to the talents of young people who are working to develop critical thinking, social responsibility, and communication skills using language, image, sound, music, and interactivity.

Statewide competitions should be developed to motivate youth media organizations to make digital and media literacy a focus topic for community advocacy. Working collaboratively, youth media organizations, high school video production programs, and local access centers, working with cable providers in coordination with Channel One schools should host an annual statewide public service announcement (PSA) competition, inviting video, audio, or script/storyboard submissions from youth media organizations, public access centers, and individuals. The contest might involve telling a story in 30 seconds about the benefits that come from thinking critically and being socially responsible about digital media, mass media, and popular culture, using the tagline "Get Media Smart." Winning entries should be produced, hosted by a prominent celebrity, and distributed via local access and public television stations across the state.

Local libraries and public media organizations should host community screenings featuring the local producers who contributed to the project. A social media Web site could showcase all entries and offer "one-stop shopping"–style information about digital and media literacy concepts that can be effective in the home and community. A group of young leaders should be recognized at a special event sponsored by the White House.

10. Support an annual conference and educator showcase competition in Washington, DC, to increase national leadership in digital and media literacy education.

To build a community education movement for digital and media literacy, visibility is needed among media professionals, members of Congress, federal and state officials, and business, trade, and civic membership associations. It is important to nurture the development of professional associations for digital and media literacy education, enabling educators to share experiences about "what works," showing how digital and media literacy education is relevant to a wide range of stakeholders. At present, NAMLE hosts a national conference every two years, with the next event scheduled for July 2011 in Philadelphia. An annual conference based in Washington, DC, would support the increased visibility of digital and media literacy education among leaders in K–12 education at both the state and national levels. Because of rapid growth in this field, an annual conference is needed.

A national leadership conference with an educator showcase competition will substantially raise the visibility of digital and media literacy among policymakers, federal officials, and leading nonprofit and charitable organizations. It could help bring new leaders into the field and enable the membership organization to sustain a full-time executive director. This organization could easily triple its membership within one year with an annual national leadership conference, especially if coordinated with a larger association like the NCTE, the American Library Association (ALA), or the International Society for Technology Education (ISTE). This should be combined with a visibility campaign targeted to reach college and university faculty, K–12 educators, media professionals, youth media advocates, and other stakeholders with interests and experience in digital and media literacy. A major philanthropy or charitable foundation should support NAMLE over a three-year period for it to position itself as a unifying force for digital and media literacy as a national and community education movement.

Who Should Do What

To review key action items, following is a summary of what each of the different stakeholders should do.

Executive Branch

The White House should raise visibility for digital and media literacy by asking Congress to support major initiatives in digital and media literacy. The president and first lady could host a Rose Garden event that showcases the winners of the youth-produced PSA competition.

Congress

Congress should dedicate funding to support a network of in-school summer learning programs in digital and media literacy for public charter schools in low-income communities. This would help close the achievement gap. Direct federal funding should be used to build, sustain, and expand the national network. Federal investment could be matched one-to-one by university, local, state, and private dollars.

Congress should pass the Healthy Media for Youth Act (H.R. 4925), which authorizes $40 million annually to support educational programs in media literacy programs for children and youth.

Congress should dedicate 10 percent of Americorps funding to support the development of a DML service outreach program that offers training and professional development in digital and media literacy to a group of recent college graduates and places them, in teams, to work in public libraries, school libraries and technology centers, local public access centers, and other community nonprofit organizations.

U.S. Department of Education

The Department of Education should initiate funding to support an online test requiring no more than 30 minutes to complete that could measure students' ability to (a) use digital tools; (b) identify the author, purpose, and point of view of messages in print and digital formats; (c) engage in ethical reasoning about social responsibility as producers and consumers; (d) make judgments on the credibility of information sources; and (e) create simple media composition activities using language, images, and sound.

Federal support for the development of an online video documentation tool is needed. Such a database would dramatically improve knowledge of "best practices" in teacher education for digital and media literacy education.

The Department of Education should support research on district-level teacher education initiatives in digital and media literacy to help develop a rigorous base of scholarship to support the field.

State Governments

State departments of education should make available a competitive pool of monies exclusively for university and college partnerships to support cross-disciplinary teacher education programs in digital and media literacy education. This would enable intensive collaboration between faculty and students in education and communication/media studies programs to support in-school community education programs in digital and media literacy.

States should make available matching funds, on 2:1 match basis, for school districts that invest in teacher education programs in digital and media literacy.

Local Governments

School districts should dedicate funding to support a fast-track 12-month coordinated staff development program at the district level. Training should make use of the instructional practices of digital and media literacy education. School districts could offer opportunities to "catalyst teachers" who would participate in 10 full days of professional development in partnership with a college or university over the course of an academic year. Some of this training should be offered online.

Each local government should assemble a small community leadership panel with interests in digital and media literacy education. In each participating community, a local group should be charged with mapping a community's existing programs in digital and media literacy, with a special focus on youth media programs.

Libraries and Museums

The Institute of Museum and Library Services (IMLS) and the American Library Association should coordinate a DML service outreach program to host a "Silver Surfers Week," a library-based program designed to support the development of digital and media literacy competencies among Americans aged 55 and older.

Local libraries should host community screenings featuring the local youth media producers who contributed to statewide competition. In larger cities, a social media Web site could showcase all entries and offer localized "one-stop shopping"–style information about digital and media literacy concepts that can be effective in the home and community.

Federal Communications Commission

The FCC can informally encourage media companies to support an entertainment-education campaign to target an ethically problematic but common online behavior (like teasing, spying, harassment, intolerance, cyberbullying, or sexting) for exploration in subplots of prime-time programming.

A Web site that archives and offers examples of this programming could help parents and educators use TV clips to promote discussion and extend the learning experience in the home and classroom.

Philanthropies and Charitable Foundations

Support for local government is needed to map a community's existing programs in digital and media literacy, with a special focus on youth media programs for underserved populations.

Support for the development of an online video documentation tool is needed. Such a database would dramatically improve knowledge of "best practices" in teacher education for digital and media literacy education.

Foundations should support research on district-level teacher education initiatives to help develop a base of scholarship to support the field.

A marketing/visibility campaign is needed to target college and university faculty, K–12 educators, media professionals, youth media advocates, and other stakeholders with interests and experience in digital and media literacy.

A major philanthropy or charitable foundation should support NAMLE over a three-year period for it to position itself as a unifying force for digital and media literacy as a national and community education movement.

A foundation should provide support for research that measures the impact of an entertainment-education campaign, demonstrating how mass media can support knowledge and skill development in digital and media literacy.

News Media Organizations

Using a host of innovative online news tools already on the market that help teachers and students to use and analyze news and current events as part of general education, companies should offer modest grants to support partnerships with key educational groups. School districts, community colleges, museums, libraries, colleges, and universities could be invited to apply for these funds, which would support teacher education and outreach activities.

ISPs and Technology Companies

Support is needed for professional membership associations to develop a national leadership conference with an educator showcase competition to raise the visibility of digital and media literacy among policymakers, federal officials, and leading nonprofit and charitable organizations.

The Creative Community

The creative community should host an entertainment-education collaboration over a four-year period to integrate exploration of ethical and social responsibility issues as they relate to digital media. The goal would be to integrate social norms about responsibilities and rights of producers and consumers into prime-time program subplots, scenes, and dialogue.

Youth Media Organizations

Working collaboratively, youth-oriented media organizations should host an annual statewide PSA competition, inviting video, audio or script/storyboard submissions from youth media organizations, public access centers, and individuals. Winners would attend a White House event recognizing their achievements.

Professional Membership Associations

Working collaboratively and with support from charitable foundations, professional organizations should develop an online video documentation tool so that educators and researchers can upload clips of their own teaching practices and download clips for use in teacher education.

Working collaboratively, professional organizations should develop a national leadership conference with an educator showcase competition to raise the visibility of digital and media literacy among policymakers, federal officials, and leading nonprofit and charitable organizations.

Public Television and Local Community Access Centers

Statewide competitions of youth-produced works will result in winning entries in each of the 50 states, which should be distributed via both local access and public television stations across each state.

Conclusion: Imagining the Future

A global movement for digital and media literacy education is developing all over the world (Frau-Meigs & Torrent, 2009). For example, in the European Union, media literacy has been identified as a priority for the 21st century. Media literacy encompasses all media, including television and film, radio and recorded music, print media, the Internet, and all other new digital communication technologies. It is a fundamental competence not only for the young generation but for people of all ages, for parents, teachers, and media professionals. This issue is seen as so critical to the development of European social and cultural development that by 2011, all the countries of the European Union will have developed preliminary metrics to measure the levels of media literacy among their citizens.

Here in the United States, we are finally beginning to move beyond the "gee-whiz" phase that's been keeping us drooling over the just-beyond-the-horizon transformative potential of the Internet, hungry for the latest game, gadget, or online widget to change our lives.

It is now time for Americans to pay equal attention to the human competencies and skills that people use when becoming effective authors, audiences, and active participants in the digital age.

Many educators have been wary of the well-publicized hype about the unsubstantiated benefits of digital media in education because of their own real-life experience spending six hours a day with children and teens whose lives are more or less infused with cell phones, iPods, and laptops. They know that simply using digital media tools is no educational panacea. A recent study of students in Grades 5 through 8 showed that those from disadvantaged families got lower math and reading scores once the Internet arrived in the home. Analyzing the test scores of more than 150,000 students in North

Carolina, Duke University researchers compared children's reading and math scores before and after they acquired a home computer and compared those scores to those of kids who never acquired a home computer (Vigdor & Ladd, 2010). The test scores of low-income kids who got computers at home declined more than children who did not get computers. For middle-school students, social networking, YouTube videos, and online games can be a potent distraction from homework and other activities.

Even young people themselves are recognizing some limitations of life online. Some are concerned that screen interaction will replace face-to-face social relationships and others wonder if online civic acts are merely "token activism," creating an illusion of civic engagement while actually distancing people from their causes. "Such nuanced stances reveal that teens and adults are engaged in thoughtful consideration of the civic potentials of online life" (Global Kids, 2009: 17).

Generation after generation, we keep having to discover the obvious: Technology itself is no savior. Cell phones, video games, social networking, electronic whiteboards, and the Internet will not automatically improve education any more than radio or television did. Although children and young people are using digital media, they are not necessarily becoming either smarter or more digitally literate. Novel forms of digital technologies may actually widen the achievement gap by offering potent time-consuming distractions that interfere with homework and other activities. We must not confuse just owning technology, playing video games, or using online social networks with having the habits of mind, knowledge, skills, and competencies needed to be successful in the 21st century. As the Duke University study showed, computers at home are used primarily as an entertainment device unless an active, learning-oriented approach is cultivated.

Fortunately, it is possible to imagine that, in the next few years, our appreciation of the delicate balance of protection and empowerment will lead us to better manage our "constantly connected" lives. When digital and media literacy become a fundamental part of contemporary education both in and out of schools, we will achieve the following results:

- Parents will pay attention to why and how screen media are used by their children and teens at home and balance on-screen activities with other forms of play and learning to both protect and empower children and youth.
- People of all ages will internalize the practice of asking critical questions about the author, purpose, and point of view of every sort of message— whether it be from political campaigns, pharmaceutical advertisements,

reports and surveys issued by think tanks, Web sites, breaking news, e-mail, blogs, or the opinions of politicians, pundits, and celebrities.

- Teachers will use engaging instructional methods to explore the complex role of news and current events in society, making connections to literature, science, health, and history, building bridges between the classroom and the living room that support a lifetime of learning.
- People of all ages will be responsible and civil in their communication behaviors, treating others with respect and appreciating the need for social norms of behavior that create a sense of personal accountability for one's online and offline actions.
- As a fundamental part of instruction, students will compose and create authentic messages for real audiences, using digital tools, images, language, sound, and interactivity to develop knowledge and skills and discover the power of being an effective communicator.
- People from all walks of life will be able to achieve their goals in finding, sharing, and using information to solve problems, developing the ability to access, analyze, evaluate, communicate and share ideas and information, participating in meaningful social action in their neighborhoods, communities, nation, and the world.

In the process, teamwork, collaboration, reflection, ethics, and social responsibility will flourish. Teachers will not have to complain about a generation of young people who lack the ability to identify appropriate keywords for an online search activity, those who are not aware of which American city was devastated by Hurricane Katrina, and those who cannot identify the author of a Web page.

Media professionals in news and journalism, digital media, advertising, and cable and broadcast television are beginning to recognize that everybody wins when consumers are more active, engaged, intentional, and strategic about their media use habits. When people have high expectations for the quality of news and entertainment, there will be more opportunity to produce quality products. By working together to build coalitions and partnerships, we must support digital and media literacy as a community education movement for all people in the United States.

References and Bibliography

Alvermann, D. (2004). "Media, Information Communication Technologies (ICT), and Youth Literacies: A Cultural Studies Perspective." *American Behavioral Scientist 48*, 78–83.

American Academy of Child and Adolescent Psychiatry. (2002). *Children and the News. Facts for Families* (No. 67). Retrieved from http://www.aacap.org/cs/root/facts_for_families/children_and_the_news

Arnold, M. (2010). *NIE in 2010: Leaner + Locally Focused + Digital.* Alexandria, VA: Newspaper Association of America Foundation.

Bazalgette, C., Harland, J., & James, C. (2008). *Lifeblood of Democracy? Learning about Broadcast News.* Retrieved from the Office of Communications (OFCOM), Great Britain, Web site: http://www.ofcom.org.uk/advice/media_literacy/medlit pub/lifeblood/

Becker, S., Crandall, M., Fisher, K., Kinney, B., Landry, C., & Rocha, A. (2010). *Opportunity for All: How the American Public Benefits from Internet Access at U.S. Libraries.* Retrieved from the U.S. Impact Studies: http://impact.ischool .washington.edu/documents/OPP4ALL_FinalReport.pdf

Berends, M., Cannata, M., Goldring, E., & Penaloza, R. (2009, April). "Innovation in Schools of Choice." Paper presented at the annual meeting of the American Educational Research Association, San Diego, CA.

Berry, A., & Wintle, S. (2009). *Using Laptops to Facilitate Middle-School Science Learning: The Results of Hard Fun* . Retrieved from the University of Southern Maine Center for Education Policy, Applied Research and Evaluation: http://usm .maine.edu/cepare/pdf/Bristol_Final_Copy_cover.pdf

Buckingham, D. (2007). "Media Education Goes Digital: An Introduction." *Learning, Media and Technology* 32, 111–119.

Cantor, J., & Nathanson, A. (1996). "Children's Fright Reactions to Television News." *Journal of Communication* 46, 139–152.

Cavanaugh, S. (2009, September 14). Tech Group Critical of Proposed NAEP Standards [Web log post]. Retrieved from http://blogs.edweek.org/edweek/curri culum/2009/09/tech_group_critical_of_propose.html

Centers for Disease Control and Prevention. (2008). *Electronic Media and Youth: A CDC Issue Brief for Educators and Caregivers.* Retrieved from http://www.cdc .gov/violenceprevention/pdf/EA-brief-a.pdf

Cheney, D. (2010, June 24). Fuzzy Logic: Why Students Need News and Information Literacy Skills. *Youth Media Reporter.* Retrieved from http://www.youthmedia reporter.org/2010/06/fuzzy_logic_why_students_need.html

Cheney, D., Knapp, J., Alan, R., & Czapla, P. (2006). "Convergence in the Library's News Room: Enhancing News Collections and Services in Academic Libraries." *College and Research Libraries* 67, 395–417.

Coiro, J. (2007). "Exploring Changes to Reading Comprehension on the Internet: Paradoxes and Possibilities for Diverse Adolescent Readers." Unpublished doctoral dissertation, University of Connecticut. Retrieved from http://proquest.umi

.com/pqdlink?did=1372023711&Fmt=6&VType=PQD&VInst=PROD&RQT=3
09&VName=PQD&TS=1286780762&clientId=79356

Common Core State Standards Initiative. (2010). *English Language Arts Standards.*
Retrieved from http://www.corestandards.org/the-standards/english-language-arts
-standards/introduction/key-design-considerations

Dewey, J. (1923/1999). *Democracy and Education.* New York: BiblioLife.

Eysenbach, G., & Kohler, C. (2002). "How Do Consumers Search for and Appraise
Health Information on the World Wide Web? Qualitative Study Using Focus
Groups, Usability Tests, and In-Depth Interviews." *British Medical Journal,* 324,
573–577.

Finn, C. (2010, March 20). "The Case for Saturday School." *The Wall Street Journal,*
p. W1.

Fox, S. (2006). *Online Health Search 2006.* Retrieved from the Pew Internet &
American Life Project Web site: http://www.pewinternet.org/PPF/r/190/report_
display.asp

Frau-Meigs, D. (2008). "Media Education: Crossing a Mental Rubicon." In U.
Carlsson, S. Tayie, G. Jacquinot-Delaunay & J. Manuel Perez Tornero (Eds.).
Empowerment through Media Education: An Intercultural Dialogue (169–180).
Goteborg University, Sweden: The International Clearinghouse on Children,
Youth and Media, Nordicom in cooperation with UNESCO.

Frau-Meigs, D., & Torrent, J. (2009). *Mapping Media Education Policies around the
World: Visions, Programmes and Challenges.* New York: United Nations Alliance
of Civilizations.

Freire, P. (1968/1996). *Pedagogy of the Oppressed.* New York: Penguin.

Gainer, J., & Lapp, D. (2010). *Literacy Remix: Bridging Adolescents' in and out of
School Literacies.* Newark, DE: International Reading Association.

Global Kids, The Good Play Project and Common Sense Media. (2009). *Meeting
of Minds: Cross-Generational Dialogue on the Ethics of Digital Life.* Retrieved
from http://www.globalkids.org/meetingofminds.pdf

Gray, L., Thomas, N., & Lewis, L. (2010). Teachers' Use of Educational Technology in U.S. public schools: 2009 (NCES 2010–040). Washington, DC: National
Center for Education Statistics, Institute of Education Sciences, U.S. Department
of Education.

Hargittai, E., & Walejko, G. (2008). "The Participation Divide: Content Creation
and Sharing in the Digital Age." *Information, Communication and Society 11,*
239–256.

Harris, F. (2008). "Challenges to Teaching Credibility Assessment in Contemporary
Schooling." In M. Metzger & A. Flanagan (Eds.), *Digital Media, Youth and Credibility,* 155–179. Cambridge, MA: MIT Press.

Hobbs, R. (1998). "Building Citizenship Skills through Media Literacy Education." In M. Salvador & P. Sias (Eds.), *The Public Voice in a Democracy at Risk* (57–76). Westport, CT: Praeger.

Hobbs, R. (2001). "Media Literacy Skills: Interpreting Tragedy." *Social Education 65* (7), 406–411. Retrieved from http://downloads.ncss.org/lessons/650702.pdf

Hobbs, R. (2007). *Reading the Media: Media Literacy in High School English.* New York: Teachers College Press.

Hobbs, R. (2008). "Debates and Challenges Facing New Literacies in the 21st Century." In S. Livingstone & K. Drotner (Eds.), *International Handbook of Children, Media and Culture,* 431–447. London: Sage.

Hobbs, R., Ebrahimi, A., Cabral, N., Yoon, J., & Al-Humaidan, R. (2010). *"Combatting Middle East Stereotypes through Media Literacy Education in Elementary School."* Unpublished manuscript, Media Education Lab, Temple University, Philadelphia, PA.

Hobbs, R., Jaszi, P., & Aufderheide, P. (2009). "How Media Literacy Educators Reclaimed Copyright and Fair Use." *International Journal of Learning and Media* 1(3), 33–48.

Horton, F. W. (2007). *Understanding Information Literacy: A Primer.* Paris, France: Information Society Division, Communication and Information, UNESCO.

Ingersoll, R. (2009). *The Aging Teaching Workforce: A Snapshot.* Retrieved from http://www.nctaf.org/documents/NCTAFAgeDistribution408REG_000.pdf

Ito, M., Horst, H., Bittanti, M., Boyd, D., Herr-Stephenson, B., Lange, P., Pascoe, C. J., & Robinson, L. (2008). *Living and Learning with New Media: Summary of Findings from the Digital Youth Project.* Retrieved from the John D. and Catherine T. MacArthur Foundation Web site: http://www.macfound.org/atf/cf/%7BB0386CE3-8B29-4162-8098-E466FB856794%7D/DML_ETHNOG_WHITEPAPER.PDF

Jenkins, H., Clinton, K., Purushotma, R., Robison, A., & Weigel, M. (2006). *Confronting the Challenges of Participatory Culture: Media Education for the 21st Century.* Retrieved from the John D. and Catherine T. MacArthur Foundation Web site: http://digitallearning.macfound.org/atf/cf/%7B7E45C7E0-A3E0-4B89-AC9C-E807E1B0AE4E%7D/JENKINS_WHITE_PAPER.PDF

Johnston, J., Brzezinski, E., & Anderman, E. M. (1994). *Taking the Measure of Channel One: A Three-Year Perspective.* Ann Arbor, MI: Institute for Social Research.

Kaiser Family Foundation. (2003). *Children and the News: Coping with Terrorism, War and Everyday Violence.* Retrieved from www.kff.org/entmedia/upload/Key-Facts-Children-and-the-News.pdf

Kaiser Family Foundation. (2010). *Generation M2: Media in the Lives of 8- to 18-Year-Olds.* Retrieved from http://www.kff.org/entmedia/mh012010pkg.cfm

Knight Commission on the Information Needs of Communities in a Democracy. (2009). *Informing Communities: Sustaining Democracy in the Digital Age.* Washington, DC: The Aspen Institute.

Levin, B. (2010). *Universal Broadband: Targeting Investments to Achieve Meaningful Broadband Access for All Americans.* The Aspen Institute Communications and Society Program. Washington, DC: The Aspen Institute.

Levine, P. (2008). "A Public Voice for Youth: The Audience Problem in Digital Media and Civic Education." In W. L. Bennet (Ed.), *Civic Life Online: Learning How Digital Media Can Engage Youth* (119–138). Cambridge, MA: MIT Press.

Manzo, K. (2009, March 7). Testing Tech Literacy [blog post]. Retrieved from http://blogs.edweek.org/edweek/DigitalEducation/2009/03/testing_tech_literacy.html

McDevitt, M., & Chaffee, S. H. (2000). "Closing Gaps in Political Communication and Knowledge: Effects of a School Intervention." *Communication Research 27*, 259–292.

Media Education Lab (2010). Powerful Voices for Kids. Retrieved from http://mediaeducationlab.com

Metzger, M. J. (2007). "Making Sense of Credibility on the Web: Models for Evaluating Online Information and Recommendations for Future Research." *Journal of the American Society for Information Science and Technology 58* (13), 2078–2091.

Metzger, M. J. (2009). Credibility Research to Date. Retrieved from the Credibility and Digital Media @ UCSB website: http://www.credibility.ucsb.edu/past_research.php

Mihailidis, P. (2009). Media Literacy: Empowering Youth Worldwide. Retrieved from the Center for International Media Assistance Web site: http://cima.ned.org/sites/default/files/CIMA-Media_Literacy_Youth-Report.pdf

National Association for Media Literacy Education. (2007). Core Principles of Media Literacy Education in the Untied States. Retrieved from http://namle.net/wp-content/uploads/2009/09/NAMLE-CPMLE-w-questions2.pdf

National Communication Association. (1998). *Competent Communicators: K–12 Speaking, Listening and Media Literacy Standards and Competencies.* Washington, DC: Author.

National Council for the Accreditation of Teacher Education. (2007). *Professional Standards for the Accreditation of Teacher Preparation Institutions.* Retrieved from http://www.ncate.org/public/standards.asp?ch=4

National Council of Teachers of English. (2003). *Position Statement on Multi-Modal Literacies.* Retrieved from http://www.ncte.org/positions/statements/multimodalliteracies

Newspaper Association of America Foundation. (2004). *Growing Lifelong Readers: A Study of the Impact of Student Involvement with Newspapers on Adult Readership.* Retrieved from http://www.nieworld.com/lifelongreaders.htm

Office of Communications, OFCOM. (2010). *Silver Surfers Day*. Retrieved from http://www.ofcom.org.uk/consumer/2010/05/silver-surfers-day-2

Partnership for 21st Century Skills. (2009). *Professional Development: A 21st Century Skills Implementation Guide*. Retrieved from http://p21.org/documents/p21-stateimp_professional_development.pdf

Parentership for 21st Century Skills. (2010). *American Association of Colleges for Teacher Education*. Washington, DC. Retrieved from http://www.p21.org.

Partnow, J. (2010, June 24). Media and News Media in Seattle. *Youth Media Reporter*. Retrieved from http://www.youthmediareporter.org/2010/06/media_and_news_literacy_in_sea.html56 Digital andMedia Literacy: APlan of Action

PBS. (2010). *Digitally Inclined: Teachers Increasingly Value Media and Technology*. Washington, DC: Grunwald Associates.

Pew Internet & American Life Project. (2009). Teens and Sexting [press release]. Retrieved from http://www.pewinternet.org/Press-Releases/2009/Teens-and-Sexting.aspx

Pinkham, C., Wintle, S., & Silvernail, D. (2008). *21st Century Teaching and Learning: An Assessment of Student Website Evaluation Skills*. Retrieved from the University of Southern Maine Center for Education Policy, Applied Research and Evaluation website: http://usm.maine.edu/cepare/pdf/Sanford_rpt_dec_08.pdf

Place, E., Kendall, M., Hiom, D., Booth, H., Ayres, P., Manuel, A., & Smith, P. (2006). *Internet detective: Wise up to the web*. (3rd ed.). Intute Virtual Training Suite. Retrieved from http://www.vts.intute.ac.uk/detective

Rothkopf, A. (2009, October 15). Keynote address to the National Forum on Information Literacy. Washington, DC.

Salomon, G. & Perkins, D. (1989). "Rocky Roads to Transfer: Rethinking Mechanisms of a Neglected Phenomenon." *Educational Psychologist 24*, 113–142.

Staksrud, E., Livingstone, S., Haddon, L., & Ólafsson, K. (2009). *What Do We Know about Children's Use of Online Technologies? A Report on Data Availability and Research Gaps in Europe*. (2nd ed.). London: EU Kids Online, London School of Economics and Political Science.

Stephens, R., & Scott, E. (2009). White Paper: Ensuring Workforce Skills of the Future. Retrieved from http://birth2work.org/main.php

Texas Education Agency. (2006). *Texas Educator Certification Preparation Manual. English Language Arts and Reading 8–12*. Retrieved from http://www.texes.ets.org/assets/pdf/testprep_manuals/131_elar8_12_55003_web.pdf

Trotter, A. (2009, January 21). Tech Literacy Confusion. *Education Week*. Retrieved from www.edweek.org/dd/articles/2009/01/21/03techlit.h02.html

21st Century Skills Incentive Fund Act, S. 1029, 111th Cong. (2009).

U.S. Department of Education. (2010). *Teachers Use of Educational Technology in U.S. Public Schools: 2009* (NCES 2010–040). Retrieved from http://www.nces.ed.gov/pubs2010/2010040.pdf

U.S. Department of Education, Institute of Education Sciences, National Center for Education Evaluation and Regional Assistance. (2008). *Improving Adolescent Literacy: Effective Classroom and Intervention Practices: A Practice Guide.* (NCEE #2008-4027). Retrieved from http://ies.ed.gov/ncee/wwc/pdf/practiceguides/adlit_pg_082608.pdf

U.S. Department of Education, Office of Educational Technology. (2010). *Transforming American Education: Learning Powered by Technology.* Retrieved from http://www.ed.gov/technology/netp-2010

Vahlberg, V., Peer, L., & Nesbit, M. (2008). If It Catches My Eye: An Exploration of Online News Experiences of Teenagers. Retrieved from the Media Management Center, Northwestern University Web site: http://www.mediamanagementcenter.org/research/teeninternet.pdf

Vaidhyanathan, S. (2008, September 19). Generational Myth: Not All Young People Are Tech Savvy. *The Chronicle Review.* Retrieved from http://chronicle.com/article/Generation-Myth/32491

Vigdor, J., & Ladd, H. (2010). *Scaling the Digital Divide: Home Computer Technology and Student Achievement.* Retrieved from http://www.hks.harvard.edu/pepg/PDF/events/colloquia/Vigdor_ScalingtheDigitalDivide.pdf

Walma van Der Molen, J. (2003, May). "Direct Fright or Worry? A Survey of Children's Fear Reactions to Violence in Fiction and News." Paper presented at the annual meeting of the International Communication Association, San Diego, CA.

Winsten, J. (2009, December 28). *The Designated Driver Campaign: Why It Worked.* Retrieved from http://www.huffingtonpost.com/jay-winston/designated-driver-campaig_b_405249.html

Witherspoon Institute. (2010). *The Social Costs of Pornography: A Statement of Findings and Recommendations.* Princeton: NJ.

Wojcicki, E. (2010, Summer). Journalism: English for the 21st Century. Nieman Reports. Retrieved from http://www.nieman.harvard.edu/reportsitem.aspx?id=102407

Appendix: Portraits of Success

Dozens of digital and media literacy programs are taking hold across the nation and around the world. The following portraits of success offer some illustration of the many creative initiatives that bring together diverse stakeholders. This list, assembled from information provided by the author and the organizations' Web sites, is intended to illustrate the variety of programs engaging people of all ages in acquiring the critical skills for digital citizenship.

Adobe Youth Voices. Launched in June 2006 by the Adobe Foundation, Adobe Youth Voices is designed to provide youth in underserved communities with the critical digital communication skills they need to become active and engaged members of their communities and the world at large. Participating youth aged 13 to 18 use cutting-edge multimedia tools to create videos, animations, photo essays, presentations, music, and other pieces and share their ideas about topics that concern or interest them, such as peer pressure, religious and cultural identity, substance abuse, environmental degradation, and the impacts of war. These works are then shared through Youth Voices' global network of more than 500 participating sites, grantees, and organizations in 32 countries that engage youth and educators in schools and out-of-school programs. Visit http://youthvoices.adobe.com/about

BBC School Report. One of the most ambitious news literacy programs ever developed is the BBC School Report project. This program enables 25,000 children in more than 700 UK schools to learn about the practice of journalism and news production. Children develop community-based television and radio news reports that air locally and nationally during a specific time period. School Report's mission is to engage young people with news, bring their voices and stories to a wider audience, and share some of the public service values behind content creation, such as fairness, accuracy, and impartiality, because so many young people are content creators and distributors. The main aim of BBC News School Report is to interest young people in news of all sorts, and the world around them, by giving them the chance to make their own news. The program helps students develop skills of gathering information, teamwork, and time management, while providing an opportunity to discuss the responsibilities involved in broadcasting to a worldwide audience. Visit http://news.bbc.co.uk/2/hi/school_report

Center for News Literacy. The Center for News Literacy at Stony Brook University teaches students how to use critical thinking skills to judge the reliability and credibility of news reports and news sources. The Center recruits experienced journalists in career transitions to be News Literacy Fellows for two years and works with them to launch new undergraduate courses with curricula that meet the needs of the host universities. With initial funding from the John S. and James L. Knight Foundation, the center also is at work developing curriculum materials for high schools and the general public and a National News Literacy Web site through which students can collaborate on news literacy projects. Visit http://www.stonybrook.edu/journalism/newsliteracy

City Voices, City Visions. Since 2000, the University at Buffalo's Graduate School of Education has been working in collaboration with the Buffalo Public Schools to help bring digital and media literacy to teachers and students through the project City Voices, City Visions (CVCV). CVCV promotes student academic achievement and empowerment through the use of digital video tools and an emphasis on visual and analytic thinking and understanding. The program includes professional development for urban teachers to learn the use of digital video arts and communication technologies to help students meet higher learning standards in literacy and the academic disciplines. CVCV publishes and archives digital videos produced by students and teachers as curriculum and community resources. Visit http://gse.buffalo.edu/org/cityvoices

Common Sense Media. This San Francisco-based nonprofit organization provides independent information and tools about media and technology in the home so that families can make informed choices and have a voice about the media they consume. The Common Sense Media Web site includes reviews and ratings of movies, games, mobile apps, Web sites, books, and music by professional reviewers, parents, and kids. There are also resource materials specifically designed for parents and educators. Visit http://www.commonsensemedia.org

DigMe. The Digital Media (DigMe) Program at Roosevelt High School in Minneapolis uses digital media to help urban high school students learn to think critically, build meaning, and demonstrate their understanding across the subjects. The curriculum is based on the national standards in Media Literacy and 21st Century Skills. Students participate in daily reading, writing, analyzing, and discussion activities, and design and produce projects that demonstrate learning in a variety of ways, often using digital media tools. The school partners with faculty from the University of Minnesota from the fields of education, new technologies, and journalism. They aim for strong school-to-work connections by establishing relationships and internships with local technical schools, artists, studios, and businesses in the field of new media and digital media. Visit http://roosevelt.mpls.k12.mn.us/Digital_Media.html

Finding Dulcinea. This Web site addresses the "context deficit" that occurs with online searching. The name of the Web site is a reference to Miguel Cervantes's classic work of fiction, whose hero Don Quixote searches for an imaginary, idealized woman named Dulcinea. The Web site offers a section, "Behind the Headlines," which provides contextual background information on news and current events, and another section, "Suspicious Sites," offers an analysis of how sites with inaccurate and misleading information can be made to seem credible. Visit http://www.findingdulcinea.com

Global Kids. This organization uses digital media to promote global awareness and youth civic engagement. Students develop digital literacy competencies, engage in substantive online dialogues, and participate in civic action. For example, in the Virtual Video Project, students learn about critical human rights issues and filmmaking and then create educational "machinima"—short animated films created using virtual worlds—to promote awareness and action. Visit http://www.globalkids.org

IFC Media Project. This television series airs on the Independent Film Channel (IFC). This documentary series examines America's news media and seeks to uncover the truth about the news. In its first two seasons it was hosted by award-winning journalist Gideon Yago and featured in-depth reporting on controversial topics facing today's media, including how the United States is portrayed in world media and the impact of the economic downturn on the news industry. Visit http://www.ifc.com/about

Kids Voting. A media education program that gets students involved in civics, this program offers K–12 curriculum for use during an election campaign. The program integrates civics education and preparation for voting with newspaper reading and media analysis. The program now reaches an estimated 4.3 million students, 200,000 teachers, 10,600 schools, and 20,000 voter precincts. Students are encouraged to analyze and critique political advertisements, news stories, and candidate debates. Careful studies of Kids Voting show that after children are involved in the program, there are strong increases in reading newspapers, paying attention to campaign and related news on television, and discussing campaign-related issues with peers and parents (McDevitt & Chaffee, 2000). Visit http://www.kidsvotingusa.org

Know the News. Developed by Link TV, Know the News is an online learning tool for journalism students and citizen journalists, exploring the issues that shape television news, including bias, authorship, authenticity, ethics, and media ownership. Funded by the John S. and James L. Knight Foundation, the Web site is designed to help users think critically about TV news by framing news coverage in a global context based on Link TV's original productions, *Global Pulse* and *Latin Pulse,* which compare, contrast, and analyze news coverage from more than 70 broadcasters worldwide.

National Association for Media Literacy Education (NAMLE). This national membership organization is dedicated to ensuring that all people have the skills needed to critically analyze and create messages using the wide variety of communication tools now available. NAMLE brings together a broad-based coalition of media literacy practitioners and advocates from diverse fields, professions, and perspectives in a national, nonprofit membership organization to act as a key force in bringing high-quality media literacy education to all students in the United States, their parents, teachers, health care providers, counselors, clergy, political representatives, and communities. It holds conferences every two years and publishes an online, open access, peer-reviewed journal, the *Journal of Media Literacy Education.* Visit http://namle.net

National Writing Project. The NWP is a nationwide network of educators working to improve the teaching of writing and learning in the nation's schools and communities. They provide high-quality professional development programs to teachers across disciplines and at all levels, from early childhood through college. NWP's national network includes more than 200 university-based sites located in all 50 states. They have begun to explore digital and media literacy with a special program for their members called "Digital Is" where educators share work and practice and think across a variety of learning environments about elements that support effective digital writing and learning for students. Visit http://www.nwp.org

The News Literacy Project. This is an educational program that is bringing experienced journalists into middle school and high school classrooms to teach students the critical thinking skills they need to be smarter and more frequent consumers and creators of credible information across all media. Students are learning how to distinguish verified information from raw messages, spin, gossip, and opinion and are being encouraged to seek news and information that will make them well-informed citizens and voters. The project was founded in early 2008 by Alan Miller, an investigative reporter for the *Los Angeles Times,* after speaking to his daughter's Besthesda, Maryland, middle school class about why journalism matters. Visit http://www.thenews literacyproject.org

Powerful Voices for Kids. This university–school partnership is a collaborative program supported by the Media Education Lab at Temple University's School of Communications and Theater and the Russell Byers Charter School in Philadelphia. The program offers a comprehensive media literacy and technology integration program for children aged 5 to 12 that includes a four-week summer learning program for children, a staff development program for educators, in-school and after-school mentoring, and a research and assessment component. The program is designed to strengthen children's abilities to think for themselves, communicate effectively using language and technology tools, and use their powerful voices to contribute to the quality of life in their families, their schools, their communities, and the world. Evidence from the program reveals statistically significant gains in children's ability to identify the author, purpose, and target audience of a media message. Visit http://mediaeducationlab.com/powerful-voices-kids

Project Look Sharp. Developed at Ithaca College, this program provides materials, training, and support for the effective integration of media literacy with critical thinking into classroom curricula at all education levels. It offers professional development programs to educators across the state of New York, working in close coordination with the local school districts in the surrounding communities. Their multimedia materials enable social studies and science teachers to integrate critical analysis of news media into the K–12 curriculum. For example, Media Construction of War includes a 125-page kit that analyzes *Newsweek* magazine's coverage of the Vietnam War, Gulf War, and the war in Afghanistan. The kit includes three dozen slides of carefully selected *Newsweek* covers with teacher guides for each, histories of all three wars, a 12-minute video, and a lesson plan on media coverage of the Persian Gulf War. Students score information about the wars in Vietnam, the Persian Gulf, and Afghanistan while examining how media influence public opinion of current events and how to ask key media literacy questions about author, purpose, and point of view. Visit http://www.ithaca.edu/looksharp

Project New Media Literacies. Located at USC's Annenberg School for Communication, this program explores how to best equip young people with the social skills and cultural competencies needed for full participation in an emergent media landscape. They have developed resources for both in and out of the classroom for educators and learners who are interested in further understanding the new media literacies and integrating them into their learning environments. Visit http://newmedialiteracies.org

Salzburg Academy on Media and Global Change. This summer education program gathers 60 university-level students and a dozen faculty from five continents for three weeks in Austria. The program explores media's role in global citizenship, examining these questions: "How do news media affect our understanding of cultures and politics?" and "How can media better cover global problems and report on possible solutions?" The program was created by the International Center for Media and the Public Agenda, an academic institute based at the University of Maryland. Students and faculty work together to create a series of curriculum materials to explore the intersections of global media, freedom of expression, and civil society. The first half of the curriculum emphasizes basic media literacy skills—comprehension, analysis, and evaluation. Students learn to identify what news is and how media, as well as other actors, decide what information matters. They monitor, analyze, and compare media coverage of people and events and understand media's role in shaping global issues. The second half of the curriculum highlights the connections between media literacy and civil society and informs individuals about the importance of exercising their rights to freedom of expression. Visit http://www.salzburg.umd.edu/salzburg/new

Silver Surfers Day. In England, the Office of Communications, the British national government agency responsible for communications regulation, hosts a national event, Silver Surfers Day, with more than 1,500 events across the country specifically for people aged 55 and older to get a gentle introduction to the Internet. Participating businesses and organizations in the community determine how they will participate and what events they will offer. Older adults may learn about sharing photos, online banking, finding health care information, or other activities tailored to their needs and interests. Visit http://silversurfers.digitalunite.com

St. Louis Gateway Media Literacy Partners. This collaborative partnership brings together educators, parents, media professionals, and citizens in the St. Louis metropolitan area. For four years, they have hosted Media Literacy Week, which offers myriad public events supported by nearly a dozen community organizations, including universities and colleges, school districts, nonprofit organizations, and health care organizations. The partnership helps spread the word on the importance of media literacy and media literacy education, including the connection between digital and media literacy skills and economic development, with partners sharing the costs of developing programs and services for the community. Their citizen base includes public and private pre-K–12 teachers, parents, and administrators; higher-education faculty and administrators from various academic disciplines; after-school program leaders and employees; arts and culture leaders; health and allied-health professionals; media businesses; media communicators and producers; public-policy makers; public and private librarian-technologists; and business professionals. Visit http://www.gmlpstl.org

The News Literacy Project. This is an educational program that is bringing experienced journalists into middle school and high school classrooms to teach students the critical thinking skills they need to be smarter and more frequent consumers and creators of credible information across all media.

Students are learning how to distinguish verified information from raw messages, spin, gossip, and opinion and are being encouraged to seek news and information that will make them well-informed citizens and voters. The project was founded in early 2008 by Alan Miller, an investigative reporter for the *Los Angeles Times*, after speaking to his daughter's Besthesda, Maryland, middle school class about why journalism matters. Visit http://www.thenews literacyproject.org

Youth Media Reporter. YMR is a professional multimedia journal that serves practitioners, educators, and academics in the youth media field. The journal helps to build the field by documenting the insights and leading lessons in engaging young people in video, film, television, radio, music, the Internet, art, and print. Managed by the Academy for Educational Development and supported by the Open Society Institute and the McCormick Foundation, YMR is a multimedia Web journal that publishes six to eight high-quality articles every other month. Visit http://www.youthmediareporter.org

3. Stance of the AAP and Media Literacy

Marjorie J. Hogan, MD,
and Victor C. Strasburger, MD

For more than two decades, the American Academy of Pediatrics (AAP) has recognized both the public health risks and benefits of mass media for children and adolescents. (APA Committee on Public Education, 1999; APA Council on Communications and Media, 2010). The breadth of mass media subtypes is burgeoning and includes television, film, video and computer games, the Internet, music lyrics, and videos, as well as print media (newspaper, magazines, books), the new social media, and advertising in all of its forms. The potential benefits offered by media use are clear—from selected educational television programs to thought-provoking magazine articles, to the creativity encouraged through computer use. However, pediatricians are increasingly aware of and concerned about negative media influence on children and youth (Strasburger, Jordan, & Donnerstein, 2010). Media education, or media literacy, has the potential to reduce the harmful effects of media and promote the positive effects. Accordingly, the AAP has published several relevant policy statements summarizing the evidence-based research about the effects of media and encouraging media education for parents, adolescents, and children as an approach to encouraging a healthy media diet and mitigating potentially harmful effects.

American children and adolescents spend more time with a variety of media than they do with any other activity except sleeping. A 2010 survey of 8- to 18-year-olds revealed a staggering amount of media use—more than 7 hours daily. For multitasking teens, the daily time spent with media approaches 10 hours (Rideout, Foehr, & Roberts, 2010). And early research demonstrates that multitasking is not efficient (Small & Vorgan, 2008). By the time today's youth reach age 70 years, they will have spent 7 to 10 years of their lives watching television (Strasburger, 2006b). Even a majority of children under age 2 watch television between 1 and 2 hours daily, despite the AAP's recommendation (Vandwater et al., 2007). Today, more American homes have television than indoor plumbing, and a typical child lives in a home with multiple television sets (four), DVD or VCR players (three), video game consoles (two), and computers (two). The same survey found a disturbing pattern of bedroom-located media: More than 70 percent of teens have a television in their bedrooms; 50 percent have a video-game player; 50 percent have a VCR or DVD player; and a third have a computer with Internet access (Rideout et al., 2010). In addition to concern about the messages and images viewed, time spent with media often displaces involvement in creative, active, and social pursuits.

For more than two decades, evidence-based research, including longitudinal studies, find media messages and images to be associated with several serious health and behavioral problems in children and adolescents.

- Media are rife with violent images and messages, from top-grossing movies to popular video games to the evening news broadcast. More than 2,000 scientific studies and scholarly reviews have shown that certain children and adolescents exposed to violent media are at risk for aggressive behavior, desensitization to violence, and to view the world as a "meaner and scarier place" than it actually is (Anderson et al., 2003; Cantor, 1998; Christakis & Zimmerman, 2003; Strasburger et al., 2009). Whether from real-life or animated figures, children learn powerful lessons from viewing or using violent media: Violence is justified; violence is the first response to resolve a conflict; violence is often humorous and without long-term consequence. Especially for young or otherwise vulnerable children, violence used for entertainment purposes or news reports of real-life horrors, such as bombings, murders, or earthquakes, may cause fear, anxiety, or nightmares (Cantor, 1998).

- American media—both programming and advertising—are highly sexualized in their content. On prime-time television, more than 77 percent of shows contain sexualized material and themes, yet for only 14 percent of sexual incidents is there any mention of the risks or responsibilities of sexual activity (Kunkel et al., 2005; Strasburger, 2006b). Recent research adds the concern that exposure to this sexual content may contribute to an early sexual debut during adolescence (Brown et al., 2006). Other cumulative messages to young people seem ironic—companies making erectile dysfunction drugs advertise widely on prime-time television, making sex seem to be a harmless, recreational activity; at the same time, many of these stations are reluctant to promote condoms, birth control methods, and emergency contraception (Brown et al., 2006; APA Council on Communications and Media, 2010). How confusing for children and adolescents: to make sense of the behavior of adults on soap operas and prime-time dramas and the scantily clad folks selling everything from cars to beer but to hear few coherent messages about safe and responsible sexual behavior.

• Increasingly, media messages and images normalize and glamorize the use of tobacco, alcohol, and illicit drugs. Manufacturers of the legal drugs, tobacco, and alcohol spend $15 billion and $6 billion yearly to entice youngsters into "just saying yes" (Tobacco Free Kids, n.d.). On television and in movies, media operates as a "superpeer"; that is, sympathetic characters are shown drinking and smoking, making these behaviors seem normative and desirable (Strasburger et al., 2009). Although smoking in movies peaked in 2005 and has decreased steadily since, more than half of PG-13 movies in 2009 still contain smoking scenes (Glantz et al., 2010). On American television, drinking scenes are common; many are humorous, and few portray any negative consequences of drinking. Furthermore, teens hear 85 explicit drug references daily through popular music (Primack et al., 2008). Advertising and enticements to smoke and drink are also easy to find on the Internet (and buying these products online is easy for savvy youth). A recent meta-analysis estimated that 44 percent of smoking initiation among children and teens is attributable to viewing smoking in movies (Millett & Glantz, 2010), and alcohol advertising is adept at convincing teens to begin drinking as well (Grube & Waiters, 2005).

• Excessive television use is shown to be one factor leading to obesity, one of the major health problems facing children and youth today (Harris et al., 2009; Jordan, Strasburger, & Kramer-Golinkoff, 2008). Interestingly, distorted body image and even eating disorders may also be related to media messages absorbed by children and teens (Hogan & Strasburger, 2008a). The look and body shape of models and celebrities gracing youth-oriented magazines and in movies and on television define the impossible perfection today's youth cannot attain.

Increased television use may also lead to decreased school achievement (Sharif, Wills, & Sargent, 2010), and new research is investigating the relationship between overstimulation from high levels of media use and attention deficit/hyperactivity and sleep disorders (Swing et al., 2010). Indeed, several studies conclude that infants and toddlers may suffer developmental deficits as a result of media exposure at these young ages. Within this context, the Disney company is offering to return money to parents who purchased "Baby Einstein" products, which advertised that the products would promote the brain power of their babies.

- What is on the media horizon? Today, children and youth spend many hours with the Internet, especially on the popular social networking sites (Facebook, MySpace, Twitter) and YouTube (Mitchell & Ybarra, 2009). Clearly, these sites offer positive opportunities for youth to define themselves and stay connected to "friends" and their youth culture. In addition, cell phones, which are owned by a majority of today's youth, allow connectivity (and some peace of mind to parents who want to know where the children are). But at the same time, both the Internet and cell phones have become important new sources of sexual information, pornography, "sexting," and networking. Recent studies have shown that nearly a quarter of MySpace profiles have sexual references (Moreno et al., 2009), and a troubling number of teens reported having sent or received nude pictures or videos. Many of the social networking profiles also include alcohol or illicit drug use. Recent information about "new media" being used as a forum for bullying adds concern to the reach of these technologies. Furthermore, Web sites promoting anorexia nervosa may put teens at risk for eating disorders (Borzekowski et al., 2010).
- The potential harmful outcomes of excessive or inappropriate media use are well researched. School readiness and learning basic preschool concepts, role modeling of tolerance and respect, mediated journeys to far-away lands, explanations and portrayals of nature or science—all of these are positive opportunities afforded by high-quality media programming or products. But unfortunately, the prosocial benefits are less well understood and are at risk of being overwhelmed by the antisocial applications of popular media (Hogan & Strasburger, 2008b).

How should parents, pediatricians, and other professionals concerned about the influence of mass media on children and adolescents approach this issue? How can harmful media messages be minimized and prosocial, educational programming be maximized? Media education does have the potential to reduce harmful media effects, but more research is needed. In the past two centuries, to be "literate" meant that a person could read and write. In the new millennium, to be literate means that a person can successfully understand and decode a variety of different media. Given the volume of information now transmitted through mass media as opposed to the written word, it is now as important to teach media literacy (media education) as it is to teach print literacy. The major tenets of media education include (McCannon, "Media Literacy," 2009) the following:

- All media messages are constructed.
- Media messages shape our understanding of the world.
- Individuals interpret media messages uniquely.
- Mass media have powerful implications.

A media-educated person will be able to limit his or her use of media; make positive, deliberate media choices; select creative alternatives to media consumption; develop critical thinking and viewing skills; and understand the political, social, economic, and emotional implications of all forms of mass media (Hogan, 2011).

Moreover, research suggests that media education may make young people less vulnerable to the harmful effects of media exposure. Some media education programs have led to less aggressive attitudes and behaviors, increased sophistication about advertising, fewer requests for commercial products, less alcohol and tobacco use, better nutritional habits and less obesity, better body self-image, few sexual disclosures on social networking sites, and less overall television viewing. Many countries have successfully implemented media education in school curricula. Even though media education is a key factor in limiting the potentially harmful effects of media use, scrutiny of the media industry's responsibility for its programming and advertising must not be ignored.

Parents, pediatricians, and other professionals also can play key roles in educating and advocating about media (Strasburger, 2006a):

- First, adults themselves need to become educated about the public health risks of media exposure.
- Pediatricians should ask two key media-related questions at each well-child visit.
  - How much entertainment media per day is the child or teen watching?
  - Is there a television set or Internet access in the child's or teen's bedroom?
- Pediatricians and parents should recognize health or behavior problems in children or teens that may relate to media exposure, including aggressive behavior, early initiation of smoking difficulties in school, or obesity. In addition, a recent study found that office-based counseling is effective (Barkin et al., 2008).
- Advice to parents should include the following (APA Council on Communications and Media, 2010; Hogan, 2001):
  - Limit screen time to 2 hours or less per day.
  - Encourage a careful selection of programs to view.

- ○ Coview and discuss content with children or teens.
- ○ Teach and model critical viewing skills.
- ○ Understand ratings systems for various media.
- ○ Be good media role models.
- ○ Emphasize alternative activities.
- ○ Keep media out of children's and teen's bedrooms.
- ○ Avoid use of media as an electronic babysitter.
- Parents should avoid television or video viewing for children under age 2 years.
- Adults should promote literacy programs widely, including Reach Out and Read.
- Schools should include innovative media education programs into curricula, especially programs on sex education, drug use prevention, and bullying.

So that all of us (children, adolescents, and adults) can enjoy the richness offered by mass media into this millennium, a commitment to media education can't be delayed or minimized in importance. Parents and other stakeholders in the development of healthy youth bear this responsibility—and we must not ignore the fact that media are driven by great financial reward, without consideration of the impact of media images and messages on young consumers.

References

American Academy of Pediatrics, Committee on Pubic Education. (1999). "Media Education." *Pediatrics 104*, 341–343.

American Academy of Pediatrics, Council on Communications and Media. (2010). "Policy Statement—Media Education." *Pediatrics 126*, 1012–1017.

Anderson, C. A., Berkowitz, L., Donnerstein, E., Huesman, L. R., Johnson, J. D., Linz, D., Malamuth, N. M., & Wartella, E. (2003). "The Influence of Media Violence on Youth." *Psychological Science in the Public Interest 4*, 81–110.

Barkin, S. L., Finch, S. A., Ip, E. H., Scheindlin, B., Craig, J. A., Steffes, J., Weiley, V., Slora, E., Altman, D., & Wasserman, R. C. (2008). "Is Office-Based Counseling about Media Use, Timeouts, and Firearm Storage Effective? Results from a Cluster-Randomized, Controlled Trial." *Pediatrics 122*, e15–e25.

Borzekowski, D., Summer Schenk, L. G., Wilson, J. L., & Peebles, R. (2010). "e-ANA and e-MIA: A Content Analysis of Pro-Eating Disorder Web Sites." *American Journal of Public Health* 100: 1526–1534.

Brown, J. D., L'Engle, K. L., Pardun, C. J., Guo, G., Kenneavy, K., & Jackson, C. (2006). "Sexy Media Matter: Exposure to Sexual Content in Music, Movies,

Television, and Magazines Predicts Black and White Adolescents Sexual Behavior." *Pediatrics 117*, 1018–1027.

Cantor, J. (1998). *Mommy, I'm Scared.* New York: Harcourt Brace.

Christakis, D. A., & Zimmerman, F. J. (2003). "Violent Television Viewing during Preschool Is Associated with Antisocial Behavior during School Age." *Pediatrics 120*, 993–999.

Glantz, S. A., Titus, K., Mitchell, S., Polansky, J. R., & Kaufmann, R. B. (2010). "Smoking in Top-Grossing Movies: United States 1991–2009." *Morbidity and Mortality Weekly Report 59*, 1014–1017.

Goodman, Steven. *Teaching Youth Media: A Critical Guide to Literacy, Video Production, and Social Change.* New York: Teachers College (2003).

Grube, J. W., & Waiters, E. (2005). "Alcohol in the Media: Content and Effects on Drinking Beliefs and Behaviors among Youth." *Adolescent Clinics of North America 16*, 327–343.

Harris, J. L., Pomeranz, J. L., Lobstein, T., & Brownell, K. D. (2009). "A Crisis in the Marketplace: How Food Marketing Contributes to Childhood Obesity and What Can Be Done." *Annual Review of Public Health 30*, 211–225.

Hogan, M. J., & Strasburger, V. C. (2008a). "Body Image, Eating Disorders, and the Media." *Adolescent Medicine State of the Art Reviews 19*, 521–546.

Hogan, M. J., & Strasburger, V. C. (2008b). "Media and Prosocial Behavior in Children and Adolescents." In L. P. Nucci & D. Narvaez (Eds.), *Handbook of Moral and Character Education.* New York: Routledge, 2008.

Hogan, M. J. (2011). "Parents and Other Adults: Models and Monitors of Healthy Media Habits." In D. G. Singer & J. L. Singer, *Handbook of Children and Media* (2nd ed.). Thousand Oaks, CA: Sage.

Jordan, A. B., Strasburger, V. C., & Kramer-Golinkoff, E. K. (2008). "Does Adolescent Media Use Cause Obesity and Eating Disorders?" *Adolescent Medicine State of the Art Reviews 19*, 431–449.

Kunkel, D., Eyal, K., Finnerty, K., Biely, E., & Donnerstein, E. (2005). *Sex on TV 4: A Biennial Report to the Kaiser Family Foundation.* Menlo Park, CA: Kaiser Family Foundation.

McCannon, R. (2009). "Media Literacy/Media Education: Solution to Big Media?" In V. C. Strasburger, B. J. Jordan, & A. B. Jordan (Eds.), *Children, Adolescents, and the Media,* (2nd ed.), 519–569. Thousand Oaks, CA: Sage.

Millett, C., & Glantz, S. A. (2010). "Assigning an "18" Rating to Movies with Tobacco Imagery Is Essential to Reduce Youth Smoking Rates." *Thorax 65*, 377–378.

Mitchell, K. J., & Ybarra, M. (2009). "Social Networking Sites: Finding a Balance Between Their Risks and Benefits." *Archives of Pediatric and Adolescent Medicine 163*, 87–89.

Moreno, M. A., Parks, M. R., Zimmerman, F. J., Brito, T. E., & Christakis, D. A. (2009). "Display of Health Risk Behaviors on MySpace by Adolescents." *Archives of Pediatric and Adolescent Medicine 163*, 27–34.

Primack, B. A., Dalton, M. A., Carroll, M. V., Agarwal, A. A., & Fine, M. J. (2008). "Content Analysis of Tobacco, Alcohol, and Other Drugs in Popular Music." *Archives of Pediatric and Adolescent Medicine 162*, 169–175.

Rideout, V. J., Foehr, U. G., & Roberts, D. F. (2010). *Generation M2: Media in the Lives of 8- to 18-Year-Olds.* Menlo Park, CA: Kaiser Family Foundation.

Sharif, I, Wills, T. A., & Sargent, J. A. (2010). "Effect of Visual Media Use on School Performance: A Prospective Study." *Journal of Adolescent Health 46*, 52–61.

Small, G., & Vorgan, G. (2008). *iBrain: Surviving the Technological Alteration of the Modern Mind.* New York: HarperCollins.

Strasburger, V. C. (2006a). " 'Clueless.' Why Do Pediatricians Underestimate the Media's Influence on Children and Adolescents?" *Pediatrics 117*, 1427–1431.

Strasburger, V. C. (2006b). "Risky Business: What Primary Care Practitioners Need to Know About the Influence of Media on Adolescents." *Primary Care 33*, 317–348.

Strasburger, V. C., Jordan, A. B., & Donnerstein, E. (2010). "Health Effects of Media on Children and Adolescents." *Pediatrics 125*, 756–767.

Strasburger, V. C., Wilson, B. J., & Jordan, A. B. (Eds.). (2009). *Children, Adolescents, and the Media* (2nd ed.). Thousand Oaks, CA: Sage.

Swing, E. L., Gentile, D. A., Anderson, C. A., & Walsh, D. A. (2010). "Television and Video Game Exposure and the Development of Attentional Problems." *Pediatrics 126*, 214–221.

Tobacco Free Kids. (n.d.). Home page. Retrieved from http://www.tobaccofreekids.org/research

Vandwater, E. A., Rideout, V. J., Wartella, E. A., Huang, X., Lee, J. H., & Shim, MS. (2007). "Digital Childhood: Electronic Media and Technology Use among Infants, Toddlers, and Preschoolers." *Pediatrics 119*, e1006–e1015.

4. A Bicycle Riding Theory of Media Literacy

Erica Weintraub Austin

Learning to use media is a lot like learning to ride a bike: Both can transport the user to exciting destinations or to nowhere in particular. Both require capabilities that develop only with physical and cognitive growth. Both require competencies that must be learned. In addition, some of the skills for using media and riding bicycles at first require lots of effort but with practice can become like reflexes. As a result, both bike riding and media use can seem almost effortless even though they require important skills. Finally, users of both media and bicycles benefit from observing safety precautions. Unlike riding a bicycle, however, people can use media even without having the necessary capabilities, competencies, or skills in place—and without using any head protection. This makes media use deceptively hazardous.

Media are powerful tools that can educate and motivate. Preschoolers can learn how to call 911 and thereby save a stricken parent. Citizens of an autocratic regime can organize and inspire one another to undo a dictatorship. Students can research a topic using dozens of sources ranging from popular media to scholarly publications. Although every media message is educational, however, not all potential lessons are healthy ones. A message may be intended to entertain or sell instead of to teach, but children and adults learn regardless. Media literacy comprises the ability to distinguish beneficial and truthful information from unhealthy or deceptive information. An explanation of how people make these distinctions can be called a theory of media literacy, and this theory has many parallels to learning to ride a bicycle.

This theory of media literacy postulates that effective use of media requires capabilities, competencies, and a skilled application of abilities. Media-literate media use requires reflective thinking but does not require a continuously high level of cognitive engagement—that simply is not realistic in our media-saturated environment. As of 2010, children 8–18 years of age used media an average of 7.5 hours per day, and with multitasking considered, that figure rose to 11-3/4 hours (Rideout, Foehr, & Roberts, 2010). Adults watch television about 5 hours per day in addition to increasingly using media over Internet and mobile devices (The Nielsen Company, 2009). Who would want to think deeply and critically for all of that time even if they could? We often use media to relax. This means that media-literate individuals have some abilities that operate in the background, much as skilled bicycle riders can maintain their balance without much effort when the terrain is easy and the course is uncrowded.

Capabilities

Capabilities include elements of cognitive sophistication, ranging from language development to the ability to control attentional processes. Even infants pay more attention to things that seem relevant to them, such as baby talk, contrasting colors, and things they can touch or taste. They pay less attention to things that hold little meaning for them, given their cognitive sophistication—for example, we would not expect an infant to find a mathematical proof very interesting. Nevertheless, young children do not yet have the ability we expect of adults to control their reactions to things they like or do not like, or to ignore things that might not be good for them. They may try to toddle after things that adults know are not safe. Their lack of ability to hold certain types of things in memory also makes it difficult for them to understand a story that includes subplots. Capabilities ranging from walking, running, and pushing small buttons on a remote to understanding symbols and another person's intentions all develop as the body and brain mature.

Competencies

Competencies are lessons that we learn from experience—vicarious or personally experienced. For example, children begin to learn what distinguishes a commercial from a program. They also learn what cues indicate that a scene in a program is a flashback to a previous time or, perhaps, a dream sequence. They learn that visual symbols or musical cues such as a darkening sky and thundering music can signal that something bad is about to happen in a story. They require certain capabilities to develop these competencies, but the competencies do not necessarily develop automatically with the capabilities. Media literacy education can provide considerable help here, such as teaching children lessons, for example, how to identify common techniques used by advertisers.

Skills

Skills are competencies applied as appropriate. It is a skill, for example, to react differently to a message about how great a product is depending on whether that message is delivered by a paid endorser or by an independent reviewer. People need to have the capabilities and competencies in place to be able to make such a distinction, but individuals also need to make use of them. Unfortunately, plenty of research exists to show that people do not always think things through in a purely logical way. Often we make a choice based on its convenience or appeal instead of on its functionality. For example, we may buy shoes that look great but don't fit very well, convincing ourselves that they will be fine after we break them in a little bit. We might buy a chair that is inexpensive but will not last very long. We might buy a brand of cereal because we like the picture on the box. We might vote for political candidates who seem trustworthy without learning every detail of their positions on the issues that matter to us. Some of these shortcuts in decision making may not matter much, and others may be costly.

The theory of media literacy presented here holds that we do these things for two reasons. The first is that we cannot put maximum effort into everything we do—we must and do allocate resources, and so we often rely on cognitive shortcuts (Lang, 2000). The second is that we are people, not purely logical algorithms—we make decisions based on affect in addition to logic (Austin, 2007). These two limitations—which also are strengths helping us manage our resources—mean that we cannot be expected to make perfect choices all the time. This theory of media literacy offers that those with greater media literacy skills will make fewer errors in judgment, because they will use shortcuts more effectively and will be more likely to forgo shortcuts when deeper reflection would be advisable.

A Menu of Media Literacy Skills

Research on information processing, decision making, and media effects suggests that, at minimum, the following skills are necessary elements for media literacy. I cite brief examples for each to illustrate their relevance:

Using Multiple Sources
A national study by Kohut, Morin, and Keeter (2007) found that the use of multiple sources explained greater knowledge about public affairs. Regular audiences of programs attracting the most knowledgeable viewers, including late-night talk shows, tended to use an average of 7 sources for their news, compared to an average of 4.6 sources for the full sample.

Questioning Assertions Made without Supporting Evidence
In a media literacy program designed to facilitate sex education, students who had the media literacy curriculum were less likely to overestimate sexual

activity among teens and were more aware of myths about sex that appear in the media (Pinkleton et al., 2008). Another experiment demonstrated an increase in reflective thinking about media messages (Pinkleton et al., 2007).

Considering the Motivations of Sources

A brief media literacy lesson focused on an in-school news program produced especially for teenagers and that included advertising targeted teens, increased recall of news program content and increased skepticism toward advertisers. Seventh graders benefited somewhat more than eighth graders, suggesting that those with more to learn benefit more from media literacy education (Austin et al., 2006).

Taking Notice of Message Structure, Such as Production Techniques

Scholars often note that children have difficulty understanding persuasive intent before age eight years, but a rudimentary understanding of the difference between a program appears to begin by understanding where a program stops and an ad begins (Kunkel et al., 2004).

Reflecting on How Media Messages Relate to Other Information and Real Life

Many scholars believe that media effects tend to be channeled through interpersonal discussion that compares media messages to past experience and prior knowledge (e.g., Cho et al., 2009; Kim & Kim, 2008; Southwell & Yzer, 2007). Others (McDevitt, 2005; McDevitt & Chaffee, 2002) have shown that adolescents who get public affairs information through entertainment often discuss issues with their parents and benefit even more from discussion they initiate than from discussion parents initiate.

Increasing Awareness That Emotion Can Bias Our Decision Making

An evaluation of a media literacy intervention focused on tobacco use prevention showed that curriculum participants' perceptions of peer norms about tobacco use were no longer affected by how desirable tobacco messages seem, whereas control-group participants' perceptions were affected by the desirability of messages (Austin et al., 2007). The messages still seemed desirable to both groups.

Summary: Media Literacy Education Provides Safer Transportation

The theory of media literacy advanced here asserts that media literacy education has value because it provides opportunities to develop and practice the competencies briefly enumerated above. People often will apply media literacy competencies learned and internalized as heuristics or instinctive responses, similar to the ways people learning to ride a bike internalize the skills of staying upright, turning, and braking. In music and athletics, we speak of muscle memory; in media literacy, we might speak of analytical memory. Much as bike riders increase their concentration when hazards appear, skilled media users can increase their active critical thinking processes when they identify a decision-making hazard. These include things such as a persuasive message or an assertion about something important made without supporting evidence. With media literacy capabilities, competencies, and skills in place we can arrive safely at the remarkable destinations where the media can take us.

References

Austin, E. W. (2007). "The Message Interpretation Process Model." In J. J. Arnett (Ed.), *Encyclopedia of Children, Adolescents, and the Media*. Thousand Oaks, CA: Sage.

Austin, E. W., Chen, Y., Pinkleton, Bruce. E, & Quintero Johnson, J. (2006). "The Benefits and Costs of *Channel One* in a Middle School Setting and the Role of Media Literacy Training." *Pediatrics 117*, e423–e433.

Austin, E. W., Pinkleton, B. E., & Funabiki, R. P. (2007). "The Desirability Paradox in the Effects of Media Literacy Training." *Communication Research 34*, 483–506.

Cho, J., Shah, D. V., McLeod, J. M., McLeod, D. M., Scholl, R. M., & Gottlieb, M. R. (2009). "Campaigns, Reflection, and Deliberation: Advancing an O-S-R-O-R Model of Communication Effects." *Communication Theory 19*, 66–88.

Kim, J., & Kim, E. J. (2008). "Theorizing Dialogic Deliberation: Everyday Political Talk as Communicative Action and Dialogue." *Communication Theory 18*, 51–70.

Kohut, A., Morin, R., & Keeter, S. (2007). *Public Knowledge of Current Affairs Little Changed by News and Information Revolutions: What Americans Know: 1989–2007*. Washington, DC: Pew Research Center for the People and the Press.

Kunkel, D., Wilcox, B., Cantor, J., Palmer, E., Linn, S., & Dowrick, P. (2004). *Psychological Issues in the Increasing Commercialization of Childhood: Report of the APA Task Force on Advertising and Children*. Washington, DC: American Psychological Association.

Lang, A. (2000). "The Information Processing of Mediate Messages: A Framework for Communication Research." *Journal of Communication 50*, 46–70.

McDevitt, M. (2005). "The Partisan Child: Developmental Provocation as a Model of Political Socialization." *International Journal of Public Opinion Research 18*, 67-88.

McDevitt, M., & Chaffee, S. (2002). "From Top-Down to Trickle-Up Influence: Revisiting Assumptions about the Family in Political Socialization." *Political Communication 19*, 281–301.

The Nielsen Company. (2009). A2/M2 Three Screen Report: 1st Quarter 2009. Retrieved from http://blog.nielsen.com/nielsenwire/wp-content/uploads/2009/05/nielsen_threescreenreport_q109.pdf.

Pinkleton, B. E., Austin, E., W., Cohen, M., Chen, Y., & Fitzgerald, E. (2008). "Effects of a Peer-Led Media Literacy Curriculum on Adolescents' Knowledge and Attitudes Toward Sexual Behavior and Media Portrayals Of Sex." *Health Communication 23*, 462–472.

Pinkleton, B. P., Austin, E. W., Cohen, M., Miller, A., & Fitzgerald, E. (2007). "A State-Wide Evaluation of the Effectiveness of Media Literacy to Prevent Tobacco Use among Adolescents." *Health Communication 21*, 23–34.

Rideout, V. J., Foehr, U. G., & Roberts, D. F. (2010). *Generation M2: Media in the lives of 8- to 18-year-olds.* Kaiser Family Foundation. Retrieved from http://www.kff.org/entmedia/upload/8010.pdf.

Southwell, B. G., & Yzer, M. C. (2007). "The Roles of Interpersonal Communication in Mass Media Campaigns." In C. Beck (Ed.), *Communication Yearbook* (Vol. 31), 420–462. Lexington, KY: International Communication Association.

5. History of U.S. Media Literacy Education

Sam Nkana

The push for media studies dates back to the early 1930s. In the 1930s, F. R. Leavis and his student Denys Thompson championed the protectionist or inoculative view that students and society must be protected from the presumed negative influence of the mass media (Buckingham, 2003: 6–7). According to Buckingham, the central objective of Leavis and Thompson was to preserve the literary heritage, language, values, and health of the nation (p. 7). The media were seen as a corrupting influence that offered superficial pleasures in place of authentic art and literature.

Masterman (1997) describes this phase of media studies as encouraging students to "develop discrimination, fine judgment, and taste" by learning the differences between the timeless values of authentic "high culture" and "low culture," in which mass media was believed to fit (p. 21). This view of the media as a catalyst to cultural decline prioritized what teachers believed to be media topics worth teaching. Advertising was perceived as an important topic for discussion because it typified all that was most dangerous about the media—their manipulation of audiences, materialistic values, and destructive influence on language. In addition to distrust of the advertising segment of the media, literary forms such as stories in women's magazines and children's comics came under scrutiny because their plots were often geared toward stereotypical issues (p. 22).

Educators claimed that the future of society depended on "the simple task of analyzing an advertisement" and helping children develop the capacity to stand back from the text, reflect upon the motivations behind the procedures used, understand the ways in which the text was affecting them, and then determine what were authentic and inauthentic uses of language. Pedagogically, this inoculative approach placed the teacher in the role of protector of acceptable culture and arbiter of good taste (Masterman, 1997: 21).

In the late 1950s and early 1960s, according to Buckingham (2003), Williams and Hoggart spearheaded a challenge to the Leavisite ideology of "inoculation" and "protectionism." Culture was no longer viewed as a fixed set of privileged artifacts of significance—"an approved 'canon' of literary texts," but as a whole way of life; and cultural expression was seen to take a variety of forms that ranged from the exalted to the everyday. This more liberal and inclusive approach began to challenge the distinctions between high culture and popular culture, as well as between art and lived experience (Buckingham, 2003: 7).

Masterman (1997) notes that the 1960s met with success as a new generation of teachers who enjoyed popular cultural forms entered the school systems. Although these teachers did not view the media as corrupting mechanisms, their objective was not to abandon protectionist approaches to media education but to modify and extend them (Masterman, 1997). The acceptance of film by educators in the 1960s set the stage for the introduction of film appreciation courses in classrooms both in Europe and North America (p. 22). However, media education continued to be "protectionist."

When media studies were introduced in the early 1930s, the concepts of *media education* or *media literacy* as they are understood today were nonexistent. However, as television gained international significance, the 1962 International Conference on Screen Education concluded the following:

> Because television is already a major channel of communication, and will increase in scope and power, we believe it is the responsibility of educators to teach our young people to use this medium in a constructive way. (Hodgkinson, 1964: 78)

Goodman (2003) states that media education in the early 1960s emphasized teaching about the media instead of through the media. Students were encouraged to develop critical attitudes toward the media, specifically toward advertising and television (p. 13). He continues:

> Cultural critics such as Vance Packard (*The Hidden Persuaders*), Marshall McLuhan (*Understanding Media, The Gutenberg Galaxy*), and John Berger (*Ways of Seeing*) contributed to this sense, arguing for the need to move beyond the instrumental approach of using instructional medias as a didactic tool. (p. 13)

Curricula began henceforth to emphasize development of skills for analyzing television as a mass media text (Goodman, 2003: 13).

A major turning point in the growth of media literacy in the United States occurred in 1972 when the Surgeon General's Advisory Committee on Television and Social Behavior linked television violence and antisocial behavior

(Goodman, 2003: 13). The following year, the Ford Foundation (Goodman, 2003) issued a report on children and television stating that

> there was an important need for widened and improved instruction about the mass media in the public schools. We decided that literacy of young persons in regard to the mass media is the proper concern for educational instruction analogous to their concern about language literacy. (p. 31)

Thus, in the 1970s a period of transition from film studies to the study of television took place. According to Masterman (1997), "the study of television and newspapers raised quite different, and, in many ways, much more urgent problems" (p. 27).

In 1978, instigated by the Surgeon General's report and a subsequent call for research on children and television violence, the United States Library of Congress and the United States Office of Education hosted a national conference on "Television, the Book and the Classroom" (Tyner, 1998: 135). As a result of that conference, there was a request for proposals to develop four major critical viewing projects in the United States aimed at elementary, secondary, and adult education. The following year, the United States Office of Education funded the following critical viewing skills (CVS) proposals: Far West Laboratory for Educational Research and Development (secondary education); WNET/Channel 13, New York (middle school education); and Boston University (a critical viewing package for adults) (Tyner, 1998: 135).

Tyner (1998) states further that Educational Testing Services (ETS) in the United States was designated to take charge of designing and conducting formative research and evaluation of the critical viewing curriculum created by Far West Laboratory for Educational Research and Development in San Francisco in the early 1980s. ETS had selected 25 reviewers, all teachers or public school administrators. At the close of the reviewing session, it was concluded that the curriculum was "of high interest to students, relevant to teaching critical viewing skills, and a good addition to courses already offered" (p. 135).

Despite the positive rating by the reviewers, 46 percent of them thought that teachers would not be enthusiastic about using the curriculum, and approximately 41 percent thought that administrators would not consider using it in their schools. One of the administrators in the panel stated, "I believe this curriculum is not only important but necessary. . . . I'm not sure my colleagues would agree" (Tyner, 1998: 135).

As cited in Tyner (1998), Donna Lloyd-Kolkin, the lead researcher on the Far West project, commented that despite plentiful funding, high marks from reviewers, community support, and the push to train teachers, little implementation was ever achieved (p. 135). Government funding continued, nonetheless, to support the activities that were active at the time. However, as soon as funding ran out for the projects around 1981, media activities ground to a halt in the United States (Goodman, 2003; Tyner, 1998).

Goodman (2003) points out that, in contrast to the general lack of interest in media education in the United States in the 1980s, major media development was taking place internationally. Throughout the 1980s, media education continued to expand in the United Kingdom. Goodman credits the expansion to "the work of grassroots organizations such as the Association for Media Education in Scotland, the Association for Media Literacy in Canada, and the Australian Teachers of Media." In due time, the theoretical and practical work of the Canadians, as well as that of the British media education practitioners such as Len Masterman, David Buckingham, and Cary Bazalgette, began to alter how media literacy functioned and was assimilated in the United States (p. 13).

According to Goodman (2003), during the 1992 Aspen Institute Leadership Forum on Media Literacy, media literacy representatives from Canada spearheaded a new emphasis on staff development "as media literacy courses and institutes for teachers were soon offered by the Harvard University Graduate School of Education, Columbia University's Teachers College, New York University, Appalachian State University in North Carolina, the New Mexico State Department of Education." He notes that, although a few of these programs have continued, "many were short lived." He also notes that this conference lacked the participation of public school teachers and administrators, which underscored the continued disconnect between media literacy education and American schools (p. 14).

It is important to note that the success of the Canadian media literacy program continued to fuel an interest in the field within the United States. The Harvard Media Literacy Institute was organized in 1993 by the Harvard University School of Graduate Studies under the direction of Renee Hobbs. Barry Duncan (1993), president of the Association for Media Literacy (AML) in Canada, was one of the teachers during the Institute. He states, "I had the privilege of helping to teach the first major Media Education Institute to be held in the United States." According to Duncan, the Institute attracted 85 participants from across North America, including teachers, journalists, and church leaders.

In 1986, the Ontario Ministry of Education invited 10 members of AML to prepare a *Media Education Resource Guide*. This guide was translated into

Spanish, French, Italian, and Japanese. With this guide in hand, AML members organized conferences in Canada, the United States, Japan, Europe, and in Latin America to promote media education. In 1989, according to Duncan, Pungente, and Anderson (2002),

> The AML held an invitational think tank to discuss future developments of media education in Ontario. This led to two successful international media education conferences at the University of Guelph in 1990 and 1992. Each conference attracted over 500 participants from around the world. (paragraph 8)

Francis Davis (1992), a media education specialist on the staff of the Center for Media Literacy from 1989 to 1992, gives credit to AML for its contribution to the growth of media education in the United States. He states,

> The present is an exciting moment for media education in the United States. However, one non-U.S. organization deserves mention also because of its contribution to U.S. efforts: Ontario's Association for Media Literacy (AML) is now recognized as a world leader in media education.

Noting the many publications AML has produced for secondary media education since 1988, Davis (1992) states that "the AML is responsible for much of the growing U.S. knowledge in the field, either through direct imitation or through having introduced U.S. leaders to British and Australian educators."

Goodman (2003) notes that in the 1990s, American efforts to promote media literacy came mainly from such government and private agencies as the National Drug Control Policy, the Center for Substance Abuse Prevention, parishes of the Catholic church, lobby organizations for regulation of children's TV such as the Center for Media Education in Washington, and medical practitioners such as the American Psychological Association and the American Academy of Pediatrics (pp. 14–15). Attempts to bring more grassroots teacher participation to the media education field resulted in the collaboration of the Educational Video Center with the Annenberg Institute for School Reform to cosponsor a national conference at Wingspread Conference Center, Racine, Wisconsin. The purpose of the 1995 conference was to explore how the emerging practices and principles of media education could help promote school reform efforts throughout the United States (p. 15).

Despite the effort put forth to find common ground, Goodman (2003) notes that media literacy had little impact on the new models of education designed by the national school reform networks. Although media literacy had been advocated numerous times by educational associations such as the National Council of Teachers of English and the Speech Communication Association, it failed to become a priority for most professional education associations (p. 15).

In their article, "Has Media Literacy Found a Curricular Foothold?" Kubey and Baker (1999) note Ernest L. Boyer's definition of media literacy.

> It is no longer enough simply to read and write. Students must also become literate in the understanding of visual images. Our children must learn how to spot a stereotype, isolate a social cliché, and distinguish facts from propaganda, analysis from banter, and important news from coverage. (p. 38)

A 1998 report in *The New York Times* indicated there were 12 states with media literacy curricular frameworks. However, the following year, Kubey and Baker (1999) reported that "at least 48 state curricular frameworks now contain one or more elements calling for some form of media education" (p. 38). They concluded:

> The drive for improving curriculum standards, and the process of involving those who teach in writing those standards, have produced near unanimity in this country on the inclusion of elements of what many call "media-literacy education" in the state frameworks. (p. 38)

In their study they examined the curricular objectives and educational goals from available frameworks by direct query to state departments of education or via the Internet. They noted where the media education elements in a state's framework appeared and if such elements fell under one or more of four different categories. They found most states' frameworks contained elements that fell under at least two of the categories. In exploring the frameworks, Kubey and Baker (1999) spotlighted some impressive elements. For example, North Carolina's framework states:

> It is an important goal of education for learners to be able to critique and use the dominant media of today. Visual literacy is essential for survival as consumers and citizens in our technologically intensive world. Learners will appreciate various visual forms and compositions, compare and contrast visual and print information, formulate and clarify personal response to visual messages, evaluate the form and content of various visual communication(s) [*sic*]. (p. 38)

West Virginia calls for students to "analyze media influence on tobacco and alcohol [use] and develop counter-advertisement for peer education." Kubey and Baker caution, however, that no one should interpret their enthusiasm as a belief that any of the state's media education goals are being met. They do, nonetheless, claim that "New Mexico and Massachusetts, followed by Utah and Minnesota, probably have the greatest proportion of students actually receiving media education" (Kubey & Baker, 1999: 38).

This research highlights the needs of our education systems in the area of media literacy education. Educators must recognize communication in our society has changed enough in this century that traditional training in literature and print communication is no longer adequate. Therefore, teachers should be provided with in-service training on the integration of media education into their curriculum.

References

Buckingham, D. (2003). *Media Education: Literacy, Learning and Contemporary Culture.* Malden, MA: Polity.

Davis, J. F. (1992). "Media Literacy: From Activism to Exploration." Background paper for the National Leadership Conference on Media Literacy. Retrieved March 9, 2010, from http://www.medialit.org/reading_room/pdf/357_Aspen Bkgnd_Davis.pdf

Duncan, B. (1993, Fall/Winter). "Harvard University Hosts First US Media Literacy Teaching Institute." *Telemedium: The Journal of Media Literacy.* Retrieved March 9, 2010, from http://www.medialit.org/reading_room/article535.html

Duncan, F. D., Pungente, J., & Andersen, N. (2002). *Media Education in Canada.* Etobicoke, Canada: Association for Media Literacy. Retrieved March 9, 2010, from http://www.aml.ca/articles/articles.php?articleID=272

Hodgkinson, A. W. (1964). *Screen Education: Teaching a Critical Approach to Cinema and Television.* Reports and papers on mass communication, no. 42, p. 78. Paris: Department of Mass Communication, UNESCO. Retrieved September 9, 2009, from http://unesdoc.unesco.org/images/ 0005/000595/ 059573eo.pdf

Kubey, R., & Baker, F. (1999, October 27). "Has Media Literacy Found a Curricular Foothold?" *Education Week*, 38–56.

Masterman, L. (1997). "A Rationale for Media Education." In R. Kubey (Ed.), *Media Literacy in the Information Age* (pp. 15–68). New Brunswick, NJ: Transaction.

Tyner, K. (1998). *Literacy in a Digital World: Teaching and Learning in the Age of Information.* Mahwah, NJ: Lawrence Erlbaum.

6. Standards, Media Literacy Education

Frank Baker

As part of the maturation process of media literacy education, the identification of a consistent set of standards and objectives across media literacy programs is becoming a major area of interest.

National Standards

One of the organizations that has consistently recognized and promoted media literacy education has been the National Council of Teachers of English (NCTE). Various actions and publications over the years have demonstrated that NCTE recognizes the value of teaching with and about the media. As early as 1932, the organization saw the potential of film as a teaching tool with the creation of the Committee on Photoplay Appreciation, a group that made recommendations about which films to use and developed film study guides.

From 1961 through 1964, NCTE produced the monthly *Studies in the Mass Media*, a publication designed to introduce students and teachers to using the mass media of communication as a teaching resource.

In 1961, Neil Postman authored *Television and the Teaching of English*, a book with recommendations for teachers on how to incorporate television into the English language arts classroom.

The next year, NCTE's Committee on the Use of Mass Media published *Using Mass Media in the Schools*. One of the questions the book sought to answer was: What are teachers doing to help students learn to discriminate, evaluate, and live with mass media?

By 1963, NCTE had established a Committee on Motion Pictures and the Teaching of English, an acknowledgment that film could be used as another teaching tool.

At its 1970 annual meeting, NCTE's board passed a Resolution of Media Literacy, recognizing the powerful force of media in the lives of young people. The board urged the organization to "explore more vigorously the relationship of the learning and teaching of media literacy to other concerns of English instruction."

In 1973, NCTE passed the resolution "On Preparing Students with Skill for Evaluating Media," urging its members to teach "television and radio evaluation" in grades K–12; it also urged colleges and universities to prepare teachers to help students develop evaluation skills.

In 1975, NCTE passed a Resolution on Promoting Media Literacy. It grew out of an "awareness among educators that understanding the new media and using them constructively and creatively actually required developing a new form of literacy—new critical abilities 'in reading, listening, viewing, and thinking' that would enable students to deal constructively with complex new modes of delivering information, new multisensory tactics for persuasion, and new technology-based art forms."

The resolution urged:

- That NCTE continue to encourage teacher education programs that will enable teachers to promote media literacy in students; and
- That NCTE cooperate with organizations and individuals representing teachers of journalism, the social sciences, and speech communication to promote the understanding and develop the insights students need to evaluate critically the messages disseminated by the mass media.

By 1979, NCTE had created a "Commission on Media," composed of educators interested in media literacy and related issues. In 1988, the new Assembly on Media Arts, was publishing a newsletter for members titled *Media Matters*, which covered news about media literacy projects, books and film reviews, interviews with experts, and lesson plans.

In 1984, NCTE and the Commission on Media endorsed media literacy: "We are recognizing a need to integrate all communication media into the teaching of English and the language arts" *Telemedium (2006 Summer) 53* (1), 28.

In 1991, NCTE's Commission on Media warned that students who lack the tools to evaluate and work with nonprint media will be unprepared to live thoughtfully and productively in the present and the future.

In 1996, the NCTE and the International Reading Association copublished "Standards for the English Language Arts." The two groups listed 12 standards. Embedded within these were several references to media and media literacy. For example, Standard 1 says: "Students read a wide range of print and *nonprint* texts." The inclusion of the word *nonprint* is a clear reference to everything from photographs, to video, sound, television, and motion pictures.

Standard 3 reads: "Students apply a wide range of strategies to comprehend, interpret, evaluate, and appreciate texts," specifically mentioning the textual features of texts, including graphics—another reference to the use of visuals to support text.

Standard 4 says: "Students adjust their use of spoken, written, and visual language (e.g., conventions, style, vocabulary) to communicate effectively with a variety of audiences and for different purposes."

Standard 6 makes a direct reference to media literacy: "Students apply knowledge of language structure, language conventions (e.g., spelling and punctuation), *media techniques*, figurative language, and genre to create, critique, and discuss print and nonprint texts." Knowledge of "media techniques" most certainly includes the manner, tools, and methods used by media producers to create meaning.

Standard 8 also refers to media: "Students use a variety of technological and information resources (e.g., libraries, databases, computer networks, video) to gather and synthesize information and to create and communicate knowledge."

Finally, Standard 12 notes, "Students use spoken, written, and visual language to accomplish their own purposes (e.g., for learning, enjoyment, persuasion, and the exchange of information)."

In 1996, the NCTE passed a resolution urging language arts teachers to consider the importance of bringing visual texts into the classroom. The resolution said:

> Viewing and visually representing (defined in the NCTE/IRA *Standards for the English Language Arts*) are a part of our growing consciousness of how people gather and share information. Teachers and students need to expand their appreciation of the power of print and nonprint texts. Teachers should guide students in constructing meaning through creating and viewing nonprint texts.

Three years later, in 1999, the Mid-Continent Research for Education and Learning (McRel) organization added two new strands to its national Language Arts standards—thus continuing the recognition of the importance of visual and media literacy:

- #9: Uses viewing skills and strategies to understand and interpret visual media.
- #10: Understands the characteristics and components of the media.

Additional information about incorporating the McRel standards can be found at: http://www.frankwbaker.com/mcrel

In 2002, the Partnership for 21st Century Skills was organized. The organization began as a collaboration between the US Department of Education and some large media and technology companies. Soon afterward, educational organizations (such as AASL and ASCD) also joined the partnership. The project's homepage (http://www.p21.org/) says it "advocates for 21st century readiness for every student."

The partnership recruited teachers in every discipline to assist in the development and publication of what it calls ICT (information, communication, and technology) curriculum skills maps. The maps provide specific recommendations about how instruction should address skills previously identified as being necessary for students to compete in a 21st-century world. One of the first maps P21 released was the ICT map for the English Language Arts.

Included in this multipage document was a page devoted to "information and media literacy" skills.

Since the release of the ELA map, other maps have been published and all have included recommendations for incorporating media literacy into instruction.

In 2003, the National Board of Professional Teaching Standards (Adolescent and Young Adult, English Language Arts standards) recognized the importance of media and visual literacy when it declared:

> Accomplished teachers know that students must become critical and reflective consumers and producers of visual communication because media literacy has become an integral part of being literate in contemporary society. Teachers understand how words, images, graphics, and sounds work together in ways that are both subtle and profound. They understand that students need to learn the power of visual communication, from the uses of typefaces and white space on a written report to the uses of graphics and video in multimedia productions.

In 2004, "viewing" and "producing digital media" were components of the English & Communications benchmarks document produced by the American Diploma Project. The benchmarks "describe the skills needed for success in postsecondary education and work."

By the summer of 2011, 44 states had endorsed the Common Core Standards for the English Language Arts. By endorsing these standards, those states agreed to teach from the same national document. Although it did not specifically list "viewing," "visual representation," or "media literacy," the ELA document did include some language that could be construed as referring to the importance of teaching about the media. The document's introduction says:

> To be ready for college, workforce training, and life in a technological society, students need the ability to gather, comprehend, evaluate, synthesize, and report on information and ideas, to conduct original research in order to answer questions or solve problems, and to analyze and create a high volume and extensive range of print and nonprint texts in media forms old and new. The need to conduct research and to produce and consume media is embedded into every aspect of today's curriculum. In like fashion, research and media skills and understandings are embedded throughout the Standards rather than treated in a separate section.
>
> To read more specific references to and about media, embedded in the "Listening and Speaking" section, see: http://www.frankwbaker .com/media_core.htm

Some other elements of media literacy can also be found in the newly created national core standards for English Language Arts. Although media literacy is not specifically mentioned, elements of it can be found under the following sections:

Speaking and Listening: 8th Grade
- 2. Analyze the purpose of information presented in diverse media and formats (e.g., visually, quantitatively, orally) and evaluate the motives (e.g., social, commercial, political) behind its presentation.

Reading and Literature
7th grade
- 7. Compare and contrast a written story, drama, or poem to its audio, filmed, staged, or multimedia version, analyzing the effects of techniques unique to each medium (e.g., lighting, sound, color, or camera focus and angles in a film).

Informational Texts
7th grade
- 7. Compare and contrast a text to an audio, video, or multimedia version of the text, analyzing each medium's portrayal of the subject (e.g., how the delivery of a speech affects the impact of the words).

State Standards

In 1999, this author, in a collaboration with Rutgers University media studies professor Robert Kubey, conducted the first national study of media literacy in state K–12 teaching standards. The impetus for this study had been my participation in the 1998 National Media Education Conference, where I declared that if we wanted young people to become media literate, we should examine what each state's teaching standards say about what teachers should teach and students should learn. The result was a content analysis and subsequent op-ed published in the industry trade newspaper *Education Week,* "Has Media Education Found a Curricula Foothold?" (Baker & Kubey, 1999). We reported, that for the first time "elements of media literacy" could be found in the teaching standards of almost every state. Our survey examined the curriculum frameworks of English Language Arts, social studies and health. (Media literacy most certainly fits in every discipline, but we chose these three because, we theorized, it was represented strongest in those three.)

Writing in the piece, we said:

> Nearly all states now have one or more media education elements in their curricular frameworks[; this] represents a watershed moment in the country's educational history. Writers of the state frameworks have recognized the overwhelming and pervasive presence of media in our lives and are increasingly including language that allows teachers to integrate media education into the formal classroom setting. (Baker & Kubey, 1999)

As part of our survey, I created a Web site, with a map of the United States, where readers can locate the exact verbiage from each state's standards:

> In our original op-ed, we agreed that Texas, with its "viewing and representing" standards in English were the best in the United States. In support of those standards, in 2000 and again in 2003, Texas created and distributed a number of instructional support materials, including the following. (Baker & Kubey, 1999)

Teaching the Viewing and Representing Texas
Essential Knowledge and Skills in the English Language Arts Classroom. The state of Texas opted out of endorsing the Common Core ELA Standards, thus leaving in place the opportunity to continue to write its own standards. In this author's opinion, its "Reading/Media Literacy" standard remains one of the strongest in the United States.

For example, the standard now reads:

Students use comprehension skills to analyze how words, images, graphics, and sounds work together in various forms to impact meaning.

> In 5th grade, students are expected to:
> (a) explain how messages conveyed in various forms of media are presented differently (e.g., documentaries, online information, televised news);
> (b) consider the difference in techniques used in media (e.g., commercials, documentaries, news);
> (c) identify the point of view of media presentations;
> (d) analyze various digital media venues for levels of formality and informality.

For an excellent overview of media literacy in K–12 as well as a specific examination of the Texas media literacy standards, see this college student's thesis paper: http://digitalarchive.gsu.edu/cgi/viewcontent.cgi?article=1057 &context=communication_theses

Many language arts teachers have found success engaging students by studying advertising (both print and nonprint); analyzing informational texts (newspapers, maps, menus, etc.); identifying author bias; and analyzing and deconstructing film. Teachers have access to all kinds of media (e.g., newspapers, magazines, music, Web sites and streaming video) to meet standards, benchmarks and frameworks. The popularity of small, inexpensive cameras means more students are learning not only how to "take" pictures, but also how to upload and manipulate them for various purposes and audiences.

Textbooks are including more activities that include popular culture texts, which appeal to young people, and many include DVDs or CD-ROMS with video clips from films, commercials, and TV programs:

- McDougal Littel's *Media Focus*
- *Media Smart,* and *Media Analysis Guides*
- Holt Rinehart and Winston's *Elements of Language*
- Harcourt's *Media Literacy and Communication Skills*
- Glencoe's *Writer's Choice*
- Prentice Hall's *Media Studio*

Media literacy can also be found in many states' standards for *Social Studies*. In 2009, the National Council of Social Studies approved a position statement on the importance of media literacy. This document, authored by Jeff Share (UCLA), Joseph Braun (Illinois State University), and Joseph O'Brien

(University of Kansas), declares, "Media literacy is a pedagogical approach promoting the use of diverse types of media and information communication technology (from crayons to webcams) to question the roles of media and society and the multiple meanings of all types of messages. Analysis of media content is combined with inquiry into the medium. This approach is analytical and skill-based. Thus, media literacy integrates the process of critical inquiry with the creation of media as students examine, create, and disseminate their own alternative images, sounds, and thoughts" (Share, Braun, O'Brien).

State standards for Social Studies make many references to media, including:

- Primary sources
- Media as institutions
- Propaganda
- The rise of mass media throughout American history
- The role, influence, and impact of the media in the political process

To illustrate, Social Studies Standards in California (Grades 9–12) include:

- The growth and effects of radio and movies and their role in the worldwide diffusion of popular culture
- The role of polls, campaign advertising, and the controversies over campaign funding
- The process of lawmaking at each of the three levels of government, including the role of lobbying and the media
- Students evaluate, take, and defend positions on the influence of the media on American political life
- The meaning and importance of a free and responsible press
- The role of electronic, broadcast, print media, and the Internet as means of communication in American politics
- How public officials use the media to communicate with the citizenry and to shape public opinion

Media literacy can also be found in many states' standards for *health*.

Numerous curricula have been developed in the United States around health issues related to body image, sexual media messages, media violence, and alcohol and tobacco marketing, as well as messages about food choices.

In the State of Colorado, the health standard for middle and high school says: "Students should be able to identify and explain how the media may influence behaviors and decisions."

The State of Georgia's standard declares that students will "identify ways various forms of media, such as movies, glorify drug use."

In Missouri, the standard reads, students will "evaluate the idealized body image and elite performance levels portrayed by the media and determine the influence on a young adult's self concept, goal setting and health decisions."

Media literacy also includes many elements that make it a perfect fit in Visual and Performing Arts classrooms. This discipline is where students begin to appreciate the techniques and methods used to create productions.

Understanding "visual literacy" by studying painting, for example, is a skill that is applicable to the analysis of still images, such as photographs and posters. It is also in the arts classroom, where students put their knowledge of these techniques to work, creating and producing their own media work. Media art (aka media production) has also become a part of several states' arts standards: Minnesota, for example, has a strong media arts curriculum.

But media literacy fits across the board, in every subject and discipline. Media literacy, like reading and writing, can and should be a part of all instruction—not relegated to one or two curriculum areas.

References

Adolescence and Young Adult English Language Arts Standards of the National Board for Professional Teaching Standards. http://www.nbpts.org/the_standards/standards_by_cert?ID=2&x=57&y=11

The American Diploma Project. (2004). http://www.achieve.org/ReadyorNot 2004.

Baker, F., & Kubey, R. (1999). "Has Media Education Found a Curricula Foothold?" *Education Week.*

Common Core Standards for the English Language Arts. (2010). http://www.core standards.org/ 2010.

http://www.frankwbaker.com/mcrel

National Core Standards for English Language Arts. http://www.frankwbaker.com/media_core.htm

National Council of Teachers of English (NCTE). http://www.citejournal.org/vol10/iss1/languagearts/article1.cfm)

National Council of Teachers of English. (2009, December 1). Committee on Motion Pictures and the Teaching of English. 1963 http://myglobaleye.blogspot.com/2009_12_01_archive.html

National Council of Teachers of English Resolution of Media Literacy. (1970). http://www.ncte.org/positions/statements/medialiteracy

National Council of Teachers of English. (1973). "On Preparing Students with Skill for Evaluating Media." *Telemedium*, July/August 2006.

National Council of Teachers of English. Resolution on Promoting Media Literacy. (1975). http://contentdm.lib.byu.edu/ETD/image/etd3105.pdf.

National Council of Teachers of English. (1979). "Commission on Media." http://www.xtimeline.com/timeline/History-of-Media-Literacy

National Council of Teachers of English and the International Reading Association. "Standards for the English Language Arts."

Neil Postman, "Television and the Teaching of English." (2009, December 1). http://myglobaleye.blog spot.com/2009_12_01_archive.html

www.ncte.org/positions/statements/visualformofliteracy

Partnership for 21st Century Skills. (2010, July). http://www.p21.org/

Reading/Media Literacy standard, Texas. http://ritter.tea.state.tx.us/rules/tac/chapter 110/ch110b.html

Share, Jeff, Braun, Joseph, and O'Brien, Joseph. National Council of Social Studies Position Statement on Media Literacy. http://www.socialstudies.org/positions/medialiteracy

State of Colorado Statement of Standards-Media Literacy. www.frankwbaker.com/colorado.htm)

State of Georgia's Statement of Standards—Media Literacy. www.frankwbaker.com/georgia.htm)

State of Missouri's Statement of Standards—Media Literacy. www.frankwbaker.com/missouri)

State of Minnesota Statement of Standards—Media Literacy. http://www.pcae.k12.mn.us/pdr/facs/media.pdf)

Telemedium. (2006 Summer). *53* (1).

Walker, T. R. "Historical Literacy: Reading History through Film." (2006, Jan-Feb). *The Social Studies*, *97* (1).

http://web.archive.org/web/20041018201131/http://www.ira.org/advocacy/elastandards/standards.html

7. The Visible, the Vulnerable, and the Viable: The Case for Media Literacy in Middle School

David M. Considine

Today's middle school students are bombarded with messages, both good and bad. Now more than ever they need the tools to help them make sense of all the information they are seeing and hearing. (Swaim, 2002: 6)

A decade has now passed since Sue Swaim, executive director of the National Middle School Association (NMSA), endorsed media literacy as an important skill to develop in early adolescents. Media literacy, she said, "isn't an isolated special class, or a 3 week unit of study." It is, Swaim wrote, "an important educational imperative to be integrated throughout the curriculum."

A decade earlier, the *Fateful Choices* report from the Carnegie Council on Adolescent Development (Hechinger, 1992) noted that although teenagers were under a constant barrage of media messages, "usually in isolation from adults, schools have hardly begun to teach them how to view and listen critically." These competencies, they said, "ought to be a major component of life skills education" (p. 53).

Three years later, in 1995, the council published *Great Transitions: Preparing Adolescents for a New Century*. That report contained a vital statement for the nation's middle school teachers, focused as they are on the creation of "developmentally responsive" schools. According to the Carnegie Council (1995), "the world of the adolescent cannot be understood without considering the profound influence of the mass media" (p. 118). Bringing their experiences of mass media into the classroom provides a powerful generational bridge to help students and teachers explore issues of identity and intertextuality (Duff, 2002).

Whereas the earlier Carnegie report had addressed the potential impact of mass media on impressionable children and teens, this one specifically identified media literacy as an instructional strategy that "deserved widespread consideration in schools and community organizations as an essential part of becoming a well-educated citizen" (p. 118).

At the same time, NMSA (1995) revised its major position paper, *This We Believe: Developmentally Responsive Middle Schools*. In it, the organization said young adolescents are "socially vulnerable, because as they develop their beliefs, attitudes and values, the influence of media . . . may compromise their ideals and values" (p. 40). Middle-level educators should "understand the dynamics of an ever-changing youth culture" (p. 13).

It is worth noting that these reports describing media influence and the need for media literacy were all published before the advent of Google (1998), Wikipedia (2001), the iPod and iTunes (2001), MySpace (2003), YouTube (2005), Facebook (2006), Twitter (2006), and the ubiquitous cell phone—that handheld mobile device that is today regarded as an absolute necessity by any self-respecting adolescent.

By 2010, the wired world of American adolescents had accelerated to such an extent that a study by the Kaiser Family Foundation found that 8- to 18-year-olds spent 7.38 hours a day interacting with media and because of multitasking their daily exposure to media topped 10 hours and 45 minutes or more than in a workweek. Kaiser Foundation vice president Victoria Rideout said, "It's more important than ever that researchers, policymakers and parents stay on top of the impact it's having on their lives" (Rideout, Foehr, & Roberts, 2010: 2).

Beyond the Kaiser report, and despite the oft-stated claim that these so-called digital natives are "media savvy," evidence suggests otherwise. A 2008 report commissioned by the British Library concluded that despite widespread access to information technology, the information literacy skills of the Google Generation had not increased. Their search strategies were limited to highly branded search engines and they spent "little time evaluating information either for relevance, accuracy or authority" (p. 12). In a conclusion that would sound familiar to many teachers, the study noted that young people tended to skim information rather than read deeply or reflectively (Joint Information Systems Committee, 2008).

A study of weight-loss advertising and adolescent females, reported in *Health Education Research*, concluded that the girls were "cognitively vulnerable," with limited ability to recognize "persuasive construction strategies, including message purpose, target audience and subtext" (Hobbs et al., 2006: 1). The Pew Internet and American Life Project (2006) monitors and researches media and technology in American society, including American youth. During a presentation in Boston, the project director said, "They are not all tech-savvy. They are often unaware of and indifferent to the consequences of their use of technology. . . . they are often uncaring about their own privacy. . . . It would be good to model media literacy for them, before someone gets into real trouble" (p. 42).

But when and where should this model commence? Which teachers in what subject areas might be best prepared for this kind of modeling? How might this best be integrated into both pre-service and in-service training and staff development for middle-level educators? These are crucial logistical questions that need to be addressed to avoid the inevitable concerns about turf and time that emerge when teachers are confronted with the prospect of having to teach something else in addition to what they are already doing.

In Canada, Australia, and the United Kingdom, where media literacy (sometimes called *media studies* or *media education*) has been in the curriculum for several decades, it has typically been housed in English departments and taught during the high school years. Secondary education in these nations is often a six-year experience from Year 7 to 12. Media literacy has often been the focus of study only in the final years of school, which might well be a case of too little too late. In the United States, the unique philosophy and practice of the middle school would appear to be highly receptive to the knowledge and skills developed through media literacy. In the past decade, publications of the NMSA have begun to address the relationship between middle schools and media literacy (Considine, 2002, 2010; Considine & Baker 2006; Hobbs, 2001). This work articulates an alignment between the philosophy, practice, and mission of the NMSA, the nature and needs of early adolescents, the rapidly changing contemporary media landscape, and the knowledge and skills fostered by media literacy.

This We Believe (NMSA, 1995) argues that the early adolescents undergo significant changes during this phase of life and that, as such, schools should recognize and respond to these developments. In part that requires a "full understanding of the cultural context in which youth grow to maturity" (p. 10). As the studies from the Kaiser, Pew, and Carnegie organizations indicate, media and technology constitute a significant part of that cultural context.

An awareness of this bidirectional relationship between young people and contemporary media can be a significant factor in shaping curriculum and pedagogy that nurtures NMSA's vision of schools that "help students become good citizens, lifelong learners, caring, ethical & intellectually reflective individuals" (1995, p. 5). These goals, the organization believes, are best achieved through a curriculum that is "challenging, integrative and exploratory" (p. 11).

One college of education that has attracted national attention for its middle school program is Appalachian State in North Carolina. The Department of Curriculum and Instruction houses both an undergraduate and a graduate middle school program. At the 2010 NMSA annual conference, the program was honored by the National Association of Professors of Middle Level Education. Undergraduates in the program are required to take one course (Media and Young People) that focuses on media literacy. The graduate program, which provides in-service courses for classroom teachers, infuses media literacy content and competencies into the required Instructional Technology class.

Two decades ago, the Aspen Institute recognized Appalachian's pioneering efforts in media literacy, describing it as "perhaps the most sustained institutional effort within formal schooling" (1992, p. 4).

Today, media literacy is a significant component of a required core course in the college of education, where all students, irrespective of their concentration, must take Teaching and Learning in a Digital Age, a course that includes compulsory assignments in both media analysis and evaluation, as well as media design and production.

The college is also home to the nation's first masters program in media literacy, which in recent years has hosted free intensive, weeklong summer institutes for North Carolina teachers. These outreach efforts are considered to be important initiatives that not only promote media literacy within education but seek also to recognize and respond to potential negatives attitudes teachers might hold about media's impact both inside and outside of the classroom. This includes the need to recognize and rectify established "non-optimal" use of film and other media in the classroom which can often make it difficult for media literacy advocates to win the support of administrators and parents (Considine, 1985; Hobbs, 2006; Mangram, 2008).

Appalachian State's integrated rather than isolated approach to media literacy is consistent with the literature of the middle school movement. James Beane's (1990) *From Rhetoric to Reality* articulates a theme-based approach to middle school education, focused on the developmental changes of adolescence. One of those themes, which clearly invites a study of advertising, tools, techniques, and influences, is the "commercial pressures" and "effects of media" faced by impressionable early adolescents. A framework for teaching early adolescents to analyze and evaluate advertisements appeared in *The Middle Ground* (Considine, 2010). This type of template to foster critical thinking about key components of advertising is a necessary strategy to activate skepticism that may be dormant in many students. "Evidence suggests that even though children may have skeptical attitudes about advertising, unless they are cued to respond cognitively to an ad, they may not activate this knowledge" (Hobbs, 2007: 115).

Given that all of our students, irrespective of geographic location, socio-economic status, or ethnicity, will be lifelong consumers of media, could nurturing discerning consumers be more relevant or meaningful as a lifelong 21st-century skill? Media literacy has in fact been identified by the leaders of the 21st-century skills initiative as one of those skills. The Partnership for 21st Century Skills is a national organization that advocates for local, state, and federal policies that support the implementation of skills necessary for the nation to remain competitive in a global economy. A student who is media literate, the partnership argues, can "understand both how and why media messages are constructed," "how points of view are included or excluded," "ethical and legal issues surrounding the access and use of media," "use media creation tools to create compelling and effective communication projects," and understand "how media can influence beliefs and behaviors" (Trilling & Fadel, 2009: 67).

One project that reflects this approach was a three-year study funded by the National Science Foundation and reported in *The Middle School Journal*. It involved collaboration between university researchers, middle school teachers (language arts, math, and science), and their students. The study examined "the media messages about information technology and careers that middle school students receive from television, popular magazines, books, videotapes, movies and Web sites." What the study was designed to determine was whether these messages reinforced or hindered "the development of gender and racial diversity in the information technology workforce" (Bernt, Turner, & Bernt, 2005: 38).

This student-centered, project-based interdisciplinary approach was consistent with NMSA's belief in students becoming "active participants in the teaching learning process," which in turn is consistent with the social constructivist pedagogy ("active inquiry and critical thinking") articulated by the National Association of Media Literacy Education (NAMLE). Both NMSA and NAMLE articulate instructional strategies that are student centered, not content driven. Research suggests this approach results in significantly higher rates of learning ("retention transfer and application") than what is yielded by chalk and talk, teacher-centered instruction (McEwin & Thomason, 1989: 17).

What studies like this demonstrate is that the skills of media literacy (the ability to comprehend, analyze, evaluate, and communicate), like traditional literacy, are not limited to a single course or class but work best when integrated throughout the curriculum where they are routinely reinforced and practiced. The most obvious traditional subject area to incorporate media literacy is clearly English Language Arts. The National Council for Teachers of English (n.d.) recognizes that "media/digital literacy has become central to life and work in society," as a result of which "today's educators recognize that the words 'text' and 'literacy' are not confined to words on a page." Functioning competently in the contemporary media environment requires skills "reading, listening, viewing and bthinking that . . . enable students to deal constructively with complex new modes of information . . . new multisensory tactics for persuasion."

Although this progressive perspective is welcomed by media literacy advocates, not everyone is on board. It is still possible in this day and age to find outdated definitions of literacy and the skills it entails showing up in academic publications. *Adolescent Literacy* (Parris, Fisher, & Headley, 2009), for example, defines comprehension as "a meaning-making process through which readers acquire information and seek to understand concepts presented in PRINTED text" (p. 14). Despite the fact that the focus of the book is the very adolescents that research tells us spend increasing parts of their life engaged in a media landscape, this textbook's index makes no reference to media literacy or to any of the various forms of modern media where young people encounter today's diverse multimodal texts.

Integrating media literacy content and competencies into the classroom can often be done while teaching traditional texts and skills. Lois Lowry's *Number the Stars* and Jane Yolen's *The Devil's Arithmetic*, for example, both offer opportunities to examine propaganda and persuasion techniques in World War II and a chance to update the subject to modern methods of persuasion. S. E. Hinton's *The Outsiders* (1967) has long been a staple of young adult literature and is still the focus of academic study (Modleski, 2008). Although it is common for teachers to use the Francis Ford Coppola film version in their classes, comparing and contrasting the book and movie, there are other possibilities as well. At the beginning of the book and the film, Ponyboy Curtis exits a movie theater after seeing Paul Newman in *The Hustler*. At this point in the movie, we see his handwritten journal and hear his voiceover. The use of the first-person male voiceover is a common narrative technique evident in *Stand by Me*, *Holes*, and many other films.

Female students can be asked to find examples of female protagonists whose voiceover introduces a movie. Twenty years ago this would have presented a challenge. Today, it won't take them long to point to Bella in *Twilight* or Lily Owens in *The Secret Life of Bees*. Students might also be intrigued that Susan Eloise Hinton chose not to use her full name as an author. Could it be perhaps that boys would not respond to male-centered novels (*Tex*,

Rumblefish) if they knew the author was female? How could Hinton's decision be updated to J. K. Rowling and the Harry Potter novels?

The Outsiders is a film that also offers many opportunities to examine the role of media in the lives of its young characters. In the course of the narrative, they attend a drive-in movie, their exploits are covered in a newspaper, and Ponyboy (one of the major characters) reads *Gone with the Wind* to his friend Johnny Cade. Teachers who are fortunate enough to have a copy of the 1980s VHS version of the film will find the beginning of the movie strikingly different to the version available today on DVD. In its first theatrical release, the title of the movie scrolled across the screen from right to left, in an homage to the opening credits of *Gone with the Wind*. Rather than isolating the media moments in *The Outsiders* to the time and place of the setting, it is easy to seize on the title of another Hinton novel (*That Was Then, This Is Now*), to have students compare and contrast their own media habits and media environment today with those of the boys and girls in the novel. Although media venues, outlets, access points, and even genres may have changed in 35 years since the book was published, media as a significant presence in the life of teenagers has not.

Another NMSA publication that is compatible with media literacy is *Interdisciplinary Teaching in the Middle Grades* (Vars, 1987). This work describes an approach to curriculum development that identifies problem areas and learning units suitable for study in a middle school program. Several of these easily lend themselves to key concepts of media literacy, including the study of media depictions or representations, media values and ideology, media influences, and of course media audiences. Among the topics identified are Staying Healthy, Personal Social Relationships, Teenagers around the World, My Role as a Consumer, and The Citizen's Role in Policy Making.

This last topic, which explores democratic government, lends itself to an examination of the relationship between young people and the news media. A language arts approach could develop skills in comprehending texts that are read, heard, and viewed. Comparing how the same stories are covered in print, Internet, radio, and TV reports could help students analyze and evaluate the role of words and images in communicating information. A template for helping students analyze and evaluate broadcast news includes lower-order thinking skills that identify what stories are told in what sequence, with what degree of scope or depth. Higher-order thinking skills from the same framework include developing critical criteria for distinguishing balance from bias, along with recognizing how the target audience for the broadcast is implicated in decisions about both what stories are told and what products are sold during a TV news broadcast (Considine & Haley, 1999). Young adult literature such as Avi's *Nothing But the Truth* could also be integrated into the unit. This documentary novel chronicles the experience of Philip Malloy, a high school student who somehow becomes the focus of unwanted national media attention.

The same study of democratic government in a social studies class could examine the impact of news media on voter turnout in local, state, and national elections, FCC regulations, media consolidation and convergence, and the impact of new social media on democracy including its role in recent social and political transformations in Egypt and other countries. The National Council for the Social Studies (2009) clearly understands that these new technologies of communication shape social attitudes and behavior and must therefore be studied within the social studies curriculum. Their position statement on media literacy says: "We live in a multimedia age where the majority of information people receive comes less often from print sources and more typically from highly constructed visual images, complex sound arrangements, and multiple media formats. The multimedia age requires new skills for accessing, analyzing, evaluating, creating, and distributing messages within a digital, global, and democratic society."

From exploring news on a global perspective to understanding events closer to home, young people can be challenged to examine their own relationship with the media, including the way in which it depicts and represents people their own age. When this is applied to news media, they can be asked to evaluate and judge whether the portrait of youth contained in print and broadcast news is fair, balanced, and accurate. What factors contribute to the way the news media depict adolescents? Once again, these questions are easily connected to middle school literature. *This We Believe* actually argues that the media get it wrong. "Young adolescents are curious and concerned about themselves and their world rather than being rebellious and argumentative, as they are often portrayed in the media" (NMSA, 1995: 15). Here's an opportunity to develop a Venn diagram and challenge students to compare and contrast the lives of themselves and their friends (real-world teenagers) with the "screenagers" they see in the media.

Beyond social studies and English language arts, a third component of the curriculum that readily lends itself to media literacy is the area of health education. The Office of National Drug Control Policy (2001) at the White House is well aware of this and sees media literacy as a useful strategy in *Helping Youth Navigate the Media Age*. This report states that media literacy could provide "youth with protective skills against the negative influences of the media" (p. 7). Areas in which media messages may have a negative influence include diet and eating disorders; self-esteem and body image; alcohol, tobacco, and substance abuse; teen pregnancy; and adolescent sexuality (Brown, Steele, & Walsh-Childers, 2002; Strasburger, Wilson, & Jordan, 2009). Promising research provides evidence that instructional intervention, using the key principles and best practices of media literacy can challenge and change attitudes, perceptions, and behavior of young people in several of these problem areas (Austin & Johnson, 1997; Primack, Gold, & Switzer, 2006).

Such initiatives do more than teach young people to evaluate media messages. They adhere to best practices of media literacy that are consistent with middle school philosophy. This approach critiques the media without condemning it. Condemnation, no matter how well meaning, invites many young people to shut down or to parrot answers they know their teachers want to hear. Best practices recognize and respect that young people derive pleasure from media and technology. "Media literacy is most effectively taught when teachers respect the intelligence of youth and use a co-learning approach" (Office of National Drug Control Policy, 2001: 9). When teachers acknowledge and validate "young people's experience and familiarity with media culture . . . media literacy skills are more likely to be accepted and applied" to the media messages they are exposed to beyond the classroom and curriculum. As such, it is reinforced and integrated as a lifelong skill, not isolated to the school environment.

When we engage young people in conversations about their media use, tastes, and preferences, we gain insights into their identities, their personalities, and the ways their media choices reflect their needs and circumstances. It moves our concern from what media does *to* students to a focus on what our students do *with* media. Excellent examples of this can be found in the portraits of Marina, Christopher, and Samantha described by Joe Ellen Fishkeller (2002) in her study, *Growing Up with Television: Everyday Learning among Young Adolescent*. This study and the enthusiasm with which young people embrace the media are consistent with *Teachers as Inquirers*. In this NMSA publication, Chris Stevenson (1986) describes what happened in his classroom in 1972 when he allowed his students to explore "their television viewing tastes." Although he initially regarded the topic as trivial, student buy-in changed his mind. In the end, decades before the term *media literacy* had entered the lexicon, he concluded that this study was "possibly the most worthwhile, influential educational enterprise we undertook." As he began the study thinking he might learning something about television, Stevenson's knowledge of his students also grew. "I recognized in many of them a seriousness not previously characteristic of their response to schooling" (p. 3).

When we reinforce media literacy content and skills across the curriculum, students experience a sense of connectedness rather than fragmentation. This repetition and reinforcement promotes key facets of understanding described in another major middle school report, *Turning Points 2000: Educating Adolescents in the 21st Century* (Jackson & Andrews, 2000). Among these facets is the ability to interpret, apply, and empathize. According to this Carnegie study, students truly understand "when they have perspective: when they see and hear points of view through critical eyes and ears; when they see the big picture" (p. 75). In the second decade of the 21st century, media literacy is an instructional imperative uniquely in tune with the nature and needs of young adolescents, the ever-expanding electronic environment they live in, and the philosophy and practice of the National Middle School Association. Middle-level teachers who want their students to see the "big picture" and to develop "critical eyes and ears" are educators who must embrace media literacy.

References

Auferheide, P., & Firestone, C. (1993). The National Leadership Conference on Media Literacy. Washington, DC: Aspen Institute Communications and Society Program. 4.

Austin, E., & Johnson, K. (1997). "Effects of General and Alcohol-Specific Media Literacy Training on Children's Decision Making about Alcohol." *Journal of Health Communication 2*, 17–42.

Beane, J. (1990). *A Middle School Curriculum: From Rhetoric to Reality*. Columbus, OH: National Middle School Association.

Bernt, P., Turner, S., & Bernt, J. (2005). "Middle School Students Are Co-researchers of Their Media Environment: An Integrated Project." *Middle School Journal 37* (1), 38–44.

Brown, J., Steele, J., & Walsh-Childers, K. (2002). *Sexual Teens, Sexual Media*. Mahwah, NJ: Erlbaum.

Carnegie Council on Adolescent Development. (1995). *Great Transitions: Preparing Adolescents for a New Century*. New York: Author.

Considine, D. (2002). "Putting the Me in Media Literacy." *The Middle Ground, 6,* 15–20.

Considine, D. (2010). "This They Believe?: Adolescents and Advertising." *The Middle Ground 13*, 14–15

Considine, D. (1985). *The Cinema of Adolescence*. Jefferson, NC: McFarland Publishers.

Considine, D., & Baker, F. (2006). "Focus on Film: Learning It through the Movies." *The Middle Ground 10*, 12–15.

Considine, D. M., & Haley, G. (1999). *Visual Messages: Integrating Imagery into Instruction*. Englewood, CO: Libraries Unlimited.

Duff, P. (2002). "Pop Culture and ESL Students: Intertextuality, Identity and Participation in Classroom Discussions." *Journal of Adult and Adolescent Literacy 45*
(6), 482–487.

Fisherkeller, J. (2002). *Growing Up with Television: Everyday Learning among
Young Adolescents.* Philadelphia: Temple Press.

Hechinger, F. (1992). *Fateful Choices: Healthy Youth for the 21st Century.* New
York: Carnegie Council on Adolescent Development.

Hobbs, R. (2001). "Improving Reading Comprehension by Using Media Literacy
Activities." *Voices from the Middle, 8,* 44–50.

Hobbs, R. (2006). "Nonoptimal Uses of Video in the Classroom." *Learning Media
and Technology 31,* 35–50.

Hobbs, R. (2007). *Reading the Media: Media Literacy in High School English.* New
York: Teacher's College Press.

Hobbs, R., Broder, S., Pope, H., & Rowe, J. (2006). "How Adolescent Girls Interpret
Weight Loss Advertising." *Health Education Research 21,* 719–730.

Jackson, A., & Andrews, G., (2000). *Turning Points 2000: Educating Adolescents in
the 21st Century.* New York: Carnegie Corporation.

Joint Information System Committee. (2008). *Information Behavior of the Researcher
of the Future.* Retrieved from gg_final_keynote_11012008.pdf

Mangram, J. (2008). "Either/or Rules: Social Studies Teachers Talk about Media and
Popular Culture." *Theory and Research in Social Education, 36,* 32–60.

McEwin, K., & Thomason, J. (1989). *Who They Are—How We Teach: Early Adolescents and Their Teachers.* Westerville, OH: National Middle School Association.

Modleski, M. (2008). "Stay Gold Students: Helping Young Readers Connect to the
Outsiders." *Middle School Journal, 40* (1), 18–45.

National Association of Media Literacy Education. (2006, March 15). "Media Literacy
Defined." Retrieved from www.namle.net/publications/media-literacydefinitions

National Council for the Social Studies. (2009). *NCSS Position Statement on Media
Literacy.* Retrieved from http://www.socialstudies.org/positions/medialiteracy

National Council for Teachers of English. (2011, March 15). *Media Literacy and
the Common Core.* Retrieved from http://www.ncte.blogspot.com/2010/03/media
-literacyand-common-core.html

National Middle School Association. (1995). *This We Believe: Developmentally
Responsive Middle Schools.* Columbus, OH: Author.

Office of National Drug Control Policy. (2001). *Helping Youth Navigate the Media
Age: A New Approach to Drug Prevention.* Washington, DC: U.S. Government
Printing Office.

Parris, S., Fisher, D., & Headley, K. (2009). *Adolescent Literacy: Effective Solutions
for Every Classroom.* Newark, DE: International Reading Association.

Primack, B., Gold, M., & Switzer, G. (2006). "Development and Validation of a Smoking Media Literacy Scale for Adolescents." *Archives of Pediatric Adolescent Medicine 160*, 369–374.

Rainie, L. (2006, March 23). "Teens Technology and the World to Come." Speech to annual conference of the Public Library Association. Boston, MA.

Rideout, V., Foehr, U., & Roberts, D. (2010). *Generation M2: Media in the Lives of 8 to 18 Year-Olds.* Menlo Park, CA: Kaiser Family Foundation.

Stevenson, C. (1986). *Teachers as Inquirers: Strategies for Learning with and about Young Adolescents.* Columbus, OH: National Middle School Association.

Strasburger, V. C., Wilson, B. J., & Jordan, A. B. (Eds.). (2009). *Children, Adolescents, and the Media* (2nd ed.). Thousand Oaks, CA: Sage.

Swaim, S. (2002). "Media Literacy for Middle Level Students: An Important Curriculum Component." *The Journal of Media Literacy, 48*, 26–27.

Trilling, B., & Fadel, C. (2009). *21st Century Skills: Learning for Life in Our Times.* San Francisco: Jossey-Bass.

Vars, G. (1987). *Interdisciplinary Teaching in the Middle Grades.* Columbus, OH: National Middle School Association.

8. The Birth of the New Mexico Media Literacy Project and the Action Coalition for Media Education

Bob McCannon

Deirdre Downs, daughter of broadcast newscaster Hugh Downs, founded the New Mexico Media Literacy Project (NMMLP) at a statewide conference in March 1993. She promoted it for six months and created three active teacher-trainers (Catalysts). She then turned it over to Bob McCannon, who ran NMMLP for more than 12 and a half years, creating a vibrant, financially sound organization with eight staff members and more than a thousand Catalysts. In 2005, Bob retired from NMMLP to lead the Action Coalition for Media Education. He passed away in August 2013.

Deirdre had pioneered media education courses in Massachusetts, founding the Downs Media Education Center in 1991. She moved to New Mexico in 1993 to begin a media literacy project that she hoped would create the first media literate state. She chose New Mexico because she had lived in the state, knew people in the Department of Education, and the state had a small population, which would maximize the effect of expenditures.

The 1993 conference headlined her father, Neil Postman, and other media literacy gurus. It attracted approximately 75 interested people. Subsequently, Deirdre promoted media education around the state and nation. At the Taos Talking Picture Festival of 1993, she created panel discussions devoted to media literacy. Later she gained a small grant from the New Mexico Department of Education, which allowed her to hire an assistant and hold a two-day training for Catalysts at the Albuquerque Academy. Catalysts were supposed to be teachers who were capable of training others in media literacy. However, Deidre's grant did not cover all her expenses, reducing her personal savings. This financial deficit and health problems caused her to approach Bob McCannon in 1993.

Deidre recounts her impression of Bob in a recent interview,

> Bob's enthusiasm and distinctive interests in educational excellence made it possible for him to offer NMMLP the very best in leadership.

He had been teaching media education at Albuquerque Academy for over twenty years and had established a track record in teaching excellence well before 1993, the year he took over the leadership of NMMLP.

Bob had been teaching propaganda and media analysis at Albuquerque Academy. He was one of the first to use computers to teach history, and Apple Computer selected him to demonstrate his program in workshops around the country. His elective courses were the most popular at the academy, and he also offered a popular graduate course, "Teaching Media Education through Technology," at the University of New Mexico. He met Deirdre several times, sharing similar concerns about children, education, the media culture, and the need for media education.

In July 1993, Deirdre and Bob discussed NMMLP leadership at the Harvard Media Literacy Institute. Shortly thereafter, Deirdre asked if Albuquerque Academy would finance the project and if he would take it over.

Bob approached the school's visionary headmaster, Robert Bovinette, and he allowed Bob to present the plan to the Albuquerque Academy Board of Trustees. Albuquerque Academy is a highly regarded private school. Bob felt it would be a good public/private participation project and beneficial outreach for a richly endowed private school like the academy.

Bob's proposal to the Albuquerque Academy Board of Trustees was as follows:

1. Albuquerque Academy would pay his regular salary for running NMMLP,
2. Bob would devote his summer vacations to NMMLP, and
3. Bob would donate his honoraria and speaking fees to NMMLP.

Bob knew his contacts with public educators—gained during six years on the board and three years as president of the New Mexico Council of Social Studies—would be valuable. He also thought his colleagues at the University of New Mexico would be supportive. In September, Academy's trustees approved the project, and the next chapter of NMMLP was set to begin.

During his 12 and a half years as executive director of NMMLP, Bob did trainings and presentations; lobbied the government; created curricula, newsletters, and grant proposals; and seldom took a vacation or a day off.

NMMLP's Program

Starting with three active Catalysts from Deidre's program, Bob developed more than a thousand by creating the intensive four-day NMMLP "Catalyst

Institutes" that became famous. The New Mexico institutes were an intensive (10 hours per day) training. They were limited to 30 carefully selected applicants, 15 from New Mexico and 15 from out of state. Because NMMLP received funds from New Mexico, residents were allowed to attend for free, which was important in a poor state like New Mexico. Bob also conducted Catalyst Institutes in many other states. By the time Bob retired from NMMLP in 2005, more than 1,050 people had taken the four-day trainings, and countless others had taken shorter multiday workshops. Hundreds of media education organizations grew from those trainees who trained others.

Bob's technological background allowed NMMLP to lead the nascent media literacy presentation field. As multimedia software matured, he pioneered his "hypermedia" approach to Socratic dialogue in the 1980s when he consulted widely for Apple Computer. When Bob took over NMMLP, media educators had to carry piles of bulky one-inch videocassettes to show media examples.

In 1993, the Macintosh Quadra AV series was released. It included video input and output ports. Bob bought the first video digitizing board for personal computers. It cost $5,000, which is amazing when you consider that they are included in all computers today. With a laptop, projector (monstrous by today's standards), and a sound system, Bob was soon giving presentations with digitized video examples.

In 1996, Bob saw the potential for computerized curricula that included examples and lesson plans, so he hired a talented graphics designer and programmer, Frank Gonzales, to produce the world's first CD-ROM tool for teachers. Two years later in 1998, *Understanding Media*, a visually stunning CD-ROM that included hundreds of examples and more than 400 pages of text, covering almost all media issues and 33 media literacy skills, was introduced.

Understanding Media eventually sold more than 10,000 copies and made NMMLP world famous. It was followed by *Reversing Addiction*, which also sold many thousands of copies. By 2005, NMMLP had produced more than a dozen CD and video resources covering a wide variety of topics such as democracy, elections, smoking in movies, storytelling, consumerism, wellness, and media education skills.

NMMLP resources were recommended by the American Academy of Pediatrics (AAP), and Bob did workshops for the AAP in many states, training thousands of pediatricians as well as physicians in other specialties associated with other major medical organizations. In 2008, the APP named Bob Media Educator of the Year.

From 1994 to 2001, NMMLP held several national conferences in Albuquerque that drew more than a thousand people to learn from prominent media educators. The purpose was to promote NMMLP programs and influence students, teachers, parents, administrators, civic leaders, and members of the media. The first conference, "Teaching around Television," was held October 20–23, 1994, at Albuquerque Academy. It involved 22 of the top experts in the fields of media and education. Many of these would come to New Mexico more than once.

The group included Wally Bowen, Renate Caine, Geoffrey Caine, Brandon Centerwall, Gloria DeGaetano, Deirdre Downs, Hugh Downs, Jane Healy, Charles Johnston, Jean Kilbourne, Robert Kubey, Bill McKibben, Kathryn Montgomery, Kate Moody, Robyn Quin, Godfrey Reggio, Dorothy Singer, Jerome Singer, Elizabeth Thoman, and Kathleen Tyner. According to Bob, "This was easily the most impressive U.S. media education conference brought together as of that date."

Another conference as well as each Catalyst Institute featured nationally known media critics, researchers, and educators. That list included some of the above, as well as Susan Douglas, Stuart Ewen, Tom Gardner, George Gerbner, Jim Hightower, Sut Jhally, Naomi Klein, Bob Kubey, Bob McChesney, Jim Metrock, Peter Phillips, Neil Postman, Sheldon Rampton, Gary Ruskin, Danny Schecter, John Stauber, Victor Strasburger, Makani Themba, and Howard Zinn.

All of this ferment produced a strong desire for NMMLP presentations and products, and as Bob's schedule filled up, he hired various assistants to fill the surplus demand for trainings, presentations, and production of materials. By the time Bob retired from NMMLP in 2005, NMMLP was extremely healthy with eight employees and a surplus of $800,000.

A key reason for NMMLP's success was that, unlike other most other major media literacy organizations, NMMLP was *independent* from Big Media's money and influence. Bob said,

> NMMLP believes that media literacy requires *independence* from media corporations, so we do not take money from the global media giants who are restricting information, redefining freedom, limiting our democracy and presenting so many negative educational choices to our children and citizens.

This was in contrast to groups such as the Center for Media Literacy, Renee Hobbs's Media Literacy Project, and others. NMMLP was unafraid to take positions that ran counter to Big Media's agenda. Indeed, the project believed that the major global media corporations had become the world's biggest censors, controlling the content of information that reached the average person.

NMMLP relied on support from public and nonprofit entities, Bob's honoraria, the sales of curricular materials, and Albuquerque Academy.

NMMLP used state-of-the-art multimedia computers, CD-ROMs, videos, and DVDs to develop awareness of issues and critical skills in media literacy. Additionally, it showed teachers, students, parents, businesspeople, professionals, health workers, and others how media literacy could create freedom, relieve cynicism, fight apathy, bolster health, support communities, and build democracy.

A great deal of NMMLP's work was in health-related media issues. Grants from the state department of health supported many free in-services, as well as student and parental workshops, not to mention research into their effectiveness. By 2004, the organization had conducted eight research studies involving more than 21,500 people. These studies all followed the randomized experimental and control group model, and they always employed outside evaluators. The results showed NMMLP interventions to be effective.

A vital part of NMMLP success was Bob's development of what he calls *multimedia-based interactive Socratic dialogue.* It involves empathically asking spontaneous yet carefully selected questions about media examples that lead participants' thinking toward an understanding of the complexity of media culture and issues.

When combined with *activities that emphasize hands-on experience with small group process and media creation,* most students were motivated to further their knowledge and, often, to take action in some appropriate way. As Bob noted:

> I looked at all the research and the suggestions people were making for improvement of education. I wanted to get away from the passive processing and abstract perceiving which dominated almost all schools. At the turn of the millennium, research indicated that even schools which *said* that they valued *active* education were still mired in the passive "I speak; you listen" approach. I felt technology and questioning examples of the media culture could reverse that paradigm.

For the first five years, Bob did all of the NMMLP presenting and teaching. As the project prospered, he was able to gradually increase his staff. Some of the staff he hired were Dan Jaenks, Erica Hizel, Sandra Goldsborough, Frank Gonzales, Peter DeBenedittis, Denis Doyon, Christie McAuley, Jessica Collins, Andrea Quijada, and Damon Scott.

As noted previously, by 2005, NMMP was healthy and wealthy, and Bob decided to retire. His reasons involved a number of factors. Although loving the work, he was tired of giving NMMLP so much of his teaching job's "vacation time," and the traveling—one year he stayed in more than 80 hotels—had gotten old. In addition, Bob was a teacher, not an administrator, and running a business with eight employees involved increasing amounts of bureaucracy, which he found distasteful. Lastly, a great deal of the project's funding was in the area of addiction, particularly smoking prevention, and Bob wanted to present and teach about other media issues, such as news, democracy, corporate censorship, and the use of music.

Thus in 2002 Bob helped to found a national media education organization, the Action Coalition for Media Education. In 2005 he took his 30-year Albuquerque Academy retirement, and was pleased that the Academy gave him a post-retirement sabbatical as a reward for his sacrifices while creating the project.

Since his retirement, NMMLP has abandoned the Catalyst Institute but continues to work in prevention as well as issues of Latino and Native American justice, LBGT (Lesbian, Bisexual, Gay, Transgender) rights, bullying, relationships, protecting poor communities' media interests, and domestic violence.

Birth of the Action Coalition for Media Education (ACME)

While directing the NMMLP, Bob realized that a national media education organization was crucial to raising awareness of the urgent need for a more media literate citizenry. Thus, when Bob was invited to join the board of a new organization, the Partnership for Media Education (PME), he accepted. When the PME board met in Minneapolis to plan its 1999 meeting, it became clear that, like a number of its board members, PME would accept money from media corporations. Shortly afterward, Bob resigned from the PME's board. At its following national meeting, PME created controversy with clear favoritism toward some of the same corporations that employed PME board members. These same corporations also donated to the conference.

Then, PME changed its name to the Alliance for a Media Literate America (AMLA), and in 2001, at AMLA's founding meeting in Austin, it continued both of these unfortunate strategies, even refusing to state independence from corporate media in its bylaws. This caused a number of people to leave the conference and hold a caucus nearby; the members were determined to form another organization that would not owe anything to Big Media influence.

Independence from Big Media is a crucial issue. Global media corporations have joined the Dark Side. Their programming, movies, magazines, radio, video games, and the advertising that pays for them have become powerful influences toward compulsive and addictive lifestyles. Most despicable is the targeting of the most vulnerable among us, younger and younger children. Kids are subjected to a barrage designed to persuade them to eat McFood, smoke, drink, and value sports and celebrities above all. Hard work, saving, intellectualism, community, and healthy relationships are derided.

Furthermore, Big Media's public relations, lobbying, and campaign contributions, undermine our democratic system. As noted, Big Media has become the world's biggest censor, controlling the information, framing political debates, and consigning alternative views to the shadows.

When corporate media funds media literacy, the paramount issues of the day are not addressed. Media education cannot take on biased news if one depends on Time Warner for support. One cannot deal with corporate corruption of democracy if one depends on a corrupt corporation. An instructive example is the most widely disseminated media literacy curriculum ever produced. It was financed by a corporation, so it made no mention of corporate bias in our media culture. In fact, the only mention of corporations was in glowing positives.

The working group from Austin, formed to produce a new and independent national media education organization, grew to more than 50 people, including Wally Bowen, Aliza Dihter, Tom Gardner, Elizabeth Gleckler, Lt. Dave Grossman, Jane Healy, Sut Jhally, Carl Jensen, Jean Kilbourne, Robert McChesney, Bill McKibben, Jim Metrock, Lisa Miller, Mark Crispin Miller, Kathryn Montgomery, Neil Postman, Sheldon Rampton, Gary Ruskin, John Stauber, Victor Strasburger, Makani Themba, Frank Vespe, and Rob Williams.

The group produced the founding conference of the Action Coalition for Media Education in Albuquerque in 2002. Three hundred and fifty people came from 30 states to discuss the value of *independent* media education. Inspiring keynotes by Jean Kilbourne, Sut Jhally, and Bob McChesney praised the value and necessity of an organization like ACME, which could not be influenced by the global media cartel. Professor Jhally opined, "Media literacy is so dangerous to media corporations that they have moved to hijack the movement as it builds momentum. ACME's formation and launch therefore is an important political moment."

McChesney's stirring message included the following:

The problem we face with a hyper-commercial, profit-obsessed media system is that it does a lousy job of producing citizens in a democracy. A solution is real media literacy education that doesn't just make people more informed consumers of commercial fare, but makes them

understand how and why the media system works—so they may be critics, citizens and active participants. This is the type of media education
ACME is committed to doing.

A national board of directors was elected, and several months later, on
Super Bowl weekend 2003, it met in Montreal to create bylaws and elect officers. Rob Williams was elected president and Bob McCannon vice president.

ACME's revolutionary bylaws shattered the precedent set by AMLA
(which is now named the National Association for Media Literacy Education,
NAMLE). ACME created a Code of Ethics and Disclosure Policies to safe-
guard its independence from the global media cartel, and it takes no money
from the media.

ACME, a national nonprofit, is now widely recognized as an excellent and
independent authority for media literacy training and resources. More than
2,000 people have attended its national conferences in Albuquerque (2002),
Madison (2003), San Francisco (2004), St. Louis (2005), Burlington (2006),
Memphis (2007), Minneapolis (2008), and Boston (2011). Many more thousands have attended regional and local conferences, trainings, workshops,
and meetings of many kinds.

Bob is now president, and the current board of directors consists of Adam
Kenner, Sheryl Rivera, Elizabeth Gleckler, Amanda Shaffer, Sara Voorhees,
Ben Boyington, Jacques Brodeur, and Henry Kroll. The board of directors
bios and e-mail addresses can be found at http://www.acmecoalition.org/
board_directors. ACME's advisory board can be found at http://www.acme-
coalition.org/advisory_board.

9. What Difference Does Adding the Word *Education* Make?: NAMLE'S Contribution to Media Literacy

*Faith Rogow**

In 2001, if you had surveyed the founding members of the National Association for Media Literacy Education (NAMLE, originally AMLA) about what they expected of their new organization, you would have received dozens of different answers. So let me say at the outset that this essay is exclusively my own perspective rather than an attempt to tell the diversity of stories that will someday be recounted as NAMLE's history.

Despite significant accomplishments, NAMLE has not yet scratched the surface of its potential to be a national advocate for media literacy. Nonetheless, I predict that history will recognize it as having played a crucial role in integrating media literacy into American classrooms and that the lynchpin for NAMLE's success will have been a demand for answers to practical questions about how to teach media literacy.

The Media Literacy Context

NAMLE certainly didn't invent the idea of teaching media literacy in schools. By 2001, when NAMLE was founded, forms of media literacy had well-established curricular footholds outside of the United States in places like the United Kingdom, Canada, and Australia.

In the United States, efforts were more scattered, but the National Telemedia Council had advocated for the idea for several decades, Renee Hobbs had done important work in Massachusetts; Project Look Sharp had begun its innovative curriculum integration model working with school districts in and around Ithaca, New York; the New Mexico Media Literacy Project had reached many schools in that state; and Texas had included a "Viewing and Representing" strand into its state education standards (which was one of

* The author was NAMLE's founding president.

581

the primary reasons that NAMLE's founding conference was convened in Austin).

Although not yet widely embraced, efforts to integrate media into classrooms were being voiced in education organizations like the International Reading Association and the National Council of Teachers of English by people like Donna Alvermann and Mary Cristel. David Considine, one of the few professors of *education* working actively on media literacy, had already convened the first national media literacy conference in the United States.

Many of the most vibrant efforts, however, were not directed at schools. For example, Just Think, the Educational Video Center, and the Center for Media Literacy were all doing important work—largely outside of classroom walls.

In academe, work in media literacy was far more likely to come out of departments of communications than education school faculty, so it wasn't reaching many teachers. Media literacy discourse tended to be centered around what advocates thought was important for people to know about media, how to "read" media, or how to teach using media, but not about teaching methods or learning theories. No one was citing Vygotsky or Gardner or examining how brain-based learning might apply to media literacy. Talk of rubrics, scaffolding, standards, or developmentally appropriate practice was rare. Media literacy gatherings didn't sound like education conferences.

In the United States, the focus was on *media*, not on students or learning. We said we wanted curriculum and teaching to change, but a significant amount of what media literacy advocates actually did was about getting media to change. And despite invocations of Paulo Freire and an earnest desire to see Americans become critically autonomous thinkers, the teaching strategies we most often employed were didactic; it was common to see a "banking" model of instruction in which a media literacy "expert" simply substituted the beliefs of cultural critics for the values of commercial media. Although there was an entire literature on how to teach critical thinking, this pedagogy was largely missing from media literacy events and publications.

Still, at the turn of the millennium, there was growing energy for media literacy in the United States, with exciting initiatives in community-based youth programs, the juvenile justice system, public health projects, churches, after-school programs, and even a few colleges and universities.

Every founding member of the NAMLE Board was immersed in this world and wanted to focus on growing every aspect of it. We used the word *umbrella* a lot, thinking that NAMLE could be a unifying force for the diverse expressions of media literacy in the United States. This turned out, however, to be more of a challenge than we anticipated.

Beyond the tensions that Hobbs famously outlined in her 1998 article "The Seven Great Debates in the Media Literacy Movement," we were confronted with more than a dozen approaches to media literacy, some of which seemed to be mutually exclusive. From ensconcing film theory alongside literary theory in the English classroom to consumer education and health prevention initiatives, social justice and media reform, visual and information literacy, and even values clarification and cultural criticism, there was no shortage of things that were being done under the banner of media literacy.

Tensions arose from this diversity because people using different approaches sometimes saw themselves as being in competition with one another ("What I do is media literacy; what you do is not"), or they used the same terms but in ways that created obstacles to communication (*protection* could be about keeping people away from undesirable media or encouraging them to wade into media waters prepared to swim). People trained in different fields relied on research methods that used evidence in different ways (e.g., what an epidemiologist accepts as solid proof is very different from what a developmental psychologist would look for) or had conflicting views about appropriate funding sources (do media companies have a responsibility to fund media literacy initiatives, or does taking money from a media company present an inherent conflict of interest?).

In its early years, NAMLE reflected this uncertainty, perhaps no where more obviously than in the organization's original name. The Alliance for a Media Literate America (AMLA) described our shared goal, but there was no consensus about how best to get there. It wouldn't be until several years later that the organization would sharpen its focus and change its name to reflect an emphasis on teaching and learning.

The Shift Toward Teaching

Eventually, very practical organizational pressures about where to concentrate limited time, energy, and funds, as well as the need to make our case to prospective members, supporters, and policy makers, led NAMLE toward an examination of teaching. This was not an easy choice for an organization that hoped to take a "big tent" approach. When you start identifying good practice, you risk excluding those whose methods don't fit. Yet, without identifying what did and did not work, there would be no way to move the field forward. So, in 2007, a small group of present and past NAMLE board members gathered for a weekend and hammered out the *Core Principles for Media Literacy Education in the United States* (www.namle.net/core-principles).

Adding the word *education* to *media literacy* shifted the discourse in some interesting ways. To illustrate with just one example, Core Principle 5 acknowledges that "media are a part of culture and function as agents of socialization." In the past, that has led to an emphasis on "calling out" mainstream media for its often damaging messages and demanding change. But media reform as a goal is an anathema to schools because you can't measure teacher or student performance on how much media or media policy change. And presupposing a political agenda tied to specific actions and policies, even when that agenda is vital and just, is a direct contradiction of Freire's nonhierarchical model of teaching. So Core Principle 2.10 makes clear that "[w]hile MLE [media literacy education] may result in students wanting to change or reform media, MLE itself is not focused on changing *media*, but rather on changing *educational practice* and increasing students' knowledge and skills."

This is in no way an abandonment of media reform or media criticism. In fact, many of the principles' authors continue to be deeply committed to those pursuits. And we suspect that many media literacy students will want to engage in media reform or criticism as a way to act on their new insights. Hence the Implication for Practice just above the one on media reform, which recognizes that "[a]s a literacy, MLE may have political consequences." Education is, by its nature, a political act.

That same Core Principle goes on to make clear, however, that just because media literacy education may have outcomes with political implications does not mean that changes in media policy can be a foundational goal. As the implication goes on to say, media literacy education "is not a political movement; it is an educational discipline" (2.9). One of the shifts that NAMLE made early on was to begin identifying media literacy education as a "field," rather than as a "movement." The document doesn't set up a false dichotomy between reform or cultural criticism and education; rather it simply makes clear that they aren't the same thing. That distinction is essential if we expect schools to embrace media literacy education.

A focus on sound educational practice revealed other contradictions between media literacy instruction that comprised entirely exposing students to selected media criticism and teaching students to be independent critical thinkers who are able to examine media for themselves. It is difficult, for example, to teach students that "audiences negotiate meaning" without also accepting that students who learn more sophisticated ways to make meaning of media may or may not agree with their teacher's interpretation. There is no way to reconcile an approach in which only politically palatable interpretations of media messages are correct and also teach that audiences negotiate meaning.

To avoid this contradiction, the Core Principles includes Implications for Practice like "MLE does not start from a premise that media are inconsequential or that media are a problem" (5.5). In other words, to teach critical thinking, media literacy education starts from the neutral premise that "media are."

That neutral premise—being completely open rather than guiding students to conclusions that we have predetermined—is what provides students with essential opportunities to grapple with media texts for themselves. It is foundational for teaching students to be critical thinkers. And it is embodied throughout the Core Principles.

For example, it serves as the essence of "strong sense" critical thinking that demands the questioning of all media texts, not just those with which we disagree (1.3). It is reflected in the Implication for Practice that says "MLE is not about replacing students' perspectives with someone else's (your own, a teacher's, a media critic's, an expert's, etc.)"(1.5). It is even in the rephrasing of the familiar "Media are produced for profit and power" to "Media messages are produced for particular purposes" (1.1c).

This openness isn't an avoidance of looking at issues of money or hegemony. To the contrary, the Core Principles feature Key Questions about economics and benefits and harms. Rather, it is an acknowledgment that the way that a teacher introduces issues matters, at least if the goal is to produce critical thinkers and not just media critics. It also has the added benefit of addressing the ever-greater diversity of media in a user-generated content world where many media are still commercial but many media are not.

Utimately, the "Implications for Practice" included under each of the six main Principles are far more important than the headings, themselves. They will enable NAMLE's Core Principles to serve as a springboard for ongoing conversations about how best to teach media literacy for years to come.

The Importance of Infrastructure

In addition to expanding the media literacy discourse to look at the links (or disconnects) between ideology and real-life teaching practices, NAMLE has also done much unsung grunt work involved in creating the infrastructure that is necessary to grow and sustain media literacy education in the United States. Every grassroots endeavor relies on some basic infrastructure. Often it's a brick-and-mortar office with a computer and a phone and perhaps a paid coordinator. NAMLE opted not to go that route. It has never had an office, and its reliance on a volunteer board has both strengthened the organization and made it vulnerable. Because it relies on volunteers, what NAMLE has been able to create has been limited. But because the people running it are people immersed in media literacy, the organization has been able to create practical things that were much needed by educators.

The most visible part of that infrastructure are NAMLE's national conferences (formerly the National Media Education Conference—NMEC). These provide an opportunity for networking and interdisciplinary conversations, for those new to the field to get a broad sampling of the field, and for media literacy veterans to get their teaching "batteries" recharged.

Less well known is that the design of the program reflected the value that the organization placed on the power of bringing together people from different perspectives and experiences. In NAMLE's first decade, every conference featured at least one current or former classroom teacher as a keynote speaker, and conference planners took great care to include keynoters that were diverse in terms of gender, race, ethnicity, and profession. In addition, NAMLE committed itself to the unusual inclusion of student voices, handing over the final plenary session of every NMEC to high school students who attended the Modern Media Makers (M3) production "camp" that was held in conjunction with the conference.

Also, because NAMLE was about education, it had a natural link to parallel organizations in other countries and could function as a conduit for American teachers to share with and learn from peers in other nations. So every NMEC included a keynote from at least one person who was not American.

Even the choice to establish itself as a membership organization reflected the attention that NAMLE gave to building education infrastructure. NAMLE could have been a think tank or a research center at a university or just a group that convened a conference every couple of years, but the founders saw great value in providing ways for unaffiliated people to find and support one another. And NAMLE self-consciously set out to expand leadership opportunities for media literacy educators and advocates by writing term limits for board members into its bylaws. As an aside, this last strategy was very successful. In contrast to grassroots organizations founded by a small group of charismatic leaders where the leaders either hold on so tightly to power that no one else can exercise leadership or where the leaders eventually burn out, in NAMLE's first decade, more than 40 people served as national board members. Ten years after the organization was started, only one founding board member was still serving on the board, though many founders remained quite involved in the organization.

Bringing people together into one organization also provided a means of building the critical mass needed by educational publishers, media makers, and distributors. This was not an issue of commodifying members. It was a very practical recognition of how a field grows. For example, scholars need to publish. If we want them to devote their careers to media literacy, then there have to be presses willing to publish what they write. And for presses to be willing to publish media texts, they need efficient ways to reach prospective buyers. Moreover, if faculty can publish work on media literacy education, they are more likely to teach courses on media literacy education. And if they are teaching such courses, their libraries are likely to purchase media literacy texts for their collections, which makes academic presses more willing to publish the next media literacy title, which makes more resources available to the field, and so it goes. As a membership organization, NAMLE can play an important role in aggregating an audience for media literacy resources which will, in turn, increase the number of resources available.

Arguably, NAMLE's most significant contributions to date (in addition to the Core Principles) have resulted from a sort of informal backward mapping. For example, it was self-evident that for large numbers of schools to take on media literacy education, they needed teachers trained to teach media literacy and evidence that media literacy education worked to meet district goals. So by 2007, NAMLE convened the first U.S. Research Summit on media literacy education—not on media effects (there were other organizations that provided opportunities for that), but on the efficacy of media literacy education.

In 2009, NAMLE initiated the *Journal for Media Literacy Education*, the nation's first juried journal specifically focused on media literacy *education*. By providing a place to publish, the journal makes it possible for education professors to focus on media literacy. Without such opportunities, scholars who need to publish to retain jobs or advance would be forced to place their attention elsewhere. And if those who train teachers and investigate classroom practice can't specialize in media literacy, the field has no chance at widespread adoption. Some people viewed these initiatives as a step away from grassroots efforts. For those of us involved, it was just the opposite. It was a way to create the infrastructure necessary to sustain educational efforts on the ground.

In terms of establishing media literacy education in U.S. schools, NAMLE still has a long way to go. As it expands capacity, it will have greater ability to command the attention of policy makers. It is just beginning to use its Web site to full potential, and it will continue to struggle with its identity as more and more people get involved and expand what is already a diverse constituency.

But it is that very diversity that could be NAMLE's greatest strength. On the global stage, NAMLE has the potential to offer to the field the fruits of American creativity. Even with a move toward common standards, local control of school districts will continue to guarantee an array of teaching practices and a degree of individual experimentation as teachers try to successfully reach all students. That will undoubtedly produce some excellent models for media literacy education.

NAMLE will have many ways to measure success: the number of school districts that include media literacy in the curriculum, the amount of funding it attracts to media literacy initiatives, even the number of people who join the organization. In my view, NAMLE will be successful if teachers who are trained to teach media literacy are not only better at media decoding and production but also better teachers.

References

Hobbs, R. (1998). "The Seven Great Debates in the Media Literacy Movement." *Journal of Communication 48*, 16–32.

National Association for Media Literacy Education. (2007). *Core Principles for Media Literacy Education in the United States.* Retrieved from http://www.namle .net/core-principles

10. Print Lives: Community Newspapers

Don Corrigan

I. Still Healthy, Viable

To paraphrase Mark Twain, reports of the death of print in American publishing are very much exaggerated, particularly when it comes to community journalism. After several years of grim stories of daily newspaper woes—from downsizing, to furloughs, to layoffs, and even cessation of operations—the public can't be blamed for the widespread impression that the Age of Print Media is dead.

The big guys are in trouble. Big city daily newspapers have been losing readers and revenue year after year. However, most community papers have weathered the new digital era and America's economic downturn reasonably well. Newspaper trade organizations such as the Independent Free Papers of America (IFPA), the National Newspaper Association (NNA), and the Inland Press Association (IPA) are all working to get the message out to readers and advertisers: "We're Just Fine and We're Not Going Away." These groups say it's vital to get this information out, because the mantra about the demise of print can become a self-fulfilling prophesy if not adequately countered.

"Don't Believe the Hype: Newspapers Are Alive and Kicking" declared a headline in a 2011 edition of About.comMarketing. The article's author, Guy Bergstrom (2011), emphasized that 37 percent of the global population reads newspapers. Bergstrom noted that in America, giant newspaper chains got into a deep financial difficulties by going into massive debt before the 2008 recession to buy up other newspapers, but midsized papers and small-town papers in the United States have been doing well.

Bergstrom's analysis is echoed in the trade publications of state and national newspaper organizations. National Newspaper Association statistics show that adult readership of local community newspapers trended upward in the first decade of the new century. NNA statistics show the percentage of adults reading a local community newspaper on a weekly basis climbed to as high as 86 percent in 2008 (Kimball, 2009).

State newspaper groups report that their membership numbers have stayed steady despite the dramatic 2008 economic downturn, which ushered in the worst recession since the Great Depression. According to Lisa Hills of the Minnesota Newspaper Association, local community newspapers are doing "surprisingly" well in a weak economy. Her state newspaper group has kept a roll of about 375 newspaper members, with even a few community journalism startups in the offing (Kimball, 2009).

II. Community Journalism Defined

The tendency to lump local community journalism in with big city daily journalism constitutes the time-worn fallacy of mixing apples and oranges. That mix-up becomes even worse when media analysts blur the lines between the two and then proceed to write an all-encompassing obituary for all of the print media. Community journalism is profoundly different from that practiced by mainstream media outlets such as *The New York Times*, *Chicago Sun-Times*, or *Los Angeles Times*. Community journalism is best typified by small papers such as the *News & Guide* in Jackson Hole, Wyoming; the *News-Argus* in Goldsboro, North Carolina; or the *Washington Missourian* in Washington, Missouri.

Community journalism's traits differ markedly from big city journalism:

- *It's micro-news*. Community newspaper champion Jock Lauterer, a journalism professor at the University of North Carolina, points out that community journalism involves relentless "local coverage of city council, planning board, Boy Scout field days, church suppers and even Aunt Maude's 100th birthday. . . . [It's] an affirmation of the community's identity and its vision for itself" (Ellison, 2010)
- *It's personal*. Community journalism is extremely personal. When a tornado, flood, shooting spree, or kidnapping takes place in a smaller community, the mainstream media swoop in and out. Their reporters interview people they will never see again on stories they will likely never revisit. In contrast, community reporters live among the people they cover; they feel a special accountability for the stories they report; they can feel the hurt of local tragedy and setbacks personally; and very often they are involved in follow-up stories involving rebuilding, reconciliation, or community healing (Corrigan, 2009).
- *It's community-valued*. There are a number of journalism ethics codes that are guides for the profession. However, as Bill Reader (2008), a journalism professor at the University of Ohio, notes,

community journalism is journalism that privileges community values over professional values. That is community journalists are sensitive (but not necessarily deferential) to the wants and needs of the community they serve. That affects everything from news judgment (what is or is not worth covering) to making touchy ethical decisions (about publishing information that would be embarrassing to people who live in the community).

Finally, community journalism can rightfully lay claim to two terms that have been hyped in the new age of Internet communications. Community journalism is *hyperlocal*; it's also the original social media. Hyperlocal news is a type of journalism that covers narrow-interest stories related to a specific region, city, or neighborhood. Such stories might include repair of a giant pothole on a certain street, an infestation of cicadas in a certain neighborhood, or a block party held every year to welcome summer.

In defining what makes news, journalism academics often cite conflict, impact, novelty, prominence, timeliness, and proximity (Corrigan, 1999: 153). With community journalism, that quality of "proximity" takes precedence. Here is the benchmark question for the community journalist: Is this news that's in my own readers' backyard? That doesn't mean national and global issues are ignored, but it does mean that wider-frame issues must be localized.

Community journalism can make a claim as the original social media, no matter what the Tweeters and the Facebook crowd may contend. Quality community newspapers provide information that connects people and causes. The stories in community journals, both before and after the advent of the Internet, have given citizens the reasons to participate in their communities and the ways to be participants.

III. Economics of Community Journalism

One reason we hear so much about the struggling newspaper industry is because the reports are based on the top 100—maybe the top 250—daily newspapers, according to the National Newspaper Association's Brian Steffens. Those newspaper operations are extremely important, but that focus "doesn't tell the story of the remaining 1,200 daily newspapers or the 8,000 community weekly papers in America" (Kimball, 2009).

The big daily newspaper companies are often in trouble because of the unrealistic prices that they paid for media acquisitions before the 2008 crash. To finance debt since that time, they have often resorted to cutting fat, and then muscle, from their news operations. Additional woes for the big dailies come from the rise of the Digital Age. These newspapers began adding news Web sites, without thinking through how these digital offerings would be monetized. Advertising on their news Web sites provides a fraction of the revenue that newspaper print ads provide, and paywalls on sites to charge for access have backfired with readers.

Big dailies have lost major corporate display advertisers on the retail side; they've lost much of their classified ad base; and they've lost a lot of circulation on which advertising rates are predicated. In contrast, most community newspapers have always relied on mom-and-pop shops for display ad revenue, rather than big-box retailers. These smaller, independent shops and restaurant advertisers have remained loyal to the local community newspapers, even though they have suffered from the economic downturn.

Newspaper analyst John Morton (2009) has pointed out that large dailies once got 50 percent or more of their advertising from classified ads, with real estate, employment, and automotive being the primary classifications streaming in revenue. Now, classified Web sites such as Craigslist, eBay, and Angie's List have taken a huge bite out of the dailies. In an article for *American Journalism Review* titled, "Not Dead Yet: Despite the Gloomy News about Newspapers, Many Smaller Dailies Still Make Money," Morton (2009) observed that smaller community dailies have never relied on more than 30 percent of their revenue from classifieds, and they have not endured the loss of classified ads that have hit metro dailies. The retention of classifieds in community weeklies is even better.

Finally, metro dailies have suffered circulation loss because readers can go to Web sites and get the all-important world and national news for free. Local news is not so easy to come by—especially hyperlocal news. "Here's the deal, the Internet killed about 90 percent of what made big dailies so vital," says Jock Lauterer, who directs the Carolina Community Media Project for the University of North Carolina at Chapel Hill. Lauterer continues:

> We don't get our "news" from the morning newspaper anymore. We get it from a variety of other sources. But, the only place to get your in-depth, community, local, down-to-your doorstep news is your local community paper—be it online or print. And the fact that so many folks still crave tactile experience with a "paper"—the old portable, clippable, hold-and-fold legacy media, is a testimony to human nature and the survivability and sustainability of the community press. (Ellison, 2010)

If print has any future in the news business, it is in the arena of community journalism. Of course, a number of attempts are being made to challenge the dominance of the hyperlocal fare of community newspapers on the Internet, foremost among the challengers is AOL's Patch sites. However, Lauterer makes an important point: Newspapers are retro and after a day of working at video screens all day, many readers want retro. They want "the old portable, clippable, hold-and-fold legacy media" (Ellison, 2010).

IV. Analyzing Community Journalism Content

Community newspapers were once derided as the mangy sheet, the advertising shopper, or the weekly town rag. Reporters and editors, who once had secure berths at metro dailies, were especially prone to sneering at the community press. Now, after several years of layoffs at big city papers, the snide remarks have dissolved as journalists are happy to have jobs in the community press. And, quite frankly, the influx of their talent has improved the overall product for hyperlocal media.

In some cases, unemployed daily journalists have started or bought community newspapers to bring their talents to bear in a new fashion. M. E. Sprengelmeyer talked about the stress of being cut loose from a daily at the 2010 annual convention of the Association for Education in Journalism and Mass Communication (AEJMC) in Denver. A first-rate reporter, he lost a great job when the *Rocky Mountain News* closed its doors. "I literally went into mourning for a week when the *News* closed," said Sprengelmeyer. "I traveled a lot. I covered Iraq, Afghanistan. I knew I'd never get a job like this again."

Sprengelmeyer quit mourning. He put his life savings down to buy the Guadalupe County Communicator. He has transformed the New Mexico newspaper into a thriving community weekly and hired more reporters.

Sprengelmeyer told one of many success stories on an AEJMC panel about the flourishing of hometown journalism. The University of North Carolina's Lauterer talked about as many as 15 newspaper start-ups in his state and the rise of university community journalism programs (Corrigan, 2010).

The influx of new talent and enthusiasm into the community journalism profession should translate into a better grade of writing, photography, graphics, and layout in the future. As unemployed daily reporters seek refuge in community journalism, they will upload investigative and analysis skills into the product that once were confined to the metros. However, community journalism has to be held to a different standard than that of traditional daily journalism—not necessarily an inferior standard but a different one. There are a number of points to keep in mind when analyzing community journalism content.

- *First take.* Community newspapers do not provide the first take or first read on state, national, or international issues. Don't judge the local paper as a failure because it doesn't have the first take on peace negotiations in the Middle East or the latest scandal in the U.S. Congress.
- *Good taste.* Compared with the big city tabloids or television news, community newspapers are much more concerned about steering clear of content that could be offensive to readers and upholding community standards. It's not always because of higher ethical standards, but the local paper is much more vulnerable to swift and harsh reaction to tasteless photos and attack headlines.
- *Big scoops.* Community newspapers like to scoop the competition, but having the story first is not always paramount. A community paper is more likely to withhold the names of shooting victims until they are officially released and next-of-kin are notified than many national operations.
- *Local, local.* Community newspapers may not cover the visit of a U.S. president in a neighboring town. This is not because the story is too big or the paper too provincial. In most cases, it's a situation in which proximity will always trump prominence. The local angle is at a premium.
- *Boosterism.* Community newspapers engage in a certain amount of cheerleading for the local community because the fates of the paper and its host town or county are tied together. However, this doesn't mean the newspaper never performs a watchdog function or calls out bad actors or incompetence at the local city hall or school district.
- *Involvement.* Community newspapers are often key players in local events, from the historical society's strawberry festival to the fireworks display at the Fourth of July celebration. The paper may help underwrite the strawberries as well as the Roman candles, and editorial employees may help with the community volunteer days as well.
- *Detachment.* "The role of the enlightened community newspaper is far more demanding and complex than that of the big city paper, which can afford to be detached, remote, critical, aloof, cynical and at times, elite," writes Jock Lauterer in *Community Journalism: The Personal Approach* (2000). Community journalism operates within the fabric and is part of the landscape of the territory within which it operates; it is not above the fray, it is part of the fray.

That little line keeps moving when it comes to what is permissible in the mainstream news media in this country. "It's hard not to cross the line when they keep moving the little sucker," says the anchorman in the movie classic

Broadcast News, in reference to what is acceptable in journalism. That little line is moving a lot these days in a tough economic environment in which media outlets must try new things to stay afloat. For example, it was once considered anathema for a respectable daily to sell a portion of its front page to advertisers. Those days are now gone for many dailies.

Big city papers are more responsive and more involved in the communities they serve. They are much more defensive and self-conscious when they are accused of being "elitist," a term they might have embraced once as a badge of honor. The big city papers now want readers to know that they are involved and are concerned about the general welfare of their constituencies. Perhaps it's a compliment to local community journalism that so many large daily newspapers in this country have now adopted many of the approaches to their readers that were once the preserve of local papers.

References

Bergstrom, G. (2011, August 11). "Don't Believe the Hype: Newspapers Are Alive and Kicking: 37 Percent of Global Population Reads Newspapers." Retrieved from http://marketing.about.com/od/publicrelation1/a/Do-Not-Believe-The-Hype -Newspapers-Are-Alive-And-Kicking.htm

Corrigan, D. (1999). *The Public Journalism Movement in America*. Westport, CT: Praeger.

Corrigan, D. (2009, Winter). "When Murder Strikes a Small Community." *Nieman Reports 63*, 7–8.

Corrigan, D. (2010, August 13–19). "Community Journalism: 'The Original Social Media.' " *Webster-Kirkwood Times*, p. 6.

Ellison, Q. (2010, November 17). "Press Wars: Community Newspapers Thrive Despite Stagnant Economy." *Smoky Mountain News*. Retrieved from http:// www.smokymountainnews.com/archives/item/2577-press-wars-community -newspapers-thrive-despite-stagnant-economy.

Kimball, J. (2009, March 3). "While Major Metros Struggle, Many Newspa- pers Still Thriving in Smaller Towns." *Minnesota Post*. Retrieved from http:// www.minnpost.com/politics-policy/2009/03/while-major-metros-struggle -many-newspapers-still-thriving-smaller-towns.

Lauterer, J. (2000) *Community Journalism: The Personal Approach*. Ames: Univer- sity of Iowa Press.

Morton, J. (2009, June/July). "Not Dead Yet: Despite the Gloomy News about News- papers, Many Smaller Dailies Still Make Money." *American Journalism Review*, p. 48.

Reader, Bill. "What's The Difference?" Scripps Blogs, E.W. Scripps School of Journalism, Ohio University. November 5, 2008. Retrieved July 1, 2013. http:// scrippsjschool.org/blog/post.php?postID=57&blogID=17

11. ACME: Independent Media Education for Interesting Times

Rob Williams

We live in the most mediated-saturated society in world history. Americans spend upward of 10 to 12 hours every day immersed in an ever-more-sophisticated, networked, and convergent media culture. As we enter the 21st century, this situation might seem like a cause for celebration—more media theoretically mean more voices, more diversity, and more channels for information, entertainment, and education.

A closer look, however, reveals a more complicated reality. Most of the stories told in our media culture—by some estimates, as much as 90 percent of our media content—are ultimately owned by Time Warner, News Corp, Disney, Viacom, Vivendi, Sony, and a few other giant transnational corporations. The much-celebrated emerging world of digitally driven social media networks, meanwhile, featuring giant multimedia multinationals such as Google and Facebook, gobble up tremendous amounts of personal data, energy, time, and money in the name of "searching" and "friending," creating not just new possibilities for conversation but new opportunities for surveillance.

Media scholar George Gerbner explained that whoever is telling the stories within a culture has enormous power to shape how people think, act, and buy. Consequently, for the first time in human history, most of the stories about people, life, and values are told not by parents, elders, schools, churches, and others in the community who have something to tell but by a group of distant conglomerates that have little to tell and everything to sell. The result? Our 21st-century world has ceded much of our cultural storytelling power to a small number of large media corporations whose primary goal is to maximize their profits, rather than nurture our society's health, the vibrancy of our flesh-and-blood civic spaces, or our children's well-being. The tools of their trade are media messages, platforms, and content embedded in the increasingly convergent worlds of the Internet, e-games, television, and other media technologies. These corporations devote their energies to expensive efforts designed to mold our young people, from as early an age as possible, into brand-loyal consumers of corporately produced lifestyles, goods, and behaviors.

Spending more than $1 trillion in marketing each year, Big Media companies and their Fortune 500 allies use media to target consumers with a wide variety of products, goods, and services, wrapping their appeals in suggestive stories that model compulsive consumerism and "civic-less" cynicism; push sugar, caffeine, nicotine, alcohol, and a wide variety of addictive products; and advertise gratuitous sexual and violent content and other kinds of anti-social behavior.

Parents, teachers, and thinking citizens now find themselves on the front lines of a struggle over stories, as corporate media owners wage increasingly sophisticated advertising, branding, and marketing campaigns to win the hearts and minds of our citizens from ever-younger ages. As astute critics such as Nicolas Carr (2011), author of *The Shallows: What the Internet Is Doing to Our Brains*, have suggested, the Internet actually exacerbates these troublesome trends, functioning as an attention-dividing medium that promotes a "juggler's mind," elevating hyperengagement over thoughtful and reflective discourse.

Confronted with this emerging reality as the new millennium began, in 2001–2002, 40 media educators from all over the United States founded the Action Coalition for Media Education (ACME), a national independently funded educational nonprofit organization. ACME is a network of media educators, health advocates, researchers, reformers, media makers, organizers, and citizens who challenge the Big Media status quo with a three-part mission:

1. Teaching media education skills and issues to children and adults, so they can become more successful and healthier participants in our democracy.
2. Championing media reform as a crucial aspect of any cause. Whether it is saving the whales or curing cancer, every cause will benefit from a reformed news media supported by a more media-educated public.
3. Promoting activism (civic engagement) as a crucial component of democratizing our media system. Media "education" differs from media "literacy" in its emphasis on activism. Unlike other media "literacy" organizations, ACME accepts no corporate funding. ACME cannot be bought. ACME has a Code of Ethics and practices financial disclosure.

Since its inception, ACME has hosted four national media education conferences (New Mexico in 2002, San Francisco in 2004, Minneapolis in 2007, and Boston in 2011), bringing together hundreds of independent-minded media educators from across the North American continent to share ideas and resources, discuss and debate "best practices," and draw inspiration from one another's work. ACME also has conducted numerous workshops around the country for interested teachers and citizens, and trained hundreds of teachers through undergraduate and graduate education courses. ACME offers free resources for teachers, including our famed "language of persuasion" guide developed by ACME co-founder Bob McCannon, at its Web site: www.acmecoalition.org. Finally, during the past 10 years, ACME has championed the mission of its media education partners, including Free Press, Project Censored, the Media Education Foundation, and the Center for Media and Democracy.

When confronted with the power of the Big Media status quo, doing independently funded media education work is never easy. But the need has never been greater. "The problem we face with a hyper-commercial, profit-obsessed media system is that it does a lousy job of producing citizens," observes media scholar Bob McChesney, author of a dozen books on media reform. Communications scholar Sut Jhally, founder of the Media Education Foundation, adds:

> A solution is real media education that doesn't just make people more informed consumers, but active citizens who understand how it all works. ACME is committed to real media education. Media education is dangerous to media corporations, so they have moved to hijack the movement. [But] ACME cannot be hijacked.

Find out more about ACME at www.acmecoalition.org.

Reference

Carr, N. (2011). *The Shallows: What the Internet Is Doing to Our Brains.* New York: W. W. Norton.

12. The Role of Media Literacy in the Media Arts

Kathleen Tyner

Understanding the relationship between form and content is an essential literacy skill. Aesthetic qualities vary by medium, but in general, the media arts are used to construct meaning and to shape the reception of media texts. Artistic expression in media is used to support both narrative and nonnarrative forms of expression. In narrative forms of media, the arts support the linguistic, discursive, and stylistic conventions related to storytelling, communication, messaging, and dramatic effect. In nonnarrative expression, such as avant-garde and experimental media, the media arts inform the artistic process and explore the related structural qualities of media texts and objects. Artistic decisions made to construct and distribute digital media in social, networked spaces increasingly demonstrate the blurred line between authorship and audiences in digital, virtual experiences.

Additionally, the relationship between form and content for various media is framed within the complex intersection of the arts and sciences. The cultural production and reception of media texts is shaped by the underlying scientific, mathematical, chemical, electrical, engineering, and technological processes that both support and limit the artistic creation and distribution of human communication and mediated texts. Canadian media scholar Marshall McLuhan (1964) refers to the relationship of the media arts and media technologies in his phrase, "the medium is the message." He presents the relationship between form and content as both an affordance and a limitation for media production and reception.

Analogous to the study of the history of literacy, the media arts can be studied through the investigation of media tools, texts, and contexts. Media producers and audiences draw from the codes and conventions of broader artistic movements as they construct meaning. These movements influence production and reception across and between media genre such as still images, photography, music, moving images, simulations, interactive media, and augmented realities. Examples of artistic movements in the 20th century include dadaism, surrealism, photorealism, and street art, to name a few.

Scholars such as Roland Barthe, Michel Foucault, Rudolf Arnheim, Michele Knobel, Colin Lankshear, and many others have explored the unique aesthetics of each medium and the way that the media arts are used by producers and audiences to create meaning within historical, cultural, social, economic, and environmental contexts.

The uses of media arts and technologies to support and construct human communication have a long history. Before the widespread uses of alphabetic literacy, the ambiguous reception of mediated experience is discussed in a fictional dialogue with Socrates in an allegory known as *Plato's Cave* that appears in Plato's *The Republic,* written around 380 BCE.

Subsequently, the relationships between media technologies and the arts was explored by al-Jazari, a 13th-century Islamic scholar, engineer, and scientist, who discusses the way to use the robotic arts as a way to capture images and sounds in his *Book of Knowledge of Ingenious Devices* (Nadarajan, 2007).

In the 17th and 18th centuries, artists and scientists explored still and moving images through light shows, camera obscura, phantasmagoria, magic lanterns, and other multimedia illusions. The first photograph is often attributed to Joseph Nicéphore Niépce who captured camera obscura images with chemical techniques in France in 1816 (Harry Ransom Center, 2011).

Subsequent experimentation with art and chemistry by Louis-Jacques-Mandé Daguerre and others in the 1840s is a testament to the interlocking qualities of form, content, the arts, sciences, and their underlying contexts. These early photographs attest to the experimental nature of photographic aesthetics and the human desire to capture and share visual images of the physical world. In the late 1800s and early 1900s, experiments with moving image media by Moliere, Edison, the Lumiere Brothers, and others built on the artistic processes and technologies used to capture and render still images. Experiments with sound recording around 1910 lead to the production of sound on film in the 1920s.

Also in the early 1900s, artists such as Marcel Duchamp incorporated found objects, random juxtapositions, performative elements, and audio/optical techniques and devices in his works in the visual arts and music. His innovative, avant-garde techniques are referred to as *kinetic art* and *readymade art.* Drawing from the dadaist and surrealist artistic movements, his work was foundational for the 1960s kinetic and op art movements and is also referenced in early 21st-century remix techniques used by artists in digital, sound, and moving image media arts.

The history of media demonstrates that as the public gains access to each new communications device, *do-it-yourself production* (DYI) proliferates.

This tendency can be seen in the widespread uses of photography for rituals, milestones, and as memory triggers for social and family events. The introduction of affordable film cameras in the early years of the 20th century drove membership in local film clubs where amateur makers met to show work in 8mm, Super-8, and 16mm. Access to lightweight port-a-pak video equipment in the 1960s shaped the visual aesthetics of video art through pioneering experiments by artists such as Nam June Paik and the Raindance Media Collective. These artists introduced radical theories and philosophies of video that were alternative to the forms of cultural communication and expression found in broadcast media and promoted the creation of do-it-yourself (DIY) media projects by the public. The uses of mobile and affordable digital media in the early 21st century continue to drive experimental production and distribution models that are in contrast to the formulaic and factory-model aesthetics of corporate media industries.

Although the media arts are an established field in postsecondary educational curriculum, the relationship of the media arts to arts education in formal education has an ambiguous history in elementary and secondary education. In the 19th century, tensions between the fine arts and popular culture were used to narrow the range of media texts that were deemed suitable for formal schooling. In the late 20th century, the media arts were positioned as a subcategory of the visual arts as part of a discipline-based educational movement in the elementary and secondary classroom. As digital media became increasingly ubiquitous in the late 20th century, the media arts were increasingly referenced as important areas of study in standards-based, arts education documents from professional organizations and formal educational institutions.

Media literacy implies a working knowledge of the aesthetic qualities, vocabularies, and artistic movements that shape audience reception of a media text. The optimum development of knowledge and skill in the media arts is accomplished through a combination of critical analysis and critical production of media in a variety of forms. The interdisciplinary relationship between media analysis and production is also problematic for the integration of the media arts in the formal school curriculum.

Although the media arts aid in analysis and appreciation of media texts, hands-on production is the best way to explore the limitations and artistic processes associated with each medium. The introduction of media production as an essential component of literacy raises important questions about the optimum design of the learning environment for hands-on, interdisciplinary, collaborative, and peer-reviewed projects for literacy learning. These pedagogical qualities create tensions with the content-delivery modes of instruction and standardized assessment found in traditional schooling. For this reason, media production opportunities for students are more often found in the informal education sector in after-school, summer, and Saturday programs. These programs are designed by a loose network of organizations and practitioners who promote concepts and practices that are referred to as *youth media*. In higher education, the media arts are most often privileged in the fine arts, intermedia studies, media studies, and theater departments.

References

The Harry Ransom Center. (2011). The First Photograph. Retrieved from http://www .hrc.utexas.edu/exhibitions/permanent/wfp

McLuhan, M. (1964). *Understanding Media: The Extensions of Man*. New York: McGraw-Hill.

Nadarajan, G. (2007). "Islamic Automation: A Reading of Al-Jazari's *The Book of Knowledge of Ingenious Mechanical Devices* (1206)." In O. Grau (Ed.), *Media Art Histories* (pp. 163–178). Cambridge, MA: MIT Press.

Plato. (380 BCE). The Allegory of the Cave. *The Republic*. Retrieved from http://www .wsu.edu:8080/~wldciv/world_civ_reader/world_civ_reader_1/plato.html

Thread 2 Contributor Biographies

Erica Weintraub Austin is professor and director at the Murrow Center for Media and Health Promotion Research, Murrow College of Communication, Washington State University.

Frank Baker is an author, webmaster (the Media Literacy Clearinghouse), and media education consultant. He works with teachers and students to teach media literacy education.

David M. Considine is a professor of media studies and instructional technology at Appalachian State University in Boone, North Carolina. In 1995, he convened and chaired the first national media literacy conference and in 1999 introduced the first masters program in media literacy. His books include *The Cinema of Adolescence*, *Visual Messages: Integrating Imagery into Instruction*, and *Imagine That: Developing Critical Thinking and Viewing through Children's Literacy*. He can be accessed at www.media-literacy .net and e-mailed at considinedm@appstate.edu

Don Corrigan is a professor in the school of communications at Webster University and the editor and co-publisher of the *Webster-Kirkwood Times Inc.* in St. Louis, Missouri.

Renee Hobbs is professor of communication at Temple University's School of Communications and Theater, where she founded the Media Education Lab in the Department of Broadcasting, Telecommunications and Mass Media. Over her career, she has contributed dozens of scholarly articles, multimedia curriculum resources, and professional development programs to advance the quality of media literacy education in the United States and around the world.

Marjorie J. Hogan, MD, is in the Department of Pediatrics, Hennepin County Medical Center, and is associate professor of pediatrics at the University of Minnesota.

Bob McCannon is president of the Action Coalition for Media Education and a teacher, author, and presenter. An American Academy of Pediatrics'

Media Educator of the Year, he has done workshops worldwide. E-mail: mccannon@flash.net

Sam Nkana is a professor at Southern Adventist University and a specialist in Media Literacy Education, Curriculum and Instruction.

Faith Rogow, PhD, is the National Association for Media Literacy Education (NAMLE) founding president and co-author of *The Teacher's Guide to Media Literacy* (Corwin, 2012).

Marieli Rowe is editor of *The Journal of Media Literacy* (formerly *Telemedium, The Journal of Media Literacy*) and executive director of its supporting organization, the National Telemedia Council, Inc. She has held this position for more than 30 years since 1978 and has been involved in its activities since 1963. Her special interest is in the positive potential of media literacy education for the young child and the development of fresh new attitudes in education toward thinking and society.

Victor C. Strasburger, MD, is professor of pediatrics and family & community medicine, University of New Mexico School of Medicine.

Kathleen Tyner is associate professor in the Department of Radio-Television-Film at the University of Texas at Austin.

Rob Williams (www.robwilliamsmedia.com) is a musician, farmer, historian, consultant, journalist, and professor who teaches media and communications courses at Burlington's Champlain College and serves as editor and publisher of *Vermont Commons: Voices of Independence* statewide independent multimedia newspaper (www.vtcommons.org).

THREAD 3
Media Literacy Organizations

Thread 3 focuses on current national organizations that actively promote media literacy.

Thread 3: Media Literacy Organizations

911 Media Arts Center
909 NE 43rd Street, Suite 206
Seattle, WA 98105
(206) 682-6552
Fax: (206) 464-9009
www.911media.org
E-mail: info@911media.org
Vision-Making Media Matters
In a time of major advances in digital media, 911 Media Arts Center envisions a future in which independent voices thrive in a society that fosters diversity, innovation, and artistic excellence.

About-Face
Kathy Bruin, Founder
Jennifer Berger, Executive Director
P.O. Box 77665
San Francisco, CA 94107
(415) 839-6779
www.about-face.org
E-mail: info@about-face.org
Mission Statement
About-Face equips women and girls with tools to understand and resist harmful media messages that affect their self-esteem and body image.

Action Coalition for Media Education (ACME)
Bob McCannon, Cofounder
2808 El Tesoro Escondido, NW
Albuquerque, NM 87120
(505) 839-9702
www.acmecoalition.org
E-mail: mccannon@flash.net
robw@acmecoalition.org

Free of any funding from Big Media, ACME is an emerging global coalition run by and for media educators, a network that champions a three-part mission:

1. Teaching media education knowledge and skills—through keynotes, workshops, trainings, and institutes—to children and adults so that they can become more critical media consumers and more active participants in our democracy.
2. Supporting media reform—no matter what one's cause, media reform is crucial for the success of that cause, and because only those who are media educated support media reform, media education must be a top priority for all citizens and activists.
3. Democratizing our media system through education and activism.

Action for Children's Television

U.S. Citizens' Activist Group

A "grassroots" activist group, Action for Children's Television (A.C.T.) was founded by Peggy Charren and a group of "housewives and mothers" in her home in Newton, Massachusetts, in 1968. The members of A.C.T. were initially concerned with the lack of quality television programming offered to children. In 1970 A.C.T. petitioned the Federal Communications Commission (FCC) asking that television stations be required to provide more programming for the child viewer. A.C.T. also became concerned with issues of advertising within children's programming. Partially due to their efforts, the FCC enacted rules pertaining to program length commercials, host selling, and the placement of separation devices between commercials and children's programming.

A.C.T. was responsible for many cases brought before the courts in regard to the FCC and its policies concerning children's television. These cases include a major case in media law, *Action for Children's Television, et al. v. Federal Communications Commission and the United States of America* (821. F. 2d 741. D.C. Cir. 1987).

Alliance for Community Media

Helen Soule, Executive Director
1100 G Street NW, Suite 740
Washington, DC 20005
(202) 393-2650
Fax: (202) 393-2653
www.ourchannels.org

Mission Statement

For democracy to flourish, people must be active participants in their government, educated to think critically, and free to express themselves. The mission of the Alliance for Community Media is to advance democratic ideals by ensuring that people have access to electronic media and by promoting effective communication through community uses of media.

Alternative Media Information Center

The Media Network
39 W 14th Street
New York, NY 10011
(212) 929-2663

American Center for Children and Media

James Fellows, Founder and President Emeritus
David Kleeman, President
5400 North Street Louis Ave.
Chicago, IL 60625
(773) 509-5510
Fax: (773) 509-5303
www.centerforchildrenandmedia.org
E-mail: info@centerforchildrenandmedia.org

Mission Statement

Support a vibrant children's media industry by convening key constituencies to develop, implement, and promote policies and practices that respect young people's well-being, and are sustainable. Demonstrate accuracy in predicting emerging business, social, technological, and creative issues that will affect children's media. Produce thoughtful, objective issue analyses based on research aggregation and evaluation. Convene and sustain an Executive Roundtable of industry leaders that will serve as a forward-looking, off-the-record forum on controversial issues, including the potential for self-regulation. Establish a credible and effective voice for the industry, building visibility for children's media business realities and strengthening the perception that media is serving children's needs.

The Annenberg School for Communication at
University of Pennsylvania

Michael X. Delli Carpini, PhD
Professor of Communication and Walter H. Annenberg, Dean
3620 Walnut Street
Philadelphia, PA 19104

(215) 898-7041

www.asc.upenn.edu

"Every human advancement or reversal can be understood through communication. The right to free communication carries with it responsibility to respect the dignity of others—and this must be recognized as irreversible. Educating students to effectively communicate this message and to be of service to all people is the enduring mission of this school." (The Honorable Walter H. Annenberg, October 16, 1958)

Publisher, diplomat, and philanthropist Walter Annenberg wrote those words when he founded the Annenberg School for Communication at the University of Pennsylvania.

Throughout the past five decades, the Annenberg School for Communication has remained true to the mission articulated by Ambassador Annenberg, while responding to changes in both the nature of communication as a social process and in Communication as a discipline. Today we advance our mission through four central goals:

- Producing and disseminating cutting-edge scholarly research designed to advance the discipline's theoretical and empirical understanding of the role of communication in public and private life.
- Producing and disseminating high-quality applied research designed to advance the public's understanding and effective use of communication, and policy makers' ability to create a media environment that fosters the personal and collective development of its citizens.
- Educating doctoral students in the theories, substance, and methods of communication research and placing them in leading academic and professional positions in the field.
- Providing a first-class liberal arts education to undergraduates, designed to help them become better consumers and producers of public information, strengthening their understanding of the role of communication in their personal, professional and civic lives, and preparing them for private and public-sector leadership positions in communication-related and other fields.

Appalachian Media Institute (AMI; Appalshop)

91 Madison Avenue

Whitesburg, KY 41858

(606) 633-0108

www.appleshop.org

Appalshop is a multimedia arts and cultural organization located in Whitesburg, Kentucky, that strives to develop effective ways to use media to address the complex issues facing central Appalachia—a declining coal economy, a legacy of environmental damage, high unemployment rates, and poor educational opportunities and attainment. In 1988, Appalshop staff members founded the Appalachian Media Institute (AMI), a media training program for central Appalachian youth. Using the technological and artistic resources of Appalshop, AMI helps young people explore how media production skills can be used to ask, and begin to answer, critical questions of themselves and their communities. With opportunities to have input into community dialogues, and frame those dialogues themselves, young people develop the skills and critical thinking abilities necessary to become leaders in creating sustainable futures for their communities. Since its inception AMI has directly engaged more than 600 young people in media production.

Arts Engine, Inc.

104 West 14th Street, 4th Floor
New York, NY 10011
(646) 230-6368
Fax: (646) 230-6388
www.artsengine.net

Committed to breaking down traditional hierarchies and status-markers, Arts Engine launched one of the only online commons for filmmakers and activists, called MediaRights.org. Now MediaRights.org is one of the most comprehensive databases of social-issue documentaries in the nation, and possibly the world, with more than 7,000 films registered and more than 20,000 members. The success of this site led to the creation of a youth-focused initiative that is now called Launchpad. It also developed and launched the Media That Matters Film Festival, one of the first online film festivals, and realized the incredible potential for online showcasing and distribution. Going into its 10th year, and much more than a festival, Media That Matters reaches hundreds of thousands of people annually and hosts hundreds of Internet pages of information with "Take Action Links." The ballast for this intense activism from the early beginnings in 1997 to today is the belief that exemplary visual storytelling on social issues can make change. Arts Engine is trusted source for media that matters. We drive change by connecting film, technology, and community.

Assembly of Media Arts

http://ncte-ama.blogspot.com/

Formerly the National Council for Teachers of English (NCTE), Assembly of Media Arts blog states: the AMA has been disbanded, but we are continuing the blog for those who teach English and are interested in the role of the media/technology in curriculum instruction. This section of the NCTE serves as a resource for the teaching of media literacy in English classes. Published in blog form, the Assembly facilitates the exchange of ideas and practices between high school and college teachers. Poster Frank Baker links to stories from around the globe dealing with issues pertaining to media literacy, in addition to contributing original material.

The Association for Media Literacy (AML)
28 Sedgewick Crescent
Scarborough, Ontario
M1K 3T6 Canada
(416) 447-9553
Fax: (416) 396-4292
E-mail: info@aml.ca or neil.andersen@tdsb.on.ca
Media literacy is an educational initiative that aims to increase students' understanding and enjoyment of how the media work, how they produce meaning, how they are organized, and how the media construct reality. AML is concerned with helping students develop an informed and critical understanding of the nature of the mass media, the techniques used by media industries, and the impact of these techniques. Media literacy also aims to provide students with the ability to create their own media products. The AML has members from across Canada, throughout the United States, and from around the world. Our international membership is particularly strong in those English-speaking countries where the educational system has given some priority to media literacy, notably England, Australia, and Scotland as well as the United States. Our members and guest speakers at AML events include internationally renowned media educators such as John Pungente, SJ, of Canada; Len Masterman and David Buckingham of Great Britain; and Robyn Quin and Barrie McMahon of Australia. Neil Andersen has taught film and/or media studies in high schools for more than 30 years. Andersen has taught media courses for teachers at the University of Toronto, York University, and Mount Saint Vincent University. He is an executive member of the Association for Media Literacy (Ontario) and on the Board of the Media-Awareness Network.

Association for a Media Literate New Brunswick
Mike Gange, President
Fredericton High

300 Priestman Street
Fredericton, NB E3B 6J8 Canada
(506) 453-9987 or (506) 453-9987
E-mail: gangemin@nbed.nb.ca
www.media-awareness.ca
In October 2001, the Association for a Media Literate New Brunswick
(A-4-ML-NB) held its inaugural meeting. Presently trying to build its membership, the A-4-ML-NB plans to create professional development opportunities for media educators through workshops and summer institutes.

ATOM Australian Teachers of Media Queensland

PO Box 2040
Kelvin Grove, 4059, Queensland
www.atomqld.org
Members of ATOM, Qld have been involved in every major development
in media education in Queensland. These include the several versions
of the Senior Film and Television syllabus, the publication of Education
Queensland's Media Curriculum Guide in 1994 and the development of the
Queensland Studies Authority's Media strand of the Years 1 to 10 Arts Syllabus. ATOM Qld Inc is an organization with a rich and long history. Film
and media teachers in Queensland were represented in a formal manner by
the Queensland Council for Children's Film and Television from at least the
mid-1960s. In 1977 a Brisbane branch of the Australian Society for Education in Film and Television was first established, providing support and information to teachers of Film Appreciation and Production. By 1981, this group
had become the Queensland Media Teachers Association and its main aim
was to support teachers introducing the new Senior Film and Television syllabus. In 1982, the QMTA became a chapter of Australian Teachers of Media.
ATOM Qld has played a key role in the development of media education
in Queensland and Australia. The "Oz Media '88," "Media World '96" and
"e-Merging Realities" (2006) conferences held in Brisbane were important
events for the development of Australian media education.

ATOM—Victoria Australian Teachers of Media

www.atomvic.org
14A Dalgety Street
St Kilda
Victoria 3182, Australia

Peter Tapp, Publications Manager
(+61-3) 9525 5302
Fax: (+61-3) 9537 2325
The Australian Teachers of Media National (ATOM) welcomes the opportunity to provide feedback to the Australian Curriculum, Assessment and Reporting Authority regarding the draft document, Shape of the Australian Curriculum: The Arts. ATOM strongly supports the inclusion of Media Arts as one of five art forms to be taught to every Australian student in Foundation to Year 8 in the Australian Curriculum. Furthermore, ATOM believes that all students in Years 9–12 should have the opportunity to study Media Arts and other art forms, and welcomes the development of curriculum for these years of schooling. Our discussions with members in our states and territories indicate general satisfaction with the direction for The Arts as articulated in the Shape Paper. The Arts Shape Paper recognizes the unique, collaborative, and creative nature of arts curriculum and its value for the education of all young Australians. It recognizes the possibilities for deep learning through the connectivity between the art forms.

ATOM (WA) Inc.—Western Australia
Bob Dixon
E-mail: mediaed@iinet.net.au
Kent St SHS Kent Street
East Vic Par, 6101 Australia
(+61) 9362-1277

Australian Children's Television Foundation (ACTF)
Patricia Gauthier, Publications Coordinator
145 Smith Street, 3rd Floor
Fitzroy, Victoria 3065, Australia
(+61-3) 9419-8800
Fax: (+61-3) 9419-0660
E-mail: info@actf.com.au
The ACTF is a national nonprofit organization. It is committed to providing Australian children with entertaining media made especially for them, which makes an enduring contribution to their cultural and educational experience. The ACTF develops and produces high-quality television programs for children. It aims to create innovative, entertaining, and educational programs. ACTF programs have screened in more than 100 countries and have won more than 95 local and international awards.

The ACTF acts as a local and international distributor of children's programs. Producers seeking a distributor for a new children's television series should contact the ACTF's Head of Development and Production. The ACTF's Resource Centre contains an extensive collection of materials on children and the media. The Centre is designed for use by researchers, producers, tertiary students, and academics, but is open to all members of the public. The holdings can be searched online.

Australian Council on Children and the Media
PO Box 447 GLENELG SA 5045 Australia
(+61-8) 8376-2111
Fax: (+61-8) 8376-2122
E-mail: info@youngmedia.org.au
www.childrenandmedia.org.au
Promoting healthy choices and stronger voices in children's media

ACCM is a unique national community organization whose members share a strong commitment to the promotion of the healthy development of Australian children. Their particular interest and expertise is in the role that media experiences play in that development. ACCM is structured as a not-for-profit company limited by guarantee with a national Board representative of major child-focused organizations in Australia.

ACCM is committed to promoting better choices and providing stronger voices in children's media. ACCM supports families, industry, and decision makers in building and maintaining a media environment that fosters the health, safety, and well-being of Australian children.

Berkman Center for Internet and Society at Harvard University
23 Everett Street, 2nd Floor
Cambridge, MA 02138
(617) 495-7547
Fax: (617) 495-7641
http://cyber.law.harvard.edu
Mission Statement
The Berkman Center's mission is to explore and understand cyberspace; to study its development, dynamics, norms, and standards; and to assess the need or lack thereof for laws and sanctions. We are a research center, premised on the observation that what we seek to learn is not already recorded. Our method is to build out into cyberspace, record data as we go, self-study, and share.

The Black Film Center/Archive at Indiana University
Black Film Center/Archive
Wells Library, Room 044
1320 East Tenth Street
Indiana University
Bloomington, IN 47405
(812) 855-6041
Fax: (812) 856-5832
E-mail: bfca@indiana.edu

Mission of the Black Film Center/Archive
The Black Film Center/Archive was established in 1981 as a repository of films and related materials by and about African Americans. Included are films that have substantial participation by African Americans as writers, actors, producers, directors, musicians, and consultants, as well as those which depict some aspect of black experience. The BFC/A is a facility where scholars, students, and researchers can view films and have access to auxiliary research facilities on the Indiana University Bloomington campus. *Black Camera*, the micro-journal of the Black Film Center/Archive, serves as an academic, professional, and community resource. In order to maintain a comprehensive research archive, the BFC/A does not distribute any part of its collection. However, the BFC/A maintains a database of more than 8,000 films, not all of which are in the collection. For a minimal fee, database research information concerning those films is available to be faxed or mailed.

Objectives of the Black Film Center/Archive
- To expand the film collection of historic and current films by and about African Americans
- To encourage the continuation of creative film activity by independent black filmmakers
- To undertake and encourage research in the history, meaning, and aesthetics of black film
- To guide and support students and researchers in black film studies

Cable in the Classroom
25 Massachusetts Ave NW, Suite 100
Washington, DC 20001
(202) 222-2335
Fax: (202) 222-2336
www.ciconline.org

Mission Statement

Cable in the Classroom (CIC) promotes the visionary, sensible, responsible, and effective use of cable's broadband technology, services, and content in teaching and learning. CIC also advocates digital citizenship and supports the complementary provision, by cable industry companies, of broadband and multichannel video services and educational content to the nation's schools.

Cameo—Council of Australian Media Education Organizations Inc.

Membership is restricted to one media teacher association from each state or territory of Australia and one organization from New Zealand.

CAMEO Objectives

- To provide communication and a forum for the free exchange of ideas between media education organizations of the states and territories of Australia and New Zealand
- To promote media education to government, students, teachers, and the public at large
- To promote communication among primary, secondary, and tertiary education, industrial, professional, and arts bodies, and all government levels
- To actively seek publicity for media education
- To research and report on curriculum and equipment for use by members
- To regularly distribute relevant information to its member associations
- Through member associations, encourage students who have potential media skills and assist in the development of these skills
- To sponsor and promote an association of media educators in states or territories of Australia and New Zealand that do not have one
- To liaise with other national or international associations having similar objectives

Canadian Association of Media Education Organizations (CAMEO)

1804—77 Street Clair Avenue East
Toronto, Ontario M4T 1M5 Canada
(416) 920-3286
Fax: (416) 920-8254
John Pungente, President, CAMEO
www.interact.uoregon.edu/Medialit/CAMEO
Founded in 1992, the Canadian Association of Media Education Organizations (CAMEO) is an association of Canadian media literacy groups from

across Canada. The goal of CAMEO, through its member organizations, is to advocate, promote, and develop media literacy in Canada. A media literate person is one who has an informed and critical understanding of the nature, techniques, and impact of the mass media as well as the ability to produce media products. The current president of CAMEO is John J. Pungente, SJ, executive director of the Jesuit Communication Project in Toronto.

Canadian Association for Media Education

Dan Blake, President
1363 Fountain Way
Vancouver, BC V6H 3T2 Canada
(604) 734-9250
Fax: (604) 734-9251
E-Mail:danblake@istar.ca
www.interact.uoregon.edu
C.A.M.E. was formed by a group of teachers and media professionals and was incorporated as nonprofit society in August 1991. We have about 100 members, mostly in the Lower Mainland. Our objectives are as follows:
- to educate Canadians about the media,
- to promote media education, and
- to encourage Canadian cultural expression in the media.

Center for Democracy and Technology (CDT)

Leslie Harris, President and CEO, CDT
1634 I Street NW #1100
Washington, DC 20006
(202) 637-9800
Fax: (202) 637-0968
www.cdt.org
Mission Statement
The Center for Democracy and Technology (CDT) is a 501(c)(3) nonprofit public policy organization dedicated to promoting the democratic potential of today's open, decentralized global Internet. Our mission is to conceptualize, develop, and implement public policies that will keep the Internet open, innovative, and free.

The CDT is a nonprofit public interest organization working to keep the Internet open, innovative, and free. As a civil liberties group with expertise in law, technology, and policy, CDT works to enhance free expression and privacy in communications technologies by finding practical and innovative solutions to public policy challenges while protecting civil liberties. CDT is dedicated to building consensus among all parties interested in the future of the Internet and other new communications media.

The Center for Digital Democracy (CDD)

Jeffrey Chester, Executive Director

jeff@democraticmedia.org

(202) 494-7100

www.democraticmedia.org

The Center for Digital Democracy (CDD) is dedicated to ensuring that the public interest is a fundamental part of the new digital communications landscape. From open broadband networks, to free or low-cost universal Internet access, to diverse ownership of new media outlets, privacy and other consumer safeguards, CDD works to promote an electronic media system that fosters democratic expression and human rights. A national, not-for-profit group based in Washington, DC, CDD is on the cutting edge of new media developments, especially tracking the commercial media market. Through outreach to the press, policy makers, reports, blogs, investigative research, and organizing, CDD plays a unique and pivotal role helping foster the development of sustainable online communities and services essential to civil society in the 21st century. The Center for Digital Democracy was founded in 2001.

The Centre for Literacy

2100 Marlowe Avenue, Suite 236

Montreal, QC Canada H4A3L5

(514) 798-5601

Fax: (514) 798-5602

E-mail: info@centreforliteracy.qc.ca

www.centreforliteracy.qc.ca

The Centre for Literacy is a Montreal-based centre of expertise that supports best practices and informed policy development in literacy and essential skills by creating bridges between research, policy, and practice. We do this through learning events (including institutes and workshops), action research projects and publications, and also through our library services and Web site.

Mission

To improve literacy outcomes by advancing the integration of evidence-based literacy policy and practice.

Center for Media and Public Affairs at George Mason University (CMPA)

Dr. S. Robert Lichter, Director
2100 L Street N.W., Suite 300
Washington, DC 20037
(202) 223-2942
Fax: (202) 872-4014
www.cmpa.com
E-mail: mail@cmpa.com

Goals

The Center for Media and Public Affairs (CMPA) is a nonpartisan research and educational organization that conducts scientific studies of news and entertainment media. CMPA's goal is to provide an empirical basis for ongoing debates over media coverage and impact through well-documented, timely, and readable studies.

Center for Media Literacy (CML)

Tessa Jolls, President and CEO
Center for Media Literacy
22631 Pacific Coast Highway, #472
Malibu, CA 90265
www.medialit.org
Phone: (310) 456-1225
Fax: (310) 456-0020

The Center for Media Literacy (CML) is an educational organization that provides leadership, public education, professional development, and educational resources nationally and internationally. Dedicated to promoting and supporting media literacy education as a framework for accessing, analyzing, evaluating, creating, and participating with media content, CML works to help citizens, especially the young, develop critical thinking and media production skills needed to live fully in the 21st century media culture.

The Center for Media Studies, Rutgers

The State University of New Jersey
SCILS, Rutgers University
4 Huntington Street
New Brunswick, NJ 08901
Robert Kubey, Director (ext. 8164)
E-mail: kubey@rutgers.edu

(732) 932-7500

www.mediastudies.rutgers.edu

Mission

The Center for Media Studies is concerned with the impact of media on contemporary society. Through research, teaching, public events, and outreach, the Center seeks ways for the media to better serve the public interest. Founded by the Department of Journalism and Media Studies in the School of Communication and Information at Rutgers University, the Center brings faculty and students together from diverse departments at each of Rutgers' campuses to work with citizens, educators, foundations, government agencies, and media professionals.

Goals

- To initiate and support intellectual partnerships across departments and academic units toward new collaborative research and scholarship, teaching, and outreach efforts.
- To initiate and develop working liaisons among and between researchers and scholars, media professionals, educators, parents, and others who work with children and youth, as well as those in business and government, thereby increasing the relevance of our research and teaching efforts to the world beyond the academy.
- To address issues of public concern regarding media performance and to bring critical issues to the public's attention. To involve the public in the Center's programs and events.

Center for Social Media

Pat Aufderheide, PhD, Director and Professor of Communication

American University

4400 Massachusetts Avenue NW

Washington, DC 20016-8001

(202) 885-1000

www.american.edu

www.centerforsocialmedia.org/aufderheide.html

The Center for Social Media (CSM) showcases ways to use media as creative tools for public knowledge and action. It focuses on social documentary films and on the public media environment that supports civil society and democracy. In addition to hosting film festivals, conferences, and working groups, it maintains a Web site that serves as a clearinghouse of resources for filmmakers, activists, and scholars. Each year CSM hosts the Media That Matters conference (formerly known as Making Your Media Matter) featuring a keynote address and panels contributing to an overall theme that showcases strategies for socially engaged media. Media That Matters is a conference for established and aspiring filmmakers, nonprofit communications leaders, funders, and students who want to learn and share cutting-edge practices to make their media matter.

The Centre for Literacy of Quebec
Linda Shohet, Executive Director
2100 Marlowe Avenue, Suite 236
Montreal, QC H4A 3L5 Canada
(514) 798-5601
Fax: (514) 798-5602
www.centerforliteracy.qc.ca
Mission Statement
To improve literacy outcomes by advancing the integration of evidence-based literacy policy and practice. We look toward a society where life-long learning opportunities and community supports enable all individuals to participate fully in their communities as family members, citizens, and workers. The Centre for Literacy is a Montreal-based centre of expertise that supports best practices and informed policy development in literacy and essential skills by creating bridges between research, policy, and practice. We do this through learning events (including institutes and workshops), action research projects and publications, and also through our library services and Web site.

Centro de Investigacion de Medios Para la Educacion (CIME)
Miguel Reyes Torre, Director
Educational-CIME Facultad de Ciencias de la Educación
Faculty of Education
Universidad de Playa Ancha Universidad de Playa Ancha
Av. Playa Ancha 850, Valparaíso Avenida Playa Ancha 850
Valparaíso, Chile
(+56) 32-500-193
Fax: (+56) 32-676-424
E-mail: cime@upa.cl
Mission
To promote the use of media in education. CIME has worked to accomplish this mission through the following activities:

1. Training teachers in the development of methodologies and techniques for using social media to the classroom through courses, workshops, a postgraduate program, and two distance-learning programs.
2. Development and evaluation of various methodologies for solving problems caused by television and other media in school.
3. Training for the active perception of television programs such as "School for Parents, Family and Television" and "Learning to watch TV through the TV."
4. Radio program production line with the objectives of the Centre.
5. Development of research.
6. Organizing events for the discussion of issues related to the relationship between media and education.
7. Research dissemination activities and establishing contacts with exchange centers or similar institutions in the country and abroad.

Children's Advertising Review Unit

70 West 36th Street, 12th Floor
New York, NY 10018
www.caru.org
(866) 334-6272
E-mail: caru@caru.bbb.org

Mission Statement

As an extension of its initial mission, to help advertisers deal sensitively with the child audience in a responsible manner, in 1996 CARU added a section to its *Guidelines* that highlight issues, including children's privacy, that are unique to the Internet and online sites directed at children age 12 and under. These Guidelines served as the basis of the federal Children's Online Privacy Protection Act of 1998 (COPPA). CARU has established a Safe Harbor Program for our supporters to help them protect the privacy of children online and meet the requirements of COPPA and our *Guidelines*.

Children's Media Project (CMP)

Lady Washington Firehouse
20 Academy Street
Poughkeepsie, NY 12601
(845) 485-4480/(845) 625-2090
Fax: (845) 559-0005
E-mail: info@childrensmediaproject.org
www.childrensmediaproject.org

Children's Media Project (CMP) is a nonprofit arts and education organization with a history of empowering "at-risk" youth through the media arts. Their mission is to create a teaching/learning environment where artists, educators, community activists, and children can learn to interact with the media arts both as creators and critical viewers.

Children's Music Network (CMN)
Administrative Coordinator: Jane Arsham
10 Court Street, P.O. Box 22
Arlington, MA 02476
(339) 707-0277
E-mail: office@cmnonline.org
www.cmnonline.org
Mission Statement
The Children's Music Network celebrates the positive power of music in the lives of children by sharing songs, exchanging ideas, and creating community. In the 1980s, like-minded teachers, performers, songwriters, radio hosts, and parents who cared about the quality and content of children's music established the Children's Music Network (CMN), a nonprofit association that now has members across the United States and Canada. We recognize children's music as a powerful means of encouraging cooperation, celebrating diversity, building self-esteem, promoting respect and responsibility for our environment, and cultivating an understanding of nonviolence and social justice.

Children Now
Ted Lempert, President
1212 Broadway, 5th Floor
Oakland, CA 94612
(510) 763-2444
Fax: (510) 763-1974
E-mail: info@childrennow.org
www.childrennow.org
Mission Statement
Children Now's mission is to find common ground among influential opinion leaders, interest groups, and policymakers who together can develop and drive socially innovative, "win-win" approaches to help all children achieve their full potential.

Citizens for Media Literacy (CML)

34 Wall Street, Suite 407
Asheville, NC 28801
www.main.nc.us/cml/
(828) 255-0182
Fax: (882) 254-2286
E-mail: cml@mail.nc.us

Mission Statement

The mission of Citizens for Media Literacy is to teach young people how to think critically about TV and advertising. Citizens for Media Literacy is a nonprofit, public-interest organization linking media literacy with the concepts and practices of citizenship.

Commercial Alert

Robert Weissman, Managing Director
P.O. Box 19002
Washington, DC 20036
(202) 387-8030
Fax: (202) 234-5176
www.commercialalert.org

Mission Statement

Commercial Alert's mission is to keep the commercial culture within its proper sphere, and to prevent it from exploiting children and subverting the higher values of family, community, environmental integrity, and democracy. Commercial Alert is a nonprofit organization established under section 501(c)(3) of the U.S. tax code. Our mission is to keep the commercial culture within its proper sphere, and to prevent it from exploiting children and subverting the higher values of family, community, environmental integrity, and democracy.

Community Film Workshop

Margaret Caples, Executive Director
In Residence at the Harris Park
6200 S. Drexel, Room 201
Chicago, IL 60637-2630
(773) 752-9335
www.cfwchicago.org

Community Film Workshop of Chicago (CFWC) provides 16mm film and digital media classes. Since 1971, the Community Film Workshop has established a reputation for quality, hands-on education, small class size, individualized instruction, and cooperative learning. CFWC participants are multicultural and represent a wide spectrum of age, educational background, and experiences. CFWC has implemented successful school-to-college program for high school youth and worked with schools and community groups.

Community Media Workshop at Columbia College

600 S Michigan Avenue
Chicago, IL 60605
(312) 369-6400
Fax: (312) 369-6404
E-mail: cmw@newstips.org
www.newstips.org and www.communitymediaworkshop.org
Walk-In Location
218 S Wabash, 7th Floor
Since 1989, Community Media Workshop has worked to diversify the voices in news and public debates by providing a unique mix of communications coaching for grassroots, arts, and other nonprofit organizations and sourcing grassroots and community news for journalists. Connecting the community with media, the Workshop promotes news that matters. Democracy depends upon freedom of expression and a plurality of voices. We believe all have the right to be heard and deserve an equal opportunity to shape public debate. Diversifying the voices in public debate leads to a dialogue that portrays society more fully and accurately, and such diversity in turn enriches democracy. To meet our mission and vision we offer a unique blend of communications coaching and community-oriented journalism resources, in three areas.

The Consumer Federation of America

1620 I Street, NW, Suite 200
Washington, DC 20006
(202) 387-6121
www.consumerfed.org
The Consumer Federation of America (CFA) is an association of nonprofit consumer organizations that was established in 1968 to advance the consumer interest through research, advocacy, and education. Today, nearly 300 of these groups participate in the federation and govern it through their representatives on the organization's Board of Directors. CFA is a research, advocacy, education, and service organization.

As a research organization, CFA investigates consumer issues, behavior, and attitudes through surveys, focus groups, investigative reports, economic analysis, and policy analysis.

As an advocacy organization, CFA works to advance pro-consumer policies on a variety of issues before Congress, the White House, federal and state regulatory agencies, state legislatures, and the courts.

As a service organization, CFA assists individuals and organizations. Our principal service to individuals is through the America Saves campaign, which we organized in 2000 and have managed since then.

Digital Democracy

109 West 27th Street, #6b

New York, NY 10001

(347) 688-3336

www.digital-democracy.org

Digital Democracy (DD) works with local partners to put information into the hands of people who need it most—those neglected, disenfranchised, or abused by their rulers. Dd emphasizes *education, communication, and participation* to empower citizens to build and shape their own communities. Digital Democracy incorporated as a nonprofit organization November 20, 2008.

Educational Video Center (EVC)

Steve Goodman, Founding Director and Executive Director

(sgoodman@evc.org)

120 West 30th Street, 7th Floor

New York, NY 10001

(212) 465-9366

Fax: (212) 465-9369

E-mail: info@evc.org

www.evc.org

Mission and History

The Educational Video Center is a nonprofit youth media organization dedicated to teaching documentary video as a means to develop the artistic, critical literacy, and career skills of young people, while nurturing their idealism and commitment to social change.

Electronic Frontier Foundation (EFF)

San Francisco (Main Office)

454 Shotwell Street

E-mail: information@eff.org

(415) 436-9333

Fax: (415) 436-9993

Washington, DC (Satellite Office)

David Sobel, Senior Counsel
1818 N. Street, NW, Suite 410
Washington, DC 20036
(202) 797-9009
Fax: (202) 797-9066
www.eff.org

Mission Statement

The Electronic Frontier Foundation was established to help civilize the electronic frontier; to make it truly useful and beneficial not just to a technical elite, but to everyone; and to do this in a way which is in keeping with our society's highest traditions of the free and open flow of information and communication.

To that end, the Electronic Frontier Foundation will:

1. Engage in and support educational activities which increase popular understanding of the opportunities and challenges posed by developments in computing and telecommunications.
2. Develop among policy makers a better understanding of the issues underlying free and open telecommunications, and support the creation of legal and structural approaches which will ease the assimilation of these new technologies by society.
3. Raise public awareness about civil liberties issues arising from the rapid advancement in the area of new computer-based communications media. Support litigation in the public interest to preserve, protect, and extend First Amendment rights within the realm of computing and telecommunications technology.
4. Encourage and support the development of new tools that will endow nontechnical users with full and easy access to computer-based telecommunications.

FactCheck.org

Brooks Jackson, Director
Annenberg Public Policy Center
320 National Press Building
Washington, DC 20045
(202) 879-6700
E-mail: Editor@factcheck.org
www.factcheck.org

Mission Statement

We are a nonpartisan, nonprofit "consumer advocate" for voters that aims to reduce the level of deception and confusion in U.S. politics. We monitor the factual accuracy of what is said by major U.S. political players in the form of TV ads, debates, speeches, interviews, and news releases. Our goal is to apply the best practices of both journalism and scholarship, and to increase public knowledge and understanding. FactCheck.org is a project of the Annenberg Public Policy Center of the University of Pennsylvania.

Fairness and Accuracy In Reporting (FAIR)

104 W. 27th Street, Suite 10B
New York, NY 10001
(212) 663-6700
Fax: (212) 727-7668
E-mail: fair@fair.org
www.fair.org
Twitter: @FAIRmediawatch

Mission Statement

FAIR, the national media watch group, has been offering well-documented criticism of media bias and censorship since 1986. We work to invigorate the First Amendment by advocating for greater diversity in the press and by scrutinizing media practices that marginalize public interest, minority, and dissenting viewpoints. As an anticensorship organization, we expose neglected news stories and defend working journalists when they are muzzled.

Free Expression Policy Project

Marjorie Heins, Founder and Director
170 West 76th Street, #301
New York, NY 10023
E-mail: margeheins@verizon.net
www.fepproject.org

The Free Expression Policy Project (FEPP), founded in 2000, provides research and advocacy on free speech, copyright, and media democracy issues. FEPP's primary areas of inquiry are the following:

- Restrictions on publicly funded expression—in libraries, museums, schools, universities, and arts and humanities agencies
- Internet filters, rating systems, and other measures that restrict access to information and ideas in the digital age
- Restrictive copyright laws, digital rights management, and other imbalances in the intellectual property system
- Mass media consolidation, public access to the airwaves, and other issues of media democracy

- Censorship designed to shield adolescents and children from controversial art, information, and ideas

Free Press
Massachusetts Office
40 Main Street, Suite 301
Florence, MA 01062
(877) 888-1533
Fax : (413) 585-8904
Washington Office
501 Third Street NW, Suite 875
Washington, DC 20001
(202) 265-1490
Fax: (202) 265-1489
www.freepress.net

Free Press Basics
Free Press is a national, nonpartisan, nonprofit organization working to reform the media. Through education, organizing, and advocacy, we promote diverse and independent media ownership, strong public media, quality journalism, and universal access to communications. Today, Free Press is the largest media reform organization in the United States, with nearly half a million activists and members and a full-time staff of more than 30 based in our offices in Washington, DC, and Florence, Massachusetts.

Gateway Media Literacy Partners, Inc. (GMLP)
Jessica G. Brown, Founder, President
P. O. Box 170071
Saint Louis, MO 63117
www.gatewaymedialiteracypartners.org or www.gmlpstl.org
Gateway Media Literacy Partners, Inc., is a 501c3 organization registered in the State of Missouri. GMLP is a not-for-profit organization that is mainly, but not exclusively, a regional organization comprising public, private, volunteer, and independent-sector citizens who understand that our youths live in a complex multimedia world and require new competencies for 21st-century citizenship. Established in 2004, the GMLP's mission is to (1) promote media literacy in the St. Louis region; (2) promote community partnerships and collaborations; (3) provide support for media literacy projects; (4) act as a conduit for national initiatives; (5) initiate a sustained education campaign that defines and clarifies the need for and value of media literacy.

Globalvision
P.O. Box 677
New York, NY 10035
(212) 246-0202
E-mail: roc@globalvision.org
www.globalvision.org
Cofounded by award-winning journalists Rory O'Connor and Danny Schechter, Globalvision is a full-service, independent, international media company specializing in information, entertainment, and educational programming. For more than two decades, Globalvision has produced highly acclaimed newsmagazines, nationally televised specials, cutting-edge documentary films, leading Web sites, public service campaigns, and a wide variety of corporate communications tools and strategies.

Grade the News at the School of Journalism and Mass Communications
San Jose State University
John McManus, Director
Michael Stoll, Associate Director
Dwight Bentel Hall
One Washington Square
San Jose, CA 95192-0026
408-924-3240
Fax: 408-924-3229
E-mail: jmcmanus@gradethenews.org or mstoll@gradethenews.org
www.gradethenews.org
Mission Statement
(1) To help Bay Area residents recognize their dependence on news—democracy's most essential commodity, (2) assess news organizations' success in meeting those ends, and (3) secure quality news across the region's diverse communities.

Hands on a Camera
Amy Peter Jensen, Director
Brigham Young University
360 BRMB
Provo, UT 84602
(801) 422-2997
http://cfac-old.byu.edu/index.php?id=527

Purpose

To instill the basic principles of media literacy in local primary and secondary students by providing them with hands-on experiences with digital media. It is an ongoing service-learning, education-based project. "We put into the hands of students the tools of media so when they're bombarded [with the media] they're empowered. They don't take the media as is, but . . . its real message." (Yancy Zimmerman, Advertising Senior involved in the project)

Independent Media Center

Seattle Headquarters
1125 N. 98th Street
Seattle, WA 98103
www.seattle.indymedia.org or www.indymedia.org

History

The Independent Media Center (www.indymedia.org) was established by various independent and alternative media organizations and activists in 1999 for the purpose of providing grassroots coverage of the World Trade Organization (WTO) protests in Seattle. The center acted as a clearinghouse of information for journalists and provided up-to-the-minute reports, photos, audio, and video footage through its Web site. The site, which used a democratic open-publishing system, logged more than 2 million hits and was featured on America Online, Yahoo, CNN, BBC Online, and numerous other sites. Through a decentralized and autonomous network, hundreds of media activists set up independent media centers in London, Canada, Mexico City, Prague, Belgium, France, and Italy over the next year. IMCs have since been established on every continent, with more to come.

Independent Television Service (ITVS)

651 Brannan Street, Suite 410
San Francisco, CA 94107
(415) 356-8383
Fax: (415) 356-8391
E-mail: itvs@itvs.org
www.itvs.org

Mission Statement

The Independent Television Service (ITVS) brings independently produced, high-quality public broadcast and news media programs to local, national, and international audiences. The independent producers who create ITVS programs take creative risks, tackle complex issues, and express points of view seldom explored in the mass media. ITVS programs enrich the cultural landscape with the voices and visions of underrepresented communities, and reflect the interests and concerns of a diverse society.

International Communication Association

Michael L. Haley, Executive Director
1500 21st Street, NW
Washington, DC 20036
E-mail: mhaley@icahdq.org
www.icahdq.org
(202) 955-1444
(202) 955-1448

Mission Statement

The International Communication Association aims to advance the scholarly study of human communication by encouraging and facilitating excellence in academic research worldwide. The purposes of the Association are (1) to provide and international forum to enable the development, conduct, and critical evaluation of communication research; (2) to sustain a program of high-quality scholarly publication and knowledge exchange; (3) to facilitate inclusiveness and debate among scholars from diverse national and cultural backgrounds and from multidisciplinary perspectives on communication-related issues; and (4) to promote a wider public interest in, and visibility of, the theories, methods, findings, and applications generated by research in communication and allied fields.

ICA began more than 50 years ago as a small association of U.S. researchers and is now a truly international association with more than 4,200 members in over 80 countries.

International Development Education Resource Association

West Broadway Ave.
Vancouver, BC
604-732-1496
E-mail: idera@vcn.ca
Fax: 738-8400
Webpage: www.vcn.bc.ca/idera

Jesuit Communications Project (JCP)

1804-77 Street Clair Avenue East
Toronto, Ontario, Canada M4T 1M5
(416) 920-3286
Fax: (416) 920-8254

E-mail: pungente@sympatico.ca

http://jcp.proscenia.net/index.htm

Under the direction of John Pungente SJ, the Toronto-based Jesuit Communication Project promotes the development of media literacy across Canada. The JCP has been active in offering workshops and keynote addresses at teachers' conferences, in-services, and summer institutes across Canada, Australia, and in the United States, Europe, and Japan. Founded in 1984, the JCP has a resource library of more than 4,000 books and periodicals on the media, as well as many media literacy resource kits and curricula from around the world.

Just Think Foundation

Elana Rosen, Founder

Arthur Grau IV, Community Manager

39 Mesa Street, Suite 106

San Francisco, CA 94129

(415) 561-2900

Fax: (415) 598-1622

E-mail: think@justthink.org

www.justthink.org

Founded in 1995 as a concerned response to the ever-increasing deluge of messages youth receive from television, radio, film, print media, electronic games, and the Internet, Just Think teaches young people media literacy skills for the 21st century. Having reached nearly 7,500 students, teachers, parents, and others through direct programs, more than 35,000 individuals through screenings, exhibits, fairs, and other community events, and an additional 4,000,000 lives through unique media touches, Just Think has successfully created and delivered in-school, after-school, and online media arts and technology education locally, nationally, and internationally.

Killology Research Group

P.O. Box 180

Mascoutah, IL 62258

(618) 566-4682

Fax: (618) 566-4738

www.killology.com

Learning Matters Inc.

127 W. 26th Street, #1200

New York, NY 10001

(212) 725-7000

Fax: (212) 725-2433
E-mail: news@learningmatters.tv
www.learningmatters.tv

Mission Statement

To use media to encourage and enrich public dialogue about education, youth, and families. Learning Matters, an independent, nonprofit production company focused on education, produces reports for *PBS NewsHour* as well as documentaries for PBS.

We believe that although problems and injustices are common, solutions do exist. Our television programs, podcasts, and publications spotlight problems and celebrate their solutions.

Link TV

P.O. Box 2008
San Francisco, CA 94126
(866) 485-8848
www.linktv.org

Link Media is an independent media organization whose mission is to engage, inform, and inspire viewers to become involved in the world. Link Media is committed to (1) providing powerful stories and unseen perspectives. Link's programs encourage compassion and an imaginative empathy that reaches beyond the viewer's own surroundings and extends beyond borders, real and perceived. (2) Giving voice to people without a voice from communities underrepresented in conventional media. We connect viewers not only to the "movers and shakers" but also to the "moved and shaken"— people affected by the news. (3) Linking local to global. The stories we present help people draw the connection between themselves and others, as well as how local issues have broader implications. (4) Inspiring action. Program trailers and the Web site give viewers access to tools and connections to take action on social issues. Link programs counter the cynicism and resignation that can result from watching conventional television news. (5) Promoting dialogue across cultural and ideological divides through innovative media formats. (6) Fostering collaboration through coalition building with partner organizations and grassroots organizations around specific issues that matter to all of us.

Listen Up!

127 W. 26th Street, #1200
New York, NY 10001
(212)725-7000
www.listenup.org

Listen Up! is a project of Learning Matters, Inc., a Peabody Award–winning production company. For over a decade, Learning Matters has been producing outstanding reportage about American education.

Mission

Listen Up! is a youth media network that connects young video producers and their allies to resources, support, and projects in order to develop the field and achieve an authentic youth voice in the mass media. Listen Up! aims to provide connections, information, media tools, and services to young video producers and their allies, both inside and outside the network; work with young producers to raise production quality and tell excellent stories; implement and fund projects; cultivate meaningful partnerships with like-minded organizations to develop and promote the field of youth media; and secure broadcast venues for youth produced video.

MAME—Michigan Association for Media in Education

Tim Staal, Executive Director
1407 Rensen Street
Lansing, MI 48910
(517) 394-2808
E-mail: tstaal@gmail.com
www.mimame.org

MAME members are dedicated professionals, committed to providing the best possible media services for their students

Purpose Statement

The purpose of the Futures Strategic Plan of Action of the Michigan Association for Media in Education is to provide a planned, deliberate, and sustained effort in support of the library media profession by

- advocating for the profession,
- collaborating with multitype educational organizations and agencies,
- fostering leadership development to build leaders within the organization,
- working with decision making bodies,
- providing professional development opportunities, and
- improving service to members.

Manitoba Association for Media Literacy

Brian Murphy, President
80 Shillingstone Road
Winnipeg, MB R3Y 1J3 Canada
(204) 489-5701

E-mail: brmurphy@mb.sympatico.ca

www.media-awareness.ca

The Manitoba Association for Media Literacy (MAML) has been active since its inception in 1990. To accomplish its goals, MAML sponsors presentations and workshops for educators, parents, and members of the public at large; assists in the development of media literacy programs for Manitoba schools; provides in-service opportunities for Manitoba teachers; and publishes *Directions*, a quarterly newsletter.

Media Access Project

1625 K Street, NW

Suite 1000

Washington, DC 20006

(202) 232.4300

Fax: (202) 466.7656

www.mediaaccess.org

For more than 35 years, Media Access Project (MAP) has worked to promote the public's right to access a diversity of sources and viewpoints in electronic mass media. From protecting low-power FM radio, to fighting media consolidation, to defending "open access" and network neutrality, MAP has provided critical legal representation for the media reform and public-interest community. As a nonprofit public-interest law firm, MAP does not generally charge its clients legal fees. Nor does MAP get large donations from industry donors. MAP relies primarily on donations from citizens and on grants from public foundations. Media Access Project is a 501(c)(3) tax-exempt organization.

Media Alert!

5816 S. Lupine Drive

Littleton, CO 80123

303-738-8137

www.mediaalert.org

Media Awareness Network

950 Gladstone Avenue, Suite 120

Ottawa, ON

K1Y 3E6

(613) 224-7721

Toll Free: 1-800-896-3342 (in Canada)

Fax: (613) 761-9024

E-mail: info@media-awareness.ca

MNET is a Canadian nonprofit organization that has been pioneering the development of media literacy and digital literacy programs since its incorporation in 1996. Members of our team have backgrounds in education, journalism, mass communications, and cultural policy. Working out of Ottawa, we promote media literacy and digital literacy by producing education and awareness programs and resources, working in partnership with Canadian and international organizations, and speaking to audiences across Canada and around the world.

Media Channel

Danny Schechter, Founder
Rory O'Connor, Founder
578 8th Avenue
New York, NY 10018
(212) 246-0202
Fax: (212) 246-2677
E-mail: dissector@mediachannel.org
www.mediachannel.org
Media Channel is concerned with the political, cultural, and social impacts of the media, large and small. Founded in 2000, Media Channel exists to provide information and diverse perspectives and inspire debate, collaboration, action, and citizen engagement.

Media Education Foundation

Sut Jhally, Founder and Executive Director
60 Masonic Street
Northampton, MA 01060
(800) 897-0089 or (413) 584-8500
Fax: (800) 659-6882 or (413) 586-8398
E-mail: info@mediaed.org
www.mediaed.org

Mission

The Media Education Foundation produces and distributes documentary films and other educational resources to inspire critical reflection on the social, political, and cultural impact of American mass media. The project of the Media Education Foundation has always been informed by this notion: that language—and, by extension, images—define the limits, and possibilities, of human imagination and thought.

Media Education Lab at Temple University
Contact: Sherri Hope Culver
Annenberg Hall
2020 N. 13th Street
Office 205
Philadelphia, PA 19122
(215) 204-3255
E-mail: shculver@temple.edu
www.temple.edu

Mission Statement

The mission of the Media Education Lab at Temple University is to improve media literacy education through scholarship and research agenda to explore the educational impact of media and technology, with a focus on media literacy education. Efforts include community outreach, public programs, educational services, and multimedia curriculum resources.

Founded by Renee Hobbs, a pioneering leader in the media education field, we have two primary goals: (1) providing community outreach, public programs, and educational services and multimedia curriculum resources targeted to the needs of youth and local school and after-school educators; and (2) developing a multidisciplinary research agenda to explore the broad educational impact of media and technology, with a focus on media literacy education.

The Media Foundation
1243 West 7th Avenue
Vancouver, BC V6H 1B7, Canada
(604) 736-9401
www.adbusters.org

Adbusters Magazine

Based in Vancouver, British Columbia, Canada, Adbusters is a not-for-profit, reader-supported 120,000-circulation magazine concerned about the erosion of our physical and cultural environments by commercial forces. Our work has been embraced by organizations like Friends of the Earth and Greenpeace, and has been featured in hundreds of alternative and mainstream newspapers, magazines, and television and radio shows around the world.

Media Know All
http://www.mediaknowall.com

Description

Media Know All was started in 2000 to allow Internet research for Media Studies students. You will find a mixture of basic notes and links to other, relevant sites, plus a blog featuring media news stories. This has been designed specifically to help UK students following the WJEC GCSE, AS, and A-level syllabus, but you may find useful information here whatever course or level you are studying.

Media Literacy Clearinghouse (MLC)

1400 Pickens Street 5th Floor
Columbia, SC 29201
(803) 254-8987, ext. 229
E-mail: fbaker1346@aol.com
www.frankwbaker.com

Purpose

Created by Frank Baker, a leader in the advocacy of media literacy education, the Media Literacy Clearinghouse (MLC) strives to promote critical thinking about media messages. The MLC'S mission is to assist K–12 educators who wish to:

1. Teach standards that include nonprint, media texts
2. Learn more about media literacy
3. Integrate media literacy into classroom instruction
4. Help students "read" the media
5. Help students become more aware of the media they consume.

Media Literacy Contests for Colorado Middle School and High School Students

www.primett.org

Media Literacy Education

www.medialiteracy.com

Media Literacy Saskatchewan (MLS)

Ann van der Wal, President
Box 298 Dalmeny, SK Canada 945
306-254-4456
van.der.wal.ann@sbe.saskatoon.sk.ca
www.quadrant.net/Media_Literacy

www.stf.sk.ca

Media Literacy Saskatchewan (MLS) is a Special Subject Council of the Saskatchewan Teacher's Federation. Formed in 1990, its mandate is to support teachers who wish to teach media literacy skills in the classroom. MLS publishes MEDIAVIEW, a newsletter designed to provide members with practical ideas and lesson plans to put to immediate use. Since its humble beginning in 1933, the Saskatchewan Teachers' Federation has grown to become one of the largest professional associations in the province. Today, the Federation serves more than 12,000 members throughout Saskatchewan. It embraces and promotes a vision of the whole teacher by offering programs, services, and resources that address their economic welfare and professional growth, and the diverse affecting teachers' workplace environment.

Media Literacy Week

Media Literacy Week is an annual event that takes place in November each year. Co-led by MNET and the Canadian Teachers' Federation, the week shines a spotlight on the importance of media literacy as a key component in our education system. To get started, free downloadable resources are available on the Media Literacy Week Web site.

Media Awareness Network provides professional development and in-class resources for media education and Internet literacy. The resources are available, through licensing, to: provincial/territorial departments, school districts and boards, national and regional library systems, post-secondary institutions, and individual schools.

Media Matters for America

455 Massachusetts Avenue, NW, Suite 600
Washington, DC 20001
(202) 756-4100
www.mediamatters.org or mm-tips@mediamatters.org
Media Matters for America is a Web-based, not-for-profit 501(c)(3) progressive research and information center dedicated to comprehensively monitoring, analyzing, and correcting conservative misinformation in the U.S. media.

Purpose

Launched in May 2004, Media Matters for America put in place, for the first time, the means to systematically monitor a cross section of print, broadcast, cable, radio, and Internet media outlets for conservative misinformation—news or commentary that is not accurate, reliable, or credible and that forwards the conservative agenda—every day, in real time. Using the Web site mediamatters.org as the principal vehicle for disseminating research and information, Media Matters posts rapid-response items as well as longer research and analytic reports documenting conservative misinformation throughout the media. Additionally, Media Matters works daily to notify activists, journalists, pundits, and the general public about instances of misinformation, providing them with the resources to rebut false claims and to take direct action against offending media institutions.

The Media Network

Nhora Barrera Murphy, President and CEO
8720 Georgia Avenue, Suite 606
Silver Spring, MD 20910
(301 565-0770
Fax: (301) 565-0773
www.themedianetwork.com
The Media Network is an award-winning, full-service communications company specializing in social marketing, research, and outreach to the general market, as well as Hispanic populations. We are committed to solving your communication needs through innovative and specially tailored services that ensure your message resonates with those who need to hear it most. In doing so, we further our mission of enhancing the quality of life and well-being of people everywhere.

Media Research Center
Media Reality Check

Brent Bozell, President
325 S. Patrick Street
Alexandria, VA 22314
(703) 683-9733 or (800) 672-1423
fax: (703) 683-9736
The mission of the Media Research Center, "America's Media Watchdog," is to bring balance to the news media. Leaders of America's conservative movement have long believed that within the national news media a strident liberal bias existed that influenced the public's understanding of critical issues.

MediaRites

Dmae Roberts, Executive Producer
www.mediarites.org
E-mail: mediarites@comcaStreetnet

Mission Statement

MediaRites is a nonprofit media arts organization dedicated to telling the stories of diverse cultures and giving voice to the unheard. Through our radio documentaries, new media, and outreach projects, we create lasting legacies and connect communities.

Media Think (formerly Northwest Media Literacy Center [NMLC])

200 NE 71st Avenue
Portland, OR 97213-5664
(503) 525-1095
E-mail: info@mediathink.org
www.mediathink.org

Media Think is a Portland-based nonprofit organization that advances media literacy—the ability to interpret, understand, and evaluate media and its messages. Our programs and presentations strengthen critical thinking skills and encourage media to better serve society. Our focus is on young people—the most voracious and vulnerable consumers of media. Media Think changes how young people think about, interact with, and use media.

In addition, this all-volunteer organization offers group training, presentations, and media literacy courses, including teacher training programs and discussion boards. Their approach addresses a range of topics, including: media violence, body image, health image, health news reporting, overconsumption and the environment, globalization, corporate influence, stereotyping, sexuality, brain development, addiction, and creativity.

Media Think serves as a resource center and a catalyst for public awareness with specific interests in media literacy for organizations and individuals. The organization challenges media professionals to "raise the bar," be responsible, and be accountable for the information they produce and disseminate.

Media Watch

P. O. Box 618
Santa Cruz, CA 95061
(831) 423-6355
E-mail: info@mediawatch.com
www.mediawatch.com

Goal

The goal of Media Watch is to challenge abusive stereotypes and other biased images commonly found in the media. Media Watch, which began in 1984, distributes educational videos, media literacy information, and newsletters to help create more informed consumers of the mass media. The organization does not believe in any form of censorship, especially the silencing of marginalized groups. Instead, Media Watch believes education will help create a more active citizenry who will take action against commercial media saturation.

Media Working Group Inc.
1225 North Bend Road
Cincinnati, OH 45224
or
MWG Administration
P.O. Box 1807
Lexington, KY 40588-1807
(859) 803-9953
(859) 581-0033
Fax: (503) 218.8886
www.mwg.org

Founded in 1987, Media Working Group is a community of filmmakers that explores the cultural, natural, and spiritual dimensions of 21st-century life to bring provocative and entertaining stories to the screen and classroom. From documentaries that build bridges with marginalized cultures to explorations that shed light on the natural world, Media Working Group uncovers new worlds and unique points of view and is dedicated to personal expression, social change, and earth-centered consciousness. Through the creation of media culture, we seek to intervene in mass media and its consumer-driven message. MWG works with organizations and institutions to create media messages to catalyze social action. United by the belief that awareness inspires social change, filmmakers transcend problems to expose solutions through artistic endeavors that celebrate the diversity of life and ideas. Character-driven, multilingual documentary and drama reveal overlooked treasures of the world and inspire viewers to make a difference. Through a cooperative management model, Media Working Group supports visionary filmmakers and educators whose work reflects sophistication, integrity, and high production value. Over time it has honed its services that best serve the complex needs of independent digital video and filmmakers, journalists, digital networkers, new media makers, organizations, organizers, and writers.

Media Workshop NY
1540 Broadway
New York, NY 10036-4039
(212) 782-0300

MEME Films
Rob Williams
Waitsfield, VT 05673
(802) 279-3364
www.robwilliamsmedia.com
www.memefilms.org
Linked Web sites:
ACME: http://www.acmecoalition.org
NMMP: http://www.nmmlp.org
Free Press: http://www.mediareform.net
MEF: http://www.mediaed.org
RWM: http://www.robwilliamsmedia.com
Mission Statement
We offer media literacy education through interactive multimedia presentations and hands-on digital video production. We offer media education keynote presentations, video productions workshops, documentary film production, free teaching resources, and DVD videos for sale. As a nationally recognized media educator, Dr. Rob Williams works extensively with young people in and out of the classroom. Professional videographer and media educator James Valastro brings more than 16 years of camera, lighting, and filmmaking experience to his production work.

Midwest Center for Media Literacy
Edie Barnard, Executive Director
edie@mwcml.org
Cristle Coleman, Vice President, Program
(636) 926-2209
cristle@mwcml.org
1211 McKinley Avenue
St. Louis, MO 63119
(314) 368-1055
E-mail: info@mwcml.org
www.mwcml.org
Purpose
The Midwest Center for Media Literacy is a 501(c)(3) agency that was founded in 2007 to provide media education programs to Missouri students, as well as an affordable option to other nonprofits needing professional media services. There is a full-service media production facility that can produce every aspect of media needs.

The Center sponsors an education and advocacy program called "Back-Talk," which invites students to talk back to Big Tobacco by using media to voice their opinions. Another program, "Media Section," gives an in-depth look at the quality and type of their videos. The Midwest Center helps children, teachers, and community members to understand the ways in which the media shapes beliefs and behaviors and teaches the skills to harness the power of media in a positive way.

Their dedication is in helping nonprofit and governmental organizations utilize media to help tell unique stories. Video allows these stories to reach much broader audiences through the use of the Internet and other media sources.

MIT Media Lab
Nicholas Negroponte, Founder
communications@media.mit.edu
www.media.mit.edu
MIT Media Laboratory
77 Massachusetts Avenue, E14/E15
Cambridge, MA 02139-4307 USA
(617) 253-5960 or (617) 253-4791
Mission and History
At the Media Lab, the future is lived, not imagined. In a world where radical technology advances are taken for granted, Media Lab researchers design technologies for people to create a *better* future. Now entering its 25th year, the MIT Media Laboratory, under the direction of Frank Moss (MIT PhD, 1977), is focusing on "human adaptability"—work ranging from initiatives to treat conditions such as Alzheimer's disease and depression, to sociable robots that can monitor the health of children or the elderly, to the development of smart prostheses that can mimic—or even exceed—the capabilities of our biological limbs.

The Museum of Broadcast Communications
676 North LaSalle Street
Suite 424
Chicago, IL 60654
Mission Statement
The mission of the Museum of Broadcast Communications (MBC) is to collect, preserve, and present historic and contemporary radio and television content as well as educate, inform, and entertain the public through its archives,

public programs, screenings, exhibits, publications, and online access to its resources. The MBC is an Illinois nonprofit corporation that owns and manages two subsidiaries, Museum.TV and the National Radio Hall of Fame (NRHOF) and its Web site radiohof.org.

NAA Foundation
4401 Wilson Boulevard, Suite 900
Arlington, VA 22203
Fax: (571) 366-1195
Sandy Woodcock, Director
(571) 366-1008
E-mail: sandy.woodcock@naa.org
www.naafoundation.org

Mission Statement
The Newspaper Association of America Foundation strives to develop engaged and literate citizens in a diverse society. The Foundation invests in and supports programs designed to enhance student achievement through newspaper readership and appreciation of the First Amendment. The Foundation also endeavors to help news media companies increase their readership and audience by offering programs that encourage the cultivation of a more diverse workforce in the press. The NAA Foundation was established as the ANPA Foundation in 1961 by the board of directors of what was then called the American Newspaper Publishers Association. In 1992, it officially adopted its current name. The NAA Foundation is a 501(c)(3) nonprofit organization. Contributions are tax-deductible and may be made in the form of cash, securities, and bequests. There are no membership requirements or dues and the NAA Foundation represents all newspapers equally. Programs of the NAA Foundation are supported by an endowment funded by the newspaper industry.

National Academy of Television Arts & Sciences—Creating Critical Viewers
1697 Broadway, Suite 1001
New York, NY 10019
(212) 586-8424
Fax: (212) 246-8129

The National Academy of Television Arts and Sciences was founded in 1955. It is dedicated to the advancement of the arts and sciences of television and the promotion of creative leadership for artistic, educational, and technical achievements within the television industry. It recognizes excellence in television with the coveted Emmy® Award for News, Sports, Daytime, Public Service, and Technology. Beyond awards, NATAS has extensive educational programs including National Student Television and its Student Award for Excellence for outstanding journalistic work by high school students, as well as scholarships, publications, and major activities for both industry professionals and the viewing public.

National Alliance for Media Arts and Culture (NAMAC)

Jack Walsh, Executive Director
E-mail: jack@namac.org ext. 304
Daniel "Dewey" Schott, Senior Manager of Leadership Services
E-mail: dan@namac.org ext.302
145 9th Street, Suite 102
San Francisco, CA 94103
(415) 431-1391
Fax: (415) 431-1392
www.namac.org

Mission Statement

NAMAC fosters and fortifies the culture and business of independent media arts. Through dialogue, collaboration, research, and advocacy, we connect, organize, and develop organizations. NAMAC was founded in 1980 by an independent group of media arts organization leaders who realized they could strengthen their social and cultural impact by working as a united force. The idea was to create a national organization that would provide support services to its institutional members, and advocate for the media literacy community. NAMAC serves their membership by conducting research analysis, offering leadership training, and advocating on behalf of their field. Members offer a large range of services in support of the independent media arts including production, exhibition, distribution, education, research, preservation and archive development, and telecommunications and cultural policy advocacy. NAMAC members include community-based media productions centers and facilities, university-based programs, museums, media presenters and exhibitors, film festivals, distributors, film archives, youth media programs, community-access television, digital arts and online groups, and policy-related centers. Combined, these organizations serve approximately 400,000 artists and other media professionals nationwide. Their Web site invites participation and shares their strategies for the future.

Additionally NAMAC has a section called "Idea Exchange" where people can critically engage with ideas and other NAMAC users by commenting on favorite articles.

The National Alliance for Nonviolent Programming

Dr. Whitney Grove Vanderwerff, PhD, Executive Director
122 N. Elm Street, Suite 300
Greensboro, NC 27410
(336) 370-0407
Fax: 336-370-0392
E-mail: NA4NVP@aol.com

The National Alliance for Nonviolent Programming (NANP) is a national not-for-profit network that helps build and support grassroots initiatives to promote and teach media literacy and nonviolence in communities nationwide. Dr. Whitney Grove Vanderwerff, an internationally recognized educator, is NANP's executive director. Considering violence the endpoint of disrespect, Dr. Vanderwerff's work addresses not only media portrayals of gratuitous violence and aggression but also stereotyping, prejudice, racism, gender relationships, new research on brain development, and media ownership and production. Dr. Whitney Vanderwerff and the National Alliance for Non-Violent Programming: a superb resource for speaking, training, and presentations on media violence. Dr. Vanderwerff, a former college dean of education, is also a leading expert in selecting and applying curriculum for follow-on work in schools and communities.

National Association for Media Literacy Education (NAMLE)

10 Laurel Hill Drive
Cherry Hill, NJ 08003
(888) 775-2652
E-mail: namle@namle.net
www.namle.net

Formerly the Alliance for a Media Literate America (AMLA), NAMLE is a national nonprofit organization that is dedicated in promoting media literacy education.

Vision

The NAMLE vision is to help individuals of all ages develop the habits of inquiry and skills of expression that they need to be critical thinkers, effective communicators, and active citizens in today's world.

Mission Statement

The NAMLE mission is "To expand and improve the practice of media literacy education in the United States. . . . We define both education and media broadly. Education includes both formal and informal settings, classroom and living room, in school and after school, anywhere that lifelong learners can be reached. Media includes digital media, computers, video games, radio, television, mobile media, print, and communication technologies that we haven't even dreamed of yet." NAMLE sponsors the *Journal of Media Literacy Education*, an online journal that supports the development of research, scholarship, and the pedagogy of media literacy education. The journal provides a forum for established and emerging scholars, media practitioners in and out of schools. Renee Hobbs, PhD, and Amy Peterson, PhD, serve as coeditors of the journal. NAMLE also publishes a month newsletter, providing the latest news in media literacy education.

The National Council of Teachers of English

1111 W. Kenyon Road
Urbana, IL 61801-1096
(217) 328-3870 or (877) 369-6283
Fax: (217) 328-9645
www.ncte.org

Mission Statement

The National Council of Teachers of English is devoted to improving the teaching and learning of English and the language arts at all levels of education. This mission statement was adopted in 1990:

"The Council promotes the development of literacy, the use of language to construct personal and public worlds and to achieve full participation in society, through the learning and teaching of English and the related arts and sciences of language."

Commission on Media

As the 21st century begins, we see rapid, large-scale changes in the electronic media available to the public for everyday use. At the same time, creative teachers are enriching instruction by mixing traditional media, such as drawing and construction, with the use of new media forms and instruments. NCTE has the responsibility to make all teachers aware of these changes and the opportunities they offer for improved instruction.

The Media Literacy Award will be presented to an individual, team, or department that has implemented and refined exemplary media literacy practices in their school environment. The Award Selection Process will be based on a portfolio review by a panel from the Commission on Media.

The National Telemedia Council (NTC)

1922 University Avenue
Madison, WI 53726
E-mail: Ntelemedia@aol.com

The National Telemedia Council is a national nonprofit organization that has been promoting the concept of media literacy for five decades. From the beginning, we have taken a positive, nonjudgmental attitude and embraced a philosophy that values reflective judgment and cooperation rather than confrontation with the media industry.

The Journal of Media Literacy brings together the thinking and experiences of the major pioneers, the current practitioners, and the future thinkers in media literacy. It is produced up to three times a year and is the only in-depth North American print journal in media education. For the theme of each issue, the editorial board invites an expert guest coeditor and outstanding contributors in their field. A recent issue of *The Journal of Media Literacy* explores "School 2.0: Transforming 21st Century Education through New Media Literacies." How will schools need to change to keep up with the growth of new media? We now have Web 2.0—what will School 2.0 look like? The cover features Ken Burns, recognizing the release of his PBS series "The National Parks: America's Best Idea." With today's technology, students have the ability to produce and distribute their own videos worldwide. Like Ken Burns, their productions will have a point of view, no matter how benign. Media literacy enables viewers to be more aware and responsible in their use of media.

NBPTS Offices

Arlington Office
1525 Wilson Boulevard, Ste. 500
Arlington, VA 22209
NBPTS Processing Center
11827 Tech Com Way, Suite 200
San Antonio, TX 78233
(800) 22TEACH;
Fax: 1-888-811-3514
www.nbpts.org

NBPTS is an independent, nonprofit, nonpartisan, and nongovernmental organization. It was formed in 1987 to advance the quality of teaching and learning by developing professional standards for accomplished teaching, creating a voluntary system to certify teachers who meet those standards and integrating certified teachers into educational reform efforts. The mission of the National Board for Professional Teaching Standards is to advance the quality of teaching and learning by maintaining high and rigorous standards for what accomplished teachers should know and be able to do, providing a national voluntary system, certifying teachers who meet these standards, and advocating related education reforms to integrate National Board Certification in American education and to capitalize on the expertise of National Board Certified Teachers.

The New Media Consortium

6101 W. Courtyard, Building One, Suite 100
Austin, TX 78730
(512) 445-4200
Fax: (512) 445-4205
www.archive.nmc.org
NMC is first and foremost a community of innovators, and it provides many resources and benefits in support of the NMC community as part of the membership package.

NMC is an international not-for-profit consortium of learning, focused organizations dedicated to the exploration and use of new media and new technologies. Its hundreds of member institutions constitute an elite list of the most highly regarded colleges and universities in the world, as well as leading museums, key research centers, and some of the world's most forward-thinking companies. For more than 15 years, the consortium and its members have dedicated themselves to exploring and developing potential applications of emerging technologies for learning, research, and creative inquiry. The consortium's *Horizon Reports* are regarded worldwide as the most timely and authoritative sources of information on new and emerging technologies available to education anywhere.

New Mexico Media Literacy Project (NMMLP)

Andrea Isabel Quijada, Executive Director
6400 Wyoming Blvd. NE
Albuquerque, NM 87109
(505) 828-3129
Fax: (505) 828-3142,
E-mail: info@medialiteracyproject.org
www.nmmlp.org
The Media Literacy Project, founded in 1993, cultivates critical thinking and activism. We are committed to building a healthy world through media

justice. As a nationally recognized leader in media literacy resources, trainings, and education, MLP delivers dynamic multimedia presentations at conferences, workshops, and classrooms across the country. Our media literacy curricula and action guides are used in countless classrooms and communities, and our training programs have empowered thousands of people to be advocates and activists for media justice. Our organizing campaigns such as Siembra la palabra digna, and our role as an Anchor Organization for the Media Action Grassroots Network (MAG-Net) center communities of color, poor communities, rural communities, and immigrant communities in the creation of local, regional, and national media policy.

The Media Literacy Project is fiscally sponsored by Albuquerque Academy, a nonprofit, tax-exempt independent school (Grades 6–12). MLP receives in-kind support from Albuquerque Academy and financial support from the Center for Media Justice, Media Democracy Fund, New Mexico Department of Health, New Mexico Community Foundation, Third Wave Foundation, and other public and private donors. Additionally, MLP earns income from sales of our multimedia resources, honoraria, and trainings. In order to preserve our independence, MLP does not accept funding from media corporations.

Newspaper Association of America Foundation (NAAF)

Margaret G. Vassilikos, Sr. Vice President and Treasurer
4401 Wilson Boulevard, Suite 900
Arlington, VA 22203
(571) 366-1010
Fax: (571) 366-1195
www.naafoundation.org

The NAA Foundation was established as the ANPA Foundation in 1961 by the board of directors of what was then called the American Newspaper Publishers Association. In 1992, it officially adopted its current name. The NAA Foundation is a 501(c)(3) nonprofit organization. Contributions are tax deductible and may be made in the form of cash, securities, and bequests. There are no membership requirements or dues and the NAA Foundation represents all newspapers equally.

Mission Statement

The Newspaper Association of America Foundation strives to develop engaged and literate citizens in a diverse society. It invests in and supports programs designed to enhance student achievement through newspaper readership and appreciation of the First Amendment. The foundation also endeavors to help news media companies increase its readership and audience by offering programs that encourage the cultivation of a more diverse workforce in the press.

News Watch
www.BigEye.com
www.NewsWatch.org
Stewart Ogilby, Editor of BigEye.com
"It is not enough for journalists to see themselves as mere messengers without understanding the hidden agendas of the message and myths that surround it."—John Pilger

BigEye.com was born in October 1995, beginning as a listing of links to an increasing number of educational and interesting Web sites. In the Web's early months, this site provided a useful resource for intelligent computer users. This Web site virtually shouts the message that our airwaves, a natural resource, must be freed from corporate monopoly. Broadcasting entities, in addition to lobbyists (bribers), must be restrained legally from financial interaction with governments (local, state, and national). The wonderful inventions of Radio and TV are available for social and cultural interests in our lives. A new and uncorrupted representative government can surely determine necessary frequency and power distributions to minimize bandwidth interference. However, controls of broadcaster content by corporate entities and governments necessarily reduce our airwaves to that ages-old game of the few for more money and power. Commercial advertising is designed to increase their money, and propaganda is designed to increase their power. Airwaves are a natural resource. They require environmental protection by us. It is our responsibility to keep this resource as uncorrupted as the air we breathe and the water we depend on.

Northwest Progressive Institute
P.O. Box 264
Redmond, WA 98073
(425) 310-2785
www.nwprogressive.org
Mission Statement
We will work as a forum for progressive thought, an oasis for the promotion of peace and freedom, a warning against corruption and ignorance, and a light for others. The NPI is a grassroots think tank, devoted to researching progressive ideas and promoting progressive values.

NW Center for Excellence in Media Literacy

www.depts.washington.edu

http://education.washington.edu/areas/ep/profiles/faculty/cohen.html

Marilyn Cohen, PhD, is research associate professor in Education Psychology for the University of Washington and the director of the NW Center for Excellence in Media Literacy. "As director of the NW Center for Excellence in Media Literacy, I am greatly involved with in the field of media literacy education. Our center has been very active since the early 1990s in using media literacy as a strategy to address health issues such as teen pregnancy prevention, substance abuse prevention, and violence prevention as well as more recently, the areas of nutrition and fitness. With support from the Washington State Department of Health, I am currently able to continue my work in the area of teen pregnancy prevention, which has been one of my focus areas since 1994. With support of a National Institutes of Health grant, we are also currently working with the UW's Center for Public Health Nutrition to develop curriculum materials for elementary school youth in Washington, Idaho, and Oregon. I remain committed to fostering and promoting the area of media literacy education research and have served as chair for the nation's first media literacy education summit sponsored by the National Association for Media Literacy Education held in St. Louis (June 2007). Our center here in the College of Education has also been responsible for organizing the region's first conferences for teachers and health professionals focused on the areas of teen health and media literacy. The center continues to offer numerous media literacy workshops and institutes throughout the region."

One Economy Corporation

1220 19th Street NW, Suite 610

Washington DC 20036

(202) 393-0051

Mission Statement

To ensure that every person, regardless of income and location, can maximize the power of technology to improve the quality of his or her life and enter the economic mainstream. One Economy is a global nonprofit organization that leverages the power of technology and connects underserved communities around the world to vital information that will improve their lives.

Pauline Center for Media Studies in California

3908 Sepulveda Boulevard

Culver City, CA 90230

(310) 636-8385

Fax: (310) 397-8366

E-mail: pcms@paulinemedia.com

www.freepress.net

The Pauline Center for Media Studies is a project of the U.S.-Toronto Province of the Daughters of Street Paul that was founded to promote media mindfulness and media literacy education in schools and faith communities.

Priime Tiime Today

P.O. Box 3285

Littleton, CO 80161 1-303-770-3239

E-mail: donna@primett.org.

www.primett.org

(Parents Responsibly Involved in Media Excellence and Teens Involved in Media Excellence)

Priime Tiime Today and its partners form a team dedicated to teaching media consumers at every level, how to question, analyze, interpret, and evaluate those messages. The knowledge and skills of media literacy empower individuals and communities to become a more informed electorate and a positive force for change. Priime Tiime Today is a nonprofit 501(c)(3) organization that trains preschool- through adult-level groups to become media literate consumers.

Project Censored

Media Freedom Foundation

P. O. Box 571

Cotati, CA 94931

(707) 874-2695

www.projectcensored.org

Mission Statement

The mission of Project Censored is to teach students and the public about the role of a free press in a free society—and to tell the News That Didn't Make the News and Why.

Overview

Project Censored was founded by Carl Jensen in 1976 and is a media research program working in cooperation with numerous independent media groups in the United States. Project Censored's principle objective is training of SSU students in media research and First Amendment issues and the advocacy for, and protection of, free press rights in the United States. Project Censored has trained more than 1,500 students in investigative research in the past three decades.

Project Look Sharp (Ithaca)
Cyndy Scheibe, Executive Director
Ithaca College
1119 Williams Hall, Ithaca, NY 14850-7290
(607) 274-3471
E-mail: looksharp@ithaca.edu
www.ithaca.edu/looksharp
Primary Goals
To promote and support media literacy education at the community, state, and national levels. To provide teachers with ongoing pre-service and in-service training and mentoring in media education. To work with teachers to create new or revised teaching materials and pedagogical strategies that incorporate media literacy and enhance classroom practice. To develop and publish curriculum materials that infuse media literacy into core content. To evaluate the effectiveness of media literacy as a pedagogical approach to education. To develop a model for including media literacy in the school curriculum at all grade levels and in all instructional areas, and to show how media literacy can help teachers address new and existing learning standards. To work in collaboration with other entities at Ithaca College to promote and support media literacy integration at the College.

Project MUSE
The Johns Hopkins University Press
2715 North Charles Street
Baltimore, MD 21218-4319
(410) 516-6989
Fax: (410) 516-6968
E-mail: muse@press.jhu.edu
www.muse.jhu.edu

Rocky Mountain Media Watch
Blog
www.BigMedia.org

Goal

Jason Salzman is the cofounder of Rocky Mountain Media Watch, a non-profit organization that aims to hold the news media to their own professional standards, like those promulgated by the Society of Professional Journalists. That is also the goal of the Big Media Blog.

Sazlburg Academy on Media & Global Change

Paul Mihaildis, PhD
1828 L Street, NW, Suite 1111
Washington, DC 20036
(516) 463-5226
E-mail: pmihailidis@salzburgglobal.org
www.sazlburgumd.edu

The Salzburg Academy on Media & Global Change is a three-week summer academy that gathers 60 university-level students and a dozen faculty from five continents to explore media's role in global citizenship. The Salzburg Academy is conceived to answer two of the most pressing questions of our time: "How do news media affect our understanding of ourselves, our cultures, our politics?" and "How can we use media to better cover global problems and to better report on possible solutions?" Students and faculty work together to create a series of curricular products around the connections between global media, freedom of expression, and civil society–what the Academy calls "Global Media Literacy."

South Australia Association for Media Education (SAAME)

Grant Brindal
E-mail: bigred@chariot.net.au
PO Box 300
Ingle Farm SA 5098
(+61) 015-397451
Fax: (+61-8) 396-1968
CAMEO member
www.pa.ash.org.au

SAAME (South Australian Association for Media Education Inc.) originally began as the S.A. Association for Screen Education during the 1970s and in 1979 hosted for the first National Screen Education Conference. In 1982, SAAME again held a national conference, this time for media education.

Some of the resolutions to come out of this included the undertaking of the other states to host this biennial event and the establishment of CAMEO. At the Annual General Meeting early in 1983, a new constitution was adopted along with the name, South Australian Association for Media Education, and the organization became incorporated. Teresa Shearer (now Forest) was the inaugural president. During the early 1980s SAAME was very involved in running student film-making camps and supporting the Young Film Makers Festival.

For three years in the late 1980s, SAAME conducted the S.A.Y. Media Awards. This involved about 1,000 students across the state selecting, monitoring, and voting for the media products and personalities they thought were the "best." The culmination of this process was an awards night at which the students announced the winners (à la Oscars) and presented them with their award. In 1994, SAAME again hosted the National Media Education Conference. The success of Mediascape '94 highlighted the leading role South Australia and SAAME play in Media Education.

Southwest Alternate Media Project (SWAMP)

Mary Lampe, Executive Director
1519 West Main
Houston, TX 77006
(713) 522-8592
Fax: (713) 522-0953
E-mail: swamp@swamp.org
www.swamp.org

SWAMP is a Houston-based nonprofit regional media arts center conducting residencies in schools, community centers and art organizations since 1977. SWAMP has collaborated with the San Francisco–based Strategies for Media Literacy to develop training workshops and seminars which incorporate analysis with aesthetic and production elements of media literacy.

Mission Statement

SWAMP promotes the creation and appreciation of film, video, and new media as art forms of a multicultural community.

Studies in Media and Information Literacy Education (SIMILE)

Teen Futures Media Network
University of Washington
Experimental Education Unit
Box 357925
Seattle, WA 98195
(206) 543-9414
888-TEEN-NET (888-833-6638)
E-mail: thmedia@u.washington.edu
www.depts.washington.edu/thmedia
Much of Teen Futures' work has focused on media literacy-based approaches to major teen health issues including the prevention of teen pregnancy, sexually transmitted diseases, tobacco, alcohol and other drugs, and youth violence, and nutrition and body image.

The Teen Health and the Media Web site is a virtual meeting place for teens, parents, educators, health professionals, and others who share a strong commitment to teen health. Using the power of media literacy, we encourage young people to make healthy choices and to interact with the media both as critical viewers and creators. To become "active" rather than "passive" consumers of the media, teens need to arm themselves with the skills to become media literate.

Teen Health and the Media

The Television Project
Annamarie Pluhar, Executive Director
797 Sunset Lake Road
Brattleboro, VT 05301
www.tvp.org
The Television Project is a 501(c)(3) organization incorporated in Maryland and registered with the Office of the Secretary of State. The Television Project is an educational organization. We help parents understand how television affects their families and community, and propose alternatives that foster positive emotional, cognitive, and spiritual development within families and communities. Our primary aim is to empower parents to manage television use.

Understand Media
P.O. Box 34514
Los Angeles, CA 90034
Los Angeles: (310) 237-3925
New York: (914) 233-3531

E-mail: info@understandmedia.com
www.understandmedia.com
Understand Media was founded by Nick Pernisco with the sole intention of educating the community about media. Mr. Pernisco is an associate professor at Santa Monica College and an adjunct professor at California State University, Northridge. He has been involved in the media education community since 2005, but has been producing media professionally since 1996. Understand Media contains resources for teachers of all levels, parents, children, and the general community. Resources include lesson plans for teaching media literacy in the classroom, helpful books about media, media literacy and media issues, and links to numerous Web sites that help deepen the understanding of media in our society.

Vancouver Community Network
411 Dunsmuir St, 2nd Floor
Vancouver, BC V6B 1X4 Canada
(604) 257-3811
Fax: (604) 257-3804
E-mail: idera@vcn.bc.ca
www.vcn.bc.ca/idera
Vision Statement
The Vancouver Community Network strives to be an inclusive, multicultural, community-based organization that ensures the free, accessible electronic creation and exchange of the broadest range of information, experience, ideas, and wisdom. The Vancouver Community Network owns, operates, and promotes a free, publicly accessible, noncommercial, community computer utility in the Lower Mainland of BC that provides a public space on the Internet. Vancouver Community Network (VCN) is a nonprofit Internet service provider that provides free services to assist individuals, community groups, and nonprofit organizations in accessing and utilizing the Internet to its fullest ability.

Youth Empowerment in Action
469 Marillac Hall
One University Boulevard
University of Missouri, St. Louis
(314) 516-4603 or (314) 516-4642
E-mail: yea@umsl.edu
www.healthymissouri.net

The Youth Empowerment in Action! project is a media literacy-based program hosted by the Center for Character and Citizenship in the College of Education, University of Missouri, St. Louis.

Goals

- To help young people acquire the necessary skills to use today's information and communication technologies effectively and safely
- To teach kids to think critically about the ways in which the media impacts values, behaviors, and beliefs
- To encourage young people to develop critical thinking skills so they can become active participants rather than passive consumers in today's society
- To provide media education to teachers, health professionals, and agencies serving youth
- Develop and provide media literacy resources to schools, parents, and community members
- Promote service learning opportunities through policy analysis, media advocacy and civic engagement

Youth Radio

1701 Broadway
Oakland, CA 94612
(510) 251-1101
Fax: (510) 899-8769
www.youthradio.org

Mission and Vision

Youth Radio founded in 1990 promotes young people's intellectual, creative, and professional growth through education and access to media. Youth Radio's media education, broadcast journalism, technical training, and production activities provide unique opportunities in social, professional, and leadership development for youth, aged 14 to 24. We see Youth Radio's work as cultivating the natural resilience and strength of young people. By connecting youth with their communities through media literacy and professional development, they become active partners in civic engagement.

Youth Radio's overarching goal is to instill a long-term commitment and engagement on the part of youth as viable contributors and leaders in the media/arts, journalism, and civic life. Eighty percent of Youth Radio participants are low-income and/or youth of color. All of Youth Radio's programs and services—professional development, media education, technical training, academic support, and health services—are free. Our programs and services strengthen life skills, motivate high school graduation, support higher education goals, and prepare participants for careers in the 21st century. Our youth-produced investigative news features and compelling personal narratives air nationally and touch the lives of millions of listeners each month.

THREAD 4

Notable National Media Literacy Figures

Thread 4 identifies individuals who have made a significant contribution to the discipline of media literacy. The information is based on an online project organized by the Center for Media Literacy, titled *Pioneer Voices in Media Literacy*. The individuals included in the project consist of people who began to make a significant contribution to the field of media literacy in the United States before 1990. The print versions of those interviews are included here, with the permission of the Center for Media Literacy.

Neil Andersen

Neil Andersen has taught film and/or media studies in high schools for more than 30 years. He has been a computer resource teacher, helping teachers integrate technology into their curricula, and has given numerous educational keynotes and workshops across Canada, in the United States, Asia, Australia, and Europe. Andersen has taught media courses for teachers at the University of Toronto, York University, and at Mount Saint Vincent University. He is an executive member of the Association for Media Literacy and on the Boards of the Media-Awareness Network and the *Journal of Media Education*. He has made movies and videos, authored student textbooks, teacher resource books including *Scanning Television*, journal articles, more than 200 study guides, and designed interactive CDs, Web sites, programs, and posters. Currently, Neil is a presenter, consultant, and writer. (Source: http://cmns.athabascau .ca/featured_courses/mediaLiteracy/authors/)

Edited Transcript: Interview, March 4, 2011
Interviewer: Tessa Jolls

TJ: Neil, why did you become involved in media education?

NA: I think media education chose me rather than me choosing it. It's been a lifelong journey—a very happy experience for me because I found something that I really enjoyed. I started when I was four years old going to the Saturday matinee with a group of friends and we would trudge off through the Winnipeg winter and for 25 cents I would get movies and a chocolate bar and a drink. The movies would be six or seven items: a trailer or two, a feature but then also a cartoon, a serial, a travelogue, and a newsreel. They were really fun times with my friends as well as just watching all this stuff. And as an adolescent I had an unusual access to the university alumni movie club and I was able to see foreign movies that other people weren't seeing. They were esoteric and sophisticated, so I've had a rather long exposure that way. Also, I was able to have both a movie camera and a still camera from a relatively young age, again at 12 or 13, so I was making home movies and shooting a lot of pictures for the family. And then I used that interest to go into the high school camera club and I shot a large number of the photos for the yearbook or whatever other tasks were asked of me. So it's been a long time in terms of production, and then when I was in the university I discovered movie courses and I started taking those and even changed my major. That was because of this previous experience and attraction. Then through a further series of happenstances and luck, I discovered the Association for Media Literacy and started a lifelong association with Barry Duncan and the other people with whom I shared a common interest. It's one of those situations in which you find like-minded people and you enjoy their company, they help you grow, you help them grow, and everybody is happy in that environment.

TJ: Earlier, you said it wasn't so much that you found media literacy as media literacy found you. Can you elaborate?

NA: It's just so compelling that I can't leave it alone. Sometimes—I've become a pariah—I would object to a particular commercial or billboard, or statement in the newscast, and people look at me and say, what's your problem?! And what's happening is I'm listening, watching, and contextualizing and applying some of my theoretical understanding to it that they aren't aware of. And I have had the same feedback from my students. I had a student once tell me that she was no longer allowed to watch television with her family. They actually ordered her out of the room because she was making critical comments and spoiling their enjoyment of the experience. And I take that as a compliment but I appreciate the fact that you can become the pariah.

TJ: As you became involved in media education, what were your goals?

NA: Well, I see media literacy as life literacy because if I can't understand and use the current communications forms effectively then I'm not going to be an effective person either on a civic level, on a personal level, or on a vocational/career level. I'm just not going to be as effective. I've been able to prove that to myself. I've worked very hard in my life to become accomplished in a variety of things, so I make movies and videos, design Web sites and posters, write books, etc., partly because I want to understand the codes and the conventions and the processes that are involved in those activities. So, I've only ever done one podcast, but I did a podcast because I wanted to understand it. I did a half-hour podcast and went through all of the processes and editing for it. I don't want to make a career of it, but I've always felt that if I put myself out there and try these things out and understand them then I can be more effective. The analogy I made in my media book was, once you have played a sport, you are forever changed as a spectator because you have a greater appreciation as a spectator watching it being played. I think this is the same notion, to me significant for all of my students and I now teach teachers. But I point out to them that our students, as adults—even as teens—are going to have to be facile in a variety of media forms no matter what job they're in because now almost everybody now may not build a Web site but certainly must interact with a Web site and understand how it works. We have so many people who are blogging, texting, or tweeting. You have to understand the codes and conventions of those in order to know the effects. So many jobs regularly involved people in media production by using microphones or cameras, so this is not something that you go to California for and live in Hollywood and hope to get a job. That whole notion is long gone. This is a situation in which wherever you happen to be and whatever job you happen to be doing, you are a part of media consumption and production. Since it's life literacy, I'm very committed to try to encourage this for each and every person so that they don't end up missing out. Really, call them the disenfranchised because we actually can create poverty by design if we aren't more careful.

TJ: What are some milestones that you've seen along the way in terms of the development of the field and how that's affected you, your work, and vice versa?

NA: There have been several. I started working in Super-8 and I taught film production, using Super-8 for quite a number of years and then the change into videotape at some point, and then linear editing, then nonlinear editing. Certainly the digital change has been extremely profound. I still think it hasn't been examined to the extent that it needs to be. I don't think we appreciate the profundity of the move from analog to digital. I suspect it's because we've been affected so profoundly by it that it's hard to see it. But that's certainly one huge shift, one that has allowed some people to call it democratization. I think that's an overstatement but there is certainly YouTube and things like that which represent a move toward democratization. It's not a worldwide movement by any means, but among the privileged it might be. The other thing, however, that changed for us in the association was a profound shift from text-centered study to an audience or cultural study. We were motoring along very happily and presenting mostly a text-centered approach to media studies where we would assume that the meaning was in the text and that if we understood the codes and conventions of the text, we could tease that meaning out. Then somebody wrote an essay that criticized us, rather soundly, and said that we were making a big mistake because we were not acknowledging audience and the role of the audience. We read that with great interest and we changed as a result of it. We acknowledged that the paper was making statements that were valid, that we had been missing a huge piece, and that we needed to change. About that same time, David Buckingham visited the AML, and he was doing the same thing where he was making the point that the text is not irrelevant but it isn't as important as the various uses that people are putting it to. That reinforced that cultural studies notion and made a profound shift for the association because we started to rethink what we were doing; we started to reformulate our teaching strategies and our presentations at that point in a very positive way. Those were two really big shifts that occurred for me, and I feel I have lived the history of media literacy education because I started in the early '70s and I'm still working in it.

TJ: What has surprised you as you've gone along?

NA: What has surprised me? Oh, well there are a lot of small surprises. One of the things that I've tried to do is to make a point of paying attention to the new innovations and to try them out, to experiment with them. I think what is fun is to see how people use things for purposes that were not originally intended. I think that's very exciting: When you see somebody take a machine or a program or something that was written for this and is using it for that. And that is extremely valid and clever and personally useful, and you think how wonderful that that person has been able to subvert or exploit a text or technology for a purpose that no one else had ever imagined. Those are moments when you really understand the fun of the technological opportunities that we have.

TJ: How far do you feel the field has come and do you feel like it's moved in the directions that you wanted to see?

NA: It certainly hasn't moved as fast as I would like. The implementation of media literacy education is proceeding at a snail's pace if it's proceeding at all. I find that very frustrating. What I just can't understand is that, if this is so exciting to me why isn't it exciting to everybody else? Am I seeing something they aren't seeing, or am I missing something that they are seeing? I don't understand. I've talked to people in other countries and there is an implementation dip in other places as well. The jurisdiction I'm working in has a huge accountability issue focusing on reading and writing. It has privileged reading and writing to the point where media literacy education has suffered—as have speaking and listening education. So we've got six language strands at work in a school but only two of them are being implemented in a serious way. I can't see that changing any time soon, and it's quite unfortunate because the balance is not there.

In Ontario, we have media literacy mandated, and we have very articulate learning goals but it still isn't happening in most classrooms. The faculties of education seem to have been stonewalling this. We've got seven faculties of education in Ontario, and I work in one of those and then do some freelance work in another one. But I'm only aware of one person at one of those faculties that is doing any media literacy education. And this is at a time when it's mandated for all of the teachers, so six faculties of education are graduating teachers to whom they haven't given any preparation. So there's small wonder that this isn't being implemented well in the classroom. This has been true for quite some time. I'm talking about a curriculum that started talking about media education in 1987 in a fairly serious way, then in a very serious way in 1998, and yet here we are, these many years later and these faculties of education are not supporting it. I'm pretty disappointed in that. I was actually hoping to be a full-time person supporting media literacy education in a faculty of education but that employment never materialized. I'm teaching one course, and it's to teachers who are selecting, enjoying, and appreciating the course greatly. But it's a very small percentage of people.

TJ: Are there some steps that can be taken, or are there some ways that you think this could be remedied?

NA: One is to put proper emphasis on it and try to rebalance the various language strands in the schools. Ironically, there isn't a course that isn't involving media because they are using computers or they're showing videos or they have a smart board or whatever—all of these things are in constant use in schools. And yet these people aren't using them as effectively as they could if they just understood them a little bit better.

I don't think that this system is giving teachers the kind of support they need. It's running them down, it's exhausting them, and they are not open to new ideas because they are just in survival mode. You can't learn new things when you're in survival mode. We know Maslow's hierarchy of needs says that all learners have to have some sort of comfort level and a little bit of leisure before they can accept and start to work on new ideas. So if it's the few teachers that I work with who have self-selected to take my course and learn from it, that's fine. But the rest of them are just trying to get through the day, and if they've got any spare time, they need to relax.

The system needs to foreground new learning for teachers, and put it out there as a priority and it has to provide both time and money if it expects it to get implemented. They certainly are putting that energy into reading and writing. And the balance of language needs to be made and it isn't being made.

TJ: Could you report a bit on your experience with students on media education through the years, what you've seen in terms of their responses, and how that affected your teaching?

NA: There have been a range of responses. A number of my students have gone into the media industry. A couple of my students have gone into media education. At one end, you have people who are excited and inspired to the point where they make it a career. And I'm sure there are a large number that took it as an interest course, and that's fine too. This needs to be compulsory if not a standard course for all students and not an elective as it is in high school, so for Ontarians media education is a part of all English courses. All students take English courses, so on paper media literacy education occurs for every student, and so it should for reasons I suggested earlier. So I had that range of students, those that have said, "Okay, this is interesting, thanks very much," and others that have said, "Okay, this has changed my life and I'm going to do this ongoing for my life." I think I have to remind myself that I don't want everybody to become a media teacher or media producer—it's important that we just have that awareness, that expanded literacy, that multi-literacy, that I think everybody needs.

TJ: You had mentioned that you really saw students engaged in media education who maybe weren't engaged in school otherwise. Who are those students? And what do you think the difference is?

NA: That's a good question. There are some people who go to school because they want to get through it. They have their eye on the postsecondary, they want to become a pharmacist or engineer, and they realize they have to put their time in and complete the assignments in high school to get the marks that will get them that postsecondary entry. You can ask those students any number of irrelevant, silly things and they'll go along with you because they've got that larger goal.

There are other students who only want to do something that is currently and personally relevant. They can't see that distant goal and, in many ways, they are more interesting and fun to teach because they are genuine in their responses. Those are the students who are unaffected by a very theoretical course, something that they can't see as personally relevant. So the courses I was teaching in media were very personally relevant and I actually made an effort to do that. As I taught my high school courses, I would start off by saying, "This course is not about media. This course is about you and how you relate to the media and what you are thinking about and which things you find pleasurable and which things you don't." There was a certain attraction there, I was being very deliberate in that statement but also true.

I invite my students to talk. In fact, I think talk is really underrated in school, and I would have extended conversations with my students, whatever the issue or technology that we were discussing because, as they talked, they had to think through their relationships, their values, and their uses of things. So the talk was very useful and powerful that way, and it was also developing their ability to think and express themselves. It was a win-win in many ways.

So they would come to my class because they felt that they had an investment in it, that they were learning something about themselves rather than learning something about a subject. Those were the students, the disaffected students from the other classes, that I had no discipline problems with and who enjoyed what we were doing, and it was because they were inside the picture instead of outside looking in.

TJ: Neil, are there some thoughts that occur to you about the field or observations that you'd like to share in terms of where you think the field is moving?

NA: One of the issues that has been bandied around is whether or not media literacy education should be separate from other things, whether it should be integrated with everything that we do. It's a really tough, tough thing to consider. I was actually given an opportunity when Ontario rewrote the curriculum in 2005. I said, "Ideally, this shouldn't be media education—it should be a part of everything else. There shouldn't be a separate media strand in the English curriculum; it should be integrated with everything else." And the Ministry of Education officer said, "Well, is that the way you want to revise the curriculum?" And there was a long pause while I pondered that. Even though I believed that that's how it should be, I said, "No, because if we take the strand out, it will be easier to ignore." But the fact is that math, geography, history, and science teachers, whether they are teaching a subject in high school or elementary school, can and should be integrating media literacies into most of their lessons. So this is the point I make with my Faculty of Education people, and they are very comfortable by the time we're finished in seeing ways that you can do media literacy in five minutes in another lesson rather than having to make it a separate lesson or separate unit. This isn't an easy thing for everybody, however, and until it gets to be easy, I think media literacy education is going to have to maintain a separate position.

So it's a conundrum because, as proponents of media education, we ideally would like to see it become so integrated it becomes invisible but the reality that it wouldn't be integrated, it would be nonexistent if people didn't have to evaluate it. So I think we are in a transition and it's going to be a long one.

TJ: Yes, I hear you on that. Right now, I'm here with a colleague at the digital media conference in Long Beach, California, being sponsored by the MacArthur Foundation. The conference is really fascinating, interesting, and it's a very energetic crowd. Of course I would guess, there's probably not a single school superintendent or principal. It's a crowd that's not an education crowd, unfortunately. So we are hearing about using media, exciting new media projects, students engaging in media production, and so on. And Neil, I'm sure you've been at many of these kinds of things too, and unfortunately, I don't sense that there's really a framework for understanding media as a system or, you know, the real media literacy learning in a sense of really understanding media and seeing how to connect it to other subjects in a way that teachers can understand and learn how to do that. And so, I totally relate to what you're saying about how it becomes invisible and unfortunately the adults, the teachers, don't really have the understanding of the discipline. And since they don't, they can't translate it, they can't incorporate it, so we've got this big disconnect between what we know how to do, and yet other people not knowing how to do. They haven't had the chance to learn.

NA: I have certain sympathy for teachers who don't teach media literacy even though they are mandated to. If they never had it in pre-service or in-service, how can I be angry or disappointed that they're not doing it? The only way I can be disappointed is that they didn't do what I did and that was to put themselves out there and learn it to find either the people or the courses to take and learn it. And I've done that out of a personal responsibility and commitment in that I don't think I'm serving my students properly so I learn both. By both, I mean first of all I learn the literacy skills and then I learn the teaching skills. So I think, "Why haven't other people put themselves out there and put in the hours that I have put in to learn what I know and therefore support students in something that is important?" That's the only way I can be disappointed in them. My greater disappointment is in the system.

TJ: And it is the problem that none of us grow up learning this literacy in school, and so it's invisible in that way; and then it's not taught in teacher education, so they don't have a real way of coming where they're supposed to be. There needs to be that kind of disruption in the system to be able to really insert this; and even some of those efforts have been disappointing, like calling for mandating and it not happening. Some of that is because people don't know how, just not taking initiative, different outcomes like that but then coming and seeing how ubiquitous the technology is and the media, in a way, I guess just that is kind of forcing the issue more, and so at least there's that encouragement.

NA: It's going to be a one-by-one conversion, at least until we get some critical mass. And that's also the new marketing right? The new marketing is to sell to people individually, one at a time, and it looks like we are going to have to do the same thing. And that's why I continue with my Faculty of

Education teaching, because I can work with these people for 125 hours, each on a personal level. I can have a much more profound influence than in any other way, so when most of these people have finished with my course, I'm pretty confident that they can go back to school and work media studies into their curriculum in a valid way and help their students.

TJ: Yes, I hear you; and I guess the comfort there in what we're saying is that nothing happens without the grassroots. The grassroots has to be there, and so it's a tough and long and slow haul. At the same time when you see the effects, and you see people you know who are taking up the mantle, you know that something's gotta give at some point.

NA: How long has it been since Al Gore said that he was going to wire the nation and we were all going to be connected and it was going to be wonderful? And now that looks rather naïve doesn't it?

TJ: Yea! Although, the spread of the technology has been phenomenal.

NA: Of the technology, not the literacy.

Cary Bazalgette

Cary Bazalgette is a freelance writer, researcher, and consultant specializing in media education and media education research. She is the chair of the Media Education Association; a member of the European Commission's Media Literacy Experts Group; a fellow of the Royal Society for the encouragement of Arts, Manufactures, and Commerce (RSA); and a visiting fellow at the Institute of Education, University of London. She worked at the British Film Institute from 1979 to 2007, including eight years (1999–2006) as head of Education.

Edited Transcript: Interview, October 13, 2010
Interviewer: Dee Morgenthaler

DM: Do you think we are moving in the right direction? What would you like to see happen?

CB: In the UK right now, we are holding our breath to see what will happen next. The new government is undertaking a comprehensive review of all its expenditure, which is likely to result in enormous cuts to public services. A lot of people will be losing their jobs, and the immediate future for education and the economy in general is looking very bleak. In this context, it is impossible to describe the development of media education as moving in any direction at all, let alone the right one. But even at the best of times, here and pretty much everywhere in the world, the development of media education has been, and continues to be, patchy and is seriously hampered by any shared sense of what the desirable learning outcomes are and what learning progression looks like. We have a serious lack of good evidence about teaching and learning and an excess of optimistic assertion about what people have done in classrooms and what effect they think it has had. Until we gather better, more objective, and more sustained evidence about media teaching and learning, we can't make judgments about what movement is going on or in what direction.

For myself, I am very glad to not be working in public service any more. I am happy working voluntarily for the Media Education Association, which is an independent subject association for media teachers in England, run by its members. We aren't accountable to anyone except the teachers and the children that our members teach. We are working hard, trying to ensure that the association survives. We get together annually at a conference and we have a new Web site based on social networking principles (www.themea .org), which enables anyone to join us for nothing.

Nevertheless, there is a growing interest in the idea of media literacy—in other words, in the outcomes of media education. We do now have a government-funded body (Ofcom [the Office of Communications], our media regulator) that has a statutory responsibility for media literacy, which at least places it on the political agenda, although associating media literacy with a regulator does create problems for us because it links media literacy with the protection of children rather than with their general literacy competence.

An important factor for us in the UK is also that we have long-established specialist courses in media and in film that are offered in many schools as options to young people between the ages of 14 and 19. Each year over 100,000 students take examinations at the end of these courses, which means that there is a substantial sector of teachers in the UK who do have real expertise and experience in teaching young people about media, and a large and growing body of teaching resources produced by commercial publishers. Despite the fact that some sectors of the media and politics are contemptuous of these courses, they are in fact extremely demanding of both teachers and students, and it is hard to get high grades in the examinations.

I believe, however, that the biggest challenge that faces us is how to establish media education as a normal part of schooling for every child from the very beginning of schooling. I see the way to achieving this as being through the transformation of the literacy curriculum so that all children learn about books, films, broadcasting, photography, computer games, social networking, and whatever other media forms may evolve, as an everyday part of their schooling. It would be nice if I could start to see that happening in my lifetime, but I shan't be surprised if it doesn't.

David Buckingham

David Buckingham is currently professor of Education at the Institute of Education, London University, where he directs the Centre for the Study of Children, Youth and Media. He has directed more than 20 externally funded research projects on these issues as well as been a consultant for bodies such as UNESCO; the United Nations; Ofcom; the Department for Children, Schools and Families; the Institute for Public Policy Research. Additionally, he is the author, and coauthor, or editor of over more than 20 books and approximately 200 articles and book chapters. Professor Buckingham has also been a visiting scholar at the Annenberg School for Communications, University of Pennsylvania, and a visiting professor at New York University as well as the Norwegian Centre for Child Research. He began his career as an English teacher in secondary school.

Edited Transcript: Interview, October 29, 2010
Interviewer: Dee Morgenthaler

DB: Today, seven-year-olds can edit films on iM-movie or any other program. And in our research they are doing that. There is a danger of them confusing media education with technology. People think that if they are doing things with technology then they are doing media education and they're not. What they are doing is a very instrumental use of technology which is very uncritical and unthinking. It is driven by technology hype—over-excited view of the wonders of technology. This is a very dangerous moment for us. How do we insist on the critical dimensions of media literacy being important at a point when everybody seems to be rushing to get kids doing very functional things with technology as though by wiring them up we are somehow going to solve the world's problems?

I think it is exciting that children are capable of creating content, but it needs to be accompanied by a kind of critical thinking about what you are doing and a certain level of reflection on the choices you are making, and undertaking the process consciously. I think that often gets lost as people get carried away by creativity and the wonders of technology. All of the critical questions get pushed to one side.

The one difference between the United States and the UK is that in the U.S. system, it has been very hard to get media education into the mainstream curriculum, so when people are looking for interesting things, they are looking at after-school settings, community neighborhood settings, and so on. Whereas in the UK, we have had media education as a separate subject in school for about 40 years. It has stayed in the curriculum but let's be clear—it is not a compulsory subject. It's been an element of English, and English is obviously a compulsory subject, and that has been there since the '60s. But media studies as a subject is always optional. What happens is that children get to the age of 14 and are forced to specialize in a particular subject. At that point they drop some subjects and take up new subjects and then they specialize further when they reach the age of 16. So for four years of schooling, they specialize in one subject, and media studies has been one of those subjects. It is not necessarily offered in every school, but I think it is increasingly being offered in many schools. Aside from the media elements that happens within the subject of English, those specialist courses like media studies are only optional.

DM: Can you tell me more about the study you have going on right now and how you see your work continuing?

DB: The project is called Developing Media Literacy, and it is the first time I have ever had serious funding to do research about media education in the classroom. When I moved into teacher education, one of the first things I did was to offer continuing teacher education—what is called postgraduate education. I first set up a teacher research group because one of the problems was that Len Masterman's theory of teaching and the picture that he painted was rather different from my experience as a teacher. Masterman talked about how he would radicalize students, yet my experience was actually that the students knew a lot more about this than we tended to give them credit for. Also, what happened in my classroom was not a process of radical conversion, and I didn't see myself as a sort of political evangelist in that sort of way. So what I wanted to do was to do research on the teachers who were teaching it to study their own practice.

Around 1990, there was a book that came out called *Media Learning*. This was the first study to really give some evidence as to what was happening in media classrooms, as opposed to what people said should be happening. I have had lots of research funding for studies about youth and media, but actual research about classrooms and teaching and learning had been really quite hard to generate.

So what we are doing in the Developing Media Literacy research is working with groups of teachers—and we are actually looking across the age range—from about 6 years through to year 11 and the 15-to-16 age range. We are working with the teachers to devise curriculum, teaching materials, and classroom activities, which they then implement in their classroom. The point is that you obviously don't teach the same thing to 6-year-olds that you do with 16-year-olds, but there is a shared core, with similar aims and often some similar materials. We want to be able to compare across the age range.

What we are really trying to get at is what kids of different ages are capable of understanding. And what you find is that younger kids are actually much more capable than you might have imagined. In many ways, younger kids can do a lot of the stuff that we have been trying to teach 14-year-olds. Seven-year-olds can get quite a lot. If you provide media education in a systematic way over time, and didn't just leave it until secondary school but put it in the primary school as well—if they did media education every year all the way through—what you would get at the end of it would be something that is quite challenging and complex, which is more than students are getting at the moment. Another part of this project is that we are in two very different locations. One is broadly white middle class; the other is much more working class, and I think class differences are really crucial, to be taken into consideration, because differences are quite shocking both in the assumptions that teachers make about the kids but also in what is really possible. They are very different worlds. The teachers develop the curriculum with us.

DM: When teachers are being trained in the UK, is media literacy a part of their training?

DB: Not really. A lot of the training has now been shifted into schools. When I started teacher education in the mid-1980s, we actually had a lot of time with the student teachers. They would go off and do their teaching practice but actually they spent quite a lot of time in the university, and we were teaching both the basics of media studies but also how you teach media studies. At some point, more and more of their time is spent in school and there has been a feeling from the government and policy makers that it's people like us, the teachers, who give students these crazy ideas and we are dangerous. They want to shift the training more and more into the schools so the time that you have with students at university is less and less. When I started teaching, we had a specialist course for teachers who were going to be teachers of English and media studies. All the English teachers had a lot of time in courses on media studies. Now that course doesn't exist anymore. I also think that increasingly, there is less and less available to teachers now because it has all shifted into schools. And that is a problem.

So if you want to train to be a media studies teacher, you have to come and be a part of the training—part of the master's course. Most of our energy goes towards running a master's master's program. You might have a tiny little taste of media education when you are doing your initial training, but if you want to do this as a specialist thing then you really have to come do a master's. We work with the British Film Institute (BFI) and run modules where the students can do them as free-standing courses, but they also build up towards a master's course. Largely those teachers are paying for themselves, and they are doing the work on their own time. And that is all part of the de-professionalization of teaching I was referring to. When I first went to work in the mid-1980s at the Institute of Education, we had a group of full-time students who were all teachers who had been given a year out of school to become specialist media teachers. They were challenging to teach; they really knew what they wanted. They were often people that had been teaching for quite a long time already, and it was a great opportunity for them to have that one year; now that just does not happen anymore. Thankfully there are teachers that want to continue their studies, but it has become harder and harder for teachers to get specialized courses like that.

DM: Do you think the field is moving in the right direction?

DB: I think we are in a paradoxical place. I mean, on one hand you could say that the kind of work that I was doing as a teacher in school in the '70s or in the early '80s-—that has become institutionalized. There are now very well-recognized exam courses in media studies. Students can go to do media studies at university. It is often denigrated as being not a serious subject, but actually it is quite competitive to get into media studies, and I think it is taken seriously as a subject by many people, but not by everybody. And that is still a struggle.

Conversely, you can say that media education has arrived and has its place in the curriculum. With younger kids it is part of English but it is still not happening independently in primary schools. There are people talking about it, and people pushing at that, but it's not really sufficiently established or as established as I would like it to be in primary schools. But nevertheless, you could say media studies as a specialist subject is well established. On the other hand, you have the paradoxical presence of the regulators. If you have heard about Ofcom (Office of Communications), the government passed a communications act in 2003 that established a new, converged regulator for media to promote media literacy. Now, what they thought media literacy was is not entirely clear. But there are people within Ofcom who *do* know what media literacy is. And that has been quite striking and surprising, gaining recognition of media literacy by government. One of the culture ministers under Labor, Tessa Jowell, said, "Media literacy is as important as math and science." So you had this very high-rank recognition of media literacy, while realizing that what they describe as media literacy is not quite what we mean—there is a debate to be had. You have people say, . . . "Oh, what is *media literacy*? We don't know what it means," but the term has become much more widely recognized at a policy level. So there is one argument where you can say that media literacy is important, but there is still a struggle that goes on. And the struggle is about, "Is this serious? Is this an important area of study?" There are people who would like to denigrate media studies and see it as trivial and a waste of kids' time. I guess that has always been around and probably always will be around because there are people who find the whole idea really frightening.

I think the complicating factor is technology, which I have written an entire book about called *Beyond Technology*. There was a massive push towards technology in schools and I looked at that and compared it with when I was teaching in the late '70s and early '80s—struggling to do media production work, which for me was always the interesting thing. And you will find that Len Masterman was very negative about it; but for me that was the interesting stuff. I was trying to do it with clunky VHS videos and making animation mini-films. To me, creating and producing the media was the means to critically understanding the media; that was what it was all about. But it was a struggle because it was hard. Access to the technology was hard, technology was hard to handle.

Renée Cherow-O'Leary

Renée Cherow-O'Leary is president of Education for the 21st Century, a media consulting group in New York City that develops curriculum and educational materials primarily for children, parents, and teachers in multiple platforms; conducts qualitative research; and develops conceptual white papers for nonprofit and for-profit educational organizations. Among other university appointments, Dr. Cherow-O'Leary has served as professor of English Education at Teachers College, Columbia University and as a visiting scholar at Harvard University's Graduate School of Education. She began her career in newspaper reporting and children's book publishing.

Edited Transcript: Interview, November 23, 2010
Interviewer: Dee Morgenthaler

DM: What inspired your journey in terms of getting to the point of looking at media and media education? Generally, how did you become involved in media education, if you want to talk a little bit about what got you interested from the start?

RCO: I had been working in publishing and became very interested in the newly established public television movement and the success of *Sesame Street* and was fortunate enough to get a job there when it really was a "workshop." (The organization that produced the show was called Children's Television Workshop.) I thought these were going to be the future of education. Neil Postman had started a program at New York University in 1970 called Media Ecology. It had no track record whatsoever. He had written a book called *Television and the Teaching of English*, which had captured my attention and had written what has now become a classic, *Teaching as a Subversive Activity*, around that time. And so, I was drawn to him and rejected the more traditional graduate school PhD programs once I was accepted, even though I was offered a fellowship in English Education at another university. For better or worse—and there were some very wonderful things and some very unwonderful things about the early years of Media Ecology—I made my choice at that point to move into that arena and began a more formal study of the impact of media.

The term *ecology* came out of systems thinking, that we are all connected not only people but the Earth itself. Books such as *The Whole Earth Catalog*, the landing of spacecraft on the moon in 1969, the establishment of the first Earth Day in 1970, and the recognition that Earth was our fragile little planet became embedded in contemporary consciousness. And so, "ecology" was a hot new word, but no one quite knew what it meant, especially in relation to media. Marshall McLuhan had written his seminal book, *Understanding Media*, in 1964, and his work was also informing thinking about media. Among his ideas was that the medium itself (no matter what its content) was transforming and extending our human nervous system. He said the Earth was turning into a global village because of the way we could now reach out to each other and communicate. (Remember this was way before the Internet!) I was totally intrigued at the possibilities this seemed to foreshadow.

So we struggled with defining the term *media ecology*. It was frustrating and exhilarating to be charting a new field. As we speak, I realize that articulating this personal history is fun because you don't always think about how all the pieces fit together, but between McLuhan (on whom I had written my master's thesis at the University of Chicago), *Sesame Street*, and the work of Neil Postman, I was really immersed in some of the most forward thinking ideas about media at the time.

DM: So, McLuhan and Postman were inspiring your work. Anyone else that you can remember that kind of inspired your interest or events that were going on at the time that pushed you in that direction?

RCO: Well, yes. I mean, there were things going on in New York, like, there was a video production place called Global Village. People were just starting to use portable video equipment. Father John Culkin is gone now. But John Culkin was a huge, larger-than-life personality and based at this center. It was called the Global Village based on McLuhan's terminology. And so, I went to a lot of lectures and events and that kind of thing. The other thing that happened simultaneously with the creation of the network of PBS stations was the separate creation of cable television, an entirely new series of networks that promised a world of "500 channels." It seemed as if so many of these would be educational. I was thrilled at the prospect of all these outlets for ideas. There were also public access channels mandated by the government to hear the voices of common people who never before would have been able to produce their own programs. It was a heady time.

I for a time had worked for a company directly before *Sesame Street* that was a joining of forces of Time-Life and General Electric. It was called the General Learning Corporation, and Dr. Frank Keppel, who had been the dean of the Harvard Graduate School of Education, was the chief officer of that company. Time-Life created what today might be called software or the program side of things and GE created some kind of experimental hardware. We were working with people in poverty because there was a lot of emphasis on the war on poverty, and also the promise with cable television meant the potential for education was going to be enormous. And that also was at the start of the '70s. So I have to say there was a lot of ferment in the world of media at that time. And media studies, we take it for granted today, but it was not yet a serious academic discipline then. It had to be honed and shaped into an academic discipline.

DM: It seemed to start as a way to engage students, film studies, etc. and then evolved into a more critical stance.

RCO: It was an evolving discipline. People that were involved with these media ideas at the time kind of had to find each other. There weren't institutionalized structures for this sort of study not even for film, really, in America. I was involved very early on with the National Council of the Teachers of English (NCTE) because in my academic work, I was teaching literature and English and some of my graduate school mentors were very involved in NCTE. I used to be a member that a group of interested members called the Media Caucus, and there were literally about 15 of us in the room trying to figure out what this was. Media literacy was only a gleam in someone's eye then. There wasn't a language for this kind of study. It had to be invented.

I mean, you could always show movies to make a student interested or a reward on a Friday afternoon in a classroom. But the critique, particularly Postman's view that media were ecological, that the media interpenetrated all areas of culture, was very new at the time. That kind of growing understanding was really behind sophisticated media study among scholars. Maybe, among some people it was kind of fun to have a legitimate reason to show something, but in what we were doing in critique, that wasn't going to get you anywhere. People were upset about it. There were those who felt it was shallow and simplistic. Why, for example, would you show television in school?

New openings started to emerge for gatherings to explore these issues. And soon, given the nature of academic exploration, more and more theories started to emerge. (There was also a lot of worry too that media were going to change the nature of teaching and the primacy of the printed word. Even Postman later in his career retreated from his original embrace of media because he felt it had destroyed the nature of reasoned discourse and instead set people awash in a sea of fragmented, unconnected bits of information.

He mourned the linear nature of reasoning and the building of cohesive and persuasive argument.)

So, to explain how it was once the critique and theory started to emerged: Pick your favorite novel. Then, it became more legitimate to compare the film and the book, let's say, and to begin to understand characterization and other things through that. In fact, it was more engaging, definitely. And you could teach Shakespeare and suddenly there was a plethora of plays of Shakespeare that were made into film. By and large, I think it was film and not television that really at that point was the medium of choice for serious academic analysis.

I think that when people began . . . it's such a long conversation in terms of thinking about it. I would say that film studies, particularly in Europe, has its own cachet—the French New Wave, the Italian films that were suddenly becoming more mainstream. There was serious crossover to America from abroad. People [had] heard of Fellini and Marcello Mastroianni and *La Dolce Vita*. I think that the intellectuals in the universities became very, very interested in film first, and that seemed to have a theoretical gain which you need in a university for film here. And then all this other stuff started, also. People became aware of the value of it especially younger faculty, as I was, who saw a whole new field unfolding before us!

But I can tell you that not everyone in academia felt that way. I taught at City College. It was around 1980, the City University of New York in the English Department. I will never forget one woman standing up. People were talking about using film and she said, "I will never use a film in my class" like it was a corruption and cheapening. And I thought, you know what, you are in the 20th century. But no, no, no she was totally a defender of purity of the printed word. The image was somehow a sleazy, second-rate substitute. There's always been that little strand of thinking about media—that it is cheapening, weakening, impure, and possibly detrimental to the students' thinking.

DM: That brings me to my next question. Were there obstacles or surprises along the way that affected your teaching efforts—different viewpoints you encountered that affected your work?

RCO: Let me think for a second. You know, I guess [laughs] it's a funny question in a way because I gravitated to the people that were excited about the things I was excited about. And I went to the places where I felt that was happening. So, even though Neil's program was a little bit off the wall in those years in terms of figuring out what we were doing, I preferred to be there [rather] than studying Chaucer and the classics at that moment, as much as I loved them and had been trained in them. It was a time of seizing the day. It was our time! And we had something to say! I do love Chaucer, but I just made that choice. So, the obstacles for me . . . I don't think I had any! I don't remember them, let's put it that way. I would say my obstacles were more personal, I had a child, I was doing doctoral work, I was trying to . . . you know the story. And the feminist movement was just taking hold as well, another new consciousness to assimilate fully and act on.

You're doing it. I was working full time. I was going to school. I was starting a family and that kind of stuff. So, trying to do it all maybe was a little bit of an obstacle. But I'm a pretty optimistic person, I'd say. I am fortunate to say that I feel that I am a confident, thinking person and I did not experience that many obstacles. (It helps to have a very supportive husband who'll take over when you have to study.) When I was teaching I always looked for a place where they wanted to do English and media if I could. And I love literature, so I didn't mind doing just the literature but everybody who was an old progressive was kind of opening up to this.

DM: Have you always been in New York?

RCO: I grew up in New Jersey and always knew I was going to move to NYC as soon as I could. I went to Barnard College undergrad, the women's college at the time of Columbia University. Then, because I got a full fellowship, went to graduate school at the University of Chicago for my master's, and then I came back to New York and stayed after my doctorate at New York University. My other choices at the time were looking to go possibly either to Stanford or Harvard and then I kind of got caught up in my work and my life in New York and didn't go. But you know, those are the roads not taken, like you say. Had I been at X place or Y place, how would my career have evolved? You just don't know.

DM: Can you talk about personal milestones or milestones that you see in terms of your work in media literacy and media education—things that stand out for you as important moments?

RCO: What happened that was interesting for me was, let's see. All of the years of teaching this and trying to figure it out and creating courses I consider milestones. I'm proud that I was in the forefront in the beginning to teach this stuff along with a lot of other colleagues. But that mattered, creating courses, I love doing that. The other milestone for me was an ironic one. I was in between jobs and sometimes that happens, you know, when one thing ends and the . . . And I applied to become the national coordinator of Creating Critical Viewers at the National Academy of Television Arts and

Sciences. They were just beginning to get into media literacy at the industry level because one of NATAS's board members was very interested in this idea. (Not everyone else in the industry was as enamored of the idea of media literacy—then still a new concept!) Creating Critical Viewers was an already developed curriculum created by the well-known Yale scholars, Jerome and Dorothy Singer.

And so, I applied for this job, which at the time was advertised as part-time at the Television Academy in New York. And they chose me and I became the coordinator for a national initiative in 17 cities of this Creating Critical Viewers curriculum and approach. And it was an opportunity for me to expand it. That was in 1995. And that was the time when I actually got to know the media literacy community and began my affiliation with the group across the country of broadcasters and educators and cultural leaders such as the leaders of children's museums, libraries—who saw the potential in this new kind of literacy. Many of the people I met then are now leaders in the media literacy movement. I thought, you know, just as I had when we were 15 people in the Media Caucus at the NCTE, that I had found the kindred spirits who were going to pioneer this movement.

That lasted about three years, 1995 to 1998, and I was traveling all the time and I was meeting people in all these different cities. And my job was as the spokesperson for this media literacy project and the concept in general. I spoke to many audiences. And I began to try to make a difference in the cultural institutions of the cities where I felt that media literacy would have a natural home.

As I said, this included teachers and schools, libraries, museums, sometimes special film programs or government agencies. And that was my mandate as much as possible. There was a coordinator in every city, so let's say St. Louis, San Francisco, Philadelphia, and all the others where NATAS had a chapter around the country. And ironically, some of the people today that I know well in the media literacy movement were those coordinators who've now become leaders like Sherri Culver, the head of the National Association of Media Literacy Education (NAMLE).

Sherri was the Philadelphia coordinator, Marilyn Cohen of Seattle at the University of Washington Media Literacy Program was another, and so many other good people who are now part of a media literacy community. So it became, at that time in the mid '90s, media literacy was becoming a field unto itself and becoming recognized. I mean, it wasn't so known and understood before that time and again, others such as Renee Hobbs, Liz Thoman, and others were creating forums for these ideas to be heard and acted upon.

DM: In terms of the field of media education and media literacy, do you think we've come far enough or that we're moving in the right direction?

RCO: I think that media literacy has been stagnant. At least . . . now, I can't say totally that that's the case. I know there are pockets of very exciting work. I think people like Henry Jenkins have affiliated in some way with media literacy and certainly the new media literacy's at MIT and USC and all of that are absolutely positive and critical. We need to think much, much larger than has ever been thought about before. It's not about an ad for cosmetics, making women into objects. That was good in the old days. But we have to, again I credit Neil, whose thinking I've realized has pervaded my thinking in many more ways than I ever thought it would! [laughs] But I want to look at it much more ecologically. Media literacy got very stuck, I think, let's say five years ago. There were principles that came out of media literacy and NAMLE has tried to standardize the field and give it a base.

But I don't know, I try . . . I feel that we need to think on a much larger scale. Like when I go down to events, for example, in Washington at the Kaiser Family Foundation, I'm struck that the members of Congress, the FTC and so on, are still stuck on the kind of media literacy that, when they mention it, to me is very 20th century. I think media literacy has to connect with "21st-century skills," with new media literacy and the current movements in "new media" and "social media" (these didn't really exist a decade ago!) and with social patterns that are transforming our culture. It has to be a bigger tent. I am a person who tries very hard to think in an interdisciplinary fashion, and so I would like media literacy to link more to other transformative areas in our culture. Whether it's robotics or looking at the nature of avatars and what it means to be human today. . .

I think these are the kind of media that we're talking about now. Tools like iPads and apps are transforming how we acquire and disseminate information. Children in this age are becoming utterly adept at these things at very young ages. We're talking about another kind of literacy. This impacts everything we know about education and learning. I'll say one more thing that might be seen as heretical: In my view, media literacy doesn't pay enough sophisticated attention to the business of media. I work in media. I'm a consultant to many media organizations on educational matters and I feel that certainly in the old days, media literacy tended vilify them all. We have to understand these tools, how they originate, the business of them, and then know what we need to teach and explore to help deconstruct for the purpose of understanding and be as strong as anything that's coming out of the media industry in terms of ideas and innovation. The industries themselves are evolving at record speed. We must be as sharp as they and live inside our own creativity and challenges and not just condemn others but find our own *new* voices for this new century.

DM: What an excellent point.

RCO: Because we're in this together in some way. We wouldn't have media literacy if we didn't have media. So my sense is that we need an enlivened true 21st-century media literacy. I've been wanting to write about this. It's like all those things that you think you want to write about. Because the world is moving much faster than media literacy is. I guess that's my point. And there are some key thinkers working on the cutting edge of that domain who are not formally recognized generally as known quantities in the field of media literacy. But they would be, if we decide to think in an interdisciplinary way. I'll give you an example. Recently, there was a conference at Bard College. It's a very avant-garde, arts-oriented college about an hour or two out of New York City. The conference had Sherry Turkle as a speaker and a wonderful thinker named Ray Kurzweil whose work I've loved for years. I've always taught Kurzweil in my media studies class, but I never hear him mentioned by most people.

His name is Raymond Kurzweil. He's a futurist and an inventor. He's written books called *The Singularity Is Near*, *The Age of Intelligent Machines*, *The Age of Spiritual Machines*. The conference at Bard was about being human in an inhuman age. I ultimately couldn't go, but it was streamed and it's online. What is humanity now when soon we will be able to implant chips in our brains and we're partly robotic already and cybernetic or whatever we want to call ourselves? What does it mean to be human?

You see, those are the questions that engage me. I want to know, not just should I turn on this tele program or that program. That's OK, but I want to know what our media are doing to our consciousness. I was a major in philosophy and English, and as I get older, the philosophical questions are more important to me than the literal ones.

I thank you for letting me expound. If you don't say these things out loud, they just kind of rattle around in your brain.

DM: Right, well history is so important, in terms of figuring out, where we go, what to do now. I agree with you, it's as if we're at a standstill.

RCO: Media literacy has become oversimplified. It's oversimplified. I guess that's how I feel. Sometimes I think it's because I've been through the mill a few times and heard the ideas before. Or is it because it really just isn't growing? And I think that's really the question. It starts with the blame on the outside if it's just me. It just doesn't grab me the way it did. Maybe there will be something new. I know that if I write about this, even in an article, you're stimulating me, and maybe the transcript or something to be the basis.

It's like, how can we link to the others thinking about these issues and the media? And I have to say that some of the people from the industry are doing some of the most mind-boggling thinking. Yes, what I was going to tell you about the grant, I knew I had left something out.

The key word is called *transmedia*. There is a thinker named Jeff Gomez, who is not mentioned in any media literacy circles, but Jeff is having a huge influence on the industry. It's about mythic thinking with media. It's for branding but when I heard him speak, and he's one of the most sophisticated theorists that I have heard in a long, long time. And he's having a very large influence on the next developments of media. It's called transmedia or thinking. Henry Jenkins has articulated this vision, and Jeff Gomez is one of the entrepreneurs putting it into action. He is the CEO of a company called Starlight Runner. It's very different than what we're talking about. It appeals to me, as a teacher of English, because of the narrative scope of what he's trying to do.

It's basically, for example, media literacy could connect to narrative theory. If you look at—I mean I've been working with doctoral students as a faculty member at institutions such as Teachers College, Columbia University—if you look at some of the most interesting work theoretically, in English Education, it's narrative inquiry. Story and meaning. The humanness of story. We're not tapping into any of that in media literacy. The way we tell stories, that's what's compelling to do. We all know from media literacy that each genre tells a story in a different way, right? Something in film is different than a television story, or one in print, or a game. So, we've got a multitude of genres. But we haven't looked very much at how these genres interconnect with each other and build a much larger story. Now, when you've got a franchise—Let's say George Lucas, who is interesting, because he tries to do educational stuff as well, with Edutopia. But you know, when you're building a *Star Wars* brand—quote, unquote—you are looking at how the toy impacts the game, how the game impacts the whatever, the movie, and how the, you know. All of these are story elements.

If you look to Gomez's work, you would see that he calls this integration mythical. He's talking about, how do some stories become larger than life? They enter into our very being, our very culture; and why do they? So, I think this media literacy, we've been so narrowly focused, that we don't understand why certain story elements are so powerful and profound and why people want to use them.

For example, there is a current case before the Supreme Court on video games. Big case, it just came up before the Supreme Court. About violence and video games, and is there any redeeming social value. It's like pornography years ago. I think we have to understand violence, which is of course very abhorrent, at the same time seems to have a deep psychic connection. My husband is a psychoanalyst, and we go to a variety of psychoanalytic conferences. Psychoanalysis has always been very interested in film and the kinds of stories that we tell ourselves—both our personal stories and the cultural stories that we buy into. So, I think that media are representative of those stories, and sometimes very exploitative of those stories.

I know because I work with people who write scripts. I'm an educational consultant on a couple of different programs for children. They go through five iterations with about 20 people giving them notes on the script. Even for the most simple of children's shows. I see how these are built, and in my job as an education consultant, I look at this and I think, you know, there's a teachable moment here. How about if we do this or say this, or you know?

We're working with a culture. Media are huge communities of culture. When I do my work here in New York, there are animators reading my stuff in Toronto, there are writers in LA, and so is the company with its standards and practices division, for example. You just have to respect that media production is a huge, huge enterprise that we need to better understand and learn from, as well as criticize.

DM: Is there anything else you want to add?

RCO: No, I think the most important question might be, where is media literacy going? It is wonderful to know that there is a new generation coming up with new ideas that will invigorate media literacy and media studies. For those of us who are still alive and kicking and who can recount these histories while still looking to the future, there is a lot more to say and do. But it needs to come from some deeper spring. Perhaps this new work that you are doing with Tessa [Jolls] will be a source of that spring, to energize us. Thank you for the opportunity to speak to you.

Marilyn Cohen

Marilyn Cohen is research associate professor, Educational Psychology, at the University of Washington in Seattle, and director of the Northwest Center for Excellence in Media Literacy, within the College of Education. She was first chair for the first Research Summit for media literacy at the National Association for Media Literacy Education held in St. Louis, 2007, and has received major support through the years for her work in health issues such as teen pregnancy prevention, substance abuse prevention, violence prevention, nutrition, and fitness. She began her career in special education.

Edited Transcript: Interview: March 4, 2011
Interviewer: Tessa Jolls

TJ: So what informed and inspired your work?

MC: I found out that there was a conference going on in 1993 in Toronto, and so I went there and that was the greatest thing I ever could have done at this juncture in my career, because it pulled together everything that I knew and thought about, cared about at that point. So I met Barry Duncan and Chris Worsnop, and Neil Andersen, Carolyn Wilson, all leaders in this Association for Media Literacy; and I was so impressed with these people and so many other Canadians that I met at that time but are too numerous to mention here. They were so incredible, so giving. They were eager to share their knowledge, experience, and materials.

They encouraged me to take media literacy education back to our schools in Washington; they gave me a ton of resources and ideas, and their conference was just amazing. The people there were just so open about everything that they were doing. In 1994, I went back again; they had another conference in Toronto and it was just as wonderful as 1993 had been. Through those two conferences and the people that I met, I learned probably the basis of everything that I do today. That was really the beginning for me of everything that I do. Those were the people who really influenced me. In 1994, I knew when I went back to the second conference, I would have an opportunity here in Washington, a big opportunity to really get media literacy into the schools, to bring the word to teachers for the first time.

TJ: What has surprised you along the way?

MC: The opportunity to further media literacy education in our state came about in a very unusual way. It came from the teen pregnancy group at our Department of Health. I worked with a person at the University of Washington to do some research on teen pregnancy prevention. We showed kids PSAs prepared by a variety of groups all over the country on teen pregnancy prevention. We were asking kids to tell us what they liked or disliked about these PSAs because the state was going to produce its own PSAs. But this was a wonderful beginning to media literacy because of course the kids were telling us all these things they liked and didn't like about the PSAs. We were asking them to become little media critics. At the end of one of the sessions, some kids came up to me and said, "If this is the best you guys can do, well you're in real trouble." The kids were great. The research was really interesting, and the person I was working with was saying "Wow, these kids are just perfect for everything you told me that you really want to do."

While we were working on our research project, the state legislature was deciding to give money to our Office of Superintendent of Public Instruction to support efforts in schools that would allow students to learn how to put together their own teen pregnancy prevention media campaigns. This new funding created what came to be known as the state's Teen Aware Project.

The Teen Aware Project gave me a direct opportunity to begin working with teachers across our state since teachers who were going to run these media campaigns knew nothing about media or media campaigns. This was an opportunity to teach them about media literacy, so I was able to put together curriculum materials for the teachers and do some trainings and start working in the whole area of media literacy and teen pregnancy prevention. Although this was an abstinence-based project which is a very controversial topic in itself. Abstinence was a real in-your-face message to the kids. I mean, safer sex was not an in-your-face message. The general attitude was they knew all about how to protect themselves; they'd heard it since kindergarten (of course, without a doubt they needed to learn this information and there was much that they truly didn't know, but that's another story), but when you talked about abstinence, that was a whole different deal, "Like what does that mean; are you serious?" And of course, if you're talking about media, abstinence is an oxymoron so you really can do some wonderful things with a media literacy–based approach and leave the kids to come up with their own conclusions, which has to be the bottom line in any case. Your job as an educator is try to help them make an informed choice: Whatever that choice may be, if they decide to become sexually active or delay having sex, they've got the information.

That was 1995 when I was working on the Teen Aware curriculum with the Office of the Superintendent. In 1996, with the Department of Health's support, we began what was called the Teen Features Media Network where we started to work on various kinds of media campaigns for teenagers; the first was focused on teen pregnancy. Teen Features Media Network provided a vehicle for promoting media literacy education across the state. The Department of Health was very interested in media literacy education and the way in which it related to health education and health promotion; consequently, they allowed us to do all sorts of wonderful projects. We were able to put together our first Media Literacy institute in 1996, two of them actually. One of them was held here at UW in Seattle and the other on the eastern part of the state in Spokane. We were able to put together a series of institutes for people on media literacy and teen pregnancy prevention. These attracted a lot of attention and introduced many people across our state to media literacy education. People came to the institutes for a whole variety of reasons and the Department of Health was delighted because they found they could draw many people that had never demonstrated their interest in learning more about teen pregnancy prevention before and now were learning how they could use this material in a variety of classroom settings as well as in community organizations

It was fresh and new and a way of getting people to pay attention to this area of teen health that badly needed attention. In 1996, following these very successful institutes, the Department of Health convened an interdisciplinary task force which wrote its first paper on media literacy and why it was a very important tool for people working in areas of health. This was a groundbreaking document for representatives of the state agencies to write collaboratively because it brought media literacy to the attention of all the agencies and really helped us reach out to their constituents. In 1997, this interdisciplinary task force put together its first in a series of teen health and media conferences. These were conferences that were not just about teen pregnancy but about a wide range of teen health issues as they related to the media; therefore it was the decision to call the first conference "Images of Youth: Teen Health and Media." This was followed by more Images of Youth conferences in subsequent years.

These conferences were held alternately in the western part of the state or the eastern part of the state, so that people on both sides of the mountains would have a chance to really come and find out about media literacy education. They were able to really reach out to people all over the state and introduce them to media literacy education and demonstrate to them how it could be integrated with their work.

From these conferences and other outreach work we were able to do, a lot of people became interested in how media literacy education could apply to a whole variety of things that they were doing. And so that sort of jumps us forward to the 2000s where we not only were doing the conferences but also were starting to write curriculum for people. We were not only training people how to integrate media literacy education into their work with kids but we were actually showing them how to do it and giving them materials that made that possible. We also began at this time to train kids to deliver some of these programs to other kids. We would have kids teaching other kids about media literacy education, and using media as a hook to teach their peers about health issues. Our work really began focusing on that area and led to a whole variety of new endeavors.

With teenagers as teachers, that was probably one of the most fun things I've ever done. Each part of it has been great, but that's just been added icing to the cake because it's so terrific to see these kids become excellent presenters, talking about media and media literacy in their own special ways.

TJ: What were some other milestones you experienced, Marilyn?

MC: In 2001, we worked with NATAS (National Academy of Television of Arts and Sciences), on their CCV (Creating Critical Viewers) project. For this project, we wanted to get media literacy into a whole district so we approached the superintendent of Seattle Schools who at the time was John Stanford, a pretty amazing guy who made considerable impact on this district. We managed to get an appointment with him that was to last 30 minutes. We took in our stuff and told him about media literacy education and that we would really like to teach media literacy in Seattle's School District and he said to us, much to our surprise, "Well, let's make it happen!"

We just about fell over in a dead faint. He said "I'm sure you came here thinking that you were going to meet with all this bureaucracy, 20,000 committee meetings and all of that, but that's not the way I operate." He was just incredible; it was so tragic that he died a very untimely death about three or four years into his tenure as superintendent. He did amazing things and he has been remembered as the type of person that you rarely see, but anyway, he called up right then and there one of his chief program administrators and brought her into his office while we were still sitting there. He told her, "You see these people here; you're going to be working with these people and we're going to make this happen!" As a result, we were able to work directly with several middle and high school teachers across Seattle School District at that time, providing media literacy education training and helping them to find ways to integrate the NATAS-sponsored curriculum Creating Critical Viewers into their classroom schedule.

At that time, the national group of NATAS really wanted to introduce Creating Critical Viewers, a program created by Jerome and Dorothy Singer, into the nation's schools. NATAS named coordinators around the country who could work with Creating Critical Viewers. It was Seattle that really took the lead in getting into the schools because our superintendent was so supportive. So that was 2001, and then in 2001 we also had our first online curriculum project. Our Office of the Superintendent initiated a few pilot online classes at this time, and I was asked to be one of the first teachers and put together a media literacy education course. I really enjoyed this experience.

We can jump to 2006, when we just had another media literacy conference, our fourth. So we were continuing in various ways to keep media literacy out there, to keep refining the kinds of content because now we had people who knew what it was, and they wanted more information and more resources, so we wanted to move beyond the basic awareness level; you could go a lot further and move to a much deeper level with them. That was really wonderful! We also continued our focus on developing curriculum with an emphasis on health issues from a media literacy education perspective. As I said earlier, we started with teen pregnancy, and we continue to work on programming in that area, focusing on a comprehensive approach to sex education (e.g., includes addressing protection, birth control issues); we've also addressed many other health issues such as tobacco prevention, school violence prevention, youth suicide prevention, etc. So we've continued to look at a wide range of different health issues, including obesity and overweight prevention. That brings us to today.

TJ: Marilyn, at what point did you start the Center for Excellence in Media Literacy?

MC: The center was started in 2007 as an outgrowth of the conferences that we had been offering with the support of our state's Department of Health and other state agencies. The idea was that, rather than run another state conference, why not try to go out and work more intensively in certain areas of the state? Of course much had been going on prior to the creation of the center regarding media literacy, as we have already discussed, since we had been working on the University campus since the late '80s when we began our early efforts with the television project and throughout the '90s when we began working intensively on media literacy education with our state agencies, offering some of the first media and health conferences in the nation, along with numerous workshops, writing curriculum, conducting research, etc.

The center was designed to provide outreach to various parts of the state and provide resources in training and curriculum materials to these areas. It also has served a much broader function; through the conferences, it became a catalyst for activities, but now it could also be a place where people could come to direct their questions and seek help and advice. We could also produce and distribute material that would then be useful for these various groups that were seeking materials and resources. Teen Futures Media Network, one aspect of this center, is probably our most active arm, although the Center doesn't just work with teenagers; middle and high school students have been a major focus, but the center reaches out to work with younger children as well. The center broadly encompasses and works with all ages.

TJ: Thinking about the field in general, how far do you think the field has come?

MC: It's a highly interdisciplinary field. In my area in education, one of the last things I did that was totally education-focused before I became involved with media literacy education was to serve as interdisciplinary training coordinator for what is known today as the Center on Human Development and Disability at the University. I've always really worked on fostering interdisciplinary connections; and with the work that we do today, we are involved in a lot of interdisciplinary work across all agencies, as I described to you. It's really important to find ways to collaborate across disciplines since we all have so much to give to each other. That sharing is really important and I think what has been surprising to me and a little disappointing is the way in which groups come together in the US is so much different from what I observed initially and what I was so excited about in those early years when I was becoming involved in media literacy education with the help and support of our Canadian neighbors.

What drew me so much into this field, and created such excitement, was at last I found people who shared this passion, who really wanted to get out and do something. They weren't a huge core of people; they were substantial size for sure, but every person in Canada didn't know about them. But they realized that they had to work together to make any kind of difference. When I look at the media today and I look at all the different factions and the media literacy movement, as you might call it, it just seems that some of us are at cross-purposes with each other rather than working together toward that which we are all trying to accomplish. There is such a need to work together; so many people in our country have no idea what this is all about. And yet people really need to know, and people, once they do know, get excited and go off in their own directions to make a difference. They will do things with the resources you provide them that will surprise you. That's exciting and that's just part of making stuff your own and that's what it takes to really make things happen. However, we are still a long way from creating that critical mass that can make a tremendous impact in this country. We need to work together toward creating that critical mass.

TJ: Yes, it's all about that progression.

MC: Yes it is, but it doesn't seem like we are progressing very far, we have these groups that seem like they are each going in a certain direction; just how much stronger and bigger would we be if we spoke together in one voice or had a common language. And the field is growing, I mean the conference that you're at, the Digital Media Conference, this is a group that has other interests, yet shares many of our same core interests. There are going to be all kinds of groups that share a common core. And I don't think we're looking at that nearly as much as we should be. I think we are looking at let's stay as this group or let's stay as that; that group has a voice about this but not about that. And this person is much more important than that person, I mean one of the things I try to do, and I hope successfully, is that people in our state would say that they have learned this is the field that is open to all of you; you're each going to go about it in your own way but we need to help each other, we need to grow together. And I think that there isn't enough of that attitude. I know Marieli [i.e., Marieli Rowe, director of the Telemedia Council and chief editor of its *Journal of Media Literacy*], I admire her for all the work she's done. I know her work has always been based on that, the idea of collaboration and sharing.

TJ: Of reaching out . . .

MC: I would see her as like the group in Toronto, the Association for Media Literacy that has tried so hard to reach out and bring together groups and individuals that share different perspectives about a wide variety of issues all of continuing importance to those of us in media literacy education.

TJ: What would you like to see happen in this field?

MC: Joining a variety of groups together to try to look at what they share . . . even examples like what does ACME share with NAMLE, do they have two such radically different messages, does nobody at NAMLE care about media reform, how about the whole media reform movement? What are they each saying that is so radically different? I mean, yes, media literacy education isn't totally their message at ACME or is it the total message for Campaign for Commercial-Free Kids, for instance, or other groups I could mention. However, there's a core here in all of these groups that has a common theme and we don't seem to be searching for any kind of common theme anymore. And it's the common theme that our country really needs to hear.

We are a nation used to soundbites; we talk about the media but we're not very good at using the media to get out some standard messages and demonstrate that there is a strong core group here in the U.S. that is supporting some of the same messages and demanding some much-needed changes. Sure, each of our groups will take on a number of other issues that are of unique concern to only that group, but what do we share in common? There still aren't enough of us and we need to be spending more of our time and effort trying to find ways to collaborate with one another to achieve some common goals.

TJ: Exactly, because you know that whole role of media in society and how it's affecting us, what do we—as consumers and producers—what are we able to do?

MC: Yes, it's an issue that concerns our public health. Everybody that I've ever worked with in the field of public health understands this as a core issue, and if they don't initially they soon do when you start to educate them. I mean it crosses all the different areas. It just seems as though we haven't thought broadly enough about this. And also, how is it going to be realistically implemented in our schools—it's still not a question that is taken up enough because media literacy education as an entity by itself is not happening. We're not going to have media literacy courses in our schools anytime soon I believe. Math, science . . . we are going have to find a way to focus on them, also our students are not doing well in a lot of other areas . . . such as reading and writing. But how does all that fit with media literacy education? That's really the question; it's not can we teach you now about media literacy education—that is not the way to go about it. And it's not the approach we've ever taken in our project because it has never worked that way. I can get people to think about media literacy education when I go to what they are thinking about . . . if they are thinking about science, that's where I have to be. If they are thinking about math, that's where I have to be. It's a different way of thinking, but it's where the country is, it's where we've always been.

TJ: You're saying that, OK, if they're talking about math and science then we can definitely address math and science with media literacy, and combine those . . .

MC: Well, it's how can you make it stronger? How can it help what you're doing? Anyway, I think we need to do a lot more of that. I think that if there's any prayer of moving this forward we have to strive to integrate media literacy education with the subjects that are being stressed in the classroom. It's an approach that cannot be ignored because that's the reality of our educational system.

TJ: Exactly, and so for the field really to advance and continue to develop, we have to really go where the education system is . . .

MC: That's right. You have to look at it very realistically and listen to the people and all the problems they are dealing with; really work in the schools and find out what is it that they are dealing with, the realities of their day. What are their questions? It has to come from where the schools are instead of superimposing where we'd like the schools to be. Everybody is superimposing where they want the schools to be . . . and the schools are very used to this but that doesn't mean that they're listening any more than their kids are.

TJ: Well, that helps; I think that gives some perspectives on where things might go, and what our next steps might be in this field. So I don't want to put words in your mouth but what I'm hearing is that in terms of next steps, we really have to continue to work with the education system and really connect with their needs so that we can provide the media literacy education and do it in a way that they can accept and that they can really embrace. Is this what you'd like to see happen?

MC: Yes. I can't start off by telling you everything that I have to offer and how important it is for you because schools have heard time and again how important everything is for them. They have heard that their kids need to have science and get it out of a certain book or they have heard that they shouldn't get books at all because it should be all experiential learning. They've been told to take this particular program and run with it and then a few years later, they've been told that this program has been found not to have merit and it's another program that's gained favor, etc. etc. Now you're coming in and saying okay now this is what media literacy is and this is how you teach it, and this is what you need to do. I mean, think about that! It just doesn't fly. It can't fly. We need to remember the ongoing pressures that the schools are facing and get grounded with what is happening in the schools. Now the kids are another story. When they can find how they can talk about media in the schools as part of the curriculum, they're loving it. They would love in many cases to help make that happen. They live in a media-rich environment and to them integrating media literacy education into their regular classroom activity seems quite natural and appealing. So how do you marry what your needs are and what their needs are?

TJ: It seems like now there's more of a demand in the sense that the schools are really being forced to address media and technology. So how do we really work with them to solve that problem that they have, that integration?

MC: They absolutely have that problem and they are totally having to face that now. They're just grappling with it and having huge problems and that's exactly where the rubber hits the road for people in media literacy if they are there. If they are cognizant about some of the various problems schools are now facing and if they are able to really help and make themselves available to help, there has never been a better time than now!

There are so many people who are in classrooms who are talking to the kids about media in one way or another and having many of their own questions about how to proceed. The kids are bringing issues to school that are media related and schools have not had to consider some of these issues in the past. Many teachers would love to know and absolutely need to know that there is a whole field—media literacy education—out there, and it has never been more important than right now!

David Considine

David Considine is a prolific author and professor at the Reich College of Education at Appalachian State University (ASU), where he established the first ever graduate program in media literacy. In addition to having served on the board of directors for the National Telemedia Council, the International Visual Literacy Association and the Alliance for a Media Literate America, Dr. Considine was consultant to the White House Office of National Drug Control Policy during the Clinton and the Bush administrations. Since the beginning of his career as a schoolteacher in his native Melbourne, Australia, Dr. Considine has been an advocate for media literacy's integration into schools.

Edited Transcript: Interview, July 12, 2010
Interviewer: Dee Morgenthaler

DM: How did you become involved in media education?

DC: I had just started teaching high school—which in Australia is a six-year experience—in the early 1970s, so I might have been teaching 11-year-olds one minute and 18-year-olds the next period. So you had to be on your feet. And the kids were bored senseless. It was a fairly traditional school where they were required to do texts that they weren't interested in. And so I was just experimenting to see what worked for them—music and film—somewhere in that period of time when we also had the beginning of reel-to-reel video tape. I was able, as an audio visual coordinator, to get several taping machines, and with televisions at home I started taping programs, which meant that I had very relevant stuff in the classroom (for example, 8mm video production, which the kids loved—especially the underachieving boys).

At the same time, LaTrobe University, which is where I had done my undergrad degree, offered the nation's first bachelor's degree in Media Education so when someone actually called me and said that I could get a degree for watching film, I thought, well I do that anyway, and developed an elective in media studies—which went from year 9 to year 10—which filled up and was a big hit.

The labor government came to power in 1972. They had been out for 23 years, and they started funding money to the western suburbs, the working-class suburbs of Melbourne, where I was teaching. We got a grant which enabled funding for the first TV studio in the western suburbs so now production became a big part of media studies not just analysis. We did video and audio production also. And that's kind of where it went and it has been going on ever since . . .

I have been teaching the core skills of media literacy both online and in the classroom for decades. But in the '80s, it was called *critical viewing skills*, because I wasn't going to call the course about anything American until I knew what it even meant. So we did at least have a critical viewing skills movement or *articulation* or *awareness* in the '70s and '80s. And today if you look at things like the *Journal of Adult and Adolescent Literacy*, there is a huge body of research now that didn't exist at the time, that tells you what engages kids in the way of texts and what doesn't. And what most of it says is what I found out strictly by trial and error. If it is relevant to them, if it's got something to do with their life and connects the classroom to the real world, then they get involved. So, in many ways I stumbled into media literacy because media was an important part of my life since the kids were so close to my own age.

I also created an American history course at that time. There was none when I got there, and they told me that the students wouldn't be interested, which I thought was insane because Australian kids were being drafted to fight in Vietnam. So, they needed to be paying attention to what was going on in America. So I included a lot of media in that way—critically and reflectively. They had to evaluate and analyze that in a history/social studies context as well. And lots of them went on to be teachers and school administrators and university lecturers.

In the American history class, we used the classics like *The Grapes of Wrath*, but this period was also when Robert Redford and Mia Farrow did *The Great Gatsby,* so certainly when we were doing the '20s we did *Gatsby*. In English we did, and I was amazed because these tests are often set by state examiners, *Who's Afraid of Virginia Wolf*—a just incredibly powerful film—still is; also *One Flew Over the Cuckoo's Nest*. I know because it was part of what I was doing as part of my bachelor's degree—I surveyed students from suburban and rural Victoria, the state of Victoria. The two of the films that most resonated with them at the time were, *The Summer of '42*, obviously about an adolescent boy's rites of passage, and one of Stanley Kramer's lesser-known films, *Bless the Beasts and the Children*. They strongly empathized with the adolescent characters in those movies. And the more I saw them bond and empathize with them, that was really where my first book, *The Cinema of Adolescence*, came from. It is really why I left Australia. Because

I was watching Australian kids watching American media and being influenced by it. I came to America in the later part of the '70s. And I came to study at the University of Wisconsin in Madison to study film.

DM: Were there specific people or texts that have inspired your work?

DC: From my point of view, Neil Postman's work in the '80s, Len Masterman, Father John Pungente, Barry Duncan—it's been a privilege to know all of those folks, and in many cases, to work with them, to team-teach with them. Renee Hobbs wears me out. She has indefatigable energy. I had the privilege of working with her and team-teaching with her for several years for the Discovery Channel—a kind of dog and pony show, "No TV," that we took around the country.

She pioneered significant steps: a bond with the White House, a bond with corporate America, scholarly research that gives meaningful evidence and data that skeptical people want [supporting the fact] that media literacy does make a difference. So her work with Babson and Billerica and at Temple is just exemplary.

On a quieter, more behind-the-scenes scale, Marieli Rowe. When the flame of media literacy was flickering and threatening to go out, her work as a quiet, committed presence making sure that the first Telemedium and then the *Journal of Media Literacy* continued to grow. There are just so many ways, including that first national conference back in '95.

I wouldn't have left Australia had it not been for the work of Dr. Patricia Edgar and Dr. Ina Bertrand and La Trobe. Because my first undergraduate degree was dismal and I promised (in fact you will see it on the home page of my Web site), I swore I would never go back to university after my first degree. I hated it and these two gave me an opportunity in film and media scholarship to experience success after mediocrity and encouraged me all the way.

And finally, Kathleen Tyner. Words can't describe—she just has an incredible, not only national presence, but international presence, the book *Literacy in a Digital World*, and that's just one of them. She was one of the first people I ever invited to be part of the program. She will be back here in about two weeks. I think this will be her third gig with us. The students love her. I just think she is a remarkable person and academic.

Those are the people that have made the difference for me, both personally and professionally. You can't work with those folks and not have a personal relationship with them as well. And most of them at some point have ended up in Boone, North Carolina, which I can assure you 20 years ago, none of them had ever heard of.

DM: Can you talk a little bit about your opinion about the state of media literacy today? How far do you think the field has come?

DC: The answer is simple: Not far enough. But that doesn't tell us anything unless you ask why. You are dealing with two things. Media literacy is an innovation and you are trying to put an innovation into an institution, which is actually an institution of inertia.

The culture and climate of schools swallows innovation. Statistics tell us that by 2013, we will be spending $29 billion a year on technology and almost all of the research, with the exception of a few pockets of progress, raises very substantial questions about whether technology transforms education or not. So even though the computer promises individual self-paced learning, we've turned it into "drill and kill." In other words, the system swallows the innovation and the innovation takes on the life of what's already been there.

So, we don't have $29 billion to grow media literacy. It's hardly surprising then, that it happens in short bursts, flares up somewhere, dies down, and is subject to fad funding. The good news is that it is identified as one of the "21st-century skills." The good news is that it is not difficult these days to find media literacy in one form or another showing up in various curriculum standards. So, in North Carolina, for example, English language arts (ELA): it says chapter and verse that students will respond to and analyze texts that are read, heard, and viewed. It specifies media bias and media propaganda.

All of that is fine, but unless you do significant teacher training, and even then the latest federal research says, "OK, so we've now exposed teachers to more technology classes, more media classes than previous generations of teachers had." The problem is when they get to the schools, the young digital native teachers encounter department heads and administrators who are often unfamiliar with and not receptive to what it is they are trying to do; a case in point being social networking. And you see this. The schools are almost schizophrenic in their perspective about media and technology. So bear with me here . . . this needs to be unpacked a little.

In 2006, the Secondary Principals Association released a report on technology and media in schools and social networking—and generally they see the promise but then they also see the peril—and their dominant concern is one of caution and safety. The following year—and now these two groups ought to be on the same page—the following year, 2007, in a report called "Creating and Connecting" the National School Boards Association essentially calls on school districts and administrators to relax their policies. It integrates social networking into the curriculum and classroom. Why? Because they know students are being alienated. Basically what they say is the actual reality is that the students who have access to those sorts of tools outside the school will increasingly find school irrelevant.

So you've got a big struggle and you can sum up that struggle with two different perspectives: the group that wants to control media and technology and the group that sees media and technology in terms of challenge and creativity. And there is no clear winner. And I think in most cases, kids, the students, and their teachers are often the losers. And the PEW group basically came to the same conclusion as BellSouth in reports in 2002, 2003, basically saying the same thing. One of them called it a "startling red flag." They saw a huge gap between the way the teachers perceived media and technology in their classes and the way kids perceived it. So again, with all of the effort that's gone on for 100 years based around tools in the schools—and we still have no common vision about that—why would we expect media literacy to be more widespread and sustained when the efforts have been so recent and the financial commitment so minimal?

You've still got to educate people that media literacy is not just teaching kids with media. And you've then got to teach the other group (the one that thinks they're doing media literacy but only does it from a protectionist paradigm, only does media literacy to the extent that they see the media as the enemy and therefore they're backing the old inoculation model, you know, which really should have gone out in the 1920s). But those folks are alive and well and not just in rural North Carolina. A fairly recent study concluded that many social studies teachers regard media and popular culture as "fluff" that they need to protect children from.

One of the problems we face is that 41 states—41 states!—have not a single media or technology requirement for school administrators, and this is horrendous just fiscally, leaving out the pedagogy. Given how much money the schools are receiving and spending on media and technology, why 41 states would not require administrators to have any background in it is nothing short of staggering.

So, the problem is that the teachers may well be trying to do something with media literacy but they have to convince administrators who have no background in this at all.

In 1985, I did a piece for the *School Library Media Quarterly*, and I closed that piece by saying, "It's not the hardware or the software, it's the underwear." And the "underwear" is the underlying policies and procedures and perspectives that come into play. And there are, like, three different perspectives, and to this day, it's the first question I ask my grad classes in technology. We have media advocates, media accomplices, and media adversaries.

And the adversaries are still out there. They may be well meaning, but on the other hand, they may be technophobes. They may at times think that media literacy is incompatible with print literacy. Ask any librarian about Harry Potter's influence on kids' reading.

You know, it's that if you're pro-screen, you must be anti-page. There are so many misconceptions out there, but you know, we have this saying that "perception is reality." So for media literacy to grow we have to recognize the misconceptions and then respond to them. My general belief is that the best area, the most viable avenue for doing that, is through the National Middle School Association. I think they have the most progressive view of education. Their former executive director has endorsed media literacy. It's compatible with their three bibles, and their three bibles are *Turning Point 2000*, *From Rhetoric to Reality*, and *This We Believe*. I defy anyone to read those three things and say that media literacy does not line up with those.

The Carnegie Council on Adolescent Development in '95 in their report "Great Transmissions" put it very simply; they said, "You can't understand the world of the adolescent if you don't understand their media environment." I really think that's incredibly fertile ground for working in, because they are really interested in the whole child, not just the cognitive-intellectual child. They break child and early adolescent development into five dimensions and it's very easy.

All five of those dimensions, if you conceptualize that as spokes in a wheel, you pick up those five dimensions of adolescence and say, "Media literacy can do that, it can do that, fits there, works there."

DM: Do you think the field is moving in the direction you think best? Why or why not?

DC: Look, I think that John Naisbitt in 1982 in *Megatrends* said that we're drowning in information and starved for knowledge, and I don't see anything that tells me otherwise. If we're drowning in information and starved for knowledge, then I think media literacy is a lifeline. I think it's a lifeline for anyone who thinks they're going under.

It's not just a 21st-century skill, it's a survival skill. The whole notion, the American ideal of "informed responsible citizenship," you can't possibly think that's the first word there, "informed." You cannot be an informed, responsible citizen if you are not simultaneously media literate. It is a prerequisite for a healthy democratic society that society and its citizens are media literate.

DM: And the thing you said before, I mean the real focus, could be in identifying those misconceptions and figuring out a way to educate the change makers.

DC: Right. And we still get into fragmentation. Something came over the Internet the other day, and I said, "Oh God, are we still doing this?" It was a particular organization, and they were perfectly well meaning. I mean, the program that we're running here in two weeks is very deliberately called "Linking the Literacies," but we keep getting into splintering the literacies.

So, the Library Science Group wanted to do information literacy, which begs the question, well, information to whom? And for kids, what they seek as information is not necessarily the formal types of information that librarians focus on. So anyway, this organization was promoting what they called "news literacy." If you're media literate, you are going to be news literate. And then I've heard "teleliteracy" and "screen literacy."

I mean, if you work with the principles of media literacy—if you work with the T.A.P. model [Text, Audience, Production], if you work with Lasswell's model—you're going to get all of those things under that umbrella.

Anyway, the newness comes along, and we get distracted by the newness of the tool, and we ignore the sameness of the school. And media literacy hits the same barrier. School culture and climate either supports or subverts an innovation. If you know that to begin with, you don't runaround saying, "Look, we got this dandy new idea called media literacy. Are you interested?" Because the first thing teachers are going to go into is, the, "I don't have time to" model. "How do you expect me to do this in addition to anything else?" That's a perfectly valid question for any teacher to ask when confronted with new expectations.

It's a risk–reward ratio and the minute anyone comes to the conclusion that that change—whether it's media literacy or a whole language versus phonetics, or anything else—the minute you get into the risk–reward ratio and they conclude that it's too much trouble, then there goes the innovation. Not that it was a bad idea. We just hadn't made the idea compatible with the people we wanted to embrace it.

DM: So what is the direction?

DC: Well, I think we need a management model for targeting and growing media literacy with the constituencies that are out there: National Council for the Social Studies (NCSS), National Middle School Association (NMSA), Parent Teacher Association (PTA). These groups have already been receptive but for the most part, we have a shocking one-size-fits all approach to staff development in education, not differentiated staff development. We make these basic training mistakes when each new technology comes along so it is not likely that media literacy will be approached with anything other than the same top-down model when it comes to most single school sites or districts.

That's a model where teachers experience change as something that happens to them, not through them, which ultimately breeds resentment and resistance undermining the very change we are trying to implement.

Well over a decade ago, the Aspen Institute recognized our approach to media literacy at Appalachian State (ASU) as something of an exemplary model. I am not talking about the master's in media literacy that we introduced in 1999. I am talking about the way in which media literacy has been integrated into undergraduate teacher preparation. Our undergrads in middle school training, with a focus on English language arts, have to take Media and Young People, a class that focuses on the principles and purposes of media literacy as they relate to the nature and needs of early adolescents and the mission statement of the National Middle School Association. But even though that's a good course, it is isolated to ELA in middle schools. The reality now, the big news at ASU is that all undergrads in our College of Education must take a course called Teaching and Learning in a Digital Age. The course mandates that these young teachers engage in both media analysis and evaluation, and media design and production, using common rubrics with the projects and assessments all posted to a central site for comparison and evaluation.

So the data is available, accessible, that administrators and teachers can look at to see how these projects, these portfolios connected to state standards, to media literacy "best practices," and to a pedagogy that meaningfully engages today's learners.

But once again that's not sufficient. What about the teachers who have been in the schools for 10 or 20 years? How do we get them on board? That's tough going in this economy. My dean, Dr. Charles Duke, and my chairperson, Dr. Michael Jacobson, have supported summer institutes—free summer institutes for North Carolina teachers—connecting media literacy to different areas of the curriculum and different grade levels. The attendance, the evaluations, and the overall feedback have clearly indicated that when provided with opportunities like this, teachers value media literacy and are excited about taking it back to their classrooms.

DM: What are some milestones you noted along the way?

DC: We offer Media Literacy as a graduate course, which can be taken entirely online, again providing teachers with convenience of access. The Canadians have just started this with an online course they call Plato's Cave, which similarly addresses a perceived need in their nation.

Finally it should also be noted that we are starting to see the first doctoral dissertations in this nation that have addressed media literacy in the U.S.

Some of my own students have authored those studies while others have been the subjects of the studies. We are seeing media literacy increasingly show up in the literature in Library Science and in publications like *The Journal of Adolescent & Adult Literacy* from the International Reading Association.

One of the most consistent findings is that a key characteristic shared by teachers who get into media literacy is their personal passion, their vision, and their dedication. It's fascinating for me to see a young woman like LeAnna Swing, who teaches social studies and English language arts in a middle school in Asheville, North Carolina. I had never heard of her, I didn't know her. I'd never met her. She came to the Institute two years ago. Free.

She sat there at the end and she met with me, and she said, "I think I'd like to do this master's degree but it's my husband's money as well and I have to go home and talk to him." I said, "I understand that."

Two months later, she joins the program. And she has been remarkable, whether taking classes on campus or online, constantly contributing her own ideas and experiences, including what works with her students and what needs more polish and practice. The giving, the sharing, and the community these young teachers build, including with those outside their field or region, this is all a testament to that old movie line, "if you build it they will come."

DM: So what would you like to see happen?

DC: I would certainly like to see more teacher education programs integrate media literacy. I don't necessarily think an undergraduate program and teacher preparation needs a course called "media literacy." If we focus on the competency, not the course, we can get away from some of the inevitable turf battles about what course gets dropped if we introduce a new one and so on. But the methods classes—especially in English language arts, history/social studies, certainly the health education classes—these are all areas with relevant state and national standards that address media literacy issues whether focused on citizenship, civil rights, human sexuality, substance abuse, global awareness, and so on. The problem with putting the responsibility in a single class is that it isolates rather than integrates media literacy as a concept and reduces the opportunities students and teachers have to reinforce and utilize the intellectual skills that are part of the process of becoming media literate.

Too often, however, department heads and administrators are not aware of these skills and are too willing to see anything with the word *media* in it as dumbing down the curriculum or an invasion of pop culture.

DM: When I came into my doctoral program saying what I wanted to do, what I wanted to study, trying to explain media literacy to the education department was difficult.

DC: Right. And we even went through some similar things in Connecticut with a doctoral student who had areas of frustration there when she was trying to build support for her dissertation about media literacy. But it's the patient people like yourself that believe and are persistent that slowly get folks to open their eyes and be receptive. And to be perfectly frank, when I went to Madison in the '70s—and I was self-funded so that was certainly helpful—they bounced me back and forth between Curriculum and Instruction in the College of Education and Communication Arts where I was working with film. And they wanted to build this wall, about, "well, that's an educational film, but that's an entertainment film." And I said, "Yeah, but they are both being shown to the same kids. Can't you let me build a bridge between adolescents and media?" And they just weren't in that place. They were in these distinctive, separate spheres and even at the point after I'd done a 600-page dissertation, and sat down with the chair and the committee. And it was Michael Apple—who's brilliant—Michael Apple actually asked during the dissertation defense, "What's this got to do with schooling?" Well, you know, and given how incredibly progressive and liberal his books on curricula are, that was a stunning question, but he was simply blinded by the fact that from an American education point of view, this was not educational. And, mercifully, the major professor came in and said, "Well, David's made it perfectly clear that in his country, where he comes from, this is part of the curriculum." You know, because in the media world we talk about consolidation and convergence, and yet educators still like to put things in their old boxes, like the Dewey Decimal System.

DM: Media literacy, as a discipline, feels incredibly fragmented, and I agree with you wholeheartedly that everyone is really talking about the same thing.

DC: You've just got to put the pieces of the puzzle together. The guys that wrote *The Art of Japanese Management* back in the early '80s got it right. Somewhere in that book it says, "Management is not by just tools but by vision. We have the tools but we lack the vision." And I think that is absolutely correct.

And the problem there—if we go back to what I was saying before about schools, trying to grow media literacy in American schools that are triangulated by administrators on one side of the triangle, teachers on the other, and largely media specialists on the other—is that although all three are educated and licensed, they are each in splendid isolation from the other.

You end up with what I call the "formula for failure." How can they possibly have a shared vision about media and technology, its role in the classroom and its relevance to young people, when they have no common education experience and therefore a fragmented vision?

So the way we prepare teachers and administrators perpetuates that lack of vision. And that's why I am not optimistic that we will see anything other than pockets of progress. Certainly nothing that would look like sweeping systemic change or transformation in education.

Barry Duncan

Barry Duncan was an award-winning teacher, author, media consultant, and founder and past president of the Ontario-based Association for Media Literacy.

Edited Transcript: Interview, May 23, 2010
Interviewer: Dee Morgenthaler

DM: Describe how you became involved in media education.

BD: Well, I go back a fair amount of time. I am back in the paleolithic zone of media education. Like, I started teaching in the '60s. So, that was really the hotbed issues of civil rights, the war in Vietnam—all of those things were very televisual and had a lot of ideological implications. So, while I was not American, a lot of this spilled over into Canada, like draft dodging, draft evading. We were inspired by these situations that were being commodified by the media. So, I was an observer of that scene. And it obviously shaped what I was doing. The other source was the work of Marshall McLuhan. And I had the good fortune to study under him just as he was formulating his ideas.

DM: Where was that? Where did you study under him?

BD: Well, that was the early '60s. He published *Understanding Media* in 1964. So he was doing preliminary work for at least six or seven years before he really burst into full flame. Those ideas of looking at not just the content but the form of the media was McLuhan's unique contribution. And so I had the good fortune of being his graduate student in his class along with five or six others. Just as he was hammering out his ideas.

DM: What school was that?

BD: The University of Toronto. And of course, I applied some of those ideas to my teaching because I have always been a secondary school teacher. And I taught part-time at the university. But I am first and foremost a teacher and I was fortunate to be in an alternative school with only a small teacher population with lots of flexibility. So I was able to hone my ideas in ways that were relevant. More recently, in the last 10 years I have done a lot of part-time work at the university, teaching teachers how to teach media: what we call *provisional qualification courses*. And you get a certificate for completing these courses. The last one being your media studies certificate. So that is where I come into it.

Anyways, those were seminal events—of course with McLuhan, the backdrop of the civil rights, all of these things were being mediated by the media. All that made this very, very important. Just to add one other little factor that we haven't talked about, the people that were doing this in the English speaking world were primarily from the UK and the British Film Institute which privileged film, but they were doing some interesting things so there was a little publication called *Screen Education*. In fact, they used that word, we used it for a while up here in Canada, and even in the United States (because I was keeping track of what they were doing in the United States). And they tended to use the term *screen education* not *media literacy*; that came later. And for sake of argument, around 1980.

DM: Can you tell me a little bit about how you included it into your teaching?

BD: In the case of the media, I was an English teacher, so English has a great deal of kinship with the media because there are key parallels—whether it is aesthetic, values, or the commercial implications of publishing. English lends itself to it and the kind of sensibility that is characteristic of good English teachers makes them very, very compatible with media literacy. And so I incorporated that. There would be things like a comparison between a novel and a film. There is an obvious example. But looking not just at the similarities but at the differences—why does the director choose to have instead of 50 characters in *War and Peace,* he boils it down to only 10? Or why does William Wyler, who directed *Wuthering Heights* (the first version in black and white), why did he leave out one generation of characters? Well the answer is that he wants to have a good film. He doesn't want to have a cluttered feeling. So he makes an aesthetic judgment. So those are some examples.

The other would be, very much the production of media. And having that tie in with the notion of what skills are needed to not only analyze but also produce media.

DM: Did you have your students produce media?

BD: Oh yes. We were dealing in the early '70s with what they called the Sony Portapak, It was in the day of Super 8 still being carried on, and the Sony Portapack, that was tape—we tried the best we could with those things. It gave kids an opportunity to try—even though it was very primitive technology. It gave them a sense of the potential of the medium and that is what's important.

DM: What were your overall goals in education or personally in terms of media education?

BD: Well—let's look at the overarching notion—it would be, to quote Len Masterman, the notion of "representation." That is the central concept of media literacy. Because it is how we are represented and how we represent ourselves, or *re*-present ourselves. And that notion is being propelled through the decades—through the '60s to today—and it is central that how well we talk about representation largely determines the nature of how *good* our media literacy is. So, representation, the core principles—what we call the Key Concepts—by having those key notions, which often are turned into questions, that has kept us on track. And depending upon how well you do those things or have answers for some of those questions, that really determines how effective media literacy is in your school or in your community.

DM: After teaching, or during your teaching, were there other organizations that you became a part of?

BD: Well, you see I founded the Association for Media Literacy, back in 1978. And it was because of the work that organization did that we, first of all, got media education as a mandatory component in the curriculum from Grade 6 to Grade 12. And with the success of the Association for Media Literacy the other provinces were reviewing their curriculum. And when you have a major curriculum review you look at things that are there—what you have and what you don't have—and they realized that they didn't have media literacy. That there was obviously a gap. And so we came along and we had the famous *Media Literacy Resource Guide*. And that became—even in the United States—a kind of underground best-seller. At least in New York City. But it became the basis for encouraging people to say that "we can do this as well." And not only just in Ontario but in the United States, and certainly, all across Canada. So what it led to is the mandatory component, in English (it has always been tied in with the subject), but it became mandatory from coast to coast in Canada from K–12.

DM: And this guide focused on the Key Concepts? Were there lesson plans?

BD: Everything was generated with reference to those Key Concepts. To a certain extent there were lesson plans but we didn't have a detailed set. People would adapt them to what we called "teachable moments." The teachable moments are the things like the War in Vietnam, 9/11, the [2004] tsunami,

Katrina. All of those things are mediated by the media and need to have the structure of the media, the ideological implications of the media in order to clarify what is happening. Any current environmental crisis like the one in Louisiana and the Gulf of Mexico, etc. The way those are covered by the media—that's a teachable moment right now.

DM: Does this guide still exist in some form?

BD: It might be available online. It might be very well be. The exact title is *The Ministry of Education Media Resource Guide*. It came out in 1989. You can try "Ministry of Education." I should have a better answer. Copies are out there. It is still very useful, but naturally so much has happened in the last 15 years that if you based your course on what are the guiding principles in that document you would be doing an injustice. We need to reconcile traditional media with this new media. Henry Jenkins points out that we are into this convergence culture.

So the Association for Media Literacy is still in existence. Still very active. It started in 1978 and we held the largest conference ever held on media, called Summit 2000. And before that we had two big international conferences. We had the most dynamic, active, soul searching about media and kids and "how do you do it?" at those conferences. And the Americans, like Renee Hobbs, etc., were inspired by what we did. So at the conference in '89, they were really keen to get going. And they had a session at our conference. One for Americans about "how do we get going?" And so, you can argue quite easily that the seminal input was what *we* did at those conferences. We had 1,500 media educators attend. So that's the largest that has been held. It was held in Toronto.

DM: Major milestones in terms of your journey?

BD: A lot of the things that I have already spoken about, but my recognition of Marshall McLuhan, because he was an academic and he was dealing with elementary school teachers. Some of his ideas, when adapted and translated, were very much what was going on in education. It was at a fairly academic level.

DM: Do you feel that you were one of the few studying under him, that you were one of the first to adapt his ideas into the classroom?

BD: Yes, I think so. But I also say that his ideas were sufficiently complex that at times it was out of reach. I would be bullshitting if I said I understood everything he ever said. He had this evening class, and I went to this evening class with McLuhan and he just exhausted us intellectually because he had so many insights into what was going on in culture—that he was five steps ahead of everybody. Readings that were exhausting and raising the key questions. It was really extraordinary because he was right on the money on most things and what is interesting is that in the last 5 years there has been a major revival of McLuhan with all kinds of books coming out on analyzing his ideas, etc. And resurrecting old videotape. He anticipated some of the major things in terms of the impact of computers—you know, things like YouTube and Facebook. There is no problem in seeing the impact of his ideas on those phenomena.

Now one of the things that I see happening is that we now have an expanded definition of media study. At one point it tended to be film television, radio, popular music, that was it. We are now taking some of those things and using the term *popular culture*. In fact my textbook, which is in use all over Canada, is called *Mass Media and Popular Culture*. And we get into things like Barbie dolls, theme parks, graphic novels; we are going beyond what people used to be calling media literacy with film, etc. So back in the '60s and early '70s, you tended to have a great deal centered on film—both the making of and the study of film. So they brought with them very traditional notions of media, like they wouldn't look at things like ideology—that was too controversial. And Americans were fearful of the term that you would be a pinko communist ready to swallow up the minds of the young. A lot of nonsense. So people like Liz Thoman wouldn't use the word—she would say that "media is a business." And in doing that she left out the real cutting edge ideas—that people like Noam Chomsky and Robert McChesney and others had drawn attention to. You are not going to do anything that is cutting-edge if you avoid those particular intellectual domains.

So we have new paradigms that have emerged that try to do justice to the ecological/technological changes.

There is stuff that we found that was unproductive or inadequate. A great deal of the work done in the media in the United States was not teaching what media was *about*—it was teaching *against* the media. Media were seen as something that is negative, distraction, that has bad values, that is un-Christian, it is just bad news with no sense of pleasure in it.

So, you've got in the United States, and to a certain extent in Canada, people who thought the media was bad, and it was not easy for you to come along and proclaim its benefits because we were, in a sense, already killed in action before it really got going. So that negative view of the media was something that we wanted to avoid. It doesn't mean that we weren't concerned about sex and violence and video games—we are, a lot of those things are not too healthy, but to have those negative things driving a whole media literacy curriculum was most unfortunate. So it is no surprise that we had the break-away movement in the United States—the ACME group [Action Coalition for Media Education], which tends to have a negative view of media literacy. So a major milestone was trying to create a positive/healthy viewpoint of all of these things.

DM: How far do think the field has come? Is it moving in the direction that you think is best?

BD: There is NAMLE [National Association for Media Literacy Education] in the U.S., and they seem to be doing a fairly good job. They seem to be landing on their feet. And they are doing their best. I have been to every one of their conferences. But they seem to be on the right track and I think they have a long way to go. I think we all need to find the vocabulary, find the means to have a sensible middle ground, which means we're are not going to be totally celebratory, nor are we going to be giving the media a bad rap. We have got to find a compromise. So I think we are getting a little closer to that.

The title of the conference, "Bridging Literacies," was a good one from the Detroit conference. Because we have had all of the academics who have looked at things like visual literacy, the librarians looked at information literacy, you get aesthetics. You get all of these competing literacies, and that is not a bad thing . . . but there needs to be a way to bridge these and that has not successfully happened. Critical pedagogy has a lot to offer, but people like Henry Giroux and others have made it somewhat obscure. The important ideas behind critical pedagogy are still there. I want to see how that can be situated in a pedagogy, I want to see them having a major role in bringing the key ideas both of traditional media and new media—of bringing them together and making all of these things as meaningful in the curriculum and the so-called convergence and the culture of connectivity—all of the new directions—all of that stuff has to be reconciled with the traditional. And if we do a good job at that we will be successful.

If you look at the core principles and key concepts—there are groups out there that are doing some aspect of it. But the danger is that the richness, aesthetic, ideological, commercial—if they are not explored then we leave the major things out of the model(s) that are needed to deconstruct media and to acknowledge the complexity.

The librarians need to have an opportunity to see how publishers can determine what we get in our textbooks. We need to look at the influence of textbooks in the curriculum. Show how textbooks will limit what teachers can do simply by *not* offering, or what is absent. All of that kind of stuff needs to be debated. If we leave that out we have an impoverished notion of the media and that is a very sad situation.

DM: Where do you see media literacy fit in terms of the school day?

BD: I'd say, as an overview, in theory it should be everywhere. Like even people that teach mathematics can claim that they can do some media literacy. The most obvious places are clearly English and social science and humanities. Because there is a compatibility: You are looking at themes and values and the paradigms that govern the way we structure our courses and dialogue with kids. That's the first part of the answer. Part two is getting to the subjects that have the greatest amount of compatibility and by having an infusion of media literacy skills and by having a critical edge to what you are doing. It is not enough to get these kids to use the Internet, to get data—that is great as just the beginning—but how do you problematize? Well, we are seeing that there are all sorts of problems with Google as we speak. And so if you left out the whole business of neutrality and privacy—what's included and what's excluded (in terms of Google)—if you leave that stuff out then you are giving kids a very unrealistic view and you are not giving the teachers the skills or the kinds of questions that should be raised.

Those things will always be critical. There is a temptation to have traditional librarians that have a limited, fearful approach—and we are worse for wear.

Renee Hobbs

Renee Hobbs is an American educator, scholar, and advocate for media literacy education. She is professor and founding director of the Harrington School of Communication and Media at the University of Rhode Island. She is co-editor with Amy Jensen of the *Journal of Media Literacy Education.*

Edited Transcript: Interview, March 10, 2011
Interviewer: Tessa Jolls

TJ: Why did you become involved in media education?

RH: When I was an undergraduate at the University of Michigan in the 1970s, I was an English literature major. At that time we were reading Shakespeare and John Donne, Emily Dickinson, and Chaucer, and I remember very vividly thinking that these very powerful literary techniques that I'm learning to use would be productively applied to shows like *Gilligan's Island* and *I Love Lucy*. At that time, there didn't exist the serious study of popular culture but I remember thinking it would be so cool to do. And I didn't know exactly how to go about doing that. I thought, well I can go into journalism, and so I worked as a college reporter and editor for the *Michigan Daily* for three years. I realized I was fascinated with how news works, how news is constructed. I learned how powerful, in a strange way, the student newspaper actually was at that time. But nobody at the student newspaper was interested in reflecting on that. They were just on to the next story. I really wanted to think about and talk about how the news is made and how making the news shapes the world. At the same time, I also loved film, thanks to my two best film professors: Hugh Cohen, who really taught me how to write, and Herb Eagle, who had just written a book on Russian formalist film theory and whose ideas about film structure influenced my thinking about semiotics, helping me see the deep mystery at the heart of montage, interpretation, and meaning in a social and political context.

And then my senior year of undergrad I took a class with Barbra Morris, who was a remarkable rhetoric/composition professor at Michigan. She was teaching media literacy even without using the term, as I recall. She had us analyze a wide range of film and television genres and create short videos to write reflectively on our strategic choices as authors. I also took a media and children class with John Murray who was visiting the University of Michigan from Kansas State University, where he was directing a media violence initiative. He was in charge of the Boys Town Center for the Study of Youth Development and had a big media violence initiative. And as a humanist, I got incredibly fascinated with the idea of social science and the process of measuring media's impact on behavior, and so I got a master's degree at Michigan in communication to learn more about media effects research.

That introduced me to this really interesting Israeli psychologist named Gabriel Salomon, a joyful man full of life and heart and imagination. And he was visiting that year in Michigan, too. He was an educational psychologist at Hebrew University; he had just written a book called *Interaction of Media Cognition and Learning*, and that was in 1979. That book rocked my world! That book basically said that Israeli kids seem to learn more from television than American kids, because Israeli kids had just gotten television, and there was only one channel. Kids put in more mental effort when watching, and therefore they learned more from it. He realized that the more effort you put in, the more value you get out, which seemed completely right about everything in life, really. He introduced me to the work of Howard Gardner, who in the '70s had written a book called *Artful Scribbles* and was doing all this stuff studying human creativity at Harvard Graduate School of Education. I started looking at his work, and he and his grad students were looking at understanding how kids understood different TV genres, how they came to understand advertising, at the difference between cartoons and live action, and I thought hmm, that is cool.

So that's what took me to Harvard. Now once I got there I had the great opportunity to work with David Perkins and Howard Gardner and to be at Project Zero and to work on some projects because in the early '80s, first generation of microcomputers was coming out, and big set of questions were going on in the field as technology education shifted from the television to the microcomputer. I had come to Harvard in part because of Gerald Lesser's pioneering work in children and television (he was one of the cofounders of *Sesame Street*) and I loved his high-level boundary crossing at the intersection of research and practice. And at some point, I discovered media literacy somewhere stumbling around in the library. I saw that Father John Culkin (friend of Marshall McLuhan) had written this interesting dissertation on film study in the high school, while he was at Harvard Ed School back in 1964, basically saying that we need to teach kids about film and media. He's famous for the quote: "Kids with still and motion picture cameras, kids with audio and video recorders, are more fun than other kids." And when I went to my adviser Gerald Lesser to say I wanted to write my dissertation on media literacy, he said, "No way! No way! No way! Teaching kids about camera angles is ridiculous, find another topic." Basically his argument was there was not enough literature to build upon, and so therefore I wouldn't be able to write a good dissertation and contribute new knowledge to the field. But that was pretty depressing. So instead I went back to my interest in news and journalism and I conducted an experiment to explore how various forms of television editing could, depending on the type of editing, help people to better comprehend and remember the content of TV news. After I got the degree, I was hired as an assistant professor of communication at Babson College in 1985. Within the first year or two, I found myself at the Boston Film Video Foundation for an event which brought together media artists, K–12 teachers and college professors to talk about media in society. I remember being bored with the superficial blather throughout the whole event, at some point I got up on my high horse and said, "I'm teaching my college juniors and seniors about the First Amendment and the difference between broadcast and cable television and about the economics of the media and how advertising supports what we see on broadcast television and how radio waves work . . . I'm teaching this stuff to kids who are 20 and 21, 22 years old, they're finance and accounting majors, and you know what? I could just as easily teach the same stuff to seventh graders."

Somebody came up to me after and tapped me on my shoulder and said, "You really think you can teach this stuff to seventh graders?" I said, "ABSOLUTELY!" That was Anne Marie Stein, and she was the executive director for the Boston Film Video Foundation. We talked, we drank coffee, and we wrote a grant, funded by the Andy Warhol Foundation. At that time, Branda Miller, an experimental video artist teaching at Rensselaer Polytechnic, was exploring youth media, too, and so we collaborated on a curriculum. With Tim Wright, a terrific video artist, we went into the Taft Middle School in Boston, a really grimy, deeply troubled school. I worked for three years, in 6th-, 7th-, and 8th-grade classrooms. Working with these kids was where I made a lot of mistakes and, in the process, I really learned how to teach. I experimented. I discovered right quick that it wasn't about stuffing knowledge into their heads. It was a form of consciousness-raising and that required creating a meaningful learning environment to activate intellectual curiosity and a sense of personal agency. Kids did critical analysis activities where we deconstructed different kinds of TV shows, news, and advertising. We did production activities where kids made all kinds of narrative stories and public service announcements, little documentaries. Those three years were incredibly important for me trying to figure out how to engage 6th-, 7th-, and 8th-graders and how to connect with their experience with media and popular culture. I also learned a little about how to manage the impossibilities of an urban public school that feels like a prison for these kids who were only 11, 12, 13 years old. I knew then that there were enough messy complexities in this work to last a lifetime—I got bitten by the media literacy bug.

TJ: Once you see it in action like that, and really see that you can get those results with 7th graders, it's pretty amazing. Now, okay maybe the best thing to do is just keep on going. . .

RH: Yikes, we could be talking all day though! During this time, I think I went deep into babyland. . . Roger was born in '88, Rachel was born in '89 [Hobbs's son and daughter]. When I was raising my children, I was exploring another kind of media literacy watching them use media and technology—they were my informal research subjects, of course. But I was still trying to get tenure, so I wasn't publishing on media literacy in that period, in part because I was having trouble getting the Taft Middle School work that I was doing into publication. It didn't really fit into communication and it really didn't fit in education. So I kind of regrouped and said, to get tenure I need publications, and to get publications, something big and splashy would be good. So basically I went back to the issues I was exploring during my PhD thesis, which was looking at television editing, montage, image-sound relationships, and how this affects people's interpretation processes.

Thanks to help from my colleagues John Stauffer and Richard Frost, we were able to go to Northwest Kenya to explore a research question that had intrigued me for years. My ideas on visual literacy were deeply inflected by my undergraduate work in film/video studies at Michigan. I had a course with Rudolf Arnheim, a very influential German film theorist who was teaching at the University of Michigan when I was an undergraduate. In 1932 (yes, that's 1932!), he wrote a book called *Film as Art*, where he claimed that people needed to "learn" to "read the grammar of film." I was always intrigued by perceptual psychology and wondered if this was true or not. When John Stauffer told me about the opportunity to work with a group of tribal people, it struck me that it might be possible to test Arnheim's idea experimentally. We had a connection with a missionary who worked with the Pokot, a large group of nomadic tribes people in Northwest Kenya. Most had never seen photographs, film, or television before. So off we went to the middle of the most remote part of Kenya you can possibly imagine—with a jeep, a generator, and some portable video editing equipment. We made short video stories based on their folktales, family stories, and traditions. Some were unedited, where the camera would start and stop after five minutes of story where the story kind of acted out, nonverbally, with one long still shot. And then we did highly edited versions of that same story using close-ups, medium shots, long shots, to structure the narrative using conventional film structure.

We were absolutely convinced that the Pokot people would not be able to understand the edited version because it was so highly fragmented. Think about it: If you've never seen film or television, you live in a seamless world. Reality is not edited. How strange it must seem to have all those juxtapositions of time and space. But in fact, to our surprise, the Pokot were perfectly able to comprehend those highly edited stories. In fact, they comprehended the edited version of the story just as well as the unedited version. The next year we went back and we tested other kinds of editing techniques like flashback, where the events are presented out of time sequence, and parallel montage, where two events are portrayed as happening at the same time by cutting back and forth between two locations. They could understand nonverbal narratives told using these visual conventions perfectly well. So this research actually got me my first award recognition and publication in the top-ranked *Journal of Communication*. When I got tenure, then I realized that I could go back to media literacy.

One of my professors at Harvard asked me to do some adjunct teaching at that time, so I got to teach at Harvard for about two years, one or two courses, one course a semester. That was great because I met all kinds of smart young women and men who were going to go off and have amazing careers. Like Dorothea Gillim, the founder/creator of *Word Girl*, the PBS show, she was one of my students. At Harvard, I got the idea to do a summer institute on media education in 1992 and 1993. The people at Harvard sat me down and showed me how to write a budget, and showed me how, if I wanted 100 people to show up, it would cost thousands and thousands of dollars. I wanted Neil Postman to come and give a lecture. I wanted Barry Duncan, Kathleen Tyner, David Considine, Bob Kubey, and John Pungente to be there. These were the A-listers in media literacy that I had met in late '80s and early '90s. I reached out to Bobbi Kamil, the brand-new executive director of Cable in the Classroom, which was the new nonprofit organization founded by the cable industry. At that time, they were making available hundreds of hours of educational TV shows available without commercials for educational use by teachers and students. So I knocked on her door and said, "I need money because I want to make a film about the Harvard Institute on Media Education because it's the first-ever national-level teacher education program for media literacy. I want to document it and I need $70,000." And she said, "Well, it really doesn't work that way but I can help you with distribution." She taught me how to approach the cable industry. She connected me to Amos Hostetter at Continental Cablevision, now one of the richest people in the world. His community affairs person said yes right away. They gave me $70,000, Bobbi Kamil said we'll distribute 10,000 VHS tapes of your documentary, and basically I was off. It was my first experience with teacher education—and my first experience as an executive producer of a documentary, *Tuning in to Media*. And it was all happening at the same time! Wow!

The first year of the institute (1993) was truly magical. There were about 100 people in a sort of horseshoe-shaped classroom—very state of the art for that time period—and we had a whole glorious week together with all those luminaries that I just described, including Pat Aufderheide who was also there. I remember coming to the podium and saying, "I've been thinking about you and waiting for you and planning for this and planning to meet you for the last year and I'm so glad you're finally here!" Someone called out from the back of the room, "We've been waiting for you for ten years!" These were K–12 folks, but also people in public broadcasting, library media specialists, college faculty, media artists, and independent producers who had caught the media literacy bug, caught it hard, and who basically wanted to find a community, continue educating themselves, and come together to have meaningful dialogue. It was easy to find that first 100 people and the second year, it was easy to find the second 100 people. Now that was awesome! Both years were amazing and I really began to realize that there was a community of people who shared my passion.

In between my first Harvard Institute, and my second Harvard Institute, was the Aspen Institute where I really first got to know Liz Thoman. I had met Liz briefly some years before, but I really got to know her really well at the Wye Conference Center event hosted by the Aspen Institute. I watched how Liz cultivated and nurtured a community of media literacy stakeholders through her editorial work with *Media & Values*, a publication I greatly admired.

During that time period around 1993, I started working in Billerica, a small working-class community near Boston, which was really great learning experience. Billerica High School was one of the first seven Channel One schools, where students watched 10 minutes of news and 2 minutes of advertising and schools got a closed-circuit TV system for every classroom in the building. And Dr. John Katsoulis, an assistant superintendent of Billerica schools, came to me and said, "We're really enthusiastic about this news service. We're committed to helping our students understand news, but we can't really bring it in our schools without helping our teachers figure out how to use it well. We think that this media literacy might be what we need." This seemed important work. I was quite leery, as we all were at the time, about the kind of business model that Channel One was offering to schools. How could I help the faculty and students in these schools?

And so I was asked to do a big staff development program for all 400 members of the faculty in the district and it was actually kind of scary because we're in a big auditorium, a big assembly program. I basically did a Media Literacy 101 course on what teachers and students need to know about Channel One, how they sell audiences to advertisers, how they decide what's news, how they adapt news to be kid friendly, how to critically analyze the commercials, how to critically analyze the news programs. After an hour and half teachers left, and there in the back of the room there was this guy, in a three-piece suit, not looking like a teacher. He came up to me and introduced himself and his name was Jim Ritts, who later became CEO of Primedia. At that time, he was the vice president of something or other at Channel One. And I was like "Wow." He was in the back of the room the whole time. He said, "Let me take you for a cup of coffee." So we had a cup of coffee and I said, "Well first of all, did I accurately describe your company's goals and your business model and the economics behind it?" He said, "Absolutely, you got it right." And then he knocked my socks off. He said, "I really wish that you would go do this critical analysis and deconstruction of Channel One to every school district in America." He explained that he had been all over the country, trying to get Channel One in schools, and people in leadership positions—heads of school boards and superintendents—do not understand how the broadcasting business works, and what it takes to get programs on air. They want this, that and the other thing, but the thing is that they don't understand is how it gets paid for. He said, "I think you are doing an incredible service to the whole country and everybody in America needs to understand more about the media and how to be a critical viewer." And he basically said this will help our business because if the audience knows these things, they are actually going to be more active viewers, they're going to learn more. This is really what we need." And that really freaked me out. Until then, I was comfortable seeing big media executives as the enemy, and this was the first time I could see their work as an authentic attempt to use capitalism to support innovation in education.

So, needless to say, he introduced me to Paul Folkemer, the principal at the Benjamin Franklin Middle School in Ridgewood, New Jersey. Thanks to Channel One's support, he brought all of his faculty, a team of 10 teachers, to the Harvard Institute on Media Education in the second year. All 10 teachers were trying to integrate media literacy in the middle school. So we started having big debates about Channel One as early as 1994. And then Billerica's superintendent came up to me and said, "I like this assembly program but we really need to build a cadre of leaders. A one-shot program for 400 teachers really doesn't do it. We need a bunch of teachers who make a commitment to teaching media literacy." Basically John Katsoulis showed me how to create a Masters program in media literacy; I didn't really know how to do it at that time. We invented names and descriptions for 10 courses. And voila we got 30 teachers to sign up and we did it. In three years, we cycled 30 teachers through a master's program.

For me, this was great: again the participating teachers taught me how they learn best. My thinking about the practices of staff development changed dramatically during those three years because I had to really step away from the idea of promoting my own expertise. I had to completely change the way I taught—this is where I became all about activities and questions and open discussion of you-name-it-everything. This class became a very tight, warm, and wonderful group. Bill Walsh was the writer of our group; he would post a weekly editorial in the local newspaper, synthesizing what he was getting out of the courses in these weekly editorials that went into the town newspaper. And it was a magical time.

TJ: Can you tell me about what shaped your practice?

RH: For me, what was important about this program was that there were 30 teachers and they were equally divided among elementary, middle, and high school teachers. I could see that each group of teachers had specific needs, and I could see each group of teachers were thinking about the certain group of children that they taught; they were teaching in all the subject areas from English to Social Studies to Health to Physical Education. We had the whole gamut of folks in the room. And what we all came to understand was that the essence of the work was about connecting the classroom to the culture. In fact, it was Damian Curtiss, the head of the language arts department, who first helped me deeply understand that media literacy was an expanded form of literacy. When teachers can take advantage of the connection between what kids do when they're out of school and when they're in school, learning is robust. And the teachers had their own fantastic ride in the program, learning to analyze messages and make media as well. I remember there was one moment where I had to be absent. I came back the following week, and they had decided to meet in my absence and use that time to make a video. They basically taught each other. When I came back, they popped in the video and then we had this *amazing* conversation about what you learn when you make things. They initiated that project; they did it independently because they knew it needed to be done. So I recognized that the best thing about teaching was the opportunity to really and truly learn from my students. That was a huge "aha!" for me.

TJ: What were some other milestones for the field?

RH: Yikes! I haven't even told you the Discovery part of the story, yet. Let's talk about my earliest work with the Discovery Channel in 1994. Linda Brown contacted me totally out of the blue and said that the Discovery Channel was launching a new network called The Learning Channel and they wanted to do some kind of teacher education event and they read about the Harvard Institute. "Won't you help us try to figure out how to help us with media literacy for teachers for the Learning Channel?" I said, "Sure." By then, I had made a decision, walking one summer on the beach on Cape Cod, to invest substantial energy in the advocacy role. For me, advocacy was like being out on the water, with the boat and the waves rocking and all the wind, versus the comfort and safety and distance of being solely a researcher and scholar, gazing out at the water but not really in the game. Linda Brown and I came on to the idea of teaching teachers how to critically analyze the documentary genre, long a special interest of mine. So we settled on that.

I got to create this wonderful workshop and curriculum called KnowTV, which in 1994, won the Golden Cable Ace Award. That consisted of a curriculum book with VHS tape of clips that went next to it, that I got to produce with the guy who made my first documentary with me, a terrific media professional named Rob Stegman from Blue Star Media. He really got media literacy and we had many years of remarkable collaboration. And after KnowTV, I got to go all over the country doing these workshops; I remember doing them in Charlotte, North Carolina; in Atlanta, Georgia; in Orlando, where I met Frank Baker—where he was a superb and imaginative media specialist in the Orlando public schools. So that's where I really got the feeling that the cable industry could be useful in supporting the media literacy movement. I had a series of successes, Bobbi Kamil had supported my documentary and now Discovery was supporting the development in implementation of teacher workshops for this. So I was feeling really warm and fuzzy about the cable industry's potential. I had stars in my eyes about what they were trying to do and I was a big champion. I told my colleagues, "Let's work with these people because we can harness their money and their reach to our goals." A lot of people thought I was crazy, naïve, and I don't know, maybe I was. But it's sort of the same ambivalent way I feel today about the role of Dell, Microsoft, and Apple in the technology education business. They do have corporate agendas that shape every decision and they ARE key stakeholders in people getting smarter, more engaged, and more thoughtful about media and technology.

Of course, I didn't realize at that time that those were the years leading up to the passage of the 1996 Telecommunications Act. What I didn't understand, and now looking back at history where hindsight shows everything right, during that period 1993, '94, '95, and '96, the cable industry was really trying to tell [the] story of [its] public spiritedness so that Congress could grant them this incredible windfall of a gift, the 1996 Telecom Act. This law essentially deregulated the cable industry and enabled them to compete with the phone companies. The law reaffirmed that the cable industry didn't have to be regulated the same way broadcasters were, that is, that they didn't have any public service obligation. So I now, looking back, realize that I was enmeshed in a tiny part of that sort in terms of the industry's public policy strategy to support that legislation.

Even at the time, I was aware of that legislation moving through Congress, it wasn't like I was unaware, but I was in Washington, learning in the field about how the business gets done. I knew that members of Congress were targeted because I got to meet all kinds of Congressmen as a part of this initiative and so I definitely knew there was a political agenda regarding the regulation of the media industry. I got to meet lobbyists, PR people, and congressional staffers all thinking really strategically about policy change. (So it was déjà vu all over again with the BTOP [Broadband Technology Opportunities Program] funding from the Commerce Department and the FCC report and the Knight Commission initiative in 2011.)

As the media literacy community became a little club, we had lots of fights. Some it was the typical holier-than-thou liberal posturing and political correctness among scholars and advocacy people—stuff that I generally see as mostly worthless, self-indulgent dreck. I remember the fights. Indeed, I was the subject of some of these fights since my approach to seek external funding for media literacy by working with media companies as partners was considered particularly controversial at the time. How strange it was to be targeted by people who overtly rejected my ideas—and wrote about it. As someone who loves to be loved, this was a difficult period for me professionally and personally. But it was part of learning to be courageous and taking on the reins of leadership, too.

By then, the media literacy community began meeting at various conferences every year after that and in 1997, we formed the Partnership for Media Education (PME). I remember the phone call that started it all as vividly as if it were yesterday. I was standing in my kitchen, doing the dishes and on the phone with Liz Thoman, Lisa Reisberg from the American Academy of Pediatrics, and Nancy Chase Garcia from the Center for Substance Abuse Prevention. Lisa and Nancy pushed us in new ways to think big, and so by the end of the call, we decided to plan a national conference in Colorado Springs, connecting media literacy to public health. We raised money. We planned. We promoted. We were a very good team. In the end, over 450 people attended! By 2001, thanks to leadership from Faith Rogow and others, we decided to transform from a "gang of four" to become a national membership association.

When students were murdered at Columbine High School in 1999, yet another door opened unexpectedly. When Columbine happened, of course, many Americans were freaked out. People were watching the TV during the whole standoff, with wounded children scrambling out of the windows. It was a pretty traumatic experience and there was a whole lot of craziness. It generated a powerful kind of public reflection on the scope of the desensitized world we were becoming and loss of humanity in evidence at the circumstances that led to this tragedy.

During the months after Columbine, a lot of teachers everywhere were feeling unsafe. I remember doing a teacher workshop at about this time; we were talking about how to talk to our kids about this event. What should we do? We knew we needed to talk about it with our students, but it was really hard for the teachers. I remember a teacher saying to me, "I know what I'm supposed to say to my students, 'This is a very unusual event, and this isn't very common and this hardly ever happens, you're safe in this school.' " I nodded my agreement. And then she said, "I know that's what I'm supposed to say, but I don't feel that way, I don't feel safe in this school; I can't tell the kids something that I don't feel is true."

I looked around. I'd never been in a room where so many teachers were wounded; we were all feeling very, very vulnerable. Out of that tragedy came an initiative from Judith McHale, the president of Discovery Channel who herself had children in the Maryland public schools and was seated on the Maryland State Board of Education. She made a decision, and in the public meeting with the board members of the Maryland State Board of Education, she said, "We will do a media literacy initiative for the children of Maryland." Boom! It was decided. And then I got the call. And so that project became Assignment: Media Literacy. With the help Discovery Channel executives, Carrie Passmore and Linda Brown and Nancy Brian, it was a major multimedia production that tested all of my skills in project management. It was a year of curriculum writing and pilot-testing, 30 Maryland teachers being our advisory group—a very elaborate production and research process of getting these curriculum books and tapes and packages made and then another two years of outreach in 23 counties across the state. I was so proud to be associated with the Discovery Channel.

We did dozens and dozens of these sessions, and each one had 150 or 200 people in the room, so it was great for my ego and my Rolodex. I met a lot of Maryland teachers. Many of those folks who were there were already on their own journey with media literacy, they had already gotten on the bandwagon and this was just a small gift: a pretty box with easy-to-use lesson plans and video clips. They were ready to run with it. We got really great feedback from librarians and tech specialists and English teachers, and I remember getting amazing descriptive e-mails for a bunch of years during that time period from teachers in rural schools of Maryland, in city schools of Maryland, in Baltimore City. Teachers were saying these lessons are easy for me to use and they work. And then Bob Kubey wrote the evaluation for that project, and it was over, so we closed the project's doors by 2001. I had a chance to go do a version of the Assignment: Media Literacy curriculum in Texas. We sat with Texas educators and cable TV executives in about 2002; we revised the curriculum for the state of Texas. But by that time, the funding was cut and the program never really had a roll out . . . the material got revised for Texas but never really implemented, which is a bit of a shame.

TJ: I think what's so significant about the Discovery project in Maryland, was that it is one of the only examples of a really systematic effort. You were going for the whole state, it was being supported systematically, and you had access to this system.

RH: Again this shows the complicated multistakeholder process of making change from the top down and the bottom up. In Maryland, we had good support from the state superintendent of schools Nancy Grasmick, and we had great support from the corporation. So we had the money and the state's support but what really made the difference was at the community level. Some communities were really able to run with it like Silver Springs, Cecil County, and other places. And in other communities where the concept of media literacy was new and unfamiliar, there was less initiative. Leadership at the local level is key. In a decentralized education system, building-level leadership makes a huge difference in whether or not innovation is going to happen. I learned to appreciate the role of principals and superintendents in the change process. We made a lot of progress in Maryland with this initiative, but not every student in Maryland got to benefit from this work. It's a big state. We could've done a better job at reaching out to the principals and nurturing building-level leadership.

TJ: So the administrative level is a whole other level . . .

RH: And the problem was that we were juggling a lot of stakeholders while at the same time the principals were juggling so many other priorities. It wasn't like they were hostile; they just had lots of balls in the air, including special education, facilities issues, and curriculum issues. So, I can't blame administrators, but I don't know that we thought about them and their unique needs as deeply as we might have. When I look back at the project, that's the part of it I didn't design carefully enough.

TJ: That was a significant milestone . . . so let's see, we've gotten to late '90s–early 2000s . . .

RH: The story that I just told you happened basically with me in the role of a consultant. So, in addition to teaching my six courses, this was my other job. I guess I've been doing two or more jobs for most of my professional life. Why? This was the place of passion. For some period of time, it was really pretty separate from my day job as a professor of mass communication in a business school. The shift in my own career came in 2003 when I was able to come to Temple University and better integrate my passion for media literacy and my actual job, because I now teach doctoral students and masters students and undergraduates, and I actually get to teach and do research on media literacy. And I have a whole new crew of young scholars and teachers who are great thinkers and doers and collaborators. So for me, it's been a huge and wonderful shift because now there finally is a literature on media literacy. There are lots of teachers all over the country doing innovative and creative work. Unlike my experience in 1985, students now can write a doctoral dissertation about media literacy—and more than 50 people have in the last five years.

Now there's a new challenge that I'm still trying to figure out—and I wouldn't say I have much in the way of accomplishment after seven years at Temple—is how to make universities be more effective players in the media literacy movement. When I came to Temple, I developed the idea of the Media Education Lab so that the primary resources of the university (our students and our faculty) can help advance media literacy education through scholarship and community service. The community service part is easy: there's a boatload of needs in our local communities, and our talented graduate students and undergrads can get placed in schools and work with educators—and media literacy happens. Everybody wins. That part is easy.

The advancing scholarship part is hard because the field is still a bit compromised by its multidisciplinary or transdisciplinary nature. A young scholar who is really interested in media literacy—the big question for them is, what discipline do they enter in—communication, education, public health, sociology. What field do they enter? We don't have an answer for that, because none of those shoes exactly fit. Some part of all those shoes fit. I hope to solve that problem in my lifetime. I would really love to have an opportunity to create an interdisciplinary program where those silos don't have to interfere with the quality of scholarship for media literacy. I've been giving speeches about that based on my Knight Foundation paper, basically called "Down with the Silos." Until we can have truly interdisciplinary programs that connect English education to education to literary studies to sociology to media and communication, until you can actually study that all of a piece, then the scholarship of media literacy is going to continue to be at the margin . . . where it is right now, still at the margin in terms of public education. I hope I can get to develop this new kind of program someday . . .

TJ: What were the surprises for you along the way?

RH: Back in Aspen with a roomful of smart and passionate people who were deeply invested in media literacy, the first time, we discussed: Is this a field or a movement? And that was the big challenge. I remember at some point feeling really conflicted. I think I wanted it to be a field. I was kind of the antimovement girl in the room: "It's a field of inquiry; it's a place of research and discovery," I insisted. I was the proponent of the "big tent" idea: people from all across the ideological spectrum can engage with the power of media literacy. And other people were saying, "No, no, it's a social movement" and it's inevitably tied to core ideas of liberalism. I now think it is a movement, even though I continue to hope it can appeal to Democrats, Republicans, and everyone else. In the Knight white paper I just published, I am calling digital and media literacy a community education movement.

I continue to be pleasantly surprised at the diversity of stakeholder involvement. It's amazing. People are coming to this movement with different kinds of expertise, just the kind of expertise we actually need for a broad-based social movement. There are parents, business leaders, museum educators, computer programmers and civil rights activists and anti-poverty advocates and art teachers and school counselors. To me the idea that people are coming with this wide range of different kinds of expertise into this field is a sign that it's a full-on community education movement; plus the fact that it's happening in different settings including K–12, college, the workplace, and other settings beyond school.

Most importantly, media literacy is now a finally a part of our public discourse, and we see that so clearly now in TV shows like *The Daily Show* with Jon Stewart and *The Colbert Report*. Thank you, Jon and Steven!

Many of the important questions about how best to teach media literacy (to students and to teachers) are still unresolved. So another surprise for me is in the way the great debates I identified in 1998 are still robust and vital, even as the field is migrating toward a different theoretical formulation because of the rise of celebrity culture, popular culture, and digital literacy. I would anticipate that as more stakeholders and more folks from different points of view continue to enter the field, we are going to have to examine those key concepts and critical concepts again; I think we are going to have to have another Aspen Institute. I think the effort we've made over the past 25 years brings together people around a shared conversation despite our differences and because of our differences; therefore we need a set of strong theoretical and conceptual strands that unite us, lest we risk becoming incoherent. Indeed, all this collaborative effort has been very good for us; and I think the field has benefited tremendously from all of those efforts . . . the Five Key Questions, the CML Medialit Kit, all those things that try to connect or to identify common themes, issues, and values. We can't stop doing that. We have to keep discovering how best to bring new people and new ideas into the community so that children, young people, and all people will benefit.

Douglas Kellner

Douglas Kellner is an author, theorist, and George Kneller Chair of the Philosophy of Education at UCLA. He was an early theorist in the field of media literacy, who has since published on topics including the philosophy of Herbert Marcuse, cinema and politics, communications, and media and cultural studies.

Edited Transcript: Interview, September 13, 2010
Interviewer: Dee Morgenthaler

DM: What inspired your journey in terms of getting to the point of looking at media and media education? I'm really interested in who inspired your work in terms of texts and technology and social events.

DK: I began getting involved in media studies and education in the 1970s, around 1973, when I got a job as an assistant professor of philosophy at the University of Texas. This was before there was a field of media education, or at least I didn't know about it. After teaching there a couple years a group of graduate students and myself had a study group. Basically, we were trying to figure out how the revolution in the 1960s failed, what was the major sort of conservative cultural force that kept U.S. society together, as it were, and what was the major socializer, form of ideology, and political influence, etc.

We concluded it was media, and especially television. So I actually started studying media in the 1970s in a study group with graduate students. Then around 1977, I started to teach a course called Philosophy of Culture and Communication. This was still before I'd heard of media education or cultural studies. So I just invented this course on my own, coming out of a study group with some graduate students.

And about the same time—this was during the Carter years—in the state of Texas, which at that time had its own Democratic governor—it was pretty liberal at this time—they got a grant from the federal government on this topic of media education.

I was basically hired to go around the state of Texas to do workshops on media education, along with a woman, a Latino guy, and a black guy. We were basically covering the representation of values and ideologies in media and, in general, the politics of representation concerning gender, race, class, sexuality, and so on.

Hence, we had a woman that taught reading images of women on TV; and a Latino and a black guy who engaged representations of people of color, so that we were actually doing what later became the politics of representation and cultural studies, which engages representations and images of different groups in the media and then critiques sexism, racism, homophobia, and other negative stereotyped representations of specific social groups. In this Texas project, I started to do media education in a very classical way, teaching high school teachers how to read the media and how to teach media education in the classroom, and around the same time was trying to do this in my own course.

So I got into media education in a very practical and in a very political way, before there was an academic field, or I started writing on it, or discovered even British cultural studies.

Sometime, I think in the 1980s, I discovered that Stuart Hall and the Birmingham group were doing the same kind of media studies in this new discipline called cultural studies. Then I became part of that, connecting media education to cultural studies.

DM: When you were doing those workshops, when you were asked to go around and speak, were those to teachers, teacher groups?

DK: Yes. Very specifically it was called the Mississippi Delta Project, which was a liberal government project from the Carter administration in the late 1970s. There was poverty and bad schools in that area, and a sense that they should teach media literacy and media education to give them something they weren't getting in those schools. I was teaching teachers how to teach media education in the project, and unfortunately as soon as the Reagan administration came in, they dropped the funding of that program. So I don't know what happened to it, politically.

But it was a good program for me to interact with teachers to get a very practical orientation towards teaching media education. That is, how do I do it in a classroom as a college instructor, and then hope that future high school teachers, or maybe even grade school teachers, will teach media literacy.

DM: Where did your involvement in media education go from there?

DK: Well, I started just writing articles and books on television, on film, on media literacy. All of this accelerated tremendously when, in 1997, I got hired by UCLA to teach philosophy of education. One of the courses I did was Cultural Studies in Media Literacy. So about 1997, this became the focus of my work, whereas previously I was in a philosophy department and it was just one thing I was teaching among many things.

DM: Do you feel like the direction that we're going in now, maybe since then, is in a good direction?

DK: No. Unfortunately, media education and literacy just are not on the agenda for reforming education today, although certainly they should be.

DM: Do you have suggestions for the field?

DK: Yes. I think that education in the United States has been severely compromised and limited by not bringing media education into the curriculum. This would involve starting with K–12 and teaching media literacy as one teaches book literacy. While we're getting computer literacy teaching in the schools, somehow media literacy just never took off in American schools. This has been just a big problem, and a scandal, really. If you look at Britain, Australia, and Canada, the three other biggest English-speaking countries, all of them have some quite sophisticated media education programs in the schools K–12, whereas it's an exception in the U.S.

DM: I'm very aware of that issue, that we are very far behind in terms of media education, and it's so strange to me that we're in this society where it seems to be maybe even more influential than in the other areas where they have a much more developed literacy system. What do you think the reason behind that is? Why haven't we caught onto that? Do you think it's politics?

DK: I think it's politics and ingrained bureaucracy and conservatism in the schools. It's politics because no administration has ever brought this into the Department of Education curriculum, except for that very tiny moment in the Carter administration. I'm not even sure who it was that did this, obviously somebody in the Carter administration was farseeing enough to recognize that media education was important, and got some money to begin programs, but it just never developed.

As soon as you get to conservative administrations, like the Reagan, Bush One, and Bush Two administrations, they are just into the most conservative teaching for testing. Rudimentary reading skills and math skills are what are emphasized, so there'll be hopefully improved test scores.

DM: One of the things you touched on in your philosophical adventure piece is that, while we still need to have critical media skills and visual media skills, there's still a need for print literacy also. Can you elaborate?

DK: Absolutely. We need enhanced print literacies with computer literacy that requires even more reading and writing skills. I use the term *multiple literacies* because more than ever before, with the Internet, we have to read and write in an intelligible and coherent way and be literate in many dimensions of our life.

DM: There was this really brief moment, in terms of 21st-century learning skills, where it seemed like we were heading in a direction where the U.S. education system was finally recognizing this need, but it's kind of gotten lost in the politics of education. In terms of a policy level, one of the questions that keeps coming up in my policy classes is local control versus national control standards. If you have a little more local control over your curriculum and such, it might filter down more cleanly to the students. Now they're studying these national standards on media literacy.

DK: Right. Well, the scandal is that neither on the federal, state, or local level has anyone really taken up media literacy as an important educational reform. There may be some exceptions, but there aren't many media literacy programs. There are a couple in the L.A. area that my student Jeff Share has been involved in. Here and there you'll see some; but few, if any, have taken this up in the U.S. as an important project. So that's why it's a scandal, really.

DM: Who should be leading the effort?

DK: Everybody.

DM: In terms of our discipline or our field, I'd read that the view is that we're fragmented, and we're calling it different things, and we're not talking to the right people in order to get it. Everyone has the same goal, we want it to be in the education system, but for some reason . . .

DK: Well there's not enough "we's" on this. I think that education programs are also a scandal. It's a scandal that schools of education aren't pursuing media literacy more aggressively. Now, it's an exception at UCLA, partly because I'm teaching there; Ernest Morrell, who's been doing media literacy for years, Rhonda Hammer, Jeff Share, and others are teaching media literacy. We really have a lot of people who just came here on their own, not through us having a program. It's just individuals who happened to have media education and literacy as an agenda and have been doing it here at UCLA.

Yet we still don't even have a media literacy program at UCLA. We've had a couple of attempts to get something started. We also have a group of people in the Information Studies side of the School of Education, like Leah Lievrouw who are into media literacy, new media, and such things.

But we did sort of an informal survey, how many schools of education teach cultural studies and media education? And they were few and far between.

DM: When did you do that?

DK: Just a couple of years ago. I mean, this wasn't a systematic attempt to develop a media literacy program, just a group of us thinking that it should be done. Do you know of any systematic studies of people who have implemented media literacy programs?

DM: In terms of an overall review of who's teaching media literacy, I haven't seen any, no.

DK: I just think it'll be dispiriting when one finds out there's hardly any of these projects going on.

DM: I know. I've got my master's degree in Communication and Media Literacy. I have young children, and my interest in it was piqued from my children. I wanted to get my PhD in it. But logistically I can't move. So I forced my way into the School of Education, and they really still don't know what to do with me or where to put me. So I kind of bounced around between cultural and informational studies and things like that. I think that's just very demonstrative of how there aren't really any sustained projects of media education on the agenda of education in the U.S. today at all. People in the field of education really don't understand the term.

DK: Right. So it's really a scandal. To return to your very first question, what is the status of the field of media education at the present, I would say it's just scandalously underdeveloped in the U.S. Whereas in Canada, they have some impressive programs on different local and regional areas. In Australia, the UK, you'll get a somewhat developed field of media education. And here it's just underdeveloped. It's basically individuals are doing this here and there, and groups are doing this here and there, like the Santa Monica group.

DM: Right.

DK: But there really isn't a field in the domain of higher education or K–12 education. By the way, they're starting to do this now in China, in Taiwan, and other places in Asia, having media literacy in the school. So the West is behind almost everyone.

DM: I know, and as an infant in the academic world, I'm always trying to struggle where to put my energy. I keep coming back to the fact that it needs to go to the policy level. That is such a huge undertaking. It's very, very disheartening.

DK: Well, my response to that is, yes, it's extremely important to get some policy intervention going on. But you can do it in your own classroom. So I have a lot of students who now have jobs in education programs, and they're teaching cultural studies and media literacy as part of different courses they're teaching. Sometimes it is put in foundation of education courses, sometimes literacy ones, sometimes this that or the other course where they sneak it in. So that's the other level where we can do things. I don't want to be completely negative and pessimistic that there's nothing we can do. I mean, there's more than enough to do. We can do it in our own classes. We can fit it in one way or the other and fight to get courses in our programs.

DM: Right. In the K–12 level one way in, I see, is at the local level; creating a pilot program and trying to make changes at my local level. That's the direction I'm leaning towards, just baby steps.

DK: Right.

DM: How about interesting new areas of research that you see emerging in terms of new media? Any comments there in terms of things we need to explore further, things that are piquing your interest?

DK: Right. Actually new media is a much more exciting and encouraging field in American academia than media literacy. In other words, there are really a lot of people that are studying the Internet and are studying everything from Twitter to blogs to how we can do courses online to what kind of online components we can bring into our classes. So there's really a lot that's being done in that area. What's being given short shrift in all this is old-fashioned media literacy, teaching people how to read the media, like television, film, popular music, and so on. By the way, let me put one important point on my view of media literacy. That is Rhonda Hammer, Jeff Share, others that I'm associated with, do what we call *critical media literacy*.

In other words, it's not enough just to be able to read the media, but you have to be able to critique it in terms of the politics of representation. What are the biases in terms of representation for women, people of color, gays and lesbians, different social group? Muslims, for instance are now a demonized group in the media.

We look critically at the representations of media, but we also look at issues of power, who controls the power of representation. It's basically just a few media corporations: the big television networks, film companies, music conglomerates, advertising agencies, and the like.

Now when you turn to new media, it becomes a very different story in terms of power, that anyone can do it. So that's one of the encouraging things that anyone can make a YouTube. Anyone can Twitter. Anyone can set up a blog.

DM: I know, it's a major shift.

DK: So that's really quite an astounding dichotomy here where we have old media, media literacy, a top-down model that's been ignored in the schools, and then we have new media is like bottom up. It's something that's been engaged in the schools. It's a booming field in every way, from production to academic studies.

DM: I read a statistic about how much teens are creating media.

DK: Right, yes. So that's really encouraging. Whereas the other is really discouraging. [laughs] So it's sort of a schizophrenic field in that sense.

DM: I feel that. [laughs] That's great. OK. I always find it astounding in terms of educating educators because it's not on their radar, and they don't understand the power structures. You take for granted people assume that they are media literate. But when you tell them the actual facts about who is controlling their news channels and such, there's this look of complete shock.

DK: I mean, that's part of literacy, seeing Fox News is just straight up right-wing propaganda. That CNN tries to be middle of the road, but some of the different people have their biases. MSNBC now is being straight up left wing with Keith Olbermann, Rachel Maddow, Ed Schultz, and others. So you have to see what the biases are of the different television shows, and even networks. To be news media literate, you need to know how to read these networks. And this is, I think, another thing that's been neglected, things like news information journalism. Media education tends to focus on entertainment: images of women, blacks, gays, whoever, and neglects teaching reading news and information critically.

DM: Or being able to identify what is a message. Sometimes I think when I talk to teens about media and have them try to identify, they don't really even understand that they're seeing a message, that there's an agenda there.

DK: Exactly. So that's why you need sort of basic literacy of how to read, to see messages, to see narratives, to see biases, and things like that. But there really isn't even a field; it's so undeveloped. There are just individuals trying to do this, that, and the other thing. But there are some individuals, like the people you're interviewing, who have done a lot in their personal teaching and their writing trying to do this, that, and the other thing. So it's not that there's been a complete lack of effort, or there's no one out there doing it.

There are. Quite a few people. But just on the policy level and on the program level . . .

DM: Right, the effects of all this work is hard to see. The outcomes. The outcomes are hard to grasp.

DK: But I'll bet if you talk to people from China and Australia, you're going to get a quite different narrative. In this regard, the U.S. is underdeveloped and backward, as it were. Whereas you wouldn't say this about computer education. The U.S. is right up there. There are plenty of schools, even poor schools, that give every student a computer because they got a grant, or teach computer literacy in education.

Robert Kubey

Robert Kubey is professor and director of the Center for Media Studies in the Department of Journalism and Media Studies at the School of Communication and Information at Rutgers, the State University of New Jersey. His latest book is *Creating Television: Conversations with the People Behind 50 Years of American TV*, with other books including *Media Literacy in the Information Age* and *Television and the Quality of Life: How Viewing Shapes Everyday Experience*. He received his doctorate from the Committee on Human Development in the Department of Behavioral Sciences at the University of Chicago.

Edited Transcript: Interview, April 14, 2011
Interviewer: Dee Morgenthaler

DM: What inspired your journey in terms of getting to the point of looking at media and media education? Generally, how did you become involved in media education, if you want to talk a little bit about what got you interested from the start?

RK: I had been hearing about it (media education) going back before 1984 or so, and I remember contacting Aimee Dorr, the dean of the Education School at UCLA. Then I saw Aimee Dorr at a conference that was in Gutersloh, Germany, and this was in part looking at media literacy, and there were people from various countries there. These international conferences were very helpful, and for years, and maybe even to this day, to try and sell media literacy in the United States, some of us would bring in people from the United Kingdom, Australia, and Canada, to do tutorials, to do like a two-day workshop in media literacy. It was as if people were flown in to rescue the backward Americans. The United States has not led the way in media literacy education.

So I started looking into it and I felt strongly that it was an important cause. I learned enough about it to write my first article on the subject for *Education Week* and that was in 1991, called "The Case for Media Education."

Kathleen Tyner really liked the one-page article and that was encouraging. She had founded Strategies for Media Literacy some years before. The article then got republished a number of times. And from then on, I was fairly active in working in the area.

I've published four or five general articles in *Education Week* and other periodicals outside of the field. And I've published a number of research-related articles.

Frank Baker and I did a paper called "Obstacles to Media Literacy" in which we looked at all 50 states in terms of whether they had state standards calling for the critical study of media in students. Frank did most of the work, I must say. The article was well received and republished a number of times.

Some years later, I got a fellowship at the Annenberg School at the University of Pennsylvania to look at the obstacles to the development of media literacy in the United States. I wrote about why it's difficult to get media literacy curricula in schools.

Renee Hobbes and I started a media literacy series for Lawrence Erlbaum wherein various authors would write their own volumes. We published five volumes.

DM: Were you teaching at Rutgers when you got started?

RK: Yes, I was. I've been at Rutgers since 1985.

DM: Were there certain theoretical inspirations or certain scholars that you were reading at the time that got you thinking about media literacy in education?

RK: Len Masterman had published his book then and I found it to be very useful. He is someone I've admired for a long time. I also admired Kathleen Tyner for publishing *Stategies in Media Literacy*. Renee Hobbs and I were both fellows in media literacy at the University of Pennsylvania. Kathleen Hall Jamieson, who was the dean of the Annenberg School and one of the most powerful voices in media studies decided the first year of the Annenberg Scholars Program would focus on media literacy. Five scholars spent a semester at the University of Pennsylvania at the Annenberg School. The fellowship was helpful in getting the group of us to work on media literacy together, but mostly to publish articles or books on the subject. In a book called *Media Literacy in the Information Age,* I published chapters by all five of the fellows and a great many more.

As a result of the Annenberg School's media literacy scholars program, Renee Hobbs and I launched a media literacy series of books published under the Lawrence Erlbaum imprint.

DM: Did you have specific goals with your work? I know you were talking about the barriers to media literacy. Did you have specific goals in mind?

RK: Right. I recognized that there was a real importance to the field, but a status in schools that hadn't yet been fully realized. Indeed, most schools were doing no media education at all.

DM: Can you talk a bit about the barriers to media education?

RK: They're best covered in the two articles I've written on that subject. There was an important conference that was held in Guelph, Canada, where I first met Renee Hobbes and David Considine and others. I did taped interviews with all of them precisely on the topic of why they thought media education had been so slow to develop in the United States. What were the barriers? And also what their experience had been in their countries.

David Considine told me that in Australia, and this is true for Canada as well, that a force or lever that helped jump-start media education was the tremendous amount of U.S. media, especially television, coming into their countries.

We're all English-speaking countries, of course, and they see an awful lot of our programs and we see almost none of theirs. And that makes for a certain amount of, if not anti-Americanism, a protectionist attitude in Australia and Canada.

One of their media education goals was for kids to analyze, in part, what messages were coming from the United States and what values in TV programs were Australian values or Canadian values versus U.S. values. Many of which are, of course, the same, but some were a tad different.

And so this flooding of their countries with U.S. television programs served as a lever for Australians and the Canadians, a lever we in the U.S. did not have because our television and other media are not being overwhelmed by another media system.

American programs, particularly dramatic one-hour programs, were often doing their shooting in Vancouver because it was cheaper to get crews up in Vancouver than it was in and around Los Angeles or other U.S. locations.

They would actually put U.S. mailboxes out in these locales and remove the Canadian ones so it would look like a U.S. location, and this just really pissed off the Canadians, as you can understand. An example I often use is to imagine if 50 percent of the media coming into the United States was Australian or Japanese and what that might feel like.

I would some times get into a bit of trouble in the early days when I was speaking about this at a conference and I would talk about "American values." What I meant was "United States values" and I would upset the Canadians a bit who, of course, would point out that they were also part of

North America. I learned that I should not assume that the United States was all of America.

Another obstacle is the lack of solid quantitative "before–after" studies looking at the efficacy of media literacy instruction and whether students' scores on a number of outcome variables such as *critical thinking* increased after they had received media literacy training.

But what outcome measures exist are often reported in media literacy journals or newsletters or things like that and they don't hit the mainstream. The majority of studies use qualitative rather than quantitative measures. Much as I've published other scholars' qualitative studies, I think in the U.S. it will be quantitative measures that will win the day. If you could show that there was some statistically significant spillover effect from media literacy instruction that also helped general reading or writing scores, you could sell media literacy like hotcakes. Or at least get education schools in the country to sit up and take notice and begin to consider teaching media literacy in their schools.

This is a huge barrier. If it could be overcome, media literacy would find a place in our schools. But unless media literacy is mandated in states' standards it is not likely that media education will be taught in education schools. And even when it is mandated, in most states there is no requirement that it actually be taught.

Another big obstacle is teachers' reluctance to add still another element to the curriculum. They're already asked to teach to meet many standards and adding another meets with resistance.

They're always being told to teach more stuff and it's not very often the case that something's pulled out of all the curriculum that teachers need to teach, so they feel overburdened and they feel underappreciated across the different fields.

Then you come along with this thing called media literacy, and actually sometimes if you teach it the way it's taught some places, you would say that one of the things you want kids to be able to critique are the textbooks themselves. A lot of teachers aren't keen on kids questioning the textbook or questioning *them*. But that's part of critical thinking about media and about what media are conveying information to children. There's advertising on TV and there are movies and there are video games and all these other things.

People in schools might say "We don't want children watching more television. We don't want to bring television into our school."

Children are spending an average of three hours a day with television. When you look at all media combined it comes up that the average kid is spending something like seven hours a day in contact with media, so that includes video games, surfing Internet sites, chat rooms, all this other stuff.

Then when you look at kids multitasking: listening to music at the same time that they're goofing around with a video game, or things like that, the number of hours in contact with media exceeds seven hours. It gets to be an enormous amount of time, so many of us think schools should address this.

But schools are too overwhelmed already to address the standard curricula, and then there's the real snob effect where people say, "Oh, we sure don't want to talk about television, and certainly not video games, in our classrooms."

And many teachers, some older teachers, are sort of more set in their ways, and they don't want to try to learn a whole new curriculum or part of a new curriculum which media literacy, or media education represents.

And then some people scoff at the term *media literacy*. They go, "What do you mean being literate? Literacy is about reading. It's not about reading television."

DM: Can you elaborate on your philosophical approach to media education?

RK: It's important to recognize at this point that there are a couple types of media literacy. There's a protectionist side, which is saying, "Television's bad, video games are bad. We need to protect our children"—the inoculationist view says that we need to inoculate our children against the media. But then there's the cultural studies approach, which celebrates the media or wants to look at how the media positions different subjects. It's not about condemning the media.

And so you can have many positive things that are said about media, and then there are the people who, as part of the curriculum are teaching kids to be more selective and discriminating, and that would include me. I used to say I didn't care so much that kids were spending three hours a day with television, it's what television they were choosing to look at.

So I was sort of being a snob and a protectionist in my own right. So then there are people who cross over and do both sides, and I think both sides need to be counted on. To use a technical term, for me, and I'm joking now, it's a *mushy field*. It's a soft field, and so then it's easily attacked by people who don't know very much about it and scoff at the term *media literacy*. With the rise of the Internet, *digital literacy* is probably an easier sell.

DM: In terms of the field in general, do you have a feel for where we're going in terms of the scholarly discipline around the subject? Do you have an opinion of where it is right now? Where it should go or the direction it should go forward?

RK: When one looks at other English-speaking countries, we are the furthest behind in media literacy education.

Education schools just don't teach media literacy. But when you can't sell it very well at the university level, people ask, "Where are the next media literacy teachers going to come from?"

If it's not being taught in education schools, where's it going to be taught? That's partly because there aren't many people who've got their PhDs in media education, and there is no place that offers a PhD in media literacy to my knowledge.

Interestingly, private schools have had much more leeway to teach about media and values and things like that, whereas public schools are further behind.

Len Masterman

Known as the originator of the idea of media representation and the *Key Concepts of Media Literacy*, Len Masterman started his career as a teacher. He became an international sensation with the 1980 publication of his book *Teaching about Television*, which sold out twice on its print run in the first six months of publication and ultimately sold 100,000 copies worldwide after five years of rejection by many publishers. His subsequent book, *Teaching the Media*, applies the systematic framework he developed to media as a whole; this book was published in 1985. Masterman is now retired.

Edited Transcript: Interview, November 3, 2010
Interviewer: Dee Morgenthaler

LM: Basically, I suppose there was no such thing as a media education movement when I started. Not only that, but it seemed improbable—to me, at any rate—that there could ever be a possibility that something as heterogeneous as the mass media could be studied in a disciplined and rigorous way. That's because the whole notion of the mass media covers such a wide range of different practices that any idea that you could gather together—the fields of film, advertising, radio, newspapers, magazines, and whatever else—into a coherent field seemed unlikely.

There were, to be fair, *some* courses existing in schools and higher education on media studies, but they weren't really subjects in a traditional sense—the school ones that I knew of—and there were precious few of them (maybe one or two nationally). They would consist of an English teacher doing half a term on a bit of film, half a term on a bit of advertising, an occasional look at a newspaper or two, and that would be it.

But as for giving any thought to what connected these fields, the teachers weren't really getting very far with that. In fact, they weren't even asking the question. So the people who were doing it were really asking different questions of different media, and that meant that there wasn't really any such thing as "media studies" as a subject.

There was a branch of sociology which studied the media in terms of media effects and looked at the media in relation to different sets of social issues and so on, but that was really a branch of sociology.

And media was studied within English and English teaching (as an adjunct to literature) so that occasionally an English teacher might use a film as the basis for the kind of discussion that you would normally get through studying a book or a play.

And there's also been a strain of English teaching, which has been pretty hostile to the media, in which you would study advertising—very much from the point of view of looking at the way in which you manipulated audiences and so on.

So what existed up until about the 1960s was a sort of study of the media that was split around the different subjects, but with no coherent approach that might justify the notion that this was a subject that was actually worth studying in its own right.

I started teaching as an English teacher in the early '60s, and I did a bit of media teaching. One of the earliest pioneers of using media within English teaching was a guy called F. R. Leavis, who was probably the foremost literary critic and academic of his day. He was a Cambridge don, and his background was to look at the media as a kind of disease. He introduced what is now generally known as the inoculation approach to media study.

That is, it sees media as an almost totally malign influence, and you need to give kids small doses of it in order to inoculate them against the infection, as it were. And his background was interesting, because it's not something that ever appeared in any of his published work, but during the First World War, he was an ambulance worker, stretcher bearer; and the kinds of things he must have seen on the battlefield from the First World War are beyond imagining, really.

During virtually all wars, of course, it is pretty widely known that there is an enormous amount of propaganda and censorship. I think that, in the First World War, the degree of censorship was such that the people at home really didn't know firsthand many of the details of what was happening. So the support for the war never really wavered, and there was a great deal of censorship, and the people who were reporting it, of course, weren't inclined to write about things that might affect patriotism at home and the prosecution of the war, and so on.

So I think Leavis must have caught on to that. Although, as I said, it's all supposition; putting what I know about the man and his writing together, I would say that probably that was a sort of traumatizing experience that made him want to encourage people to look critically and closely at the media.

He was somebody who was hostile to the media but yet could see that it had a place in schools. And since he was an academic with such a formidable intellectual reputation, that gave quite a lot of impetus to English teachers to use media materials in a critical way in their classes.

His big book was one that he wrote in 1933 called *Culture and Environment*. It was still in print in '63 when I started teaching. It'd gone through about 30-odd impressions. So it was a sort of handbook for teachers on how to use the media and how to analyze adverts and so on.

The other book, I suppose, that was around when I started was a book by Vance Packard called *The Hidden Persuaders*. I don't know if you've ever come across that. It was really about the use of what he called *depth psychology* in the making of advertising and the influence of psychology within advertising.

And the idea there really came out of the use of psychological techniques by the American military. And when the Korean War ended, a lot of these people in psych (what we would now call PSYOPS) were turned back into civil society.

A lot of them found work on Madison Avenue and said, "Look. There are ways in which we can actually manipulate people." It was deliberately scary but actually the use of depth psychology in advertising was never that significant as Packard made out. It was a sensationalist sort of book. But it had a tremendous impact really at the time. It was a big seller on both sides of the Atlantic.

DM: How old were your students?

LM: When I started teaching I was teaching secondary school so that would be 11 to 18.

DM: And how did they receive your material?

LM: They loved it. As you probably know, anything from popular culture that gets into the classroom is well received. So it was always something that they liked a great deal. I suppose the big thing for me as an English teacher was moving on to work with kids who found print difficult, who were not good readers. I was sort of forced to look at what you did as an English teacher which is essentially a print-based subject . . . what you do with kids who equate print with failure and really don't want to have much to do with the written word.

So I started with students like that to use film quite a bit. And I was one of the first people, I think, to use film widely within the curriculum as an English teacher.

And I wrote quite a bit about that at the time. And just about that time film was starting to be used in the UK; in teacher training colleges where the future training teachers were being encouraged to work in film.

When I came out of a university culture where film was very important in the 1960s, late '50s–early '60s, the sort of social realism film was starting to take off, producing work of major interest and importance. The French New Wave film, European cinema was undergoing a major renaissance.

It just seemed, at the time, that some of the most significant and important ideas and aesthetic notions were coming out of film rather than out of the novel and the theater. So it was quite natural I think for teachers like me, who were just starting to use this kind of stuff in their lessons.

So that's basically how I started, as an English teacher who increasingly began to use media material. I suppose it is a similar trajectory to somebody like Barry Duncan who was also, I think, English-based, who found that the media material he used was pretty appealing and used more and more of it.

Then I got a job working in the education department of a university. One of the things I discovered in using film, particularly using foreign films, was that of course kids who had difficulty with reading, couldn't follow the subtitles.

I was using foreign films because the promise of visual medium was that they would get over the idea that print is a problem. But students couldn't follow the subtitles fast enough. That was a flop. It was a sort of massive failure on my part and sort of a major, major mistake. How stupid can you be?

So . . . I was talking about John Ford and Alfred Hitchcock and the major directors and treating them as kind of authors in the same way that you would a poet or a dramatist in literature.

But to the kids I was working with, they were as remote as, I don't know, Shakespeare, Shelly, Keats, Byron, and so on. And so it just struck me then, particularly working with more challenging students, that it might make more sense to look critically at what their primary visual experience was; and that, of course, was through TV.

What's interesting is that film started to become respectable in education at precisely the point in history where cinemas were starting to close down. And film had less and less (or fewer and fewer) credentials to be considered a mass medium, anyway.

So television was something that people were watching 20-plus hours a week. Some of the kids I was teaching didn't have a cinema within close reach. So they never went to the cinema.

So I went on teaching film on the grounds that it was close to students' experience. It wasn't close to the experience at all. So, what's interesting is the sort of progress that I made in my own thinking was based on the failure of what I was doing.

And I was trying to think, I was getting closer and closer to what might connect with the kids. When it proved that film wasn't the answer, then I was driven to look at what was more relevant.

And that's what really led me into TV, and TV teaching. I think I mentioned that I did actually teach the first examined course in television studies.

We set that up in the early '70s when I started at the University in Nottingham. That gave me the time and the flexibility to go out into a school and teach a much more kind of experimental course than would have been possible if I had been a full-time member of the teaching staff.

So I used to go out two afternoons a week to teach this course for a period of four years. The idea there was to just take a single medium and study that in a disciplined kind of way. What was challenging about that was the fact that I mentioned: the heterogeneous nature of the media.

Well that also applied to TV. It wasn't at all clear to me when I started. But television covers so many fields. It covers anything and everything you can imagine.

So you are studying television, but you could be studying football or music or a documentary of a news or an advert. It wasn't clear to me what you were studying, how could you encapsulate a field of study that was so diverse and so heterogeneous into a form of study that was focused and disciplined. In other words, TV forced me to think about what is the nature of what we are studying when we are studying. Is there a key to this that would draw these things together? I suppose the big step forward was to recognize that what we are actually studying here was television and not its subject contents. That is what we were studying, we weren't actually studying sport and music and news and documentary. We were studying representations of these things.

We were studying the ways in which these were being represented and symbolized and packaged by the medium. So that seemed a sort of major step forward. That what we were looking at was how television in particular, was trying to (and still does, and so does the press of course) present itself as being a window on the world. The analogy is with a transparent sheet of glass that you can look through. Ideally when you are looking at TV, you are actually looking through a window at reality. And what that denies is human agency, what it denies is the fact that these images are actually produced; they are selected and edited and packaged.

The seamlessness and reality of television is something that someone actually produced. In other words, what we are dealing with is a symbolic system.

And that is true of news and football and documentary film. So that thing to me came to be a fairly major step forward.

And from there it was possible to see, once you accept that what you are dealing with is a symbolic system, what you are dealing with is a construction; you take that as your focusing question. Then a whole set of satellite questions immediately present themselves.

For instance, if we are looking at representations then who is creating them, who is doing the representing? Who is telling us whose view is this of the world, who is telling us that this is the way the world is? Secondly what's the nature of the world that's being represented? What are its values? And that leads you straight into the questions of ideology.

And now that was important to me because it was one of the reasons I wanted to get into the whole thing about TV, apart from it being close to the experience of this student audience; it wouldn't have interested me if I hadn't been fairly convinced of the ideological role of the media in contemporary societies.

And there is long tradition of that. That carries on with the ideological view of the propaganda nature of the media. It carries on from the view of the Frankfurt School of Sociologists who, of course, were forced to get out of Frankfurt in the 1930s and to work in America once the Nazis got into power.

And they were particularly concerned with media study and with the importance and significance of the media because of the significance of propaganda within the development of fascism in Germany in the '30s.

So there is a strong tradition of looking at the impact of the media in mass societies, not only to encourage mass forms of production but also to encourage mass forms of thinking. The impacts of the media are of great ideological significance; that has been a strong impetus within the study of media. So that's the second sort of question, the ideological question.

Then there is the third kind of question: How are these representations made to be so seemingly authentic and true to life? How is it that we accept this as a kind of reality? And that leads you into the whole field of media language, and to learn how meaning is created.

And also the force of affective questions or questions of audience. How is the audience affected by these representations? How are they read and understood? Is it possible to read against the grain of these images, and so on?

So they were the sort of main areas of study. And pretty soon it seemed to me that I had what looked like, first of all, a reasonably coherent field to study, which is a sort of first requirement of any sort of discipline. You've got to be able to say what stands inside and outside of the field.

Any discipline worth its salt has got to have a set of key questions and issues that it thinks are important. It has got to have some key ideas and key concepts. They were already starting to form in my mind. And it's got to have a particular and characteristic mode of inquiry.

And that was something that I was talking about that developed in relation to studying the media. So you start off by actually looking at media texts, by looking at the literal meanings, the connotative meanings or what actually is being communicated here. What I was working on in early 1970 (1972–74) were things that are very familiar now: the constituents of the image. So what I was starting to get into was sort of really from the scratch, getting together the basics of what looked like a disciplined form of study. I started off by looking at constituents of the image, reading still images, reading moving images, looking at stuff that's now fairly commonplace like body language, like the way in which meaning is communicated through clothing and gesture, facial expression, and so on.

And so clarifying and making clear what the image was actually communicating at its simplest and most literal levels, then looking at connotative levels of meaning: What's being suggested here? Moving beyond the literal, reading between the lines of the image, what is it that's being presented? What's the point of view? What are the suggestions of those connotative, of those denotative levels that we've sketched out?

And then finally, can all of these connotations be pulled together to form a coherent sort of ideological position? And the idea there is that every image has a point of view, quite literally.

When you're watching television or film or looking at a photograph, there is a literal point of view. You know, where is the camera positioned? And that notion of a point of view . . . you can't have a view that's no view, as it were.

And the BBC's position is that it's sort of on Mount Olympus somewhere . . .

DM: Right. [laughs]

LM: . . . or up in the heavens with this view that is no view. And the idea there is that the physical point of view is also an intellectual point of view. If you're covering a piece of industrial action, like a strike or something like that, where you have the camera makes all the difference in the world. If the police forces are galloping towards you because you're in there amongst the strikers, that presents a very different image from the impression that you get if you're actually behind police lines and the strikers' missiles are being thrown directly at you.

Roland Barthes, a French writer, called ideology the final connotation of the connotations. That is, when you look at all of those suggestions of meanings, what does it all actually amount to? And that takes us into the field of ideology.

So when I wrote a book about that, *Teaching about Television*, I had great difficulty in finding a publisher. Nobody was interested in it. Mainly because people would, quite rightly, say, "Well, who teaches about television?" So, well, I'm hoping it might take off. [laughter]

But who would buy it? Where's the market? I said, "Well, I was hoping to create one, really." But it was really, finally, sort of published by Macmillan as a favor. Somebody at the director level at Macmillan knew somebody at the Independent Television Authority who'd actually financed some of my research, and they published it as a sort of favor. They published it in 1980, I'd finished it in about 1975, so it took about five years to get it published.

DM: Wow.

LM: And what was amazing is that within about six months I was touring Australia . . . [laughter]

. . . giving lectures about it, going to Canada and heaven knows, and all over Europe and working for the Council of Europe and UNESCO. It sold out twice on its print run in the first six months. And I think it still might be in print, actually, but it sold about 100,000 copies. And all of those publishers who'd rejected it . . .

DM: [laughs]

LM: . . . wrote back and said, "If you're ever thinking about writing anything else . . ." [laughter]

DM: Let us know.

LM: [laughs] And could you give us first refusal? So that was a kind of interesting experience, but what that opened out to me was, of course, the fact that if you could make a disciplined study of TV, then maybe, actually, the basis of this framework might work for the media as a whole. And that led me on to write the book that in a way was easier to write, because it was based on quite a lot of thinking and work that I'd already done, and that was *Teaching the Media*. It came out in 1985.

So we're up to [laughs] . . . look, we're up to 1985. We've only got 30 years to go.

DM: Right. We're doing well. And, actually, you are answering all of my questions intuitively, so there you go . . .

LM: I'm giving you a sort of chronological account as far as I can remember it really.

DM: Absolutely. It's perfect.

LM: So, yes, it just seemed to me that maybe that kind of framework might be subject to one's own interpretations.

DM: Right.

LM: So I think David Buckingham, while critical of my work, was actually, without acknowledging it as with the BFI [British Film Institute] documents, taking on the conceptual approach that I'd developed while having severe reservations about what they thought was an approach that was a bit too ideological itself.

DM: Right. Almost talking about the same things but not realizing it. [laughs]

LM: Well, what I'm trying to do is to point out that questions of ideology are central, which I would still argue, without saying that the teacher ought to encourage students to take up an ideological position.

DM: Right.

LM: It's about posing the question. It's about consciousness raising.

DM: Right.

LM: It's the same arguments with racism and feminism and I mean it's the same argument with humor. We did quite a bit of work on comedy. The last thing you can do is to say, "The jokes that you're laughing at aren't funny."

DM: Right. [laughs]

LM: [laughs] I mean you can't actually say that, because if people find it funny, then it's funny. But what you can do is raise questions about it and problemetize it and say, "Have you thought about this, and have you thought about that?" And they'll start to think about it, to muddy the water a little bit. It's to make them take things a little bit less for granted. That's what I take to be consciousness raising—raising to consciousness questions and issues that have been taken for granted.

And that's where I think ideology lies in the taken-for-granted nature of the world in which we live and our assumptions about it.

So I mean what was gratifying was, whenever I've done international conferences (I did a big international conference in Toronto in the year 2000 with representatives of some 75 countries, I think) to see people from countries that I didn't even know were countries saying, "Well, we do all the key concepts." Or somebody from India saying, "Oh, yeah, we've got a good network in India, and we're all using the key concepts," you know?

DM: Right.

LM: It's just fantastic.

DM: Right.

LM: That's just fantastic.

DM: That is. That's amazing.

LM: And I think that's the way in which, generally, the subject is now approached even with emulation to the new technologies. The key and critical questions remain the same. Where is this stuff coming from? Whose interests are being served by it? How reliable is it? How can we read it? How are we intended to read it? Can you read against it? What are the values implicit in it? And what's the ideological position that's being underpinned?

And I mean the most important ideological step of all, I think, is taken when you just actually ask the questions. That is, as soon as you crack the taken-for-granted realism of the Internet or of the TV, as soon as you say, "This isn't reality, but a representation of it," then you've made the most profound ideological step of all.

You're saying that what I previously took to be an item, an article of faith, or part of the laws of nature, are actually *representations*. They're constructs. And therefore this impinges on major questions of culture and identity and race, because issues of representation are absolutely central to that.

And representation is the key concept of all the concepts, I think, because in media we're dealing with representational systems or a representational system, and therefore, the key questions there are the key questions in relation to questions of identity and race and culture, and so on.

What is being represented, how are my views being represented, who is representing and speaking for me, and which are the voices which never get represented? And you've got there the basic [laughs] key questions for any of the most important areas of study, new areas of study, in the school and university curriculum.

DM: Right.

LM: And they'll all actually then come back to media, because that is the most important symbolic representational system in our conscience.

Barrie McMahon

Barrie McMahon has been a classroom teacher, media studies consultant, and curriculum manager with the Department of Education and Training in Western Australia. Since his retirement, he has taken up positions in the private sector and with Curtin University. He describes his current status as "author in search of a publisher." His one-year fellowship in England in 1972 led to his long career focus on media education and to his subsequent work in global media literacy. He began his career teaching English in a country town in Western Australia.

Edited Transcript: Interview, March 21, 2011
Interviewer: Tessa Jolls

TJ: How did you become involved in media literacy?

BM: There are probably a couple of contextual things that are pertinent to education in Western Australia that I should address before I get into the details of my history in media education. One is that in Australia, the state governments control education; there are six states and two territories, and they control the education systems. There are slight variations in each of the states and territories in the curriculum and there are also variations in the practices. That has been the case since time began but at this moment there are hopes to move towards a national curriculum. But even if that takes, the states will still run education. So that's what's important contextually; in the U.S. local boards run education.

In the late '60s, early '70s, the Western Australian education system was probably the most centralized education system in the world, and it is still highly centralized. So traditionally, innovation came from the top down. Western Australia is a million square miles, that's about a third of the United States, and there are only at the moment 2.5 million people. The philosophy is that, irrespective of the geography, each individual is entitled to quality education. So it is necessary to have education for those in the city and those in the remote areas of a comparable quality.

The third contextual element regarding the '60s and '70s, at the time in Western Australia (actually all across Australia), is that there were no universities offering any courses remotely connected to media education, or even media studies; it was almost a barren field to try to explore. That's the background of what education was like in Western Australia at the time.

TJ: What were some milestones for you along the way?

BM: I had taught for the first eight years of my teaching career in a country town and changed in 1967 into a working-class metropolitan school and it was a very different experience. I guess teaching in the country was a breeze because teaching kids down the street, you knew their parents and so on. Teaching in the city was much more factory-like; it was quite a different experience. I was teaching English at the time. I found that I had students in my class who were children of immigrants. They were bright enough kids, but they had little interest in traditional English values such as teaching Shakespeare and other classical literature or even of poetry, words meant nothing to them.

So this was a bit of a challenge; my whole background has been education. I'm not a film buff, although I am these days, nor am I a computer nerd or anything like that, my prime interest is education, so I was looking for a way of engaging these kids in stories that seemed to be relevant to them. One of my jobs was as the head of the department; we were going to take the kids to a camp over the weekend and I thought this is going to be a nightmare, if all we did in the camp was to try to get students to recite Shakespeare and learn poems. We were looking for something a little more lively than that.

One of the teachers said, "I know a person who makes films in drama classes with kids." And I said, "Well, let's bring that person along and see if we can have some satisfaction with the kids regarding filmmaking." At the time, in the late '60s, Super 8 was a big thing, and so at the camp, we used Super 8 and I just watched the kids engaged in narrative and storytelling in a different fashion. They spent hours and hours, not only during weekend camp but afterwards on their own time finishing their films. So when I got back to the school I telephoned the Education Department and said I needed to find someone either inside or outside of our centralized system, who knows anything about making films because I'd like to learn something about it and then build that into the English curriculum. By coincidence, someone had walked through the door almost the same day from outside the system and said he was interested in doing that.

So we got some outside help to have the students make these films and they were quite successful. What I also found was that other teachers became very interested as well because it is a great incentive to other teachers to have very responsive students who lap up at everything you put in front of them.

So that progressed for a couple of years, and at that stage, it wasn't anything more than simply making films as part of English. The idea spread a little bit so we formed an association called the Screen Education Association, which consisted of 10 or 12 people that were from various schools and we would get together from time to time and run our own professional development to learn more about what was going on with these students.

Then in 1972, I had swapped schools a couple of times since then, and had done the same things at the other schools I went to. I applied for an Education Department fellowship or scholarship; we only had one a year where they give someone a 12-month study leave to Europe, overseas, or somewhere. I applied for it and I got it.

It was really a bold move on the part of the department because the fellowship was traditionally given to some senior ranking educator who wanted to introduce a new way of assessment or something like that. But the bureaucrat that I spoke to said, "Look, I don't quite understand what you are doing but it makes sense, you've built a bit of a track record." So in '72–'73, I took my family and we went to England to study for a year, at the Hornsey College of Art in London, which later became the Kingston Polytechnic. They had a course that was remotely connected to media, something called design education. What attracted me to it was that the method of learning was incredibly flexible; you could effectively map out your own curriculum. I also found that there was another campus that was doing a film studies course so I did both courses at the same time.

Every other bit of study I've done in my life had been external study (part-time study), and here I was a full-time student at 32. It was great fun. We were used to being in such an isolated Australian city (in fact the most remote capital city in the world; the closest capital city is 2,500 miles away), and we'd never been out of Australia before, so during the breaks, we would get in a camper van that we had and trip around Britain, and I would visit schools and teachers that I heard were doing a little bit in the way of media education, things like audio tapes, slide programs, sometimes film (although film was a bit expensive). And I would do recordings and so on. So I was soaking up every little bit of experience as I possibly could. During the major breaks and towards the end of the course, we took the camper out around Europe doing the same sort of things, visiting people in different countries who either had some experience with media education; and of course as that was happening, I was gathering ideas that were a little bit beyond the original premise of film study.

I was also trying to absorb the different philosophies and ideologies and got in touch with the Screen Education Society for screen education in Britain and the British Film Institute and their equivalents to other parts of Europe as well. They were all very generous with their ideas. At the end of the 12 months in Britain, we came home via Canada and the United States and once again I did the same thing. The States I found at that time, quite disappointing, actually. I found some contacts in Canada and that was my first contact with the people in Toronto (we're talking 1973 by now). And I had even written to Marshall McLuhan, and he was the most generous with his time. We heard him give a lecture and he spent half a day with me, talking about his views on media education. One of the things that stuck in my mind . . . I said, "Well its fine if you're here in Toronto, you've got a rich environment in media, but I'm going back to a place in the bottom left-hand corner of the Earth where there's no such environment; it's going to be pretty hard to know where to start." And his comment was, "That's the best environment you can go into because you don't have to knock down any outdated monuments, you can start fresh."

So I came back to Australia full of ideas and enthusiasm. And McLuhan's prediction proved to be accurate as far as my state was concerned. Victoria, for example, had a fairly good history of film culture and the study of film which impeded for awhile (not now) the development of other areas of study in media. The education that they thought was media education was really audio visual aid material, using audio and visual aids to further science or mathematics or whatever. By this time the small Screen Education Society that we had established had collapsed. The people had gone on to do other things.

It was normal that when people had done the year's scholarship study, they went back to their previous position. But in September 1974, I met with the bureaucrats and said I wanted to pick a school and establish a viable media education program in that one school. Then we could have teachers and other interested people come in and see their lessons in action. They said, yep, that sounds pretty good (they had a vested interest in getting back the money that was spent on me.)

Yes, there were the usual blockages. With my prime interest in education rather than the gadgets, I was talking about team teaching and all those sort of things, and some of the traditionalists would say, "Ah, team teaching has never worked, we've got to have them sitting in lines in classrooms to have proper discipline." You get all those sort of arguments which just didn't suit the sort of thing that I knew would work in media education, which is having kids in groups working together with maximum flexibility, both inside and outside of the classroom. But eventually they said, "Yes, you better design a curriculum and tell us how much money you want to run it."

So I did that, and picked out a school, a school that was just starting out, that only had Years 8 and 9, so that the program could grow with the school. The condition I laid down from the start was that every student in the school did media education as a subject and that we would have a place on the time table equivalent of any other subject in the school. And they agreed to that.

So that's what we did for the first couple of years. We just grew the program within the school, and teachers from outside came in almost in uncontrollable numbers to see what was going on; and even those who weren't interested in starting media education program, specifically, were interested in building it into their English programs, their science programs or whatever. It was good that the period coincided with an era with the Australian government, when after 23 years the Conservatives were ousted in the federal government and the Labor party came into power for three years. One of the changes was that a lot of money was injected into education innovation and professional development, so we took advantage of that money in professional development and ran courses for teachers—extensive courses, five days; we worked 12 hours a day to develop some skills. And we had to do it ourselves, teachers had to do it, because as I mentioned there were no teacher institutions at all in Australia who were providing such courses.

What I've found is that the most adaptable teachers were those who had about 6, 7, 8, 9, 10 years of experience who were good teachers but looking for something new that would excite their students. We developed a group of enthusiasts amongst scores of teachers, hundreds of teachers. The program became so big that one school couldn't handle it. By this time the idea had spread to several schools and other people took it up, but on the professional development side of it, one school just couldn't keep up. So I convinced the bureaucrats in the department to give me a mobile resort, at first I thought maybe a big London bus, a big red double-decker bus, but we found that it wouldn't fit under the bridges in Western Australia, so we had to abandon that idea. And I settled for a 22-foot caravan, towed by a truck with a built-in television studio in the back. The caravan in particular, and the truck was well suited to the teachers' needs. We used to call ourselves the Mickey Mouse Multimedia Mob, I'm not sure if Mickey Mouse has the same meaning in America. We use the term *Mickey Mouse* to talk about something cheap and something nasty.

We actually thought it was a great motif to go with because what we wanted the teachers to use was equipment that was cheap and sometimes nasty because that's all they could get a hold of. If you're going to need a $30,000 mini television studio before you set this up in your school, it was never going to happen. But if we could say to them, look, you can buy a

Russian 35 mm camera for $6, you've got a chance of getting something going. So we actually had the T-shirts with Mickey Mouse on them, cameras out of his ears, everything like that. And I got the teachers themselves during the Christmas holiday (we have a long period of holiday, it's during summertime) to come in and they worked fitting out the caravan and I got some people who knew something about it, volunteers, and electricians, plumbers, to figure out the technical bits. So the television studio was all done with Portapacks. I don't know if you remember VHS Portapacks, heavy things . . . awful! But we modified them so we could use them in the studio. Then we used that truck and the caravan to go around the state and also the metropolitan area to teach teachers and also to give demonstrations.

We'd get a class of kids into the caravan and the teachers would come with them and watch the kids engage in film education, photography, audio sounds, you name it. So in that way, we were able to give the same sort of service in the country areas as the city. By this time, the Education Department has acknowledged that the program was quite a success and they gave me more staff. I think that's one of the key differences in what happened in Western Australia and what happened in Toronto. In order to beat the system in Australia, you'd have to use the system. I needed to have senior bureaucrats who were favorably disposed to what I was doing; whereas in Toronto, where it was quite decentralized, it was the Professional Teachers Association who really carried the momentum. For years, no one was employed by the Canadian education department on a salary to further media education.

TJ: It sounds like you were able to really establish media education at grassroots, provide professional development, do the modeling, really attract people to it, and then it was multiplied because it was presold. And so then people started using it, implementing it into their own classrooms, and that in turn embeds it into the curriculum.

BM: Yes, I think that's a very good summary. I wouldn't know how to go about it in the United States, because your system is so different. It would be hard, I don't think the model I used here would work in the States because it is so decentralized. I spent time with some of the great media educators in the States like Kathleen Tyner. I think that her influence is limited because of the decentralized structures. The sort of things that she does and the sort of concepts that she generates are just brilliant, and I don't know how they would spread across the system because there is no system as such. Very hard.

TJ: But back to Australia . . . what were some surprises for you?

BM: One of the things that surprised me was the lack of contest about the various ideologies that had to come into play. This started to become very noticeable once we tried to inject media education into the formal curriculum. In Western Australia now, media education is part of the formal curriculum from kindergarten, preschool if you like, through to Year 12. Every year there are some formal skills that need to be taught and understandings of the media that need to be taught. In doing that, obviously you need to adopt some ideological positions. Those who were teaching were very conscious of the visions that were sometimes in contest with each other. The people who were authorizing the curriculum didn't seem to be aware that this was contestable, and that really surprised me.

For example, some of the materials that we were drawing from then were using professional development resources by Douglas Lambs, who had the audacity to question television and its market focus. Douglas Loundes was a well-known Marxist. In fact, he later went to go work for Gaddafi, so it might not have been a good move. But obviously we weren't adopting his position; we were using his materials with a Marxist perspective in it, as well as other materials with other perspectives as well. And even a bit later on, the whole idea of cultural studies and the contest between the cultural studies approach and the more linear approach that was prevalent in the United States—they were the contests that we had to try to resolve. Some of the papers that Robyn Quin and I wrote found that, sometimes you have ideologies that completely oppose one another and you have to go with one rather that the other, but the surprise to me was that those who were approving the curriculum didn't see this. I think the reason was that at the senior level, deep down they didn't think that media education was important or significant.

TJ: What do you see as the significance of media education?

BM: Over time, we're asking students to be critical of everything and to constructively be critical of whatever they like, to search for how to make sense of the world. How do you construct meaning? That's really the position in the various contests over the ideologies that were competing. I guess that's the area that we reached eventually: The focus of media education is a sense-making process, or the making of meaning. And to me, as an educator, that was the critical factor, that was the connection between education and media. Because if it's not rote learning, education is about how to make sense of the world.

At the time that Robyn Quin came to join me in 1981, we found that there were no materials around for teachers, so Robyn and I started writing books. The Education Department wouldn't do the publishing so we published them ourselves. The first of the dozen or so books that we put out gave teachers some ideas about how to approach media education; the last resource we wrote was in 2010 on multimedia/social media. These resources are characterized by giving the teachers structures to work with, because I think that's the key in education, to give kids some kind of scaffolds. Kids know about soap operas and they know more about computer games than I do. But what they don't have are the scaffolds, the structures of how to make sense of it all, and that's the job of the teacher to do that.

TJ: Well I hope that's a criteria that people in the field will take note of because it's so essential and so often missing, really from what I've seen. That's a really essential point.

BM: And, I think those sorts of structures have got to be implied or built into the formal curriculum documents, which is sometimes an area of contest, the formality of it. Not the ideology but the formality. The other great thing that's happened in the last couple of years in Western Australia is that the professional association has revitalized itself and that's going great. The Education Department is giving the teachers a framework that's built into the curriculum but now the teachers are more in charge of their own discipline. On the east coast of Australia, Queensland always had a fairly strong professional association, so has Victoria, but for a while in Western Australia it died away.

TJ: Do you feel that the field has moved in the direction that you think best?

BM: In the mid-'80s I felt that in Western Australia media education was on a plateau. I would go into some classrooms and I would see exercises that were not only the same that we were doing in the '70s with students, but sometimes they would use exactly the same films. I thought, goodness, where's the cutting edge gone?

I think that's changed in the last few years, especially in the upper school level. There were a number of reforms made to the upper school media education syllabus. With this recent movement to a national curriculum, I think media will come in the arts curriculum, which is unfortunate, because [the] arts tend to be marginalized in Australia. I think it would've been better placed in the communication area, but nevertheless this discussion gives the chance for teachers to have a significant input into what media education will be in the future; this has injected more life into the debate. It's taken a stab at the conservative mold again, and there are young people who are forging away.

Kate Moody

Kate Moody is a lifelong educator and author who currently serves on the Alumni Advisory Council of Teachers College Columbia University (where she earned a doctoral degree in the Department of Interdisciplinary Studies in Education) and is in a private practice as a psychoeducational therapist. For the past several years, she has been researching and writing a book about educational systems in Cuba (with a travel license from the U.S. government). She has worked for public school systems, *Sesame Street*, Nickelodeon, and PBS. She was editor of Televison Awareness Training (Media Action Research Center 1979) and author of *Growing Up on Television* (Times Books, 1980). From 1994 through 2001, she developed and headed the OPEN GATES Advanced Teaching and Telecommunications Center at the University of Texas Medical School and served on the faculty in the Department of Neurology. She began her career as a third-grade teacher and reading specialist in Ann Arbor, Michigan.

Edited Transcript: Interview, March 31, 2011
Interviewer: Tessa Jolls

TJ: Why did you become involved in media education?

KM: My father was a journalist. I think that had something to do with my general interest in how people communicate. More specifically, I became interested in the 1960s in media education, meaning media broadly defined to include electronic media and all the arts. I have been a reading teacher all of my adult life. When I moved to New York from Michigan in the late '60s, it was a very interesting time. First of all, I fell into an opportunity where I began working in a television studio in an elementary school and it happens, and I verified this, it happens that the production studio at the Murray Avenue School in Larchmont, New York, was indeed the first television production studio in a school in the United States, and I presume therefore, anywhere. This was a full three-camera studio with control room, editing equipment, etc. But I became interested in that—not because I was interested in television in particular, but because I had to finish a master's thesis at the University of Michigan. I had just moved here [to New York], and I really didn't have a laboratory. My contacts were in another state. I saw this as an opportunity to use this television studio as a laboratory to observe children learning in a very pioneering way. I reported on this experience extensively in my book *The Children of Telstar*.

I subsequently wrote a master's thesis about what can be learned by working with children in a new medium—that is to say, newer than print. We were working with cameras as "process tools," i.e., to write and tell stories (late 1960s). And I found that experience to be transformative for me because I stayed interested in television as an object of inquiry—as something to study in the future—and in the course of doing that I interviewed many interesting people for the master's thesis (c. 1970). I met people who worked in major foundations here, I became involved with *Sesame Street*, and at the same time, I must point out that 1968 was one of the most interesting years of the century for a convergence of influences regarding media. Not only was that the year that I was writing this paper and working in this studio, but I also had children who were toddlers and preschoolers at the very time that *Sesame Street* went on the air. I remember watching, with my four-year-old and infant, the very first program and it was a moment you just had to think about all these things that were happening. It was a new day for children's television certainly; *Sesame Street* was a revolutionary program. Additionally, the Action for Children's Television (ACT) was founded that same year, an event which has never been paid much attention by the media literacy people. They seem to start after 1968 and discount the importance of that group, which was indeed functioning as a critic as well as a catalyst for future developments. I would point any reader who wants a broad history of media evolution to explore the history of Action for Children's Television, which was founded by Peggy Charren in 1968. The complete archive is at Harvard University's Gutmann Library. I became the founder and president of the ACT affiliate in New York, called New York Council on Children's Television. The Ethical Culture Society gave us office space for a year or so and a small grant to get started. ACT became one of the largest advocacy programs for children at any time. There were hundreds of thousands of members nationwide and the group did such things as petition FTC and the FCC regarding standards in advertising, and even at one point sued the FCC for not following through on standards they had promised. I thought then, and I think now, that parents need a little help. Teachers need a little help, by structuring our mass media in a better way.

Media has been systematically deregulated throughout my adult life. There were complaints that we had at the time about violence and advertising in particular—that isn't violence *in* advertising, but violence *and* advertising—but they're so related. Anyway it's become only worse in terms of the big picture, which means that the media literacy workers have to huff and puff and work harder. But these were the origins . . . and at the same time 1968 was the great watershed year for the whole topic for media and kids.

The Surgeon General's report on violence or aggressive behavior was funded at the national level and that was an extensive report and it was finally published in 1972. So you had the Action for Children's Television, *Sesame Street*, and, at a national level, studies on aggressive behavior taking place. About that time, I met John Culkin, who had recently left the priesthood and started the Center for Understanding Media in New York. I became involved with *Sesame Street* and with some foundations and with some writing projects for the center. It was a few years after that that I started working with Les Brown, the television correspondent to *The New York Times*. He asked me to write sections of the book *The New York Times Encyclopedia of Television* (Times Books 1977). From that experience, I was learning from senior people and working on a topic that had become of great interest. I was transformed for awhile from a reading teacher's focus, particularly on print literacy, to a person studying media, broadly defined, in terms of what were at the time new electronic media forms. In the late '70s, I was the editor of *Television Awareness Training*, which was a manual for teachers who wanted to become media educators. The construction of that manual with workshops and exercises was also a precursor to what you would call the media literacy movement which really didn't dawn until the late '70s although Liz Thoman was hard at work in Iowa.

TJ: But there certainly had to be a context and an environment where the conditions that built up, that this is what emerged and so I think your description of that watershed year is important to the story. What informed and inspired your work?

KM: Although 1968 was a watershed year in terms of actions, names, and dates, there was much before that. I was certainly reading Marshall McLuhan when his landmark book, *Understanding Media: The Extensions of Man*, was published in 1964. I still have my original copy of that text with all sorts of handwritten notes scribbled in the margins and much color-coding of content. For me that was a very important book. I found later on that a lot of people that I would meet five, six, eight years hence were also reading it. So McLuhan is part of this story. And John Culkin was very much his protégé and very good friend. The introduction to the McLuhan–Culkin way of thinking, not that it's one way of thinking, but certainly an influence was present prior to 1968.

Another important person in my early studies was Norman Cousins. He was a major philosopher, writer, and publisher of the *Saturday Review* weekly magazine. He was somebody that I was reading back when I was reading McLuhan. Later I met him and he became a good friend, in fact he wrote the introduction to *Growing Up on Television*. He was important because he really encouraged me to do further studies of television. He thought that this was enormously important, and it helps when the people you admire tell you that. Another person going way back was Professir Gerald O'Grady. He was/ is a philosopher and he was a consultant to our local schools when our local school district was doing far more with media than any place had ever heard of. They hired O'Grady as a consultant to our school district and in one of the planning memos or proposals, he put forward his own definition of media studies. I think it's very good. I certainly would take it for my own.

He wrote, "I would like to delimit media studies to mean exploration and creation, the aesthetics and the psychological, social and environmental impact of the art form of photography, cinematography, videography, radio recordings and tapes within the broad framework of general education in the humanities. I would call media studies 'the new humanities' to distinguish them from 'the old humanities'—literature, drama, fine arts, etc.—from which they often borrow and with which they continually interact, mutually influencing each other." That's the broadest view of the subject that I recall.

Others who inspired my work across the years include: Cy Schneider at Nickelodeon, Bob Geller, Dr. Calvert E. Schlick, and Kit Laybourne in the Mamaroneck Public Schools, Teri McLuhan, Thomas N. James, MD, Albert Rosenfeld, Peggy Charren, and Chester M. Pierce, MD.

TJ: I think that would be very pertinent to today's media. You could extend that list that O'Grady had.

KM: He didn't include things like cable TV, because it was not available in 1975. He was a big thinker, he certainly influenced what was going on in our school district and, believe me, our school district was the most imaginative that I have ever heard of. But there was sort of a golden age, and that's why I wrote a book, *Children of Telstar* (Center for Understanding Media). The original manuscript for that book was my doctoral dissertation at Columbia University (1993).

TJ: Are there any other milestones that come to mind as you think about how your own interests, learning, and contributions to the field evolved?

KM: As I noted earlier, the paper that I wrote on instructional television was my master's thesis at Michigan. There was also the involvement I had at Murray Avenue School, where I was the developer of the project that was of historic importance. There were affiliates developed to ACT and I was the founder and president of New York Children's Television, which was the one of the affiliates which brought me to a lot of advocacy. Then I was the editor of Television Awareness Training, followed by my numerous contributions to the *New York Times Encyclopedia of Television* and probably the work that I am most proud of, is my book *Growing Up on Television* which was published in 1980. That was a continuation of my studies with Les Brown and *New York Times Encyclopedia of Television*, but I wanted to focus just on children in that book. And though the book is quite old now, in a way it's very contemporary because all of the issues I stated there are still issues today. Sorry to say that that's true, and if there is an expectation that I had, it was that once parents and educators had certain kinds of information about the available research and the probable effects of habitual TV viewing, that they would do something about them. And I must say that all the problems are still there and I don't see that anything much has been done about them.

If you look at *Growing Up on Television*, the key issues in the table of contents go through the chapters on the effects on aggressive behavior, socialization, there's a chapter called learning and perception, another one about reading, another one about commercialization and products, considerable discussion of pace of messages, nutrition, and obesity—whatever the topics that you deal with in media literacy studies, they were named and dealt with there as concerns. And I was more of a critic than anything in that book and I saw this all coming. These were all problems. Remember, I had little kids at the time, and I was concerned about them as an educator and reading teacher. Anyway, I gathered together the existing research at the time.

The Internet and other screens are all first, second, and third cousins of television. In the 1970s, everybody was running around gleefully saying "cable is coming," this is going to be so wonderful because now we will have alternatives to commercial broadcast TV and apparently people thought that all these alternatives would be good. Well, they're not. In 1981, 1982, I was director of corporate development at Nickelodeon. NICK has disappointed me in the sense that at the time in 1981,1982 we were so delighted that this was "the first and only noncommercial channel for kids" and we kept saying that phrase over again every time because we were proud of it. But nothing stays noncommercial for very long. And I left when it all switched to an ad-supported format. I wasn't going to participate in the commodification of kids via advertising. But I was there when Nickelodeon was very small; there were only four or five of us on staff. I was there when NICK was launched on the satellite in 1982 and we thought that this was real progress because the programming was definitely designed for children and young people. There were no commercials, maybe as time went on there was an underwriting message here and there but we had strict rules as to what constituted an underwriting message and what it could not do. "No claims, no demonstrations," was the rule because then it would become an advertisement. I went on to teach about this at Hunter College, and I was a consultant to the local school district when I had the idea that I would like to teach at the university level which required a doctorate. So I did go back to school in 1988 to Columbia University where I entered a doctoral program to have the credentials to teach in the university about media.

I earned the degree and immediately went off to work with Neil Postman at NYU. He invited me to NYU to be codirector with him on something called the Institute on Media and Education. In 1994, we had a major conference in which Liz Thoman was one of the invited speakers. Then one day while I was minding my own business and doing this work at NYU, I got a phone call from somebody who was very involved with the University of Texas Medical School. This person, Al Rosenfeld, has been a good friend of mine, a scientist and a science writer doing work there for the president. He said to me, "I really want you to meet Dr. Thomas James, the president of the medical school." So my husband and I accepted an invitation to spend a long weekend so I could hear what Dr. James was aiming to develop at the University of Texas. And although Dr. James was a cardiologist, he read widely and he was very interested in telecommunications. He had a specific interest in reading and why some people learn to read easily and why other people, despite having all the best teachers, don't read well at all (dyslexia). Anyway, his concept was that we want to study the old media, that is print, and the new media, and ask questions about this in research terms. (His thinking about the definition of media studies was overarching, like Gerald O'Grady, described above.) The president saw that I had been a reading teacher all my life and continued to study dysfunctions in communication while pursing projects and studies in television as well. Of course once I heard about this, it was compellingly interesting.

So in the fall of 1994, I became the executive director of the OPEN GATES Advanced Teaching and Telecommunications Center at the University of Texas Medical Branch in Galveston, reporting to the president at the medical school with all kinds of opportunities before me. And so that was a milestone, too, in terms of where I am now. We had television studios there with the capacity of satellite connections to anywhere in the world. We did medical training with and for NASA. (NASA headquarters is just down the road.) It seemed like we could do anything. We developed a system of telemedicine clinics in the prisons throughout Texas because the distances are so great. We were experimenting with all kinds of distance learning, modes in the nursing schools, telemedicine clinics there based from the campus. And at the same time, we had a very major treatment center for dyslexia, which specialized in the treatment of dyslexia in medical students. Along with somebody else who was in Dallas, Dr. Lucius Waites, the neurologist, our group plus other people were always collaborating on things and we became the designers of the draft of a master of science degree for dyslexia therapy at a medical school. Such a degree did not exist at the time.

TJ: So you're talking about medical issues, issues that really come down to neurology right?

KM: I had an appointment in the Department of Neurology, which is probably the most appropriate academic home for such work. But, of course, as with all my work, there was an extensive interdisciplinary reach.

TJ: You were really breaking down the silos, too, in terms of being able to do cross-disciplinary kinds of projects, which I think is all part of media literacy.

KM: The bureaucracy prevents many things, but it can also provide a complexity in the environment that allows for diverse connections. So I had the great opportunity here to work for a president who was as far advanced as anybody in that kind of thinking. He was the big out-of-the-box thinker.

TJ: How do you see things developing?

KM: I am reluctant to predict. One of your questions is how far do you think the field has come, and of course the answer is not far enough. If we said we're done, we're finished.

TJ: We'd be taken for granted.

KM: And forgotten. You can't do that. So, as the field has a long way to go and I really question most of the time whether all the media literacies in the world can really counterbalance the effects of new media. There's considerable dissonance now. Because to some extent, only to some extent, Marshall McLuhan was right, and the medium is the message. When you have a medium that's jumping and changing its picture every quarter of a second, it's going to affect the brain. And I don't care whether you're talking about the weather report, or the latest war, or selling sugar products to kids. The nature of the media requires the brain to be working all the time.

There are going to be negative effects and you can talk all day about what they are and how you might need to do some yoga or you might need to understand the motive of the producer, but it's still going to have those effects. I don't think you can ameliorate some of these effects of the new media: too much data per unit—for most brains. So we can try but informing parents about certain things isn't enough. They can be just as informed as you want them to be and they'll still do certain things. The people who weren't even born yet when I wrote that book are parents now. And some of their kids are already adolescents; they were raised on television themselves. It doesn't matter if they have media literacy information or not. The media have penetrated their lives in a way that was hardly imaginable 25 years ago when you think of the studies with which you're familiar about who watches what, for how much time per day, and how many text messages, or how many this, how many that, what portion of your life is given over to this. You can't change the fact that that's a quarter of your life.

TJ: We know the media is a big part of everyone's life, there is a lifelong relationship with it. It's not going to change, it's undoubtedly affecting the brain and processing and the way young people really deal with media and so in that sense we're almost at a given and that it will continue to be there.

KM: I don't think it needs to be a given that kids will have 1,000 text messages in a day. It doesn't have to be a given unless you roll over and accept it right there.

TJ: What would you like to see happen?

KM: I would like to see one thing, the simplest one. What I would like to see is a balancing of the senses. To do that, I would recommend far less involvement with electronic media per day. And so I know certain people that don't like to hear this. But the only way to bring it down to size so that you could then work with it is to give it a proportion that is less than it currently is. I do maintain a private practice here now in which I see students that have fairly serious learning disabilities. I could tell you for sure that media is a huge interference for someone who has great difficulty with the reading and writing aspects of attending high school and passing the required tests. To remediate those things (this is a direct extension of my work in Texas), I know that they need more time and they know that they need specific kinds of lessons and work and you can't find time in their day to do this. They're too busy racing from one thing to the next. Media is a total interference; it is a daily static interference to concentration and the ability to pay attention well.

So trimming down the size of participation in media, in one's personal life is something to be addressed at home. Parents are quite crazy about this because when they see addictions developing, most can't interfere successfully with habit formation. At the public level, too, I believe in setting standards, I believe in regulation. I prefer to call it standards. I would make rules about pace and content in children's fare, and ask parents to limit the quantity of time allotted to viewing of "screens" per day.

There's still plenty for the media educators to do after that, because there are many topics of analysis and/or production to consider in school. In a slightly different vein, I would like to see music addressed as an object of inquiry to a greater extent than it has been. John Culkin and I discussed this at great length near the end of his life. We need to know more about how music works, both in the brain and in social behaviors. He felt it was a mistake to not have included this in the curricula we developed in the schools where we worked.

In the last five years or so, I've become very interested in Oliver Sacks, the brilliant neurologist and storyteller. He has written books on music and the brain. You can study music from a medical perspective but also from a social perspective, looking at what kids sing, what kids groove into their heads at an early age. Yes, the message matters.

TJ: There is a receptivity there that may not be in other kinds of media.

KM: That's right. Music is playing in their brains and developing a little groove there. I'm currently studying Cuba and education systems in Cuba. Music and all the arts hold a special place there.

TJ: In your work, you see some of the negative outcomes because of the patients and clients that you're dealing with. Does that warrant serious consideration and examination?

KM: Yes . . . but you have to understand my perspective here, having heavy involvement with dyslexia and ADHD [attention-deficit/hyperactivity disorder] both at the medical school and in my work now. There's a lot of hyperkinesis, hyperactivity around in behaviors and sometimes the behaviors are barriers to doing your schoolwork in an acceptable way, and to just getting along with others. One of the things I always do with a new client is a rather elaborate survey of how he or she uses time. It takes a whole hour to do this kind of survey. But they don't understand how media and texts infiltrate their lives. The first step is awareness.

TJ: Do you feel that teaching young people how media works as a system, teaching them the critical thinking skills, teaching them about responsible productions—how far do you think that goes in terms of addressing what we are up against here?

KM: I think it's helpful, but I'm not sure how helpful. I think to the extent that it involves "doing," it's more effective. One of the outcomes of our work in the Larchmont/Mamaroneck Public Schools with the Center for Understanding Media was the production of a paperback manual called *Doing the Media: A Portfolio of Activities*. It explained how to carry out production projects with many kinds of media—hands-on activities. But just talking to people about these kinds of things, even if it's in brilliantly thought-out lessons . . . I don't think it helps very much. I have a story that I think I wrote about when my son was a teenager. I went out to Albuquerque once for a media literacy conference, and I was telling him about what my presentation was going to be and what it was all about. He said, "Mom, I could be in one of those classes and hear about all the critical thinking points; I can do all of your exercises really well. But then I would just go home and watch television the same way after that."

I think you have to *do* the media. I don't think you can sit in the classroom and hear about it. That's it. But then it falls within, as O'Grady said, the humanities, but even more specifically the arts. And what do we cut in this country when things get rough? Music, visual arts, and physical education. That's what is closest to the media education program, because then eventually hopefully with a little help, the creative teacher could tie some of those things together, but if you don't have the "doing part" of it, it isn't worth as much.

If you are a child, you have to make and create and do something or experience it with your body first and brain second—make a motor commitment.

It isn't good enough to have these media literacy programs and arts programs in selected public schools or charter schools or private schools. That just means some people get this education and some people don't. When I say public I mean public. As my mentor, Norman Cousins, often said, "Everybody's children are society's concern."

W. James Potter

W. James Potter has been a professor in the Department of Communication at the University of California–Santa Barbara since 2001. His research focuses primarily on media literacy and media violence, and he is the author of the class textbook *Media Literacy*. He began his career as a journalist and is former editor of the *Journal of Broadcasting & Electronic Media*.

Edited Transcript: Interview, April 26, 2011
Interviewer: Tessa Jolls

TJ: What attracted you to media education?

JP: Well that's a big question. I guess it goes back to the first job I had after I graduated. I worked at a small-town newspaper and I worked on that for two years. What really made it an intense experience and what got me started on the path was that it was a small-town newspaper. When you work at a small-town newspaper, you're a photographer, you're a reporter, you're an editor, you do the layouts, you print out the pictures after you come back with the story—so you really get your hands on all the aspects of news—the police beat, the hospital beat, sports, everything. Then the other advantage of working for a small-town newspaper was that you have a lot of contact with the people, so after you write the story you continually run into the people and so I had a lot of opportunity to ask people about the stories.

It started to fascinate me that some stories I wrote that I thought were really important, nobody would read. And then other stories that I thought were really trivial, people would talk about a lot. I became fascinated by what attracts people to stories and what it is that they learn when they read the stories, and so I was interested as much in writing the stories as in talking to the people afterwards.

That led me to graduate school because I thought, well maybe there's a better way to ask questions, maybe there are theories out there that could explain this. In my first graduate program, I was focused on writing, there was a lot of psychology, education, and linguistics and things like that. After I got done with that program, I had learned a lot but then I thought, well I'm not interested only just in the general area of learning but learning in everyday experiences. So what fascinated me was a little bit less about what happens in formal situations where people learn; I was interested in that, but I think the learning that was most interesting is what happens in everyday life when people are not consciously trying to learn something with media, yet a lot of learning takes place.

That's the kind of stuff that takes place under the radar. And that became really, really fascinating so I thought, well I'd rather learn more about the communication-in-the-media side, so I enrolled in a program to study that. In all that study, I didn't really run across the term *media literacy* much if at all, but I guess that's what I was really interested in—what are the principles of learning on an everyday basis. Then, since I was planning on going on to teach in higher education, my question was how I could help people get better at that. So that, in a nutshell, is what attracted me and how I ended up in higher education.

TJ: What do you see as fitting the label *media literacy*?

JP: Even today, there's the label *media literacy*, but one of the challenges now is that everybody has heard that term and they all have ideas about what that means. If you were to interview 100 different people, you'd probably get 150 different definitions about what it really means. So we're much better off than we were maybe 30 years ago, because we've reached a rallying point, but that could mean a lot of different things to a lot of different people. But at least we have a common forum, and we're building more with organizations like yours which have done a tremendous amount, trying to bring people together and share outlooks and experiences. We really are still on the frontier; there's still so much more that has to be done.

TJ: What were some milestones that you've noted along the way, Jim, for yourself and for the field in general?

JP: The strength of media literacy is its variety, its broad-based nature; it cuts across all kinds of different fields . . . it's such an organic and dynamic kind of field. Those are the characteristics that I see out there and the down side of that is there are so many creative people out there, really sincere and motivated people who are ready to help, local curriculum development committees or PTA or individual students or people in the industry, more educational shows, policy makers . . . there are all kinds of different people and they all talk different kinds of languages, so for me, I just see almost a chaos out there that's an extreme slew of ideas that eventually is going to develop a lot of interesting insights as things move forth. But as far as traditionally what people mean by milestones, like a particular article or a particular conference that puts down a foundational pile-on that people build on, there are some that have attracted attention.

In 1998, Alan Rubin, who was editor of *Journal of Communications* at the time, asked a couple of us to do a symposium on media literacy. Bill Christ and I were able to get a really good handful of scholars who were active in that area. The individual articles in there have gotten a lot of quotes from it. Other efforts like those of Patricia Aufterheide and some other people, like Renee Hobbs, who is trying to build a professional organization. I commend those people who are trying to do that. It's so hard in this field where so much is changing so fast, there are so many competing journals and conferences out there, and with the economy the way it is, and so many demands on time. When you're interested in the media, there are really half a dozen conferences you should go to every year, and then to add another professional society, it's hard to find the time and money to go to all of those. So it's swimming upstream to pull people together.

TJ: How did the publication of your textbook *Media Literacy* come about?

JP: Every year, I taught an introductory media course. From the very beginning, I realized that you can't teach media effects without having people appreciate the media content, because it matters what you expose yourself to, and the content says something about the audience and what patterns there are and how people think. Then, to understand media, you have to know about the industry. So, to know one part or facet about the media, you have to know a little about a lot of different things. So that's how I started to teach. I was pulling the notes together, and I realized it was hard for me to find a textbook that did all of that—not just present the information, but to present it in a way where the focus of presentation was on the student rather than on the information itself. So I got a contract with Sage and published the text in the mid-'90s. At the time, I thought this is for me, to make teaching much easier and maybe help some other people to find it much easier. I guess they did, because now I'm working on the sixth edition.

Media changes so much that you have to refresh the information and the examples in order to make them viable to each new generation of students. By generation, I mean every three or four years. The student perspective changes so fast. Like right now . . . what news really means is no longer Tom Brokaw . . . what the news really means to students is tweeting where their friends are having lunch. Well, that's news! "I thought we were going to have lunch at this place and now it's at another place." That's news to me, and that's news I can use, and that's really important to me, much more important than what the city council voted on or a murder that took place in the next county or things like that, which I was taught in journalism school. There's more and more of a disconnect between what people from the previous generation used as definitions and what definitions are in use with the new generation. The new generation's whole perspective on the world and what it means to be a part of a society and what it means to contribute to that—all of that is very different than it was five years ago.

When I wrote the first edition of *Media Literacy*, desktop computers had been around for about 10 to 12 years, and that was a major breakthrough. It seems like each 2 or 3 years the shift is happening in a more pervasive way and a more fundamental way . . . it seems like the turnovers happen faster and faster. It's hard to imagine though, what the next breakthrough will be in the next couple of years. Is there going to be another Facebook, Google, something that is totally going to revolutionize the next generation of students in where they get their information and the way they interpret the world?

TJ: Are there surprises along the way that you hadn't anticipated?

JP: Well, just about everything! Ten years ago Google, I think it was in the very beginning stage, it didn't exist as a company; it wasn't until 2004 that it was publically traded. Until then people didn't understand what the company was and what it was doing, but then when it went public, at least Wall Street understood this is a major change, this is a company that is really going to change the way we think about technology. And it definitely has. I saw some figures where it was the No. 1 capitalized company in the world, where if you multiply their shares with how much people pay per share, it's worth more than any other company in the world including Exxon Mobile and companies like that. The fact that it could grow that fast and become that important financially to people who really understand business, and then if you think the impact on the society and the way people check out friends, they will Google them. Find out who this person is, or date, or a future employee. And financially the impact on the economy is tremendous. As far as the impact on the culture, it's so big that our faces are pressed right up against it. We really don't have the distance or time to understand the ramifications that it has on the society. The thing with Facebook, the second example . . . I remember the time when MySpace was bigger and Rupert Murdoch came along and bought MySpace and now that's a dinosaur, nobody is on MySpace anymore, it's all Facebook.

People don't understand the legal ramifications of Facebook. Who owns that information, how that's shared, those people who get into trouble from posting things on their Facebook? And then Twitter comes along. People spend a lot of time on Twitter and they really get something important out of that . . . and that is a brand-new phenomenon too. So if you turn the clock back 10 years, I would've never predicted, I don't think anybody could've predicted, what 2011 would be as far as the degree of social connectedness, the virtual world that a lot of people live in, games that people play. A lot of people are members of virtual communities and that's much more important to them than the real world.

TJ: Do you feel that the media literacy field has been moving along in a direction that you think is beneficial?

JP: If you really think hard about it, it could drive you crazy. Because there are literally millions of people out there who are investing in these companies who are creating new Web sites, new apps, who are dedicating large portions of their lives to creating messages and activities. Just think of Wikipedia—people are not doing it for money but doing it for internal satisfaction. There is a huge attractiveness to the media, and that's where the runaway development is coming because you just pull so many people, for so many hours, so many creative people.

Up against that you look at the challenge in media literacy. Media are just growing so fast and the number of people who are attracted to media literacy continues to grow, but not at the same rate as the amount of people who are attracted to media. So I guess there will come a time, maybe, when the new technologies and the new ways of developing information will plateau a little bit and slow down a bit. Maybe media literacy scholars and people who are socially active, maybe that will catch up. But right now, we have gone through such an explosion over the past decade especially of media outlets, of creating information, and of the explosion of messages—and not just the number of messages, but the variety and types of messages by the means that you can create those messages—that we as media literacy people really hadn't conceptualized before. I think we are really scrambling to keep up with that.

TJ: There are people who say that media literacy is not a field, it's a movement, and other people say it's a movement, not a field. What is your take, Jim?

JP: Well I've always thought that media literacy has the ingredients to be a field. I've always thought that it's important to have a rallying around a small set of theories, but right now in media we have over 100 theories. Yet only a handful of theories get mentioned more than a few times each year in the journals. So what we really have is a huge dispersion across a lot of disciplines, and that always bothered me.

Over the past few years, the phenomenon that we are studying is growing so fast and changing so much that I felt that we need to have more closure and conversion amongst scholars and more of a clustering of certain ideas in order to get the field a profile and a better definition. That could be a detriment to being seen as a field because if you're trying to be convergent and trying to build a field by trying to get everyone on the same page, with the same definitions—while the time goes by to do that, the field changes radically underneath you with the phenomenon that you're trying to study.

So for me, I've come to be a lot more comfortable with the organic nature and the fast change and the dynamic nature of the phenomenon itself. It's like riding a bucking bull. You want to take a quick photograph of it to freeze it and understand it. That might satisfy your need for closure as a human being, but it really doesn't capture the field because the field is a motion field, it's not a thing that could be captured in a snapshot.

When you're writing a book, that's what you have to do, you just have to get words down on a page. So my hope for the future is for the people who on the one hand want to get things down on paper, who want to have convergence, who want to build a field, who want us to have a high profile but who also are comfortable with a phenomenon that will change radically. Once you get things written down on paper, you've captured it for a very short period of time, and then you've got to start all over again, and you just have to be comfortable with that.

TJ: Do you feel like the field has been moving in a positive direction?

JP: Yes, I do. It has attracted lots of different kinds of people. There are a lot of people out there who are making really good contributions and who are creating consumer protection groups, trying to influence policy, trying to put together conferences or holding mini sessions and trying to get people to come to that, putting up websites. There is all kind of activity out there and the more of that we have, the better. And if people disagree with each other, as far as redefining what media literacy means, that's what's important; and people are really trying to put out their vision and share that vision with other people. And as long as they're doing that in a sincere way, not trying to belittle other people's work or for ego satisfaction but doing it because there's a tremendous need out there and they're trying to contribute in helping other people in some way to help them understand the media. Whatever that means is, as long as they're motivated by the desire to help people, what they do will eventually find an audience and I think that's another element we really have to think about. We are kind of moved to do this in a retail way rather than in a wholesale way. We have to do the best we can and hope that it's going to influence people and if it influences one or two people, then that's great. You're probably never going to be able to come up with something that speaks to everybody in the field over time. We have an impossible situation to make that happen. It just won't happen. We have too many different types of people with too many different kinds of background and different agendas.

And even if that weren't the case, the phenomenon, the field of media changes so fast. We just have to pick out target groups and help them have their "aha!" experience. That's the fun part. Although that might only happen to a handful of people each time, that's what you have to be satisfied with. You can't look at a grand scheme, OK I'm going to put out the one and only definition of media literacy and you all are going to accept it, and we are going to be carving it on monuments to be passed on for generations. In a certain way, I think most fields have to move in that direction because the way we think of our society sociologically, the economics of things, the political system across the social sciences and the physical sciences too. There's so much that's changing, it's getting more and more specialized. For example, physicists—the guy in the office down the hall from you talks a totally different language than you if you're a physicist although you're both physicists, and you both have PhDs in physics. You know you're so specialized in your training or biology or whatever the fields are that explores the information that it's so much that it's pushing us farther and farther from one another. That doesn't mean that we can't find a niche audience that we can contribute our thinking to, it's just that we can't pull everybody together and get us all thinking the same way. The world just has too much of a variety to it now.

That's why one of my biggest issues is sorting through the priority between skills and competency. Competency is categorical; either you have that competency or you don't, and then you have that competency where you're the master and that's really good. But with skills there's this huge continuum where you always get better, there's never really an ultimate end point on that. I think a lot of people look at us in media literacy and expect us to deliver competency—elementary school students, high school students, even college students. They pass the bar, they've ascended to a certain level and now they're in a category where they are a media lover and they can handle the media. But what we're really dealing with here is that we are on the continuum and we are trying to nudge people a little bit better and a little bit better as long as we can orient them to what this continuum is and how they can get better, then we can leave them alone and they will continue to work on it and continue to get better. But for outsiders who look at the media literacy movement and say "Geez, how many people have you made media literate?" That's not the right question, because the answer is "None!"

TJ: Nobody is *that* media literate!

JP: Yes, the more you study the media, the more humble you are. The proportion of the information among the media that you've mastered goes down the more you study it because as you study, you realize the media information grows at a much faster rate than your pile of knowledge does. A person's proportion of knowledge mastered is always getting smaller relative to the phenomenon being mastered, but that's a good thing because you realize how big the phenomenon is and that in itself is also an important bit of learning.

Just the explosion of books . . . I'm going to quote one of the introductions to one of my books to humble people. The number of books that are published just in the United States each year goes up but that's not publishing, but anyone could become a publisher now. The latest figure I saw was that 290,000 books were published last year in the United States. That's not articles or memoirs, those are just things that are regarded as books and that are listed in the Library of Congress. And that's probably a gross underestimation. You think, "Wow how long would it take me to just read the books that are published this year? "

If you read a book every two minutes and never slept for a year then you'd be able to get through this year's publications. And that's just books; you wouldn't be able to watch TV or news. But we are doomed further and further behind if we want to keep up with media and again you just have to get comfortable with that because if you're obsessive compulsive, which a lot of those academics are, we want to master everything, we want to pull it all together, we want to have all the great ideas on our phy sci's so we feel like we have mastered it. We're beyond that point, to get comfortable with the idea that mastery is kind of an 18th-century concept. You have to celebrate what your real interest is in and do the best that you can, you have to move on with your skills and try to put together information to give to an audience to help them and do the best you can. And then that's where your satisfaction is supposed to come from, not from mastering it. You'll never be able to do that.

What scares me the most about higher education is that in my career I've seen a real shift in focusing on a mastery of knowledge rather than development of skills. That, I think, is a big mistake. There are a lot more faculty who are dumbing down courses by focusing on conveying info-bits rather than helping students develop their skills and critical thinking. The reason for that is that there's so much pressure put on faculty to be so many different things, service and research in addition to teaching. So even as a teacher you have to automate your course and when you do that you really focus on the info-bits you don't have time to work with students to have them do writing and then you edit it and then you teach them how to format. I mean that is really detailed teaching and we have less and less and less ability to do that. Such that, when students leave college what they have learned is how to cram for an exam.

So what they have is a wheelbarrow of info-bits that have a half-life of maybe three or four years, which means that every year they're out of college, their college degree loses value as the memorized information goes out of date. Whereas if students graduate from a program with significant development of skills that they can continue crafting in their lifetime if they understood the strategies of skill development, then the value of their education gets stronger and stronger over time. But yet what we have is all of these students who have information crammed into their minds and then we dump them into the deep end of our culture which is information saturated, and a lot of them just drown because they don't know how to navigate their way through that to think for themselves and build an argument. They've been trained by professors to memorize facts rather than learning how to critically evaluate information.

Things are going to continue to go in the same direction in higher education unless we confront this situation. It's a really dangerous one. We are pressured to churn out more and more college graduates each year because administrators are interested in making sure that students are graduating on time. It's a very institutional, factory-type of mentality and that works; they put the resources behind that. But if you look at the skills that they have, can they analyze difficult problems, can they do certain things really, really well—like access new forms of media—can they develop quick contacts with other people, or can they just get a lot of superficial information on Google and Facebook? Students are very advanced in parallel processing and multitasking. So they have some significant skills that they build on their own, but those skills come from the culture and their own challenges that they set up on their own. But when they go into higher education, they have an old model that trains students in areas that are just outdated. The new models aren't there in higher ed, and a lot of the students are being turned off.

TJ: What do you feel is your most important priority to be working on right now?

JP: Well, my priority is to continue updating *Media Literacy* and to try to make my contribution with that. For myself, my challenges are to get better as a consumer of the media. I need to understand these things more, so I have to play around with Twitter and Facebook and whatever comes down the pipe next year and the year after that, and play the games online and do all that stuff. I have to do that, and each year it gets harder and harder because with some of the media, you just have to go off into a different culture. For example, with tweeting . . . To me that just looks so trivial, why would I do that? Why would I want to tell people that I'm going out to check my mail now? Who is interested in that? But there are people who are! You have to get into that mindset, and it doesn't come natural to me. I want to understand what is it that attracts people to that so much. That's been a bit of a struggle, but if I don't do that, if I don't watch *16 and Pregnant* or *Pimp My Ride*, or *Jersey Shore*—if I don't know who Snookie is—then I lose touch with the next generation and the things are important to them. If you want to be a part of today's culture, you've got to go with the flow.

Robyn Quin

Robyn Quin is deputy vice-chancellor (Education) at Curtin University of Technology. Before joining Curtin, Professor Quin was pro vice-chancellor responsible for Teaching and Learning and executive dean of the Faculty of Communications and Creative Industries at Edith Cowan University. She began her career as a teacher of English Literature.

Edited Transcript: Interview, March 22, 2011
Interviewer: Tessa Jolls

TJ: Why did you become involved with media education?

RQ: I was originally a teacher of English Literature and I found students thought it was totally irrelevant to their lives. Just like many other people who became media studies teachers, I was interested in the fact that media studies could be made more relevant to students' lives and what they were interested in, and that many of the same skills of analysis that you develop in the study of literature you could apply to the study of visual images.

TJ: What were some of the experiences that you had early on?

RQ: In the early days of media studies (now I'm talking about the '70s), it was very much oriented to practical production work. That was partly the history of its origin. Media studies in Western Australia weren't really like what happened in England or what happened in the United States and Latin America. In many other countries, media studies was either a reaction to the fear of what the media might be doing to people's psyches or intellect, or as in Latin America, that media was breaking down social values, family, and religious values. Or in England it was a kind of high-culture, low-culture divide. In Australia media studies actually started as an answer to an educational problem in that schooling—the amount of time children had to spend at school—was increased, and the school-leaving age was raised. Previous to this, schools were a sort of sorting ground, they sorted out those kids that were going to go to university and they stayed on for the whole time at school. Those that weren't left school at 14 or so and went either into trades or got a job. When they raised the school-leaving age, there were a lot of students who stayed at school but didn't intend to go to university.

This meant that the curriculum of the school was totally irrelevant to them because the curriculum was very much geared towards what you needed for university study. So media studies really came in as a curriculum answer to the problem of how do you engage young people with schooling who really would rather not be there. So media studies, in its original formation, didn't stretch their intellectual abilities greatly because it didn't require large amounts of writing or reading. And what it did have was a production orientation in the early days. So there was lots of work in filmmaking, taking your photographs, developing and printing in the darkroom, making radio programs, making Super8 films, doing animations. Its orientation was very much learning by doing and lots of production work. That was really because of the nature of the school population that it was originally designed to service.

TJ: Did you see some changes in terms of the purpose of media studies and how the subject was delivered?

RQ: Very much so. What I was just describing was a '70s conception of media, which was all about production. Conceptually, it was built on a fairly simplistic transmission model of communication, the notion that there is a message that goes through a medium and there's a receiver, the audience. Within the model that underpinned media studies, this whole notion that the message was intended.

In the '80s, there were a number of changes to the syllabus across the entire state, which had the benefit that if you wanted to introduce change, then change happens everywhere at the same time. Unlike the United States, where there are highly devolved education systems and education districts the same as in Canada or England, here it is very centralized. So what happened was that there were a number of changes to the syllabus. Those changes were brought about on the initiative of teachers who sit on the syllabus committees. What happened then, was that there was a much stronger emphasis in the new syllabus on the analysis of media and much more emphasis on the distinctive forms of the media. We spoke in terms of the skills and grammar of each media and what I described as the communication chain, the message, medium, and receiver was replaced by a new concept which looked at the construction of messages; the way that they function, the nature of each medium, and the effect on the audience.

There were two new concepts that had been absent in the previous decade . . . one was the concept of the media as a cultural agent, that the media itself had effects on culture and made changes and was both an effect upon and a reflection of changes in community attitudes, lifestyles, and social patterns. The means by which these changes were both reflected and promulgated were by such things as stereotypes, symbolism, rituals, etc.

The second major change was the conception of the audience. In the '70s, the notion of a receiver was an individual getting a message from the media that was a message intended for the individual. In the '80s the audience was conceived as not simply as individuals but as members of a shared culture or subculture. So I am suggesting that in the '80s media studies had a turn toward cultural studies and that was really influenced by the Birmingham Center for Cultural Studies under Stuart Hall and his work on television and audience, and also the work of Roland Barthes on popular culture. It got away from the behavioral emphasis in the early approaches which saw the media influence people in sort of a direct stimuli response model: You watch something violent, you do something violent. That was completely replaced by a new conception of the media as an all-pervasive, social, and political force, but the influences were indirect, subtle, and maybe even imperceptible. The earlier sort of direct correlation disappeared from the conception of the syllabus.

Interestingly, the study of audiences changed a lot, so the idea that an audience would be directly influenced didn't appear in the new syllabus; it was more David Molley's "Nationwide" studies that said that audiences are unpredictable or that you can't say how any audience will actually read a media message because people bring to any reading their own social, cultural, political, moral baggage which would determine their readings.

If we look back at the various syllabus revisions, it was a very busy time in the '80s because I think ideas were changing, pedagogy was changing, and the syllabus was trying to keep up. So by the time 1986 came around, the syllabus was organized under five key understandings. They were the problematical nature of the mass media, media products as constructions, methods of construction [that] had control of the construction, and audiences. We were seeing the media products as much more complex than had been seen in the early days. And that actually affected the way that it was taught in that there was a lot more detailed analysis of individual texts. Students were taught to look at montage, visual symbolism, the musical score, and how that influences their reaction to the images.

You've got to see that this was partly made possible by technical innovation. Previous to the '80s, you couldn't stop a frame, and so the notion of actually being able to look at a piece of footage frame by frame wasn't possible; before you had stop/start video. And so once upon a time, film was a five-minute film roll, it passed through the gate, and you couldn't go back and capture it. With video facility, with a freeze-frame facility, you could hold a single image from a film and pour over it at length. I think there is a kind of a relationship between technological advancement and the way that people were teaching because it actually made it possible to do close analysis of the image.

So what we saw coming through the '80s was a much stronger emphasis on textual analysis, so if you saw the '70s as days of production, the '80s became the days, if I wanted to generalize, of textual analysis. That appealed to a lot of teachers, especially to teachers who had been educated in traditional English studies because they were already good at textual analysis. They knew it worked. They could analyze a poem to death; they could analyze a short story to death. They could pour over language and critique it. They were transferring those skills over to visual images. So they were able to transfer their print skills of practical criticism to moving images. That meant a lot of English teachers were then happy to be teachers of media; they were previously less uncomfortable when they thought they had to do practical work and they didn't know how to use a camera. But when the emphasis came to textual analysis and what they would call practical criticism, they thought, "That's neat, I could do that because they were used to doing it before and now they could do it with films."

At the same time in Australia, there was a huge increase in the population; there was a large influx of immigrants. The birth rate had gone up in the '60s, so these children now were in high school in the '70s, so there was a much bigger demand for teachers. And we weren't training qualified media teachers at that time; we had only just started training media teachers so we saw a lot of people switch over from being English teachers to being English and media teachers or just media teachers with actually the minimum of training. They might do a workshop that Barrie McMahon and I ran, a couple of workshops maybe, but that was about all. What they were actually doing was transferring their English skills to moving image classes. So what you saw was a huge increase in the number of students studying the subject and teachers who were dedicated to the teaching of that subject. So I guess the '80s saw a real change in terms of the conception of the subject, how it was taught and what was taught within it. What was happening at the same time was that teachers, and this is partly reflective of what was being done with textual analysis, were trying to make the subject more academic.

Within Australia, there was a hierarchy of important and nonimportant subjects. The important subjects were those that led you to university—that you had to pass to get into university. The nonimportant subjects were the ones that weren't counted for university entry. So you got within schools this hierarchy of subjects. The bright students did the important subjects and got into university. The other kids took the nonimportant subjects that wouldn't get you into university. Teachers greatly resented that . . . media studies were seen as nonimportant; therefore, they wanted to make media studies more academic. They fought very hard to have it accepted as what we called a "university-entry subject." Now to do that, they had to show that media studies were a lot more than about making films. It was about higher-order thinking, higher-order reading skills, in this particular instance, it was about reading images; it was a lot more writing about reading the meaning of images because previously students were just writing about what they saw, or writing about what they heard.

And this was all a part of the effort to make the subject a legitimate university-entry subject, and therefore get the same status as subject like mathematics, science, English, history, etc. OK, that kind of effort to make a subject more academic happened in other subjects; you can read histories of school subjects and see that it happened in geography and biology in England; it happened in commercial studies in Canada, so that what was previously seen as the study for students who were going to become secretaries became business-oriented for people who might want to go on to university and study commerce. So it is something that tends to happen among teachers, they want their subjects to be seen as important. So part of it is a bit of a self-investment for those teaching the subject because they want to get the status. Of course, unless you taught one of those important subjects, it was hard to get promotion to be a head teacher, because the head of department was always the lead person in the academic subject. So, media studies tended to be within the English department, but the person who was head was always the person who was the expert in the teaching of English, not in the teaching of media studies. So there was a vested interest in the teachers trying to get their subject accepted as an academic subject for their own career and focus. So issues of status, status of the subject, status of the teachers; it was quite important in modern curriculum. It wasn't purely an intellectual move; it was a political move on the part of teachers. So there was a lot of work put in by teachers to try to have media studies accepted as a subject that would lead to university entrance.

There were a number of submissions made for university-entrance status, and they got rejected by the responsible authority. One of the reasons for rejection was that teachers insisted upon having some production work and the examining board would say, "How are we going to manage that, we can't possibly have exams and practical work in them." Mind you our art teachers have been accepting portfolios for years. They also said that the less academically able were doing the subject, so, therefore, if you put it up to the level of university entrance, then these students wouldn't pass and there would be nothing for these students so the whole reason for the existence of the subject would disappear. And there was also, let's face it, some resistance from the established subject areas who didn't want another one in their spot because, if you introduce a new subject, fewer students will do another subject, so there's a certain amount of competition between subjects about popularity.

There was also some resistance within the media studies movement from other teachers who didn't want to see media studies as an academic subject and who thought that its reason for being was about empowerment of less academically able students to have curriculum relevant to their lives and how they spent their leisure time. So the resistance was from within the movement and without.

There were two groups of teachers: those who were very keen to see it become a highly academic subject and those that weren't. And then from without, there was a certain perception that media studies was sort of like Mickey Mouse in terms of being low level, too simple, too much about having fun not enough about hard work. And so those struggles went all throughout the '80s. At the same time, the universities were introducing media studies as a discipline within bachelor of arts degrees. That was partly the British influence, where cultural and media studies had been within universities for quite some time. Here in Western Australia it hadn't been. If you went and did a Bachelor of Arts, you did traditional subjects such as geography, history, literature, American literature, Australian literature, and colonial literature, whatever. And at the university I'm now at, Curtin University (which was then called the Western Australia Institute of Technology), media studies [was introduced]. And it became extremely popular and it had very strict quotas because so many students wanted to get in. It had a both practical and theoretical side to it. You could study film, but alongside it, you had to study film criticism. John Fiske came here to what was then called the Western Australia Institute of Technology and he transformed the English department into a cultural studies department. And when that happened, the university was drawing large numbers of students, and so the other two universities in Western Australia then introduced the same subject in competition. So you had developing at university quite an academic study of the media that wasn't matched by the study that was going on at the primary and secondary schools.

There's a disjunction there in many ways. So although students couldn't get into universities with media as a subject, once they got to university, they could study media, which in itself presents as a bit crazy. And teacher education faculties were also then introducing media studies as a discipline for teaching but you weren't allowed to only be in media studies, you had to be in media studies and also in English, so there was still this notion that you had to be out there teaching something serious as well as something not serious.

At the same time, the curriculum advisory staff had in the '70s been located in a school, and the school was then kind of the hub of media studies. Barrie and I were moved into the head office, and being moved into the head office gave us a certain legitimacy because you're in the bureaucracy, because as I said, it is a very centralized system and change here comes from the top down, not from the bottom up.

So the '80s brought a huge change in what we conceived of the subject. If you look back at some of the material that came out of the years, there was a lot of work on stereotypes and representation . . . the representation of race, the visual coding in film and in television, cultural representation, sexism, genre narrative, and semiotics started to become terms being used. So the sort of work that was being done was no longer, "Go out and make a documentary of your school." It was, "Explore the concept of the representation of gender in magazines or in popular film, etc.," so the content changed quite radically.

What happened later on was that there was a reform to the whole secondary education and all subjects became eligible for entry to university. That was a fair bit later down the track. So if I then move to the '90s, there were further changes, not as radical as the change from the '70s to the '80s. When I say the '70s–'80s, it wasn't like an overnight change; I'm talking broad changes across those decades. Now media studies had been introduced at a time when education policy was really focused on the notion of a socially just and equitable society where schooling was for everybody, schooling should be relevant to everybody, schooling wasn't just about weeding out some students and putting the bright ones to university.

In the '90s that discourse virtually disappeared entirely. What was driving the nation was to be economically competitive, an industrially restructured society. And that economic imperative it was believed should drive the education of young Australians; in other words education was not geared to make you a better and more well-rounded person, it was to make you a productive earning member of society, by which I mean you would pay taxes and contribute to the whole good of society. So there was a really big change in the educational discourse. This was partly because of youth and unemployment; this had been gradually growing through the late '80s and into the early '90s, so educational discourse leaned in the direction of how we've got to make the youth more employable, they've got to have skills to get them jobs. We can't just have them good at school to make them well-rounded people; the job then of schools was to start training people for jobs. And that again had some effect on media studies. Media studies teachers tried to demonstrate that they could provide job-ready skills, which this notion of pouring over the text and analyzing it to death couldn't demonstrate. So, it happened across all subjects that they were all more vocationally oriented and everyone had to make an effort to show that they were actually giving skills to students for life post-school.

So there were a number of bureaucratic changes and one thing that happened was that the job that I had as a curriculum adviser was abolished. They abolished all curriculum advisers and said that curriculum development should be led by the heads of department in schools. The professional development money that Barrie and I used to use to run centralized workshops for staff was taken away at the center and given away to schools, and schools could use it on whatever they thought was important. So there was a change in the structure of education as well as a sense of its purpose.

What was being demanded of media studies was to incorporate traditional literacy skills: writing, reading, speaking, and listening, exactly the same as what was in the English syllabus. What people saw then was that the English syllabus also started taking on the study of visual texts; previously it had only looked at printed texts. So there was this anxiety amongst media teachers that English was taking over their ground. And as a kind of a backlash to that, they actually increased their production element to differentiate themselves. So they were trying to make themselves look different [from] English, since media studies was a wholly school-assessed subject, with the idea that these subjects needed to cater for the broad range of students and for the requirements of the workforce. So media studies became, along with a number of other subjects, slightly vocationally oriented, wholly school-assessed, for kids that weren't going to go to university but needed to be able to demonstrate specific learning skills.

This continued on right through the '90s and into the early 2000s, and what happened then was there was a total reform of what was called postcompulsory for schooling. Postcompulsory [was at] ages 16 and 17, because students could still leave school at 15 if they went into a job or training. Then postcompulsory school was reformed on the basis that every child stay in school until the year 12 at which they turned 17. By doing that, the education authority said that we should no longer be weeding kids out at a young age, saying that the choice of the subject you do determines where you can go when you leave school. Rather, the educational authority said, all subjects are equal. Any subject you do will be externally examined and will count for university entry.

Now it's not as simple as that, because some subjects are seen as harder than others and therefore are scaled, but that was the theory, and that's still what's in existence today. So if you jump forward to 2011, media studies is a subject that counts for university entry, it is externally examined, it does consist of both a production element and a written element: It's roughly weighted 50–50. The production element is done at school, but they have to produce alongside the work if it be a film or a video or images, a written discursive piece that describes the process of production, what they learned from it, the barriers, etc.

TJ: What were some of your personal milestones?

RQ: I was a teacher of media studies, then I was a curriculum adviser, then I went to the university sector and taught media studies in the university sector. And I taught teachers who would be teachers of media studies. I was probably at the forefront of some of those changes of trying to make those changes both conceptually and pedagogically. Part of that came about because there was a funny disjuncture for some years while I was teaching media studies and I was still teaching with the syllabus that had students doing a lot production work and lots of freedom to express themselves. I was studying for my master's degree in media and that was very much influenced by cultural studies and was highly analytic. I had this kind of disjuncture about teaching one thing during the day and then having a different outlook at night in my studies. I guess that was part of the push, part of why the content of media studies changed. I mean all school subjects show a history of trying to become more academic. What that actually means is determined by those who actually construct and design the curriculum. And Barrie McMahon and I were largely in control of the curriculum so what got put into it, we saw as worthwhile knowledge.

TJ: Where do you see the field now?

RQ: I'm no longer teaching media studies, I'm entirely in the administration of the university. But I'm still on the curriculum board for the subject. I see the attitude to media production now as being extremely sophisticated, and I'm not sure that the emphasis on producing polished pieces of work places a sufficient emphasis on what you're actually learning about manipulating the medium. There is so much emphasis on the students getting their work to look really good and polished that you see a lot of derivative work; that, instead of creating something new and exciting, they are copying the forms they see in the popular media and trying to get them looking as polished as feature films, music videos, etc. So I don't see much of creative imagination or using the media as a form of critical analysis or analysis of the media itself. I see a lot of reproduction of popular media and I think that's partly due to being externally examined; it does count to get into university. The students are very keen to be seen to get it right and have a good product. And the sophistication of some of the equipment now that's available for domestic use is such that they can produce highly polished products. You're not sitting any longer on a flat bed trying to stick pieces of film together with a little bit of clear tape; they're doing it digitally and they can get it wrong a million times until they get it right without any loss. So the pressure to get a highly polished piece of work out is very strong, but I'm not sure you learn as much with that focus as you do with trying to break the rules instead of trying to copy the rules. What students are doing is internalizing the conventions and very rarely challenging them.

TJ: What would you like to see happen?

RQ: I'd like to see more studies of resistance and more studies that aren't mainstream popular culture. These are easy to teach because students know them very well. I'd like to see more effort done with independent work. One of the problems quite frankly is laziness and ease of access. It's much easier to get a videotape out of the local library or copies of popular film than it is to get any kind of independent work. I'd like to see the Media Studies Teacher Association and the media department put more energy in getting access to a lot more disruptive types of work, works that challenge the thinking, because without that kind of stimulus I don't think the students can do it; they don't have that world experience to think about what a disruptive text might look like. The closest thing you would get to that is if you're looking at those Michael Moore documentaries but by and large as works go, Michael Moore's stuff is pretty conservative in terms of its form and its approach. His radicalism just lies in tilting at the windmills of big business. It's a pretty poor excuse for a disruptive text I think. But that's about as far as they'd go, and I think that's an outcome of access to more exciting and innovative works. It's about their own lack of knowledge of them and how to deal with them which is a problem of universities and the way they train teachers. And it's a fear of the power of education, the examination system. What happens if the examiners have never seen these texts and don't understand them? They fear their students are going to get marked down; it's much easier to get them to write about *Avatar* which everyone will have seen than it is about an independent text. So the external examination system brings its own restrictions.

TJ: What would you like to see with teacher training?

RQ: When students apply to do their teacher training, they earn either a bachelor of education or a diploma of education (the diploma you do on top of a degree). They have to elect what they want to become teachers of, usually they do two areas which usually match how school timetables work. So if you'll be a science teacher able to teach some mathematics, it's very rare to find some English literature teacher who teaches math. They kind of sort themselves out prior to going to do their diploma of education. But you might see a math teacher who can also teach physical education. So we still largely see social sciences teachers also able to teach media studies and English teachers able to teach media studies because that's largely how the time tables of school work in terms of how they are put onto the time table.

So once a student comes to a university, they then enroll in the course of study that they want to teach. If they already have a degree in media studies, they don't do any more content study. What they do is the pedagogy of how you teach. If they do a bachelor of education, which is a four-year degree, they do their content study alongside their pedagogical studies so they'd be studying media studies at the same time as they are studying education. That's just two ways of becoming a teacher. So they are very much predetermined, that when they leave, they will be applying for jobs that are specifically for media studies teachers. Whereas from most of what I've seen in North America, people drift over to it as opposed to being trained to do it, so although when they are doing English studies, they may do some media studies, but they are not specifically media studies teachers.

Every school here offers media studies, so therefore when students decide "I'll become a media studies teacher," they know that there will be job opportunities for them because every school offers that subject.

Marieli Rowe

Marieli Rowe has been the executive director of the National Telemedia Council since 1978 and has turned a four-page newsletter into one of today's major print journals in media education: *The Journal of Media Literacy*. Additionally, Marieli has been involved in numerous projects such as developing Children's Film Festivals in the early 1960s as well as being a part of Governor Lee Dreyfus's early 1970s Cable Regulation Committee. From her involvement with this committee she was inspired to help develop the Sun Prairie's Children's Channel in the late 1970s, which was dedicated to children's programming. As evidenced by her contributions to the world of media literacy over the past several decades, Marieli Rowe is devoted to educating children and parents to create a healthy society in the midst of the media.

Edited Transcript: Interview, June 9, 2011
Interviewers: Dee Morgenthaler and Tessa Jolls

DM: How did you become involved in media education?

MR: Of course there is never just a single answer. It is a bundle of circumstances that just seem to have happened.

I can think of three things that came together for me; one of them being that we had moved to Madison, Wisconsin, and I had the early experience of meeting the founders of the American Council for Better Broadcasts, which is the oldest ongoing media literacy organization in the United States. That was the name of the council from 1953 to 1983. It was already built upon a previous, more local group that started in the mid-1930s in Madison as a committee of the local American Association of University Women (AAUW). They studied social issues, and they decided that in the mid-'30s, one of the things that educated women should learn about was radio.

So here in Madison, the founders Leslie Spence and Jessie McCanse were the leading people in that effort. It started as a local idea and it spread all throughout Wisconsin. In 1953, the group was incorporated as a national organization, the American Council for Better Broadcasts (ACBB). In 1983, we changed the name to reflect the fact that by now there was more than just broadcasting because by this time cable had come in and the beginnings of satellite communications were there as well. Of course, we didn't have the Internet at that point. But we wanted to get away from the word *broadcast* as being the only means of communication. So the group came up with an equally obtuse name: the National Telemedia Council (NTC). We had a subtitle that would identify what it meant which was "Look, Listen, Think, Respond." This was based on our annual evaluation project that we used to do called the Look Listen Project.

I don't have to go into all of the detail behind ACBB right now, but its philosophy evolved into media literacy.

DM: What brought you to Madison, Wisconsin?

MR: I came to Madison as a wife and mother. My husband had just finished his PhD in Natural Products Chemistry in Zurich, Switzerland, so we had lived in Switzerland for four years. During this time, we had added a second baby to our family. So, we had these two little boys aged three and four when we arrived in Madison, where I knew no one. I got involved with some of the wives of the Chemistry Department and the Forest Products Lab in Madison, and they were all busy, doing the Look Listen Project. At the same time, I was also struggling with coming from no television in Switzerland to people watching *Captain Kangaroo* and who knows what else.

I was faced with this new thing—television—that the neighbor's children were watching, and we didn't have a TV; we were going to do without. We just didn't think it was necessary, and in fact, we managed for a year, but it became impossible because the kids were watching at friends' houses where we couldn't control it, so we finally decided to get a TV. At least that way we would be able to manage so that our children would watch what we wanted and when we thought it was right. This was purely without any premeditation—it was merely parenting. I had this feeling that people were using TV to keep their children quiet, to keep them busy while they were cooking dinner. To me this was an uninvited babysitter. How could I have somebody walk into my house and have them take care of my children without knowing who they were and what they were doing?

So I really came through my own personal experience to some of these ideas. At the same time I was talking to all of these people who were doing the Look Listen Project. This was an evaluation of TV programs. Every year people were asked to evaluate and fill in a little sheet of paper that asked, "Did you rate this program excellent, good, fair, or poor?" Then, there was a space where you were supposed to say why you gave it that rating. It was a qualitative evaluation and the Council's main objective was not to tell anybody what's good or bad, but to try to get people to come to their own conclusions, to develop their own criteria for excellence and apply them. They had little study groups where the moms—who in those days weren't working—would have time to meet in each others' houses and talk about programs. So this all started from AAUW.

DM: Do you know if there were other organizations going on at the same time that were doing the same thing?

MR: I probably don't know everything that was going on, but I do know of an organization that existed at the same time called the National Association for Better Radio and Television in Los Angeles, headed by a man named Frank Orme. But his attitude was not at all like ours. Leslie Spence and Frank Orme tried to collaborate, but he was more interested in censoring and telling people what was good and bad and going after the broadcasters with boycotts, which was never the approach of the NTC. We were always based on a philosophy that did not tell anyone what was good and bad but asked people to think about it, evaluate, and come to their own conclusions. You can do that with grown-ups and with children, so we had lots of high school kids doing this project throughout the United States. Eventually it became too difficult to continue it because there were many more programs around with cable coming in.

Adding to the circumstances that led to my involvement in media literacy education was my own upbringing. My family was dedicated to deeply philosophical thinking. My parents were very educated people, and scientifically oriented. For example, you didn't just express or come to conclusions without a basis for it—that is critical thinking. My dad was a neuropsychiatrist, and my mother was a PhD in zoology as well as a singer and a musician. I studied biology. We all had that science background, but with a great deal of awe and appreciation for the arts and nature. So I think I had the stuff inside of me that responded to media literacy.

This tells you something about the opportunities and joys of being a parent of young children. By your own living and your own example, your children absorb your joy and need for deeply thoughtful living and for studying. They see it. You don't even need to tell them. They see it. That's what is so beautiful about it.

DM: What were your goals in terms of media literacy?

My goals were on several levels and they evolved. I will freely admit that as I started this, I looked at TV—which was the main focus because I wasn't thinking about radio so much. Radio for me was listening to music, it wasn't so much about all of the other programs—but I looked at TV with an eye to what it was doing to my children—the media effects. I went through the process that so many people go through starting out with wanting to get rid of sex and violence or at least not wanting it in my household. So what are you going to do? Are you going to censor? Manage? Or are you going to let your children watch what they want to watch and talk about it? Not at ages three and four, I wasn't going to. But I realized eventually that you can get young children to think and to make choices by giving them limited choices. You say, "Do you want the blue cookie or do you want the red cookie?" And then they choose and you say, "Oh, you chose the red cookie, so why is that?" I could get them started to think and to become aware. You can actually start the critical thinking process at a very young age but it takes parental guidance. So my goals began on a personal level and eventually spread to a much broader stance—it went from media effects to media literacy.

It became a fascination and I began to realize that—not just for my own family—it was an incredibly important part of a healthy society in the midst of the media environment. We need to be educated about the media. This education is a process that needs to start as early as possible and it should be a lifelong process. One thing led to another and I became involved in the organization—it was my first "real job."

I was a very busy mom. So I said, "I don't think I have time for this project now, but if and when I do, it's got to be about children." Then I was invited to help plan the first ACBB Children's Film Festival, and so that became my first project. We did this Children's Film Festival in 1962 or 1963. The idea was that we were trying to prove that the broadcast industry's claim that they were airing all these cartoons and mediocre popular programs to children, "because that was what children want," was flawed. That was the industry's ploy. We decided to show them that this was not true. We wanted to show that if you give children some really exciting, beautiful programs, they will want those just as much . . . maybe even more. So we held this children's film festival at one of our local high schools where we showed films such as *Madeline*, *The Red Balloon*, *Harold and the Purple Crayon*, *White Mane*, and many other famous children's films. It was a three-day event to which we invited not only the children (and their families), but also an entire audience of specially chosen adults who sat up in the balcony—broadcasters, psychologists, teachers, FCC commissioners, journalists, and other professionals. We wanted them to watch the children watch these programs. It was a big success and that was one of our big claims to fame back in the early '60s.

Eventually my goals broadened, and I became very aware that there was a lot more to this than just on a personal level.

My goal today—and really always has been—is that we need to have media literacy throughout our society. I have an ultimate goal to take away the word *media* because reading and writing have always been a goal of all education—becoming literate. And what we are using today is just a new pen and a new book. It's the same process. There is more to learn because there are more issues involved—more complex factors such as who's paying for it and who's behind it, how is it represented and whose choice is it and all of those basic criteria that we use when teaching kids about the media—but essentially we are using a new pen, aren't we?

It seems to me that if we could get to the point where the word *literacy* means all of the media, and it pervades our education, and a goal for a healthy society is to be literate and that includes all of the media then I think they won't need organizations, nonprofits, volunteer organizations anymore—it will be part of the infrastructure and the system. That is the ultimate goal—to be obsolete.

A wonderful example of the diversity of that "new pen," the pervasiveness of "media," and their reach into our everyday lives was invented by our Canadian friend Barry Duncan. When Barry was teaching high school, he used to send his students to the local mall, and he called that event a "Mall Crawl"; and the kids were supposed to go to the mall and observe how things "worked" in the mall—where they put merchandise, what soothing music they have in there, and that it is really hard to find a clock so that you lose yourself in there. He is the one who invented the Mall Crawl. We once did such a Mall Crawl at one of our conferences in Madison. Barry Duncan was our major speaker, and he sent the whole audience out up and down the main street in Madison for about an hour and a half to bring something back that showed an illustration about media literacy. An unforgettable experience!

DM: So, what has surprised you about this journey?

MR: It is full of surprises. But it wasn't so much a surprise as it was becoming informed as each new discovery was found. For example, some surprises were learning about the various agendas, the politics, and the lack of awareness. One of the things that really keeps surprising me is the resistance that comes from education. That always goes back to the argument between media effects versus media education. And the fact that people don't seem to be able to differentiate what are media effects and what is media education. So you have people doing exercises in the classroom that are really not media education—they address media effects.

This points to the difficulties encountered in teaching the critical thinking skills that are basic to media literacy education. I was reading in the *Media L* a discussion by Faith Rogow in regards to Boy Scout Merit Badges. Having three boys myself, I got involved with Boy Scout Merit Badges. I had the Madison Scout group interested in doing a merit badge in media literacy, so we were doing that for a while but when my kids grew up, it was gone. We did it by using media production, and we found the American Family Insurance people who had a studio and were willing to help us teach scouts how to produce a program. That became a scout activity, although it was only temporary, as the insurance people pulled out eventually. Now, apparently, someone has come up again with a media literacy merit badge in the scouts, and again they do not understand what is needed. Faith was saying that this is not media literacy; it's media effects. It pervades. There is a major gap here in the need to teach the teachers. So those are the things that keep on happening. It doesn't surprise me anymore because I am so used to it.

DM: What do you think about the fact that people are creating so much media on the Internet and on their personal computers?

MR: I will go back to my earlier thought, which was that you didn't have to produce the stuff to learn about it. You could just sit there and not necessarily have to know how to wield a camera—and you know in those early days the studio cameras were huge, so I was thinking, "Is this really necessary to become media literate?" But I came to realize that just as in print literacy you can't possibly be a good evaluator until you have tried writing, so that's when I began to realize that yes, there is more to it; you have to try it yourself. Our "KIDS-4" Children's Cable Channel was an early illustration of this powerful tool. The Internet and new media have made the process of production, interaction, creation, remixing, and a host of other previously impractical or impossible activities possible, indeed easy, and in fact crucial. It has fundamentally and irreversibly changed everything.

DM: Were there specific people that have inspired your work?

MR: Some inspiring people I have met along the years are most definitely the pioneers of ACBB—Leslie Spence and Jessie McCanse. The two of them started the ACBB and worked together as teachers and innovators that started this whole effort. They taught me so much, but most importantly, they taught me the difference between media effects and media literacy. They started that whole concept of evaluation when they did the first qualitative evaluation project in the U.S. It certainly was the single most innovative thing I had ever heard of and at its peak we had 10,000 nationwide people involved.

Leslie Spence was incredibly influential in my life. To give a bit of a background, Leslie Spence was a PhD and one of those women who should have been a professor but in those days, women with PhDs got to be high school teachers. She never married but dedicated her life, money, and everything to this cause and organization. Jessie McCanse was the wife of a professor and the daughter of the president of the University of Missouri; she had two children of her own. These people were just incredibly inspiring folks who never wavered from their basic philosophy and vision.

I hesitate to try naming the many, many incredible innovators, pioneering educators, and truly exciting people who have inspired me along the way . . . they have become my friends as well, and the list is long and still growing, as we move so rapidly into new territories! . . . how can I do justice to them all without omitting!

TJ: What do you see as some important milestones?

MR: It starts out with the fact that the realization of so much of what ended up being my passion in this was really already instilled in me from childhood. I had two parents who were so incredibly reflective, globally oriented, and open to the positive things that anyone and everyone had to say. That doesn't mean that they didn't have opinions. We were living through the Nazi years in Europe, so some if it was pretty dark, but I think I grew up in a very rich environment where I had the ability to be passionate. It was a wonderful gift from my parents and probably their parents before them.

Anyway, my interest in media didn't really start until Jack and I came back to the United States after having lived in Switzerland, where we had two preschoolers. Until then, we had not even become aware of the existence of such a thing as media, and certainly not as something that touched our lives. But I began to think of it because I had those children. Now for myself personally, I hadn't studied media studies, journalism, or anything that could've pointed me in that direction. In fact, I remember meeting a woman once when I was a child in Switzerland who had said she was a journalist. She looked and sounded very autocratic and strange and I wondered what on earth kind of a weird creature a journalist would be. Anyway, I was a biology major, and that is science and nature. I was very interested in ecology. As I was studying as an undergraduate and also as a graduate student at the University of Colorado in Boulder, I was fascinated with the study of the interaction of evolving ecosystems and their impact on all living things within their changing environments. That eventually translated into my interest in my children and what constituted their world. So it was a very natural transition for me in terms of "The Ecology of Childhood." It's the process I've been talking about for years. In this light, things like television and other media were changing the traditional environment of childhood. When a baby is born, he or she faces a very limited world of the mother, father, or maybe someone else. The mother is the first impression in the environment of a newborn baby. And then the child's world grows and expands to the home, the neighborhood, churches, and school. In a natural environment all this can progress at a pace commensurate with the child's normal brain development. But today's children enter into the new media world even at birth, faced with visual stimuli that are very strong. When you put a baby in front of television or other visual media, a whole new experience is there. I think a lot of the new brain research corroborates that media can stimulate new brain synopses; there are connections made.

The milestones from this were all connected later on. I would say looking for milestones in my personal life, it's really all connected to people. First, the Wisconsin people that I met like Leslie Spence and Jessie McCanse who introduced me to their wonderfully sage philosophy of the educational and positive approach toward media, as opposed to negative reactions, such as turning off the TV or boycott—which were being done back in those days. In contrast, the point for the NTC group was to evaluate, to see what there is, and to choose wisely. That was a very big "first" for me.

Later on, I met people like Barry Duncan from Canada who put a new spin on all of this. Barry and his group of educators in Ontario had established basic criteria for teaching this thing called media literacy. We had always said, "Yes, we recognize media literacy," but there wasn't this well-defined set of basic concepts. Actually, these concepts were based on the work of Len Masterman, who was the first to put a systematic pedagogy into media literacy education.

I began to expand my own knowledge and my own horizons to see that media literacy was really a very well-definable and teachable topic. My personal journey began when I started to think in terms of getting media literacy into schools. Before that, it was all parents and teachers but on an informal level, such as developing good viewing habits and being able to say why you liked a program and why you didn't, and as a family decide what is worth your time. Now, I did believe that you could teach a very small child something about making choices. It was an evolution for me. Becoming aware through Barry's acquaintance, I went to my first conference in Guelph, Canada. John Pungente was also there, and he was very influential and people need to give him credit. At the Guelph conference, I also met Len Masterman, as well as Eddie Dick and Barrie McMahon from Australia, and many of the amazing group of Ontario educators. Several of us came from Madison, including Mary Moen and Jean Pierre Golay. I will never forget when Barrie McMahon was giving his keynote address. He said, "Before I begin, I cannot start this speech of mine without paying tribute to someone who is in the audience here, and that is Jean Pierre Golay who has been so influential." It was an incredible moment. Jean Pierre is so modest, he doesn't say these things, but he sat there. So that's one of those times that were milestones for me.

Then we began working with a new generation of pioneers later on, as the media began to become more interactive. We had started an early interactive group back in Madison in the late '70s, a children's channel. That idea came from the fact that when cable first came on the screen (and that was in the early or mid-'70s), I ended up on a governor's commission to study whether cable should be regulated or not. The chair of that commission was Lee Sherman Dreyfus, at that time chancellor of UW Stevens Point, future Wisconsin governor. Lee had also been manager of WHA-TV Public Television Station in Madison and a professor of media studies at the University of Wisconsin, and a former student of Marshall McLuhan. He was chairing that commission and he knew that I was working with the American Council for Better Broadcasts (ACBB). I got an official letter from the governor asking me to serve on this commission and I knew nothing about cable. I thought, "I'm the wrong person; they must have made a mistake." So I sent back my response saying, "I'm sorry, I couldn't possibly be on that commission." The next thing that happened was Lee Dreyfus calling me on the phone, saying, "Marieli, you've got to be on that commission. I want you on this commission because you don't already know everything about it." He had two of us from the ACBB (the other was Phyllis Young). If I was going to be involved in something like that, I would have to learn something, so I went to some workshops and learned about cable and read everything I could and pretty soon got myself fairly well informed. And that is where this idea for a children's channel was cooked up: if you're going to have that many channels, why not have one channel that would be completely dedicated to children's programming? There would be no ads and the mother could safely say, "Yes, dear, you can watch television." It's like putting a good book in their hands.

Through this idea (and it eventually took several years more) came KIDS-4, the Sun Prairie Children's Channel, which is still in existence today. It's a channel of television by and for children. They are the producers; the on-air talent, the camera crew; they do everything. This was a very early pioneering idea. Interactive TV was something that we were involved with very early, but it was still nothing like what happened much later with the era of the Internet. When you have a television station, it's a very real and physical experience; you see the people and camera and you learn how it works. People like me who need to know "why it works "and "what are the wires inside" can get a handle on it.

Another landmark for me was literally broadening my knowledge base. I went back to school to get my master's degree and experienced running conferences and assuming the role of executive director of this organization. I came from having no experience and then being told after three months of being executive director that you're supposed to put out a newsletter. So it's really been a huge learning curve for me.

Then came the age of the last real change: Working in the new virtual world there were two particular people who were incredibly influential. One was Martin Rayala, who comes as an art and design educator and artist. He came onto our board because he was interested in new media. It was Jean Pierre Golay who suggested him; he knew him from the art world. Martin opened up this world of media literacy and the Arts. And then the other person is my own son Peter. I watched him and learned from him, and I developed a definition of an artist as "someone who sees where others have not yet begun to look." For an artist such as my son, it is an innate thing, a talent they are born with. They are walking to a different drummer, which you can see when they are children.

However, while the rest of us may not be gifted with that, we can learn it. And that is media literacy. You may not become the genius or a Michelangelo, but at least you can learn to understand why he was a genius and what it was that made him a genius. So you can become a highly educated media literate person.

One thing that occurred to me was that milestones of the "movement" toward media literacy cannot just be enumerated. It's just so huge and broad because it's a whole new world culture. We need to study this from a new point of view, at least. What I say about one event and what someone else says about the same event would be really hard to match.

But I was thinking what the stages are that are needed to see change. First of all, you have to have an identity, and the second one is people following the idea . . . the third thing would be finding evidence . . . I know that the last part is reaching a critical mass. That is the question. Have we reached a critical mass? I do not know.

TJ: I feel that so much of education has been going on a different track in recent years. It's been in an environment that has been very hostile to what we are trying to accomplish. My bottom line is I think that people are seeking an innate freedom and independence that our work supports, and it feeds into a basic human need and desire. So, with that in mind eventually it will triumph because it has to.

MR: First of all, a point of view has to be identified, if we talk about how to effect change, we could say that some of the high points were the early pioneers, the educators and scholars of the '30s and '40s that I happen to know because it's in the Wisconsin history. But there were people like Louis Forsdale at Columbia Teacher's College, and Edgar Dale and Keith Tyler at Ohio State. They laid some of the foundations of what you might call critical thinking and listening skills. So on an academic level, it was an important period when people who were educators and scholars in pedagogy began to think in terms of fundamentals to critical listening and thinking. Then congressional studies were done in the '60s where Congress conducted a million-dollar study on media effects. And the FCC did an inquiry about the media, violence, and sex and one additional question that actually came about because we suggested it: It was about critical viewing skills. That was a landmark question because FCC commissioners Abbot Washburn and Kenneth Cox apparently had a very strong personal relationship with Leslie Spence, and it was at her request that they included these questions in the inquiry. That particular study at the FCC came up with the insight that media do have an effect on the viewer, etc. but the effect can be mitigated through parental or other guidance. That was, to me, the go-ahead sign for media literacy: That you didn't have to just sit there and be dumb, but rather you take that material and do something with it in your head.

Then that was followed by the million-dollar congressional allocation to develop four curricula: One was in New York with the WNET, one was in Texas, one was in Boston, and one was in San Francisco. There were four stages of schools: primary, secondary, college-age, and post-college. And our wonderful Wisconsin senator Proxmire gave the Congress one of his Golden Fleece Awards for money badly spent, because according to him, all they were doing was teaching kids how to watch television (and wasn't that a terrible waste of children's and teachers' time) . . .

A major contribution was made in developing theory and practice by the influence of Len Masterman in England and the Canadians Barry Duncan, John Pungente, their colleagues, their new organization, the Association for Media Literacy.

The last big milestone is the media explosion, which was—and is—a huge shift. All the earlier things could have been ideas that you could add into the curriculum, which were very much friendlier to the old way of teaching school. You could teach those concepts within the school curriculum, whether it was across the curriculum or a list of courses. But now, suddenly came the age of the chip covering everything from interactive media learning to literacy and learning. Much has changed in education, and we have people who say that the way we used to teach is completely obsolete and there are different ways we ought to teach.

There are people who like to teach by doing games which of course is a teaching tool, but it isn't the end-all. In my view, the games people have are a wonderful and valid approach, but it's just not the only thing. Also we have Henry Jenkins who believes in all of that, although he would agree that it's not only games. We believe that there is such a thing as media education.

These are some of the latest directions in the development of a new media literacy education, and I wanted to give you a quote from Lee Dreyfus. In 1983, as I stated earlier, we changed our name from American Council for Better Broadcasts to the National Telemedia Council because we were aware that between the rivals of cable, satellite, the new desktop computer in our office, the spectrum of 100 television channels—the time had come that our very name was obsolete. And our speaker for this big convention that we had in Madison, Lee Dreyfus, said this: "As you change your name today to the National Telemedia Council, I tell you, you are on the verge of changing an entire organization to adapt to the chip." Now this was 1983. Most people didn't even know what a chip was. Then he predicted, "The last 30 years of the explosive telecommunications growth may have just been a garden hose compared to the potential Niagara Falls of the next 30 years of telecommunication. The public defense against inundation rests in the citadel of the individual mind through education, and in selective attention to the media."

TJ: Why do you believe media literacy is important?

MR: It seems to me as basic a part of life as being alive. You need to know the air you breathe, to make sure there is oxygen in it. I mean it's that basic. The media are our path to communication and mindful and meaningful communication. So it's the literacy of the age. In the early days of writing, only the monks could write and everybody else was ignorant. Among the Native Americans or Incas, the king was illiterate and therefore didn't know anything, but his scribe was the one who had the knowledge. The power was in those people who could communicate and who were literate. And that hasn't changed. So why teach anything? We're still saying "first learn to read and write." Now in this new media age, all of these basic principles prevail. That's why we need media literacy. People say, "Why would I need to learn that, I already know how to watch television and use my cellphone." For instance, a person who wants to sing can just open his mouth and sing. But if you want to become a true singer, you have to take lessons on how to breathe so that you can keep the skill well into your life.

The most urgent—I'm convinced—is a willingness to change a decades-old atmosphere of confrontation, politics, and competitive negativism to a culture of inclusiveness and collegiality, mutual respect, and collaboration that is devoid of personal agendas in which new ideas in education in a new century can thrive.

As for achieving the goals of a multimedia-wise and reflective society, the quest goes on. Learning to be literate is a personal journey, the challenge is to be global while remaining relevant at home—to expand the vision to tomorrow while remaining grounded today, to strive for a positive nonjudgmental and passionate spirit of listening to diverse voices of individuals and cultures, and to know that achieving the goal in the age of the global village is not static but involves living mindfully with change.

The other thing about this need for media literacy that I've wanted to say is that media literacy is becoming necessary—indeed crucial—way beyond anything most of us had imagined even up until a couple of years ago. For instance, what is happening in the Middle East is an example. It has become so graphic that in a way it's an advantage for us who are trying to bring media literacy into the forefront; it's so obvious. Anybody will say you can't believe everything you see or hear; it's manufactured. A picture isn't necessarily worth a 1,000 words because it could've been manufactured. All of that is media literacy.

In a way, the extremism that is happening all around us now might just be an ally in really showing the need. People in those countries, like in Libya, etc. put their hopes on this because they had a chance to see. You cannot keep it from spreading when it's being put out there on little cell phones.

So when Lee Dreyfus talked about the "Niagara Falls," I see his Niagara Falls happening in the Middle East right now. At the same time, I also see that people are misunderstanding Americans, because we don't know other cultures. So when we walk in with our cultural ideas, it may absolutely not work for some other people.

This is a global instant and a totally invasive digital world in which all are equal, and at risk in power. We're all in the same boat. Media literacy's apex may very well be a road to new sensitivity for becoming a more civilized global society if we could develop common language through the rich variety of media.

Elizabeth Thoman

Elizabeth Thoman now devotes her time and photographic talent to Healing Petals, a collection of unique photographs to stimulate meditation, reflection, and prayer, as well as to media literacy issues. She founded *Media&Values Magazine* in 1977 and the Center for Media Literacy in 1989. She is one of four founders of the Partnership for Media Education, formed in 1997 to promote professional development in the field through organizing and hosting the National Media Education Conference. In 2001, PME evolved into a national membership organization, the Alliance for a Media Literate America (AMLA), which was renamed the National Association for Media Literacy Education. In 2002, Thoman received the Daniel J. Kane Lifetime Achievement Award from the University of Dayton (Ohio) and in 2006 received the Leaders in Learning Award from Cable in the Classroom for a lifetime of leadership in media literacy education. A Roman Catholic nun since 1964, she is a member of the progressive Sisters of the Humility of Mary, Davenport, Iowa. She began her career as a journalism and English teacher.

Edited Transcript: Interview, February 16, 2011
Interviewer: Tessa Jolls

TJ: How did you become involved in media education?

ET: I didn't, it involved me . . . When I got interested in what we now call media literacy education, the field didn't even exist. It was just something I was interested in. I later learned other people were interested in it too but in the early 1970s, none of us knew each other.

As a Catholic sister, I had been a high school teacher—English, journalism, religion—and I had had some experience in using media in the classroom and involving my students in some simple media projects. One Saturday in 1969, I remember transporting my 10 journalism students to a nearby college campus where a speaker named Marshall McLuhan was delivering a lecture. None of us, including myself, really knew what he was talking about, but somehow I felt he was important and wanted my students to hear him!

Thanks to the controversies McLuhan generated, the topic of "media and technology" and its impact in people's lives, was moving from the back burner to the front in American society. Most of the critique was negative—Peggy Charron was fighting with the FTC about children's advertising on television; the movie *Network* had coined the phrase about television, "I'm mad as hell and I'm not going to take it anymore." FCC chairman Newton Minow had excoriated the TV industry by calling American broadcasting a "vast wasteland." Most educators agreed: They saw little redeeming social value in most of media, especially television. And new technology? It was a mystery.

After a couple years of teaching high school, I was offered a job in California at a Catholic film studio that was creating innovative films for religious education. Each was short, less than 10 minutes, and designed to stimulate discussion and conversation in the classroom. It was film that didn't give answers but tried to raise questions. They took the religious education world by storm and were very successful in progressive Catholic and even Protestant educational circles.

So whenever I heard teachers (or anyone) slamming "the media," I was perplexed because I had personal experience that media products like the short films we were creating *could* be very effective in helping young people wrestle with issues that were important to them. It seemed to me that just dismissing media per se was not a smart thing to do. But I didn't know how to convince people otherwise. It was just a gut instinct.

TJ: So how did you deal with that?

ET: In 1976, I enrolled in grad school at the Annenberg School for Communication at the University of Southern California. I thought I might get some clues about how to better integrate media into education, into family life, into society at large. Things began to click when I took a class taught by the charismatic Dr. Richard Byrne called Communication and Social Values. It was a seminar course—Dr. Byrne would pose questions about communications issues, and then the class would spend three hours exploring and discussing the pros and cons.

One night he explained how the Japanese were developing half-inch videotape recorders. (Remember the first VCRs used two-inch tapes, and the equipment was humongous and not at all useable in schools). He asked—if in the near future, you could buy a highly portable half-inch VCR at an affordable price of say, $150, at K-Mart—what would you use it for? Where would the tapes come from? How would they be distributed? (Blockbuster had yet to be invented!) Some of my classmates immediately thought of pornography! Others thought movies might be put on tape for screening in the home. There was conversation about advertising and about issues of ownership. I suggested that the VCR might very well replace the 16mm film projector in classrooms. Educational film was big business in more progressive schools. Certainly the films I had been working on the last few years could be distributed on tape. I thought if a smaller VCR would be easier for teachers to use, then maybe more of them would use media resources in the classroom to engage their students more effectively.

There were other issues we discussed in that class too. The desktop computer was a new idea. Cable television. The introduction of broadcast satellites bringing education to parts of the world that didn't even have telephones. For me the course was an exciting time of discovery. But I had no idea how foundational it would turn out to be.

TJ: You mean *Media&Values*?

ET: Yes. I think you know the story. One night Dr. Byrne asked us to come back the next week with an idea for a culminating project. I thought and thought and finally decided I'd start a magazine for teachers—to try to prepare them for the world to come, the media culture that was evolving. It would be called *Media&Values* because it would "explore the values questions raised by the transition from the Industrial Age to the coming Information Age." I didn't presume to know the answers to the questions, I just wanted a forum (for myself if no one else) where we could explore, wrestle with, try to figure out the implications of this coming shift. I figured there were people who could write on one topic or another and we could publish them and get a conversation going.

Dr. Byrne just said, "Turn the first issue in for credit." I did and got an A! *Media&Values* continued for 63 quarterly issues until 1994.

TJ: What did you publish first?

ET: The year before I had given a presentation at the annual convention of the National Catholic Education Association, which I called "Television and Listerine: I Hate It but I Love It." It was my first attempt to articulate this dilemma about the potential power of media and technology to educate and inform but at the same time be so problematic. I decided this would be the key article in the first issue. It was like laying down a gauntlet.

TJ: Was that the beginning of media education?

ET: Not specifically. In the speech, I proposed that we needed teachers who knew how to deal with the media and to help kids who were growing up in a more mediated world. I didn't have a name for it, I think I called it "media awareness" . . . and I certainly didn't have a program for it! I was just trying to raise consciousness about a new kind of teaching in the world to come.

TJ: . . . and what year was that, Liz?

ET: The speech was in the spring of 1976; the first issue of *Media&Values* was fall, 1977. I had kept that speech realizing that it could be an article in a magazine. I didn't think I'd have to create the magazine, too!

TJ: But it was a kind of recognition, a kind of turning point in recognition awareness.

ET: It probably was but I don't think I recognized it was a turning point, I was just trying to articulate what I had instinctively come to—that education and educators needed to do something about preparing the next generations to live and learn in a mediated world. And it had to be positive, not negative.

TJ: Now, would you say then that this was your goal . . . to build under-standing that media IS our culture and that we really have to understand the implications of that?

ET: Right. I think I'm the one that coined the use of the word *navigate*—we have to teach young people (and ourselves) how to *navigate* media culture. As I said, most people took *navigate* to mean *avoid*—how do you avoid the danger in the rocky shore? How do you *tame* media's *powerful* influence? I didn't buy that. I knew effective teaching is never about avoidance, it's about creatively exploring and implementing new ideas in one's world.

TJ: Well along that line, what were some milestones that you noted along the way, for yourself and for the field? Maybe the best way to approach it is to share your story in terms of how you went along after founding *Media&Values*. That will help provide some perspective in terms of your early experiences as well as some of the things that may have later on turned out to be milestones.

ET: Well, one of the greatest influences, right about that same time, '76–'77, was in the Protestant church world. The Methodists, Presbyterians, Luther-ans, Episcopalians all had very professional communications programs and often worked jointly with the National Council of Churches. They published magazines, produced television shows, radio productions, etc. Led by the prophetic Dr. Everett Parker of the United Church of Christ, they also had a very active advocacy presence with the FCC and the media industry around issues of "representation" in the media—gender, race, age, ethnicity—as well as economic and ownership concerns. In the early '70s, several denomi-nations jointly created a nonprofit organization to be an umbrella for projects that they could do together—thus saving duplication of cost and having more impact. It was called the Media Action Research Center (MARC) and the first project was an education program known as Television Awareness Training or "T.A.T."

The plan was to find and train a team of regional trainers who in turn would do workshops and programs for parents and teachers at the local grassroots church level. The program would have a comprehensive book for participants and a collection of film clips from TV and movies for trainers to use to spark discussion. Do you remember seeing the books in our library?

TJ: Yes I do.

ET: Well MARC was in the midst of writing it and asked me to help create the program. But they had no money to pay me so I couldn't take it—they all had paid staff positions with their denominational offices so it wasn't a problem for them.

TJ: Yes, the freelancer's dilemma!

ET: But we stayed in touch and I contributed several small pieces to the book. I also took the T.A.T. leader training. In retrospect I think the book itself and the process of working on it helped refine some of the things I felt merited further exploration in *Media&Values*. So Television Awareness Training was one important milestone.

TJ: What were some other early influences?

ET: In the world of *public* education, there were a number of other initiatives in the late 1960s and early 1970s that contributed seeds to what has become the media literacy movement. Many of these were highly localized—usually one or maybe several teachers who created innovative programs to involve students in media projects—making Super 8 films, creating slide shows, even building small broadcast studios and involving students in creating and producing morning news shows or broadcasting sports to the local community.

A good example is the work done by teachers and parents in the Larchmont/Mamoroneck school district just north of New York City. In the early 1960s, supported by progressive administrators, they actually built a small broadcast studio in an elementary school and even involved first graders in producing a morning news show. There's a famous photograph of a 10-year-old standing on a stack of *books* to peer through the viewfinder of studio camera on a rolling tripod! In her book, *Children of Telstar*, Kate Moody, who was one of the community volunteers who helped design and implement the program over several years, tells the whole story—it's pretty fascinating.

Many of these 1960s teachers were themselves influenced by the magazine *Media&Methods*, a controlled circulation publication that served the burgeoning audio-visual and instructional media departments in public schools and school districts at the time. But in the midst of all the ads for overhead projectors and TV carts were some great articles about kids making Super-8 movies and teachers using media in the classroom. I was an avid *Media&Methods* reader myself when I was teaching and like many readers, I'm sure, felt that the magazine validated my early instincts about media as a creative educational agenda. I guess it also impressed on me the power of the printed word as a way to disseminate new ideas about education!

TJ: Was there any effort to actually create classroom curriculum?

ET: One extremely interesting project I found out about a few years ago actually came from the middle of the heartland—outside of Des Moines, Iowa—not far from where I had taught a few years earlier. Apparently Vice President Spiro Agnew visited Iowa in 1970 and delivered a speech where he used his famous phrase "nattering nabobs of negativity" to describe the so-called liberal news media. Two high school teachers from Red Bud, Iowa, decided that if the growing media world was such a problem, they ought to be teaching their students about it.

Eventually they secured a Title III grant from the United States Office of Education (USOE) under the Elementary and Secondary Education Act (ESEA) to support the prototyping, research, evaluation, and dissemination of *Media Now,* a pioneering curriculum that covered everything from how cameras worked and production basics to genre study, analyzing visuals, and developing criteria for evaluating media messages. It was rather amazing!

But the program's uniqueness was its three large cardboard boxes containing 50 self-contained learning activity packages—each containing materials, resources, and directions to complete a specific instructional exercise. The boxes could be delivered to any classroom as a permanent placement or transported from site to site within a school or district. I have been told that over 500 copies of the program were manufactured by hand and sold to schools throughout the U.S. about the same time that *Media&Values* was being gestated. I had never heard of it at the time but there is one copy in our archives and it's a fabulous artifact of early attempts at curriculum development!

A later attempt was a four-part *Critical Viewing Curriculum* (elementary, high school, college, and adult, I believe) funded by the U.S. Department of Education itself with the help of several universities and regional educational labs. It had a copyright date of 1980 and had the potential to be influential nationally but if you recall who was elected president in 1980?—Ronald

Reagan—and what his educational philosophy was?—"back to the basics"— anything as innovative as "critical viewing" just never found a foothold in U.S. educational policy even though at the very same time in Canada, Australia, England, and many other countries, media literacy was really taking off. Indeed, a year or two after it was published the curriculum was awarded one of the infamous Golden Fleece Awards for wasting tax-payer money to "teach kids to watch television."

TJ: Why do you think media literacy developed in other countries but not so much in the U.S.?

ET: Others may have their own insights, but there are two that I think are the most significant. The first was the growing influence of U.S. media around the world in the 1970s. I first became aware of this through the broad religious community I talked about earlier. There are two international religious organizations that operate in the field of media. One was called "UNDA"— a Catholic organization and the other is the World Association for Christian Communication (WACC) that at the time was headquartered in London. Funded heavily by European churches, both WACC and UNDA helped to organize many projects in what we then called the Third World—to foster the use of communications technology for building community and giving people a voice in their own future.

This was necessary because as television spread around the world, few countries had the trained personnel or the educational and economic infrastructure to produce their own programs about their own issues or culture. The U.S. media industry, of course, stepped in to fill this void by repackaging Hollywood movies and network TV programs and selling them cheaply. "Who shot J.R.?" was probably the first "cliffhanger" recognized everywhere around the world!

Educational leaders everywhere quickly realized their own cultures (and cultural values) were in danger of being lost in this onslaught of thousands of hours of U.S. "storytelling." It appears that media literacy was born simultaneously in dozens of countries all through the 1980s. When I went to a UNESCO sponsored-conference on media education in Toulouse, France, in 1989, I was stunned to meet teachers from 30 or 40 countries all carrying around published textbooks and teaching materials in their own languages. The next year when I went to Manila for a WACC congress, I met hundreds more *religious* educators and communicators with a similar commitment to media education.

What became obvious to me was that almost everywhere outside the U.S., educators had taken what was a *negative* problem for their cultures (loss of cultural values) and transformed it into a *positive* program of educational awareness and insight.

The U.S. of course didn't recognize television as a cultural invasion because it was *our* media. Stories reflected the world outside our windows, at least to some extent. We were blind to the extent that visual media was transforming the culture and values of American life.

But the greatest issue in the U.S. was simply size. Unlike other countries which have maybe a few thousand schools all teaching from a national curriculum, the U.S. education system is organized locally—50 states with 160,000 independent school districts, 4 million teachers, 50 million students . . . we still see it today . . . very little gets done quickly or efficiently. Media literacy didn't have a chance until the Internet transformed everything—and then suddenly the importance of teaching "21st-century skills" became obvious—and critical. It's just media literacy wrapped up in a new package—and improved of course by time and experience.

TJ: So was anything going on in the U.S. in the 1980s?

ET: Well lots of things were happening but not in any coherent way across the country. For example, more people in education began to explore the potential of television and visual media in how children learn—especially after *Sesame Street* became such a success. But this was about *using media to teach* rather than teaching about media itself.

There was a growing citizen activism around media issues—cable access, advertising to children, depiction issues (race, gender, etc.), which helped build awareness by parents and teachers of the influence of economic and political forces in what appeared on television.

And with the arrival of lightweight video systems and the rise of community television stations and access channels provided by cable companies, everyday citizens began to make their own video and produce programming. This demystified the whole production process for people of all ages. In schools, the field of instructional technology developed to also teach production skills and many gained support because they could be justified as job and career training.

Perhaps the most significant work with schoolchildren was Foxfire, a teaching experiment that came out Appalshop, a regional media arts center in Kentucky. And I should also mention the work of what is now called the National Telemedia Council in Madison, Wisconsin, founded by a group of women more than 50 years ago to promote education by and about television and media. They've been a small but mighty force in raising awareness, developing workshops for teachers, publishing, and networking.

Kathleen Tyner once wrote an article about the media education field using the analogy of the blind men and the elephant. Each one touches one part of the elephant—the trunk, an ear, a leg—and thinks that's what an elephant is. Of course, they're all missing the big picture.

I don't believe educators missed the big picture because of any real fault or even blindness. The enormity of the cultural shift driven by ever new technology along with the sheer geographical size of the American landscape made it impossible for *any* one person, group, or organization to get a handle on everything that was happening.

Plus no one had a mandate, much less the time and travel money, to think or organize nationally. I was lucky, I guess, that *Media&Values,* gave me a perfect excuse to try to find out who was doing what where. Our subscription list was really the first collection of names and addresses of people interested in media education—which, of course, was useful a few years later when we started holding conferences. In the late '80s we were printing about 5,000 copies of every issue. In 1994, when we stopped publishing, it was over 10,000.

TJ: What about the educational philosophy of the field? Was there any attempt to try to unify all these individual efforts pedagogically?

ET: Looking back, I see now a struggle to identify what were the core issues for the U.S. What could/should kids actually be taught? There was a *lot* of concern in the culture about the influence of television and advertising on children and how to "protect" them from any potential harm. This concern would evolve ultimately into the "protectionist" approach in the 1990s. Peggy Charren at Action for Children's Television, the PTA, the American Pediatric Association all developed advocacy positions and got a lot of headlines so that whenever anyone said "media education," there was a tendency to confuse it as advocacy for or against some aspect of media.

But the Canadians, and educators in England, too, kept pushing us not to fall into the protectionist trap—what they called "moral panics." The Canadian movement was heavily influenced by Toronto native Marshall McLuhan and led by classroom English teachers in Toronto who saw films and TV shows and ads as a new kind of "text" that needed to be analyzed just like print texts. This was a new idea for the U.S., but as a former English teacher myself, it made sense to me and was influential in developing the editorial policy for *Media&Values* which ultimately produced a third approach to media education—a recognition of issues, yes, but in an analytical approach that uncovered the complex economic, political, social, and cultural connections involved. We didn't take positions but tried to understand and help readers understand that simply "banning" media products—or television itself—was ultimately not effective.

For this, media educators were seen as advocacy "wimps" which made it harder to be taken seriously by the news media (always looking for controversy), the foundation community (which began to tie funding to behavioral change), or the organizations that were grabbing headlines with their "sky is falling" press releases.

At the same time, without a comprehensive, researched-based curriculum (which takes years to do and millions of dollars), the professional world of American education—state and district leaders who wrote policy that controlled what teachers were expected to do in the classroom—could easily ignore any call for media education as not being educationally sound.

TJ: Sounds like a no-win situation!

ET: On the surface it was. And there were dark days. But at the same time, the '80s were some of the most intellectually challenging years for me. Through some of my feminist and religious connections, I began to read the work of Brazilian educator Paulo Freire whose book, the *Pedagogy of the Oppressed,* talked about education as "banking" (depositing facts for later recall/withdrawal) rather than empowering people to think for themselves. The Liberation Theology movement, also out of Latin America, further offered a model for empowerment that is applicable in any society to any topic from scripture study to school reform. It's a four-step process of Awareness—Analysis—Reflection—Action.

TJ: That's the Empowerment Spiral. How did you make the connection?

ET: I remember precisely where I was in 1986 when I had a great "aha!" and connected the exploration of media issues with the process of educational change and reform. I was reading a book about social analysis and it dawned on me that if we could apply an educationally sound process of inquiry to media issues, then we finally had a foundation to build curriculum around. I further realized that education in a media world would not be about teaching *facts* but about exploring *questions*. So teachers didn't have to know all the answers, they just needed to know how to ask the right questions to get students thinking!

Then I thought . . . *Media&Values* could become a resource for learning how to ask the right questions! The whole mission of the magazine shifted and it became a vehicle for helping readers learn to ask questions about all the media issues facing us in the late 20th century—advertising and consumerism, the trivialization of news, sexism in the media, ageism, ethnicity and race, violence—the topics were almost unlimited. At one time we had 20 file drawers chock-full of newspaper clippings and highlighted articles and book reviews and half-done interviews and teaching ideas . . . we collected cartoons too because sometimes a cartoon could raise a question better than words could. We added columnists from different fields and a two-page tear-out with a teachable activity for the classroom.

That's when *Media&Values* began to take off because people saw something practical coming out of it.

TJ: Yes, well, and it brought a lot of people together and it got a lot done.

ET: I feel really privileged to have been part of that part of history. There were a lot of late nights, but it was rewarding especially when we got a congratulatory letter from Bill Moyers (we framed it!) or a $5,000 check from a foundation. My Rolodex was a hodgepodge of Catholic and Protestant communicators, film teachers, foundation executives, journalists and TV broadcasters, advocacy groups, authors, media professors and, of course, anyone trying to actually do something in the field. Somehow it all worked.

Meeting so many people around the U.S. and from different countries was also exciting . . . and satisfying, too. Many are still good friends. I remember going on a trip to London in, I guess it was '85. I had heard that the British Film Institute was developing some media education resources so I looked up their address and kind of knocked on the door and said "Hello." Cary Bazalgette, now head of the BFA's media education program, invited me for tea at her home, and we talked for hours. She told me about work going on in Australia—and Canada. That was my first introduction to what was developing in Canada.

TJ: What are some of the highlights of the '90s?

ET: There are so many—we were really galloping along . . .

In 1990, we added a Leader's Guide with lesson plans to each thematic issue of *Media&Values* and called it a "Media Literacy Workshop Kit." The kits were the first generation of teaching tools created for use in the U.S. and we sold thousands of them on topics like sexism in the media, media and politics, parenting in a TV age, and finally *Beyond Blame: Challenging Violence in Media*, which became a blockbuster in the field.

The kits were not full-blown curricula but more like individual units built on an underlying pedagogy of the Empowerment Spiral and Five Core Concepts of Media Education, which we adapted from the Canadians' original version of eight "Key Concepts."

The Canadians sponsored their first big conference in the summer of 1990. Five hundred Canadian teachers came, but only 15 of us came from the U.S.

Two years later a second conference drew 500 Canadians along with *50* Americans. By 1995, there was enough involvement to start holding conferences in the U.S.—and there have been over a dozen since.

The Aspen Institute's Leadership Conference brought 25 leaders in the field together in late 1992 to hammer out some definitions and guiding principles—and introduce us to one another! The resulting report from the weekend was a major document for the field even today.

Following up her pledge at the Aspen Conference, Renee Hobbs directed the first weeklong summer institute for teachers at the Harvard Graduate School of Education in 1993. It set the model for many other conferences for teaching teachers how to integrate media literacy across the curriculum.

Although it started out modestly in 1990, the Center for Media Literacy's mail-order Media Literacy Resource Distribution Service gathered teaching materials from dozens of publishers into an annual catalog many called an "illustrated bibliography" of the field. For many time-strapped teachers, it was a boon to be able to get everything from one place on one purchase order.

And then in 1997 came the formation of the Partnership for Media Education (PME) by four women leaders in the field: Lisa Reisberg (Miller) of the American Academy of Pediatrics, Nancy Chase (Garcia) from the Center for Substance Abuse Prevention, Renee Hobbs, and myself. PME was chartered to coordinate professional development conferences to advance the field. By 2001 it evolved into a professional membership association—the Alliance for a Media Literate America (AMLA). Now it's NAMLE—the National Association for Media Literacy Education.

TJ: That really captures a lot of the early development of the field and how things came along. Maybe we can switch gears and talk about what you see happening now. Do you feel like the field has moved in the direction you were hoping for and that you think is best?

ET: Well, I don't know if I even knew what we were hoping for . . . it just seemed the right thing to do, to keep on keeping on. Looking back on 30 years I don't see very many wrong turns. I think the directions we took as *Media&Values,* then the Center for Media and Values (1989) and finally the Center for Media Literacy (1994), helped the field find a foothold in American education even though it took 30 years.

The big challenge was (and is) to keep our spirits up when funding was tight and we had to lay off staff or drop projects. Ceasing publication of *Media&Values* after 15 years was really a blow, but it was the right thing to do at the time. Not having to meet quarterly publication deadlines opened up time to explore what was to be a critical next phase of the field—an emphasis on professional development and teacher training. With support from TV producer Norman Felton, we developed the Felton Media Literacy Scholars Program (1996–1998) as a first attempt at working with teachers. For many reasons it was not sustainable but through it we learned better what would be needed to prepare teachers for teaching in a 21st-century media culture.

TJ: For you, what were some surprises along the way? When you think back on things, do you say, "Oh my gosh! Wow! I never expected that"?

ET: Yes I think even now I'm amazed by the number of people that subscribed to *Media&Values* and how widely influential it was. Renee [Hobbs] told me that in 1986, she picked up a copy in the University of Michigan library and said to herself—"I want to know who's doing this." We've been friends for 20 years. Because I loved doing the magazine and it consumed more than 15 years of my life (1977–1994), *Media&Values* is probably the project I am most proud of—and it absolutely delights me that it was so helpful to others.

Then the national conference we hosted here in Los Angeles at UCLA in 1996 was a wonderful surprise. It was a gathering of nearly 400 people in U.S. media literacy—many who met each other for the first time. I remember opening the conference with the comment, "Wow, this is like my Rolodex come to life!" We didn't have people submit presentations as NAMLE does now. Rather my staff was great at mining the Southern California media community for speakers and panelists. We had a panel of media critics—Elvis Mitchell, Howard Rosenberg, Ella Taylor. We worked with the Writer's Guild to put together panel of TV writers with high school teachers who were teaching filmmaking. It went two hours overtime and everyone missed lunch but they wouldn't stop talking! Renee did the opening address and that's where she first outlined her "7 Great Debates in Media Literacy." That was (and is) one of the most important documents about the media literacy field, I think.

Just one more! The coming together of the founding board of AMLA was a delight. Faith Rogow was very instrumental in pushing us forward and saying it was time for a national organization. I was surprised; I didn't think it would happen so soon. But in every meeting of the board, no matter how difficult the issues were that we had to face, there was so much respect for each other's expertise and contributions! We had fun, too! All of [the members of] that board continue to be dear friends.

TJ: When you look forward, are there some things you'd like to see happen?

ET: Well you know since I pulled back considerably, I'm not as up to date on what's going on. And that's OK. In my religious community [Sisters of the Humility of Mary] there is a tradition of encouraging and supporting sisters to do innovative things, especially in education. And then when the idea or project is ready to be turned over to competent people who can move it forward, we move on to the next challenge. I always said I'd stay with the center until "media literacy becomes a household word." There were many years when I'd say it, and people would say, "Huh?" Now the idea of media literacy education is widespread. I'm content to have contributed a few steps toward where [the] field is now and I'm confident this generation of teachers and leaders will take it wherever it needs to go.

TJ: Well it's interesting, I remember at one of the meetings of the Felton Scholars, somebody brought up the question of what's next. I remember saying and thinking that our job is to make sure that media literacy becomes part of everyday life, it's something that's happening all the time.

ET: And what made that happen was the Internet. Until the Internet came along, everything was about television. As long as media literacy was about television, it could be dismissed as not being very important because television was not being used by educated people (or so they say!).

But as soon as the Internet hit everyday grassroots families, then we transformed into a totally different culture. It took a while for many of us to realize how important the shift was, except that I had some sense of it because of my work at Annenberg. In cleaning out my files recently, I came across a speech I gave in the '80s where I talked about in the future we'd have handheld screens . . . mobile devices . . . I didn't know it was going to be a phone, but that's what it's turned out to be. When I came across it I thought, "Geez, did I write that?" I guess I must have, it was in my handwriting.

Kathleen Tyner

Kathleen Tyner is associate professor in the Department of Radio-TV-Film in the College of Communications at the University of Texas at Austin. As author of texts such as "Literacy in a Digital World: Teaching and Learning in the Age of Information" and "Visions/Revisions: Moving Forward with Media Literacy," Tyner is an expert on media literacy and the uses of new media in formal and informal learning spaces. She began her career in journalism and media production in San Francisco.

Edited Transcript: Interview, September 23, 2010
Interviewer: Dee Morgenthaler

DM: How did you become involved in media education?

KT: I had a teaching credential, but went into journalism and media and production rather early. In San Francisco, I worked at the City Station to do political programming with multiple shows per week. One of the news programs was a roundtable with local journalists, and we analyzed the top local stories of the week. During that time, I could see that news and information was packaged—I could see the spin factor at work. When I was in undergraduate school, I worked with politicians and knew that this was just part of the political profession. So, I thought that given my teaching background and my background in news, that it would be really important for people to understand that reporting is not only about being able to read and write newspapers and TV news but is mostly about being able to deconstruct sources and analyze an argument and make decisions in a civic arena. So I'm interested in the craft of production, as well as the content.

During the course of my work, I've also been motivated by my strong interest in the arts. In particular, in nonnarrative, experimental, and avantgarde art. With the decline of art in public schools, people don't have a lot of opportunity to appreciate and use and understand the artistic process. They have easy access to a limited range of production models that are familiar to television and the Hollywood factory model. But they don't have a lot of opportunity to experience the media arts—things like Super 8 or 16mm film and other kinds of archival media forms that have inspired artists over time.

I have written about the *tyranny of the narrative* as an emphasis in media education of narrative over aesthetics. It is one thing to deconstruct literature, but especially when we get into the realm of virtual worlds and gaming, most people do not yet have the aesthetic vocabulary to really discuss and thoroughly enjoy what they are seeing and to share that in the public realm. So I always thought that the best way to teach about media was to marry production with analysis.

Since the early 1980s, I've worked on projects that rely on innovative computer applications and have witnessed the shift to digital literacy firsthand. It's been an interesting ride. In 1984, I worked on one of the first U.S. videotex projects for the *San Francisco Chronicle*. We were trying to do something like the French "Minitel." The *Chronicle Videotex* was created with cables and kiosks all over the city in San Francisco long before we had the Internet. The problem was that they didn't quite have a coherent business model. They were still trying to use the newspaper model of classified advertising and display ads and they didn't quite know how to leverage—or even really to count—their user traffic data. So it was really a starting point in the history of the Internet and developed a lot of processes through localized, connected new media that people have since tried to refine. I'm still not sure if the business model is there yet!

The question remains: Where do people get news that's reported in a professional way with gatekeepers who understand the journalism profession versus bloggers—some of whom are very professional, some of whom are not? This extends to broadcast news. When there is a need for local news, television and radio are not "dead" at all. People still depend on broadcast media. So the forms overlap, but don't necessarily die out. Except when they do. I will miss Kodachrome.

There is a lot of research done on the ubiquitous, pervasive nature of information flow and the fact that it has just proliferated to the extent that people have a lot more choice. But like anything else—when you go in the supermarket, for example—a lot more choice isn't always an efficient way to make decisions.

And so as the print, analog, and digital collided I decided to start a non-profit organization called Strategies for Media Literacy in the late 1980s to support media literacy education. It lasted until the dot-com crash and created a lot of resources, support, and workshops for teachers that are still used today.

DM: Were there specific texts and scholars that inspired you?

KT: I was inspired by the scholarship of Walter J. Ong who actually did have an astute vision of the Internet before he stopped writing. I think that the linguistic work of James Paul Gee was groundbreaking and really important for media studies. Rudolf Arnheim's work on film theory and aesthetics is as important today as it was when he wrote it. When I started the nonprofit, I had a lot of help from the Canadian Association for Media Literacy, the British Film Institute, and the Australian Teachers of Media along the way. The key concepts, critical questions, and rubrics that they used to organize media education efforts were useful to me then and are still the basis for the critical questions that media literacy advocates use today.

I also learned so much from the experimental film community in San Francisco, which has been very inspirational and supportive of my media education work, especially the Pacific Film Archive, San Francisco Cinematheque, and Other Cinema in the Bay Area. I am inspired by 20th-century artists like Marcel Duchamp and also by contemporary experimental filmmakers.

When I look to new media, I draw from a broad palette of pop culture insights, as well as from academic scholarship. I am inspired by things like Ray Kurtzweil and Vernor Vinge's ideas about singularity and Gordon Moore of Intel who came up with Moore's Law. I value archival media as a way to provide important contextual information for my students. Brewster Kahle's concept of the "Wayback Machine" and Rick Prelinger's curating of ephemeral media on the Internet Archive have been inspirational and helpful in my teaching.

I realize now that unless you know something about software programming, you cannot be completely literate in today's society. Most of us don't know how to program—including me—so in order to maintain high levels of literacy, it's good to try to keep on top of structural trends and to sort the long trends from the short trends. Right now, younger kids are more likely to learn programming at home or in a nonprofit organization than they are during the school day.

I do admire the scholars who take both the long and the broad view of digital literacy. In the context of media education, I like David Buckingham's work because he takes a longer view and also understands the aesthetic component. Sonia Livingstone's work is groundbreaking and writers like S. Craig Watkins, Mimi Ito, Lissa Soep, and Steve Goodman always give me new insights into the social uses of new media with young people. I like the work of Gunther Kress because he understands the history of literacy and puts digital literacy in a multiliteracy context with a design element. Right now I am following the work of Daniel Pink, who calls for interdisciplinary, blurred boundaries between art and science, which makes a lot of sense to me.

DM: Any obstacles or surprises?

KT: Human nature doesn't surprise me so much anymore. But in terms of media literacy education, I expect surprises because I never considered media literacy to be a field or a movement. When you define a field, it has certain characteristics before it becomes a field. One of these characteristics is an agreement on professional practices—common shared knowledge of professional practices. For example, journalism has broadly recognized professional practices that define the field. Media literacy doesn't have a comparable consensus. This is because media literacy is an extension of literacy and it has always been a messy subject. You can tell the same story around Gutenberg and his invention of the printing press.

I mean, is literacy—writ large—a movement? Is literacy a field? So, why would media literacy be a field? And who can agree on the mission of a media literacy movement? In their groundbreaking 1996 essay, "A Pedagogy of Multiliteracies: Designing Social Futures," the New London Group brilliantly represents literacy as a complex, multiliteracy concept of design. Similarly, I have represented literacy as a multiliteracy mandala with an emphasis on multiple pathways to literacy and the tension between content and contexts. I think that the emphasis is on dialogues of literacy as a concept in process and so we jump in and examine it from various perspectives. Instead, people get hung up arguing about the definitions and purposes of media education instead of jumping in the flow of dialogue about the strategic and pleasurable uses of literacy.

I do understand that field-building techniques are a way to exert awareness and influence in academic circles or workplace development circles or political circles, or policy circles. That's to be expected and for the most part, it stimulates dialogue about literacy. These dialogues can't be expected to define media literacy, but they do provide useful support and strategies for practitioners. But in this rapidly changing media environment, I doubt that anyone is going to corner the "market" on media literacy definitions, purposes, policies, or critical questions.

At its core, literacy is still simply about human communication and the need for human beings to use it to gain social capital and exert power and influence and so on. Literacy helps us to look out for and balance collective interests with our individual interests. Literacy is a tool of strategy, negotiation and expression. It is an essential skill. If you study the history of literacy, the need to control and shape the educational process around the uses of literacy tools and texts is always attached to literacy attainment. But the path is unique to every person. Scholar Harvey Graff explains this in *The Labyrinths of Literacy*.

DM: So, do you think media education belongs in the education system?

KT: Of course it belongs in education. Like print literacy, it shoots across the curriculum. It is disappointing that it is so often narrowly conceived and ghettoized in "educational technology" courses. Again, if you think of the need to analyze and use both technical skills and artistic processes to create new media, then it makes sense that media education is an integral, interdisciplinary basic for formal education. But part of the problem is that we have diminished the role of the arts in public education to the extent that you have to ask, "What's the point?" If we don't have time for project-based learning and if we are going to rely on standardized test scores as the main way to design learning environments, then why not just do distance education in the comfort of your own home?

Content delivery is fine, but when it is the only pedagogical goal, it does not serve media education in either formal or informal learning environments. Instead, it blunts critical dialogue and hands-on expression. Even when production takes place, I've seen media education in public schools used mostly as vehicles for information or public service messages or other kinds of values inculcation. There's no joy in this. This type of media production may be useful for social activists and it may be well intended, but artists sometimes feel bullied by the pressure to narrowly use their skills to deliver a message, especially when the message might be amorphous. Instead, they are exploring color, or maybe they are exploring a process around montage, or maybe they are exploring the artistic process of specific media. And so when production is introduced in K–12 education, it can be very heavy-handed and adult-driven. This kind of values inculcation extends to analysis when the goal of analysis is framed as a way to influence broader social and cultural issues.

So it must be very frustrating because people don't have any consistent outlets for their preferred literacies in school. Instead their uses of media look more like ed-tech lessons or life skills education or something. Especially now, kids create and share and critique media all of the time, especially with gaming, but until recently, no one taught them this or talked about it in school. They are hungry to learn about media and to exercise their literacy skills. When they find kindred spirits in their online communities, they talk about different things, not only about the narrative of the game or the rules of the games but how they are created and the pleasure they get from the aesthetic and who did it well and how it was done and audience issues. They compare and critique and defend their preferences. They create their own avatars and use Maya or Alice software to understand the way that games are created. It's not enough to simply create "educationally acceptable" games and introduce them in the formal classroom as a new form of textbook. I asked a teenager if he liked to play educational video games. He told me, "I love to play video games but do I play educational games? Uh, that's OK." He thought that educational games were kind of pathetic because they didn't have the same degree of risk and challenge and learning opportunities that he experienced in commercial games. James Paul Gee writes about this all the time.

Formal education has somewhat lost its way and part of it is because it was so intertwined with print literacy. As that connection unraveled the school system hasn't yet found its footing in new media. There are people that understand this connection between literacy and learning very well, like Henry Jenkins and Katie Salen. But others have yet to come to terms with the integration of new media across the formal school curriculum. A whole generation of teachers raised on print media is retiring, but I don't necessarily see that new generations of teachers are embracing new media in the current school system—even though teachers use it outside of school all the time.

DM: Are they [teachers] being constrained?

KT: Constrained by the system, I can see that. Or perhaps in some cases they are book people who gravitated to the education system because that's where the print is. I am not sure. It's not necessarily about the literacy tools or access. It's about the design of learning environments that are out of sync with contemporary communication practices. But the point is that kids are desperate for a place that is meaningful and resonates with their prior literacy experiences and incorporates their really valuable skills in production and knowledge creation and sharing.

DM: Do you see a specific outlet, for example, digital storytelling, or something along those lines?

KT: Storytelling is a good bridge for people who understand narrative structure and interpret media from that cognitive lens. When we talk to teachers about narratives I think they are in a comfort zone, so storytelling is a way to introduce the integration of more types of media in the classroom.

But media education can't stop with learning about storytelling techniques. We can't forget the fact that film or video production isn't only about the story. In fact I would argue that especially in virtual worlds, the characters as well as the aesthetics could spontaneously drive the narrative. Also, narrative structure is peculiar to each medium, and in order to be really broadly literate, you might be able to negotiate the different discourses of each of those media not only in a narrative structure with dialogue, but in their aesthetic values and the limitations of the technologies that create them. These media forms also create the meaning in a very McLuhanist way. Once you have an opportunity to discuss these things with people in media education courses, then

I do think that people are really smart and have been immersed in all these media for their whole lives now and are kind of dying to talk about it—even if they don't quite have an opportunity or might not have the vocabulary to address it at first. But once you find a bridge, or what teachers would call a scaffolding process, like digital storytelling, it can open a portal and all kinds of discussion about the various discourses of each media that help people to become more broadly and deeply literate.

DM: In regards to the field of media education, what you would like to see happen in the future?

KT: I would like to see more integration of media arts and project-based learning across the curriculum in public education. I'd like to see more emphasis on the artistic process, including critique and apprenticeships. We need more opportunities to teach about programming and computer systems for young people who want to explore those areas. Sometime in the future, I think that people will simply say *literacy* and assume that all media forms are included in this term. I'd like it very much if the phrase *media literacy* would fade into a broader and dynamic concept of literacy. It is already an anachronism in its own time.

Chris Worsnop

Chris Worsnop is now running a weekly film program at the local Cobourg Ontario library and chairing the committee for the Marie Dressler Foundation Vintage Film Festival. He is author of two books, *Screening Images: Ideas for Media Education* (2nd ed., 1999) and *Assessing Media Work: Authentic Assessment in Media Education* (1996). His background is in high school teaching and K–12 curriculum development, implementation, and evaluation in English language arts, drama, and media education.

Edited Transcript: Interview, February 24, 2011
Interviewer: Tessa Jolls

CW: My father was a projectionist, and then I misspent three years getting an undergraduate degree in England, going to the movies every night instead of studying literature. When I was an undergraduate there were no film or media courses that I could have taken.

Afterwards, I just gravitated to something I loved. In 1965, I discovered 16mm projectors in the Ottawa high school where I taught, and the geography teachers thought that they belonged to them. I disabused the geography teachers of that idea and got in touch with the National Film Board of Canada http://www.nfb.ca/ and the Canadian Film Institute, http://www.cfi-icf.ca/ and made some good contacts there who gave me access to their entire libraries. I just kept driving downtown and picking up films that they recommended and bringing them back to my classroom and teaching them as if they were poems or short stories. I found that they were tremendously effective with all kinds of students. They seemed to understand better what I was trying to do with literature.

This branched off then into the formation of the film society at the school where we rented 16mm feature films and showed them in the auditorium. The next year, I got an English headship at another school and immediately formed another film society. That year the Ontario Ministry of Education allowed the teaching of a unit on film as a part of the graduating year English course. I immediately put in a proposal to teach this course. All the films I wanted to put in the film curriculum, I put in the film society program. Half of the members of the film society were parents, so their memberships helped to fund the materials we needed for this film course. We did an auteur study on Arthur Penn http://hcl.harvard.edu/hfa/films/2008janfeb/penn.html: *Miracle Worker*, *Left Handed Gun*, *Mickey One*, *The Chase*. *Bonnie and Clyde* was a hot film that year.

TJ: How great! It really was a combination of the parents, you as the teacher, and your students who made it happen!

CW: Well, I really had an enthusiastic staff. It was a brand-new school and we'd hired very enthusiastic teachers who were, many of them, very strong in media. Of course we kept up with the connection with the National Film Board and the Canadian Film Institute.

Around that time, too, I got invited to join the board of the Film Federation of Eastern Ontario. That's a mouthful. That was an organization that bought 16mm films—there was no videotape then—and placed them in blocks that it rented to public libraries. These blocks circulated around eastern Ontario and people with a library card could borrow them with a projector, take them to their homes or church or whatever organization they represented, and show them as a public screening. It was an ungainly way of having media at home, but it worked. It had actually been set up earlier by the NFB, but when they gave up circulating their own blocks the federations in different parts of Ontario took it over.

Now from there I went on to the Ontario Film Association which existed to promote nontheatrical film to libraries, colleges, universities, and school boards and museums and all the organizations with a collection of nontheatrical films. The Ontario Film Association organized an annual marketplace that lasted for four days. The OFA later set up the John Grierson http://www.griersontrust.org/john-grierson.html Documentary Seminar, using the model of the Flaherty Seminar http://www.flahertyseminar.org/. It ran at the same location for a few days before the marketplace. So this went on for several years, we invited people like Basil Wright http://www.griersontrust.org/john-grierson.html to come and be our guest speakers. The German animator, Lotte Reiniger (http://www.awn.com/mag/issue1.3/articles/moritz1.3.html), who did the shadow animation *Prince Ahmed*, came one year. Well, eventually, the OFA disappeared because VHS came in and then of course DVD, and it was unnecessary for people to come to a central place. The whole model for the marketplace became no longer viable.

While all this was going on, I was working in school to change the use of media in the classroom from audiovisual aids into a subject of its own. The argument I've always used is that a large and increasing part of our modern culture is visual.

Nowadays we'd call it screen-based, but we didn't then. The British Film Institute http://filmstore.bfi.org.uk/ at the time had a name for the subject—*screen education*. I'm talking about the mid- to late-1960s now. Of course in Europe and the UK, media education had existed since the 1930s, in fact, F. R. Leavis (http://archive.waccglobal.org/wacc/publications/media_devel opment/archive/2003_4/visions_of_media_education_the_road_from_dys topia), who was one my teachers at university, had written some seminal material about it promoting the use of films in the classroom, but he came from a kind of an elitist base wanting to talk about The Canon rather than about popular culture. But still it was something that got the BFI engaged in education, and the BFI did a lot to support media education/media studies, whatever you want to call it, in the UK.

Sorry for the digression: I was trying to get media established in its own right because modern culture is no longer exclusively print based. I insist on that word *exclusively*. It's still very much print based, but in the 19th century when a lot of our educational institutions were formed, and our institutional assumptions were created, our culture *was* almost exclusively print based and it made sense for our education to be print based. But that doesn't make sense anymore.

It hasn't made sense for quite a long time. I reckon any culture that wants to thrive should really educate its children and its young people within the culture that they exist. They should be encouraged to swim in the water that actually forms their culture rather than look backwards; some would call it the rear view mirror, after McLuhan, looking back to the ancient Greek and Roman culture, plays from the 17th century or the novels of the 19th century. As a footnote here, I am really enjoying reading all of these again now, but I rarely enjoyed or understood or appreciated them as much as I should have when I was young.

So I was involved along with people like Barry Duncan (http://www.aml .ca/aboutus/speakerBios.php?speakerID=283) in the very early movement in Ontario to establish screen education or media literacy—I think we still called it screen education then—in Ontario. I wasn't involved as much as Barry; he was very definitely more involved than me. There was a big media literacy conference at York University in Toronto with John Culkin (http:// www.medialit.org/reading-room/john-culkin-sj-man-who-invented-media-literacy-1928–1993) as the keynote.

I ran some sessions in Ottawa too, little weekend or single-day sessions. A man called Tony Hodgkinson (http://www.jstor.org/pss/30217409) who was then in Boston doing work in screen education, he came up from there to do the keynote in Ottawa for us. Tony was an ex-BFI leader who had been involved in selecting the materials that BFI made available to British teachers: extracts from feature films and such. Those still might be available. Tony was a great guy.

We had a little ruse that we used. We had one $250 honorarium, and we kept offering it to each other to go and speak for each other. But the idea was that nobody would ever spend it, but they would make it available to somebody else. So we only ever needed one $250 but created the impression that there was a lot of activity going on and funds to support it; $250 was quite a bit of money in those days, but there were no travel expenses, and Tony came very cheerfully on his own dime.

Around that time, 1969–1970, I moved and became a curriculum coordinator in a school board on the St. Lawrence in a town called Brockville. I was working for a director of education, Lloyd Dennis (http://agora.lakeheadu .ca/agora.php?st=331), who was the best-known progressivist in the province, which made him either a prince or a target; you know how it goes with progressivists. I was one of his fans. In 1968, this is just before I went there, I went to a NFB summer institute and spent six weeks immersed with filmmakers, editors, sound experts, animators, and the whole nine yards of what was going on then at the national film board. There was a very memorable session with Norman McLaren (http://www3.nfb.ca/animation/objanim/en/ filmmakers/Norman-McLaren/overview.php). We were 20 to 25 people from across Canada who were very keen to be teachers of media, and I think that summer really gave me the bite to keep moving on because I knew that I wasn't alone.

TJ: That sounds understandable because I think, when you are trying to advance some ideas, as you were, it's very important to have compatriots who also are working on some of the same issues and feeling like you can make some progress.

CW: Thank you, you feel as if you're not isolated. Barry Duncan had been on this same course either the year previous or two years previous. 1967 had been a pivotal year—the year of Canada's centennial and the year the Montreal world's fair. A very, very exciting time in Canada, around that time. Of course, Marshall McLuhan was also quite prominent then. He was teaching at Toronto University. He was one of Barry's teachers.

When I became a curriculum coordinator, I was in charge of English, which meant I had a lot of teachers to relate to, secondary and elementary, but of course I was still very interested in media, but I had to ration the amount of time I allowed myself to spend on it. I kept up with my work with the OFA, all through those years in Brockville and started writing a bit then. I wrote reviews of Canadian short films, nontheatrical in the OFA newsletter. I even produced a book of reviews once, in 1975, with the intention of doing one of every year, but of course those intentions fell upon stony ground. It was too much work because it was all done on a Selectric typewriter. My wife retyped every one of the reviews—there were about 400—into camera-ready copy. And that was the year our daughter was born, 1979. Yes, enough of that.

TJ: Oh, nevertheless, your writings have been so terrific. I know we always thought of your book on media literacy, really the pocketbook that everybody should read. So I really do hope you do talk some about that.

CW: Oh well, that's very kind of you. OK, I had moved in 1975 to a new school board, an even bigger one and was able to be more influential with schools in promoting media studies because there was a very good collection of 16mm films. I started writing classroom materials for publication we wrote for English teachers through my office. Some of the first things I wrote became chapters in *Screening Images*. The ones about different approaches . . . "four ways not to teach media, one way that might work," "the camera always lies," and so on. Film distributors had me writing study guides for teachers. There must have been a couple of hundred of them. I used the study guides to encourage teachers to use activities rather than just question and answer. I didn't write 20 questions, true or false; I wrote study guides that had students work in groups, make storyboards, try to reorganize or reedit the narrative. A lot of those activities are at the back of *Screening Images* both editions, in part 3. Where shall I go from there?

TJ: Well you were walking through how you were approaching media education as you were taking on more responsibilities in school . . .

CW: Thank you for putting me back on track . . . in the late '80s, the Ontario Ministry of Education formed a writing team to produce a curriculum document on Media Literacy. Barry Duncan and the Association for Media Literacy, which had been working for 10 years promoting media literacy were given the job of writing what became *The Media Literacy Resource Book* (http://www.media-awareness.ca/english/resources/educational/recommended/books/media_lit_resource_guide.cfm) in 1989. It was really written in 1988, but that's a political story. Ontario was one of the first jurisdictions to provide teachers with resources for media and Barry Duncan was right in the forefront; we can't give Barry enough credit for that.

Later in that time, just a year after the *Resource Guide* was published I was seconded to the Ministry of Education and I was able to do some stuff there for elementary schools in media, providing funds for others to do things. I went back to my own school board after that secondment, and got heavily involved in assessment.

Now, my first involvement in assessment was when I was doing my masters of education degree in the early 1970s. I was involved in assessment in reading and actually did some pretty heavy research in reading. The procedure I developed became known as Retrospective Miscue Analysis (http://www.rapidintellect.com/AEQweb/oct2750.htm). In the 1990s, we were involved very much in assessment because there was this evaluation fury going on all over North America. Locally we were determined not to use the standardized test route for assessing reading and writing. In the last two years I was working full time—I retired in 1995—I concentrated on a project for writing assessment and happily worked with Dr. Judith Fine who taught me an awful lot about assessment while I taught her about language and writing. In those two years we supervised a million-dollar research project and came up with what we were convinced was an instrument for assessing writing in an authentic fashion, the Peel Writing Scales (http://www.readingonline.org/newliteracies/worsnop/three.html). As soon I retired, I took that model for assessment and I wrote *Assessing Media Work*.

It did well for a few years. I sometimes hope that there are still copies of it that are being found and used and kids are benefiting from authentic assessment in their media classes.

TJ: How far do you think the field has come?

CW: I think that everything that needs to be said about media education has already been said. If you go back to principles, you can't go wrong. And you know we can call the principles whatever we like, the key concepts, underpinning principles, what we believe about education, children, learning. These really are the things that need to be driving what we do in all of education. It isn't really about the newest telephone or the newest kind of screen or whether 3D will revolutionize television or produce a cure for housemaid's knee. We have to stick with principles and that's one of the reasons I stopped writing, because I've already said all I have to say and anything else would just be repetition with different examples and different contexts.

And of course I have a strong belief that media education ought to be education about media rather than using media as a tool in another subject area. I absolutely can see that media education can be useful to people in other subject areas, but when media education is used to try to get to kids to stop using drugs, that's a drug education curriculum not a media education curriculum. And when it fails, it's not a failure of media education.

TJ: Do you feel like the field has moved in a direction you would hope to see?

CW: I've always been attracted to enterprises in education which encourage people to be progressive. And the one that's given me the most encouragement has been media. But I've also been very involved in drama and theater because that's another area where progressive ideas can find fertile soil and nutrition. So, I live in constant fear that progressive curriculum areas are going to be appropriated into the traditional; for when that happens people with progressive ideas seek for a new area where they can be progressive again. They don't want to toe the line of traditionalism. Traditionalism in education is not going to go away because there's too much profit for publishers and test makers for them to let go of it. And no government in its right mind wants to a have a population of young people thinking for themselves, which is what progressive education is trying to create. I mean take a look at what's happening in the Middle East right now where people have all of a sudden started thinking for themselves and the government has no idea what do with them.

So, I would like to see media education maintain its progressive stance. More important than media education is progressive education: treating young people in schools as thinking, reasoning, decision-making, creative, autonomous individuals and acknowledging that and encouraging it, accepting it in ways that don't demand that they toe the line like we had to. So, that's one of the chief reasons I've been involved, apart from the passion I've got from my dad, the projectionist, and all the evenings I spent in the 1950s watching a lot of the trash Hollywood was churning out . . . and enjoying it . . . and now I've come full circle.

In my retirement I'm doing a lot of film stuff again. I spent 10 years working with the International Baccalaureate developing a film course (http://www.ibo.org/diploma/assessment/subjectoutlines/documents/d_6_filmx_gui-out_0803_1_e.pdf) for the International Baccalaureate Diploma. I volunteer at the local public library running a weekly program of feature films, mostly for seniors like myself, and I am the chair of the Marie Dressler Foundation Vintage Film Festival www.vintagefilmfestival.com.

TJ: Have there been surprises for you along the way when you think about the development of the field and, looking back, what surprised you?

CW: Oh nothing surprises me! I'm a cynic, a cynic is a person who always expects the worst and only gets good surprises. I've watched media education stand on the edge of the cliff for so many years, and I've always been encouraged by the enthusiasm of those who are holding it from falling over the edge. Those people are always exciting to know and to mingle with and to bash minds against. I don't always agree with them but gosh it's fun.

There are awful and nasty, nasty powers in education that keep media literacy at bay. And I've fought with that. We had things like Channel 1, that's dead now isn't it? We had one here in Canada and soon after I retired, I put every ounce of energy I had into fighting the Youth News Network as an insidious and despicable plague that was getting ready to infect our public education. I quite enjoyed the fray.

It's starting up again because schools lack funds and they naturally turn to find funds anywhere they can get them. But in the end the principle to follow is that public goods belong in public hands.

I'll say it again: no government in its right mind wants a populace of young people who can think for themselves. Unfortunately, there is a big divide between good sense and common sense. The problem with common sense is that it isn't very good and the problem with good sense is that it isn't very common.

TJ: What would you like to see happen?

CW: I'd like people to read A. S. Neil (http://www.summerhillschool.co.uk/pages/asneill.html). I'd like people to read some educational philosophers and get away from worrying about test scores and start thinking about young people and what they can be, and how we can best help them become that. Get back to Dewey (http://dewey.pragmatism.org/and Jean-Jacques Rousseau and http://www.infed.org/thinkers/et-rous.htm), some of the people who write about the fundamentals of education. Think about how these ideas read in today's world . . . sure, these guys came from the print world, they came from the old society but they had a view of humanity and of learning that we can still treasure.

TJ: It really comes back to the timeless principles that we were talking about, the fundamental human need to learn and to explore and to really kind of push the limits on just what you said, what people can be.

CW: Absolutely, you see in the end it isn't so much about media and education as it is about education. I'm passionate about media, I'm still spending money on all the toys that keep coming around, but I'm not foolish enough to think that these toys and the use of them has changed the way people's brains work. I keep seeing people writing about that. Lord help us, the brain doesn't evolve that fast, we still have the same brain as before, homo sapiens sapiens.

I think we have all got ways of understanding and interpreting the world. Some people do it through numbers, paintings, sports; I choose to do it through different forms of cultural and artistic expression. I'm still a huge consumer of literature, but I adore movies, I keep an eye on the pulse of developments of media. I don't like them all, but I keep an eye on it and try to understand it. I like to understand and interpret the world through culture and art but other people do it a different way. We have to acknowledge those differences.

THREAD 5
International Media Literacy Programs

Efforts were made to contact as many countries as possible with media literacy programs. Surveys were sent to individuals in these countries identified as active and prominent in the field of media literacy. Although not all countries that are involved in media literacy are included in this section, the countries included in this thread provide insight into the historical, cultural, and political context that promotes national media literacy programs.

Australia

*Prepared by Michael Dezuanni
and Barrie McMahon*

I. Overview

School education in Australia has, until now, been the responsibility of the six states and two territories. Attempts in recent years to map the various curricula have revealed marked similarities that have led to a push toward an Australian curriculum. This will be progressively developed over the next decade. Media education in Australia reflects that educational history, and, as an emerging discipline developed independently across the states and territories, the field reveals significant differences that will need to be accommodated in the new Australian curriculum. The variations have occurred as a result of the discipline being introduced at different times that affected the conceptual frameworks that underpinned the subject. There are also differences in pedagogical approaches, particularly in regard to the appropriate balance between theoretical and practical work. The level of systemic support for the emerging discipline has affected both the roles played by the professional associations and the age at which students commence their media literacy studies. In some states and territories, media literacy objectives are identified through years K–12, but in other states, the focus has been on the senior years of schooling. There are also variations regarding the identity of the study, with some states having a specific media studies course in secondary schools while others integrate the study into established disciplines, particularly English and the arts.

Media literacy education as a specific focus was informally introduced in some states during the 1950s by teachers with an enthusiasm for film appreciation and production. On the east coast of Australia, this led to the formation of the Australian Teachers of Film Appreciation (ATFA), which later became Australian Teachers of Media (ATOM). The ATFA began publishing the *Film Appreciation Newsletter* in 1963, which supported teachers across the country through the distribution of lesson ideas, practical advice, and international developments in film education.

Official curriculum policy documents were developed as early as the 1950s. The Tasmanian English curriculum first required students to study aspects of "mass media" including film and television appreciation in 1956. Western Australia offered a Media Studies course in 1974; in Victoria, a Film and Media Studies curriculum was developed and implemented in 1981; Queensland introduced a Film and Television syllabus in 1981; the South Australia Department of Education released the K-12 Media Studies policy in 1982; and the New South Wales Department of Education published All about Mass Media Education K–12 in 1985. New versions of media curriculum documents and policies were subsequently introduced in these states throughout the next two decades.

Currently, media literacy education is well supported in the Australian school system, with all states requiring students to complete aspects of media literacy as a requirement within the English curriculum or the arts. Media literacy education will be further enhanced by the "Australian Curriculum" being developed to replace these state curricula. From 2013, this national curriculum will require all Australian children from "foundation" (preschool) to Year 8 to complete mandatory media literacy education in a new curriculum area called Media Arts. The Australian Curriculum, Assessment and Reporting Authority (ACARA) has chosen to locate media literacy within the arts in recognition of the importance of digital media participation and production to the development of media literacy. Critical analysis and reading will be an essential component of Media Arts and media literacy will continue to be developed through aspects of English curriculum. A Media Arts curriculum will also be developed by ACARA for Years 9 to 12 for those students who choose to study the area as an elective.

Media literacy in Australian schools and the broader community is advanced by research into media, communications, and cultural studies within universities with many undergraduate and graduate courses with a focus on this area. Pre-service teacher education programs that include a media literacy focus exist at several universities around the country. The Australian Communications and Media Authority (ACAMA) also promotes media literacy in the broader Australian community through its Digital Media Literacy initiative, which aims to help Australian citizens to effectively participate in digital media culture.

National Media Literacy Programs
The ATOM Awards are an annual competition hosted by the Australian Teachers of Media to recognize excellence in Australian and New Zealand media produced by students and for students.

The **ScreenIT** competition is an annual competition hosted by the Australian Centre for the Moving Image that invites students from preschool to Year 12 to share their work in the areas of animation, live action, and computer games.

II. Notable Media Literacy Organizations

1. Australian Teachers of Media (ATOM)

Contacts: http://www.atomvic.org; http://www.atomqld.org; http://www .metromagazine.com.au; atomwa@edna.edu.au)
The purpose of this organization is to promote media literacy education in Australia.
Affiliations: The National Advocates for Arts Education (NAAE)

ATOM began in the early 1960s in Victoria as the Australian Teachers of Film Appreciation (ATFA). In the early 1980s, state-based ATOM associations were established in Victoria, Queensland, Western Australia, and New South Wales. South Australian media teachers formed the South Australian Association for Media Education. During the 1980s, an umbrella organization called the Council of Australian Media Education Organisations was formed to advocate for media education in Australia and New Zealand. In 2010, ATOM National was formed to advocate for the inclusion of media literacy education in the Australia national curriculum.

ATOM organizations are professional bodies of media educators and industry professionals who advocate for media literacy education in Australian schools; advise education authorities on policy and curriculum development; provide students with opportunities to engage critically with the media; and promote the ongoing development of an innovative and diverse screen and media culture in Australia by providing debate and analysis through its various publications, both print and online, the ATOM Film TV and Multimedia Awards, and a broad range of professional development and training opportunities.

III. Notable Individuals in National Media Literacy Programs

Barrie McMahon

Author; mcmahon.b1@optusnet.com.au; Tel. 0407471751
McMahon is co-author of several foundational Australian media education texts, including *Real Images* (1986), *Stories and Stereotypes* (1988), *Australian Images* (1990), and *Advancing English Studies with Multimedia* (2009). Internationally regarded as a founder of the Media Literacy education movement.

Professor Robyn Quin

Deputy Vice Chancellor (Education) Curtin University of Technology in Western Australia; R.Quin@curtin.edu.au; Tel. 0417930780

Quin is coauthor of several foundational Australian media education texts, including *Real Images* (1986), *Stories and Stereotypes* (1988), *Australian Images* (1990), and *Advancing English Studies with Multimedia* (2009). Internationally regarded as a founder of the media literacy education movement.

Professor Carmen Luke

Retired; previously professor of Education at the University of Queensland.

Luke is a leading international scholar in the field of media literacy and new media, feminist studies, globalization, and higher education. Her work on multiliteracies and media literacy is used by educators in Australia, the United Kingdom, and the United States.

Professor Graeme Turner

Director, Centre for Critical and Cultural Studies, University of Queensland

Turner is an ARC Federation Fellow and professor of Cultural Studies. He is one of the key figures in the development of cultural and media studies in Australia and has an outstanding international reputation in the field. His work is used in many disciplines—cultural and media studies, communications, history, literary studies, and film and television studies—and it has been translated into eight languages.

Professor John Hartley

Distinguished Professor at QUT and Research Director at CCI

Hartley is the author of 20 books and upwards of 200 papers, translated into more than a dozen languages, including *Television Truths* (Blackwell 2008), *TV50: Fifty Years of Australian Television* (2006), *Reading Television* (2003), and *Communication, Cultural and Media Studies: The Key Concepts* (3rd ed., Routledge 2002).

Michael Dezuanni

Lecturer in Film and Media Curriculum at Queensland University of Technology; m.dezuanni@qut.edu.au

Dezuanni is the "media arts" adviser to the Australian Curriculum, Assessment, and Reporting Authority responsible for developing key aspects of media literacy policy for the Australian curriculum. Author of several research articles about media literacy in Australian schools and author of a textbook for use with middle years students: *Media Remix—Digital Projects for Students*.

Belgium

Prepared by Hans Martens

I. Overview

Belgium is a federal state that consists of three regions and three communities. Both media and educational policies are (mostly) regulated at the community level. In this report, we therefore separately describe the state of media literacy in the two largest Belgian communities: the Flemish community (approximately 6 million citizens) and the French-speaking community (approximately 4.2 million citizens).

Status of Media Literacy in Belgium

As with many European countries, Belgium has a long history of film educational and (more recently) audiovisual training activities. During the past decade, media education and media literacy have increasingly gained ascendency at both the Flemish and the French-speaking community level.

In the Flemish community, media literacy is most often broadly conceived as the necessary media-related knowledge, skills, and attitudes to actively participate in a mediated society. Although most policy makers emphasize the importance of a broad view on media literacy (including, for instance, the ability to analyze and evaluate more traditional media messages in newspapers, on the radio, or on television), the so-called second generation digital divide is at the center of current developments.

Recent policy documents, government initiatives, and curricular developments point to the increasing importance of media literacy in research, in formal and informal education, and in the broader social-cultural field. To illustrate, in Flemish secondary education the cross-curricular part of the core curriculum has recently been revised to include key media literacy competences such as "being alert when using media" and "thoughtful participation in the public sphere." Also, the Flemish Minister of Media is currently considering founding a Flemish knowledge center of media literacy.

In the French-speaking community, since 1995, media education has been progressively integrated in different curricula levels. Here again, the general approach is to introduce media education as a transversal or cross-curricular topic. In this way, first language courses, geography, history, ethics or religion, aesthetics, and social sciences open up many opportunities to introduce specific aspects of media education. In some schools, media literacy also appears as a separate subject, with more precisely delineated learning goals and competencies. However, for now, there is a generally shared overall pedagogical framework for media education.

Some schools, educational networks, and the Conseil supérieur de l'Education aux Médias (the Higher Council for Media Education) are currently developing a more general frame of reference for media education, based on the main informational, social, and technical skills needed to use, read, write, and navigate through (present and future) media messages. Also, the Conseil supérieur de l'Education aux Médias attached a label of "public interest" to a limited number of high-quality projects and actions. Finally, some teacher training programs include evaluations of teachers' media literacy levels, and some researchers and students lead experimental research on media literacy level assessment in different (younger and older) populations.

In both the Flemish and the French communities, media literacy training for teachers is limited and often depends on the goodwill and initiative of individual institutions, organizations, and educators. That said, as illustrated in the following section, teachers and principals have a wide range of opportunities to implement extracurricular projects (often in collaboration with nonprofit organization in the social-cultural field) and to introduce specific aspects of media literacy in everyday classroom life.

II. Notable Media Literacy Organizations

The following organizations and agents are actively involved in various media literacy initiatives inside and outside formal education. It should be clear that this list is not exhaustive. In both the Flemish and the French-speaking communities, a large variety of social-cultural organizations contribute to specific aspects of media literacy. It is beyond the scope of this report to give a full overview of all these initiatives and activities.

On the federal level:

- As *Belgian Safer Internet Centre* (http://www.saferinternet.org/web/ guest/centre/-/belgium), Child Focus initiates different campaigns on Internet safety in collaboration with the industry, ministries, and other partners. Child Focus organizes and participates in a broad range of activities and initiatives in order to raise awareness in the area of online safety and child abuse images. Child Focus develops awareness-raising tools on safe and responsible use of the Internet and informs parents, teachers, and the public about children's use of the Internet and new technologies. The aim is to provide children and their educators with information and tools for guidance and to empower children using information and communication technologies.

- *The Interactive Software Federation of Europe* (ISFE; http://www. isfe.eu) is an international association with scientific and pedagogical purposes. It represents the interests of the interactive software sector throughout the 27 EU Member States plus Norway, Iceland, Switzerland, and Liechtenstein. Today, ISFE membership comprises 13 major publishers of interactive software as well as 14 interactive software trade associations throughout Europe. ISFE created the Pan-European Game Information or PEGI (http://www.pegi.info) and PEGI online (http://www.pegionline.eu) systems. The PEGI system provides European parents with detailed recommendations regarding the age suitability of game content in the form of age labels and content descriptors on game packages. PEGI Online, its addendum for online gaming, aims to address risks associated with real-time player interaction and changing content of online games.

- The *Cinematek* (the Royal Belgian Film Archive; http://www.cin ematek.be) is a bicultural institution (for both the Flemish and the French-speaking community) supported by the Federal Ministry of Science Policy, the National Lottery, and the city of Brussels. It collects, conserves, and screens films of aesthetic, technical, and historical importance. Also, its public library has a large collection of books, specialized journals, press articles, pictures, and so forth. Often in collaboration with the (Flemish) *Vlaamse Dienst voor Filmcultuur* (VFDC) and the (French-speaking) *Service de Culture Cinématographique* (SCC), it hosts and organizes thematic lectures and other film educational activities for the public in general and for schools in particular.

- The *Evens Foundation* is a philanthropic public benefit organization based in Antwerp, Belgium, with offices in Paris and Warsaw. The Evens Foundation initiates, develops, and supports projects that encourage citizens and states to live together harmoniously in a peaceful Europe. In this way, it aims to promote respect for cultural and social diversity and hopes to strengthen social cohesion among European citizens. Since 2009, the Evens Foundation has awarded a biannual prize of Media Education for European organizations that attempt to raise critical awareness and encourage creative media production.

In the Flemish community:

- *Vlaams Steunpunt Nieuwe Geletterdheid* (VSNG; the Flemish Foundation of New Literacy; http://www.vsng.be) aims to regroup Flemish organizations that are active in the field of e-Inclusion and new media literacy. The VSNG pursues three main objectives: to promote local initiatives in the field of e-Inclusion, particularly for vulnerable social groups; to be a center of excellence where good practices can be exchanged; and to be a partner of the public authorities in the development of public policies in the field of e-Inclusion and new media literacy.
- In 2004 *CANON Cultuurcel* (the cultural unit of the Flemish Department of Education; http://www.canoncultuurcel.be) and IAK (the former Flemish Initiative for the Audiovisual Arts, now BAM) published an extensive report (Audiovisual Training in Flemish Education 2004) on the state of audiovisual education in both Flemish formal education and the Flemish social-cultural field. This report clearly illustrated how media literacy education is of interest for many educators and social-cultural actors. Following this publication, CANON launched INGEBEELD (http://www.ingebeeld.be), a four-part media educational initiative in cooperation with the Flemish media educational field, which provides offline and online media educational teaching materials for nursery, primary, secondary, and teacher education.
- *Lessen in het Donker* (Lessons in the Dark; http://www.lesseninhet donker.be) is a nonprofit film educational organization that reaches approximately 80,000 students in nursery, primary, or secondary education every year. The organization compiles a yearly film program of nonmainstream films, often with a focus on social problems, facilitating both topical and stylistic discussions in a classroom context. Furthermore, the organization provides ready-to-use teaching materials that can be used by teachers for activities of film analysis.
- *Jekino* (http://www.jekino.be) is a nonprofit organization that offers media analysis and media production workshops for children and adolescents. These practices take place both in in-school and out-of-school contexts. Workshops mainly focus on the "building blocks" of audiovisual language. Typically, participants are coached to make a short film or an animation film. Other sessions more explicitly focus on film analysis. Sometimes media educational tools are also used to deal with broader topics. Furthermore, Jekino distributes (nonmainstream) children's films and youth films.

- *Kranten in de Klas* (Newspapers in Education; http://www.kranten indeklas.be) is a joint project between the Flemish government and the Flemish Newspaper Press. Over two weeks, teachers introduce students to various newspapers. On one hand, the project aims to stimulate pupils' interest in reading the newspaper. On the other hand, students learn to critically deal with information in the media. Each year, approximately 100,000 students participate in the Newspapers in Education project.
- Next to the organizations and initiatives previously mentioned, many other nonprofit organizations are active in the media literacy field, at both the larger community and the more local level. Often these organizations cooperate. For example, in the city of Antwerp alone, among others, *StampMedia* (a youth press agency), *VideAntz* (a video production house for youngsters), *REC Radiocentrum* (a radio center), *Piazza dell'Arte* (an art education organization), and *KifKif* (an intercultural youth platform) work together on a regular basis (or have worked together in the past) on a variety of media-related projects.

In the French-speaking community:

- Since 1995, the French-speaking community has had an official coordinating body for media literacy education: the *Conseil supérieur de l'Education aux Médias* (CSEM) (the Higher Council for Media Education; http://www.csem.cfwb.be). In 2009, this coordination body was reformed and officially established by the law. The council currently associates representatives from research, media, industry, civil society, and public administrations fields. This council is in charge of giving advice about, promoting, and coordinating media education in the French community. The CSEM also has at its disposal budgets to support specific media education initiatives, mainly in a school context or in lifelong learning programs.
- Three official resource centers (the *Centre d'Autoformation et de Formation Continuée de l'Enseignment* for the French-speaking community public school network (http://www.lecaf.be), the *Centre Audiovisuel Liège* for the subsidized official public school network (http://www.cavliege.be), and *Media Animation asbl* (http://www.media-animation.be) for the free denominational subsidized school network are responsible for designing and promoting lifelong learning activities on media education for teachers of elementary, secondary, and higher education. These resource centers are responsible for assisting in the training of

media literacy educators, developing and coordinating programs of life-long media learning, informing educational officials and organizations, lending and producing media educational documents, engaging, under the auspices of the Conseil Supérieur de l'Education aux Médias, in research to promote media literacy, and so forth.

- *Média Animation* (http://www.media-animation.be) is an important resource center and lifelong learning organization in media and multi-media education. It has published a series of guides and files dedicated to media education and developed numerous educational activities in schools, families, and civil society. Its director, Patrick Verniers, is also a member of the media literacy expert group of the European Commission and is actively involved in several European media education networks (such as Euromeduc; http://www.euromeduc.eu) and European media education projects (such as Media Coach; http://www.media-coach.eu).

- Since 1996, the *Service Général de l'Audiovisuel et des Multimédias* (the General Service of Audiovisual Media and Multimedia; http://www.audiovisual.cfwb.be) has organized public auditions of television channels on topics related to media education (violence in fiction, in the news, etc.) and collaborates with other initiatives on that subject matter. It also completes studies and edits informational publications for all audiences: children, teenagers, educators, and the general public.

- The *RTBF* (French-speaking public broadcaster; http://www.rtbf.be) has a legal media education mission, although limited, stated in its management contract. The French-speaking public broadcaster has two main TV channels, La Une and La Deux, and several radio stations which are accessible to the whole French-speaking population (through television, radio, and the Internet). Although the RTBF does not produce programs that are specifically dedicated to media education, it has carried out some programs that contribute to media education in different forms and formats (debates regarding media issues, comments on breaking news–handling by the media, knowledge about media production practices, documentaries about the history of the medias, and so forth). Moreover, the RTBF is sometimes involved in media educational activities carried out by educational organizations. Likewise, *local television stations* often (implicitly) contribute to media literacy, by giving the possibility to the citizens to participate interactively in their own programs (e.g., neighborhood television).

- The *Association des Journalistes Professionnels* (AJP; The Association of Professional Journalists; http://www.ajp.be) coordinates

Journalistes en Classe (Journalists in the Classroom). Here, pupils from primary and secondary education have the opportunity to hear professional journalists talk about their métier in the classroom. The initiative is supported by the Ministry of Education of the French community and developed in consultation with the Conseil Supérieur de l'Education aux Médias.

- *La Médiathèque de la Communauté Française de Belgique* (MCFB; http://www.lamediatheque.be) is a large and accessible media library. The Mediathèque has developed thematic collections for media literacy and distributes educational resources. It played a major role in the development of media education by taking many initiatives in pilot projects and expert groups in the late 1980s and early 1990s.

- The *Cellule Culture-Enseignement* (the cultural unit of the General Secretariat of the Ministry of the French Community; http://www.culture -enseignement.cfwb.be) aims to initiate and facilitate synergies between the educational and cultural world. Within this context it actively collaborates with the *Conseil Supérieur de l'Education aux Médias* and is in charge of a number of media literacy projects such as school prizes for films, for young journalists, and so forth.

- At the UCL (Université Catholique de Louvain) the research center *GReMS* (*Groupe de Recherche en Médiation des Savoirs*) conducts research on media literacy and organizes special courses on media literacy at the university level. Likewise, media literacy courses are organized at FUNDP (Facultés Universitaires Notre-Dame de la Paix/ Département des Sciences Politiques, Sociales, et de la Communication), IHECS (Institut des Hautes Etudes en Communications Sociales), and ULg (Université de Liège/Agrégation en Education aux Médias).

- As in the Flemish community, a variety of social-cultural (nonprofit) organizations (such as, among others, *Action Cine Medias Jeunes*, *Union des Fédérations des Associations de Parents de l'Enseignement Catholique*, *Centre d'Animation par Audiovisuel*) organize a wide range of media educational activities for specific target audiences.

III. Notable Individuals in National Media Literacy Programs

1. Flemish Community
Dirk Terryn
Contact person at Interculturality, Media, and Literature at CANON Cultural Unit; project leader INgeBEELD and Network Teacher Education
Contact information: dirk.terryn@ond.vlaanderen.be

Particular contributions to the field of media literacy: project leader of INgeBEELD, one of the first comprehensive media literacy initiatives in Flemish formal education.

Christine Debaene and Simon Smessaert
Both work at the Flemish Department of Culture, Youth, Sport, and Media
Contact information: chirstine.debaene@cjsm.vlaanderen.be and simon .smessaert@cjsm.vlaanderen.be
Particular contributions to the field of media literacy: actively involved in current policy work on media literacy and media literacy education.

Laure Van Hoecke
Coordinator *Vlaams Steunpunt Nieuwe Geletterdheid* (VSNG)
Contact information: laure.van.hoecke@linc-vzw.be
Particular contributions to the field of media literacy: as a network organization, VSNG brings together the many fragmented initiatives on new media literacy in the Flemish community.

Marie-Anne Moreas and Jan Pickery
Both work at the Research Department of the Flemish Government
Contact information: marieanne.moreas@dar.vlaanderen.be and jan.pick ery@dar.vlaanderen.be
Particular contributions to the field of media literacy: have recently edited (in collaboration with a variety of Flemish communication scholars) a (Dutch-language) publication on antecedents and consequences of (online) media literacy, based on a yearly randomly sampled survey on social-cultural changes.

Professor Dr. Katia Segers and Professor Dr. Joke Bauwens
Both work at the Center of Media and Cultural Studies (CEMESO) at the Free University of Brussels
Contact information: katia.segers@vub.ac.be and joke.bauwens@vub.ac.be
Particular contributions to the field of media literacy: have recently edited (in collaboration with a variety of Flemish scholars) an accessible (Dutch-language) book on media literacy (education) for policy makers, teachers, parents, and so forth. Are both members of the European EU Kids Online network.

Hans Martens
Researcher at the Visual Studies and Media Culture Research Group at the University of Antwerp
Contact information: hans.martens@ua.ac.be

Particular contributions to the field of media literacy: author of several national and international publications on media literacy and media literacy education in the Flemish community. Is actively involved in national and international networks of media literacy researchers and practitioners.

2. French-Speaking Community
Tanguy Roosen
President of the Conseil Supérieur de l'Education aux Médias
Contact information: csem@cfwb.be
Particular contributions to the field of media literacy: expert and institutional manager.

Patrick Verniers
Vice President of the Conseil Supérieur de l'Education aux Médias and director at Média Animation.
Contact information: info@media-animation.be
Particular contributions to the field of media literacy: expert, institutional leader, developer of media literacy programs.

Professor Dr. Thierry De Smedt and Professor Dr. Pierre Fastrez
Both are professors at GREMS at the Université Catholique de Louvain
Contact information: Thierry.Desmedt@uclouvain.be and Pierre.Fastrez@uclouvain.be
Particular contributions to the field of media literacy: experts, researchers, theorists, developers of media literacy programs, teachers.

Professor Dr. François Heinderyckx
Professor at the Université Libre de Bruxelles (Departement des Sciences de l'Information et de la Communication).
Contact information: Francois.Heinderyckx@ulb.ac.be
Particular contributions to the field of media literacy: expert, researcher, theorist, institutional manager

Myriam Lenoble
General Director at the Service Général de l'Audiovisuel et des Multimédias
Contact information: myriam.leboble@cfwb.be
Particular contributions to the field of media literacy: institutional manager.

Michel Clarembeau
Position: former director at the Centre Audiovisuel Liège

Contact information: cav.liege@sec.cfwb.be
Particular contributions to the field of media literacy: expert, teacher, teacher trainer, developer of media literacy programs.

Jean-Luc Sorée
Works at the Centre d'Autoformation et de Formation Continuée de l'Enseignement
Contact information: jean-luc.soree@lecaf.be
Particular contributions to the field of media literacy: expert, teacher trainer, developer of media literacy programs.

Jean-François Dumont
General Secretary at the Association des Journalistes Professionnels
Contact information: jfdumont@ajp.be
Particular contributions to the field of media literacy: expert, teacher trainer, develops media literacy programs, institutional manager.

Bhutan

Prepared by Monira A. Y. Tsewang

I. Overview

The Royal Government of Bhutan recognizes the potential benefits of information and media in today's information age and fosters transparency and accountability for promoting good democratic governance. In pursuit of these objectives, the government is strengthening the media.

Media literacy education is one of the alternatives to promoting the quality of a vibrant and responsible media. Media shapes perceptions, beliefs, and attitudes. Media can play a professional role only if the consumers of media understand and know how to use them effectively; media consumers must be aware, skilled, and capable of analyzing content and quality of media.

Although citizens are consumers of media, they can also be producers of media and engage in discourse and participate actively. They should be able to think critically and make the right choices and express themselves also through the media platforms.

The Department of Information and Media, Ministry of Information and Communications is the lead agency in creating an enabling environment for a vibrant information and media sector and has initiated and is coordinating the Information and Media literacy education program in Bhutan. The main agencies collaborating with us are the Department of Curriculum, Ministry of Education and Royal University of Bhutan, and the Royal Education Council.

We have developed a Strategic Framework for Media Literacy Education program (involving many stakeholders). The program is targeted to be implemented nationwide for all Bhutanese citizens, dividing society into two categories for implementation.

The target audiences for these programs are

1. school students, teacher trainees, and trainers in training schools and colleges and
2. other members of the general public (literate and illiterate).

We have developed curricula for media literacy education from pre-primary to class XII, and the curriculum board has approved media literacy to be introduced as an optional subject in Grades XI and XII.

Media studies was introduced as an undergraduate course at Sherubtse College in Kanglung in July 2011, with a previously developed curriculum.

We have introduced information and media literacy in 16 (pilot) schools across the country and have raised awareness on what is media literacy to about 2,000 teacher trainees and teachers around the country. Annually we train all final-year teacher trainees from the two teacher training institutions; we also train teachers and principals at the Dzongkhag Education Conferences.

Although we are constantly refining the curriculum, we would like professional input to finalize it. We are also working on developing resource materials for schools and the general public—both printed and audiovisual programs. This has become a challenge as we lack the professional resources to develop such high-quality local resources. We have developed some educational brochures and visual teasers on media literacy. Much remains to be done.

We also developed and introduced media literacy into the non-formal or continuing education system that is very popular in Bhutan. We also plan to work closely with civil society organizations and international experts besides our local counterparts to take this program forward. We are also trying to demonstrate how critical thinking can be integrated into other subjects and not just for media literacy.

All activities involve core group members from Ministry of Education, Curriculum specialists and officers, Department of Information and Media, Royal University of Bhutan, lecturers, Royal Education Council, and nonformal education.

II. Notable Media Literacy Organizations

As mentioned above, media literacy is for all citizens in Bhutan but is categorized into two broad categories: (1) schools, teachers, teacher trainees, and lecturers, and (2) the general public.

The lead agency is the Department of Information and Media, Ministry of Information and Communications, Royal Government of Bhutan, and Ministry of Education, Curriculum Division.

III. Notable Individuals in National Media Literacy Programs

Mr. Wangchuk Rabden

Specialist, Curriculum Division, Ministry of Education, RGOB; emss@druknet.bt; 00975-17605318

Mr. Rabden is chair of the media literacy Core Group. He drafts curriculum on media literacy for schools and Grades XI and XII and plays a lead role in all training programmes for media literacy. He trains and builds awareness on media literacy at all levels and is an active advocate for media literacy and critical thinking in general.

Monira A. Y. Tsewang

Chief, InfoCom and Media Development Division, Department of Information and Media; monira@doim.gov.bt; 00975-17536187/00975-2-321093

Ms. Tsewang is responsible for taking the program forward with a team of three dedicated staff members who work with the core group members and experts and media personnel. She facilitates all media literacy activities and ensures that funds are available and builds institutional linkages. Tsewang played a catalytic role in finalization of Sherubtse College curriculum for media studies involving all stakeholders and getting expert professional advice as well.

Canada

Prepared by Barry Duncan
and John Pungente, SJ

I. Overview

Introduction

As a country whose population of some 33 million is mostly contained in a narrow band that stretches for about 4,000 miles across the northern part of the North American continent, and as a country that uses two official languages, English and French, and numerous aboriginal languages, Canadians are critically aware of the importance of communications. Canadians, in both English and French, have made major contributions to communications technology (the creation of the Anik satellite and Telidon); media theory (the work of Harold Innis, Marshall McLuhan, and André H. Caron); and media production (The National Film Board of Canada [www.nfb.ca], the Canadian Broadcasting Corporation [www.cbc.ca], and our English and French film industries).

Over the past few decades, media literacy has become part of the basic curriculum for all elementary and secondary school students in Canada. Because of the research, teaching, and promotion of media literacy by Canadian educators and the provincial ministries of education, media literacy has also become an essential building block for many postsecondary areas of study—lifelong learning programs, continuing education programs, professional development and training programs, and specialized programs for the at-risk or marginalized population.

The Status of Media Literacy in Canada

Canada's 10 provinces and 3 northern territories are each responsible for their own education system. The launching of media education in Canada came about for four major reasons: (1) critical concerns about the pervasiveness and influence of American popular culture; (2) a system of education that fostered the necessary contexts for new educational paradigms; (3) the professional education and political sectors' acknowledgment of the need for curriculum and pedagogical reevaluation and reform required by technological, social, and political developments in Canadian society; and (4) the preoccupation by teachers and administrators with the new digital media.

In Canada, in the late 1960s, the first wave of media literacy education began under the banner of *screen education*. The Canadian Association for Screen Education (CASE) sponsored the first large gathering of media teachers in 1969 at Toronto's York University. As a result of budget cuts and the general back-to-the-basics philosophy, this first wave died out in the early 1970s but returned with a renewed impetus in the early 1980s. In 1989, Ontario, where more than one-third of Canada's population lives, became the first educational jurisdiction in North America to make media literacy a mandatory part of the basic school curriculum.

By 2002, all Canadian provinces and territories had mandated media literacy in the curriculum as part of the English language arts courses, and some provinces also supported independent courses. For detailed information on provincial curriculum guidelines for media literacy, please consult the study done by the Media Awareness Network at http://www.media-awareness.ca/english/teachers/media_education/index.cfm

Defining Canadian Media Literacy and the Key Concepts

Media literacy's raison d'être is to help students develop an informed and critical understanding of the nature of the mass media, the techniques used by the mass media, and the impact of these techniques on individuals and society. Media literacy also aims to help students develop skills in creating and publishing media products.

The following eight key concepts, which provide a theoretical base for media literacy, give teachers a common language and framework for their pedagogical practices and professional development. These concepts are the foundation of Canadian media literacy educational practices and initiatives.

1. All media are constructions. Media are not simple reflections of external reality. They present productions that are carefully crafted.
2. The media construct versions of reality. Media messages come with observations, attitudes, and interpretations already built in.
3. Audiences actively negotiate meaning in media. Each of us interacts in unique ways to media texts based on such factors as gender, age, and life experiences.
4. Media messages have commercial implications. Media education includes an awareness of the economic basis of the media industry. The issue of ownership and control is of vital importance.

5. Media messages contain ideological and value messages. Media education involves an awareness of the ideological implications and value systems of media texts.

6. Media messages have social and political implications. Media education involves an awareness of the broad range of social and political effects stemming from the media.

7. Form and content are closely related in media messages. The meaning of the content is shaped by the form. Making the form/content connections relates to the thesis of Marshall McLuhan that "the medium is the message."

8. Each medium has an unique aesthetic form. This enables students not only to decode and understand media texts, but also to enjoy the unique aesthetic form of each.

Canadian Media Literacy

Canadian media educators have been influenced by trends in education and cultural theory around the world. There is an international consensus that cultural studies is the most relevant paradigm for media literacy because it addresses gender, race, and class; the centrality of "representation" in media studies acknowledges this triad, which has become the dominant organizer of Canadian media studies. Implicit in current media literacy is the necessity of combining analysis with student media production, especially through new digital media.

An important Canadian contribution is found in the work of Marshall McLuhan, who investigated the unique properties and impact of new communication technology. McLuhan also recognized Canada's low profile on the world stage, especially in our relationship to the United Sates, to be advantageous, allowing us an ironic, semidetached and often satiric perspective of popular culture.

Finally, Canadian media education accesses areas such as semiotics, social media, critical literacies, and critical pedagogies, all articulated against a background of audience studies. It is characteristically Canadian to serve as a synthesizer of important ideas while at the same time fulfilling our role as reflective skeptic.

In Canadian elementary and secondary schools there are four principle approaches to teaching media literacy.

1. *Medium (or format)-based approach*: here the characteristics, strengths, and weaknesses of a particular medium are focused on.

2. *Thematic approach*: A theme-based study involves several media. An issue, such as gender representation, can be identified and examined in terms of how it is communicated in a variety of media.

3. *Stand-alone approach*: For many teachers, a media studies unit is either a stand-alone unit within an English language arts course or a separate course in itself. The class may choose a genre, issue, or theme and study it exclusively for a specific period of time.
4. *Integrated units*: Integrating media studies into or across other classroom activities or subject areas creates the most authentic learning environment for media literacy. This pedagogical strategy connects the newer media, such as Web 2.0, to traditional forms of communication, such as television, radio, print, or speech.

Canadian Criteria for Successful Media Education

A study of media education around the world shows that there are nine factors which appear to be crucial to the successful development of media education in secondary schools.

1. Media education, like other innovative programs, must be a grassroots movement and teachers need to take a major initiative in lobbying for this.
2. Educational authorities must give clear support to media education programs by mandating the teaching of media studies within the curriculum, establishing guidelines and resource books, and making certain that curricula are developed and that materials are available.
3. Faculties of education must hire staff capable of training future teachers in media education as well as offering courses in media education. There should also be academic support from tertiary institutions in the writing of curricula and in sustained consultation.
4. In-service training at the school district level must be an integral part of program implementation.
5. School districts need consultants who have expertise in media education and who will establish communication networks.
6. Suitable resources—textbooks, Web sites, and AV material—that are relevant to the country/area must be available.
7. A support organization must be established for the purposes of workshops, conferences, dissemination of newsletters, and the development of curriculum. Such a professional organization must cut across school boards and districts to involve a cross section of people interested in media education.
8. There must be appropriate evaluation instruments that are suitable for the unique quality of media studies.

9. Because media education involves such a diversity of skills and expertise, there must be collaboration among teachers, parents, researchers, and media professionals.

II. Notable Media Literacy Organizations

There are a number of national and provincial media literacy organizations across Canada. What follows are some of these organizations and some of the people connected with them.

CAMEO: Canadian Association of Media Education Organizations

In 1992, representatives from Canadian provincial media education groups met in Toronto to form the Canadian Association of Media Education Organizations (CAMEO). The purpose of this umbrella group is to promote media education across Canada and link together Canadian media education organizations. For more information, visit http://interact.uoregon.edu/MediaLit/CAMEO/

Eight provincial media literacy organizations in Canada make up the membership of CAMEO. The first organization to be founded was the Ontario Association for Media Literacy in 1978 and the latest, the Association for Media Literacy in Newfoundland and Labrador in 2002. Other media literacy organizations have joined as associate members of CAMEO.

Although each provincial organization works provincially to develop and promote media literacy through conferences, workshops, and publications, the provincial organizations work together under CAMEO to pursue national initiatives such as the presentation of briefs across Canada to the CRTC on the issue of media and violence. Here are a few other such initiatives.

Media Literacy Week

Since 2005, CAMEO has been a contributor to Media Literacy Week organized by the Media Awareness Network (MNet) and the Canadian Teachers' Federation (CTF) by encouraging youth, parents, educators, community leaders, governments, and media industries from across the country to participate in and support media and digital literacy initiatives in their regions. For further information: Media Literacy Week Contact CAMEO. The mailing address is:

MediaSmarts
950 avenue Gladstone Ave.
Suite / Bureau 120

Ottawa, Ontario K1Y 3E6
Canada

The International Media Literacy Research Forum
May 2008 marked the start of a new international venture by Ofcom, the British telecommunications regulator. The initiative, called the International Media Literacy Research Forum, is run by a steering committee made up of one representative each from Australia, Britain, Canada, Ireland, New Zealand, and the United States. John Pungente, SJ, was invited to represent Canada on the steering committee. For the founding conference, the provincial CAMEO groups contributed to a lengthy history of media literacy in Canada. A delegation of Canadian media educators attended the first conference in London. See http://www.imlrf.org

Understanding Media Literacy: Inside Plato's Cave
Produced by Face to Face Media and The Jesuit Communication Project, *Understanding Media Literacy: Inside Plato's Cave,* is a 13-unit, 3-credit course for those wishing to know more about the nexus between children and media literacy. The course, offered through Athabasca University, is especially designed for those who teach at the Grades 7–12 levels and for students of media and communication. The 13 units that make up the online course were written and field-tested by members of the Canadian Association of Media Education Organizations (CAMEO). For more information, see www .athabascau.ca/platoscave

Provincial Members of CAMEO
Following is information on some of the provincial CAMEO groups. Please contact the individual group to find out more about the history, activities, and members of each group.

British Columbia Association for Media Education (BCAME)
Our Mission is as follows:

1. To educate Canadians about the media
2. To promote media education
3. To encourage Canadian cultural expression in the media

Formed by a group of teachers and media professionals, the British Columbia Association for Media Education (formerly the Canadian Association for Media Education) was issued its certificate of incorporation as a nonprofit society by the British Columbia Registrar of Companies in August 1991.

Some notable accomplishments:

1. Produced a document for BCAME in 1994, under contract to the BC Ministry of Education. "A Conceptual Framework for Media Education and Cross Curricular Interests" was intended to be used by the various Ministry of Education committees that were engaged in reviewing all curricula at that time. BCAME members Dan Blake and Kevin McKendy wrote the media education learning outcomes, which appeared in the final draft of the English language arts curriculum document.
2. Held a series of public fora in Vancouver between 1995 and 1997 to educate Canadians about the role of the media.
3. Participated in the development of a constitution for the Canadian Association of Media Education Organizations.
4. Presented workshops for teachers at conferences across British Columbia.
5. Coordinated four biennial Media Literacy Summer Institutes between 2001 and 2007, held in Vancouver.
6. Actively involved in developing, piloting, and promoting Plato's Cave, an online media education course for teachers.

Contacts for BCAME

1. Dan Blake, President, BC Association for Media Education: deblaca@telus.net
2. Stuart R. Poyntz, Ph., School of Communication, Simon Fraser University: spoyntz@sfu.ca
3. Kym Stuart, Sessional Lecturer, Capilano College: Kyms@sfu.ca

Alberta Association for Media Awareness (AAMA)
Wayne Blair—wblair@planet.eon.net

Manitoba Association for Media Literacy (MAML)
Brian Murphy—bmurphy@mts.net

Association for Media Literacy (AML)
Dede Sinclair: dasinclair@rogers.com
Founded in 1978, The Association for Media Literacy was the first comprehensive organization for media literacy teachers in Canada. AML Ontario

has helped establish several other provincial media literacy organizations, all members of the CAMEO national network (Canadian Association of Media Education Organizations).

The AML serves the needs of its members through a variety of services:

- AML provides a network for media literacy teachers throughout the world. Our founder, Barry Duncan, is an internationally recognized leader in the media literacy movement. Several of our executive members have also published student textbooks widely used in Ontario and throughout Canada.
- AML publishes an online newsletter for its members.
- AML organizes workshops and conferences. We were co-organizers for Summit 2000: Children, Youth and the Media: Beyond the Millennium, which was held in Toronto and attracted over 1,500 participants from 54 countries. Previously, two international conferences were held in Guelph, Ontario, and we cosponsored the Media Literacy Summer Institutes with Ryerson Polytechnic University in Toronto. We also organize workshops in the Toronto area, as well as Ottawa and Vancouver, and throughout southwestern Ontario, including London, Stratford, and Windsor.
- AML publishes curriculum anthologies and other support material for media teachers.
- AML lobbies and communicates with government, school boards, and the media industry about mutual concerns.

For more information, visit www.aml.ca

Association for Media Education Quebec (AMEQ)
AMEQ is a small, bilingual organization. Formed in September 1990, the members of the association have long contended that media literacy should be included in the curriculum from kindergarten to Grade 11. To this end, AMEQ members worked with the education ministry to develop the media education components of the Quebec Education Program (QEP).

AMEQ members are leaders in media education, providing:

- Media literacy conferences for teachers, parents, and community workers
- Student media festivals
- Daylong workshops and parent information evenings
- Workshops at provincial and national education and parent conferences, and in school board professional development programs

- Media education courses in faculties of education at Bishop's University and McGill University

Contacts:

Maureen Baron, Co-President: Maureen.baron@gmail.com
Lee Rother, PhD, Co-President: irving.rother@mail.mcgill.ca, (450) 508-9563

Media Literacy Nova Scotia (MLNS)
Peter Smith: smithps@gov.ns.ca

Association for Media Literacy New Brunswick (A-4-ML NB)
Mike Gange: sportsjounr@yahoo.com

Association for Media Literacy Newfoundland and Labrador (AMLNL)
Leslie Kennedy: lesliekennedy6525@yahoo.com

2. Associate CAMEO Members
Centre de resources en éducation aux médias (CREM)
Michel Pichette: pichette.michel@uqam.ca

Concerned Children's Advertisers (CCA)
Linda Millar: ibmillar@magma.ca
www.cca-kids.ca

Jesuit Communication Project (JCP)
John J. Pungente, SJ: pungente@sympatico.ca

Media Awareness Network (MNET)
Jane Tallim: jtallim@media-awareness.ca

Concerned Childrens' Advertisers
Founded in 1990, the Concerned Childrens' Advertisers (CCA) has developed more than 35 child-directed television commercials on topics ranging from substance abuse prevention and active living to bullying and self-esteem. They have developed study guides for all of these and present workshops across Canada. In 1997, the CCA, working with the Jesuit Communication Project, produced its first media literacy public service announcement, "Smart As You." And, in 2001, the CCA released its second media literacy

public service announcement, "The House Hippo." Both announcements speak to children directly about the importance of "watching carefully, thinking critically and navigating safely" with all media.

In addition to the PSAs, CCA has lesson plans in English and French for K–8, and a parent/community program that provides tips, tools, and strategies to help Canadian children and families understand, interpret, and use media. For more information, visit www.cca-kids.ca

CTVglobemedia

In summarizing CTVglobemedia's (CTVgm) activities, we need to speak as well about those of CHUM Television, a broadcasting company that CTVgm acquired in 2007. CTVgm is upholding CHUM's commitment to media education. Beginning in the mid-1980s, CHUM Television's support of media literacy was a key component of the company's corporate philanthropy. They operated on the belief that the ability to better understand media is a fundamental part of citizenship, and that as a public broadcaster they have a role to play in encouraging media literacy as part of good corporate citizenship.

What began as an effort to help viewers become more literate about what they watched, by producing programs that explored the nature of screen-based content, grew into a wider support of Canada's media literacy community. CTVgm provides commercial-free original programming free of charge for use in the classroom, funds media literacy initiatives and not-for-profit organizations, and donates airtime and Web space in an effort to provide tools and resources to everyone and encourage a heightened awareness about the nature and role of the media.

Noteworthy contributions to media literacy in Canada made by CHUM Television included, over the years, creating and telecasting Public Service Announcements; sponsoring the Media Education Pillar during the Summit 2000 conference, a landmark international conference about Children, Youth and the Media; becoming a founding member of Canadian Cable in the Classroom (CITC); funding teacher training institutes; organizing a National Colloquium on Cultural Diversity and Media; and partnering with the London Public Library in Ontario to create a media literacy center—the first of its kind in North America—to provide media literacy materials to the local community and surrounding area. CHUM also sponsored both Scanning Television and Scanning Television (Revised)—two award-winning educational resources for classroom use.

As well, CTVgm's national arts channel, Bravo!, aired 10 seasons of *Scanning the Movies* as well as two seasons of *Beyond the Screen*, two media literacy series hosted by John Pungente, SJ, which analyzed contemporary film.

MuchMusic, Canada's only 24-hour music channel geared specifically to teens and young adults, creates award-winning programming that addresses media and social issues from a pop-culture, youth-oriented perspective. www.muchmusic.com/mediaed

The Jesuit Communication Project (JCP)

For more than 25 years the Jesuit Communication Project has been involved in developing and promoting media literacy across Canada and around the world. John Pungente, SJ, the executive director of the JCP, has coauthored *Media Literacy: A Resource Guide* (1989), *Meet the Media* (1990), *More Than Meets the Eye: Watching TV Watching Us* (1999), and *Finding God in the Dark: The Spiritual Exercises of St. Ignatius Go to the Movies* (2004). He has contributed to international journals and books on media literacy.

Pungente was creator, producer, cowriter, and host of the award-winning media education national television series *Scanning the Movies*, which ran from 1997 to 2007 on Bravo! His new media literacy television series, *Beyond the Screen*, which he created, writes, coproduces, and hosts, began airing on Bravo! in May 2008. Each of these films is accompanied by study guides written by media educator Neil Andersen. Pungente is producer of the award-winning video *A Heart to Understand*, as well as the 1996 award-winning media education teaching resource, *Scanning Television* and the 2003 award-winning resource *Scanning Television 2*. *Scanning Television 1* and *2* were coproduced with Face to Face Media.

He is coproducer and cowriter of *Understanding Media Literacy*: *Inside Plato's Cave*, an online university full three-credit course for media literacy teachers available from Athabasca University (www.athabascau.ca/platoscave).

Since 1985, he has given many presentations across Canada and Australia, in Europe, Great Britain, the United States, and Japan. He has served as a consultant to media professionals including TV Ontario, the CBC, the NFB, CHUM Television, and Warner Bros. Canada. He is a sessional professor of media literacy at Regis College and St. Michael's College, University of Toronto.

Contact: John J. Pungente, SJ, pungente@sympatico.ca; www.beyondthe screen.com

The Media Awareness Network/Réseau Éducation-Médias

MNet is a Canadian nonprofit organization that has pioneered the development of media literacy programs since its incorporation in 1996. The site contains more than 300 teaching lessons for K–12, searchable by topic and grade or province and learning outcomes; more than 100 essays on topics such as gender, racial, and aboriginal stereotyping, media violence, online hate, electronic privacy, and Canadian cultural policies; and extensive Web awareness resources with teachers' guides.

In 1999, just as Canada was declared the first country in the world to connect all of its schools and public libraries to the Internet, MNet launched its Web Awareness Canada program, which included a professional development program for teachers and public library staff. The goal was to help young Canadians learn to be safe, wise, and responsible Internet users.

In 2000 and 2001, MNet's research initiative, "Young Canadians in a Wired World (Phase I)," surveyed, for the first time in Canada, 1,100 parents and then 6,000 students, on how kids are using the Internet and what they think about it. In 2003, MNet conducted focus groups in Montreal, Edmonton, and Toronto to track the fast transformation of the Internet from a new technology to an accepted and central part of young people's lives. This research continues to inform and support the development of MNet's education programs.

Members of the MNET team have backgrounds in education, journalism, mass communications, and cultural policy. Working from Ottawa and Montreal, in English and French, MNET promotes media literacy and Internet education by producing online programs and resources, working in partnership with Canadian and international organizations, and speaking to audiences across Canada and around the world. Since 2005, MNET and the Canadian Teachers' Federation organize a yearly Media Literacy week. For more information, visit http://www.media-awareness.ca

England

Prepared by Cary Bazalgette

I. Overview

1. England is the largest of the four nations that comprise the United Kingdom of Great Britain and Northern Ireland: its population is around 51 million—84 percent of the whole UK population.

2. *Media literacy* is specified in UK law under the Communications Act 2003. The media regulator, Ofcom, has a duty to work with others to promote media literacy. However, the UK has a long tradition of media education (i.e., the process that should lead to media literacy, and the preferred term in the UK) dating back to the 1930s (see Bolas, T. [2009]. *Screen Education: From Film Appreciation to Media Studies*, Bristol: Intellect Books). In England, there are elements of media education within subject English in the National Curriculum for 11- to 16-year-olds, whereas formal, examined courses in media studies are widely available as options to 14- to 18-year-olds and are taken by more than 100,000 students annually (i.e., about 5 percent of this age group). The status of media education in primary schools (for ages 5 to 11) and in other secondary curriculum areas is generally growing among teachers and other informed professionals. However, there is still some prejudice against it from traditionalists.

3. Examination specifications, which provide a framework for course planners in schools, are provided by Awarding Bodies, which also set and mark examinations. Media Studies and Film Studies are offered by these bodies as options at GCSE (for 16-year-olds), at AS/A2 level (for 16- to 18-year-olds), and in the Creative and Media Diploma (for 14- to 18-year-olds). The Awarding Bodies involved are WJEC (www.wjec .co.uk), OCR (www.ocr.org.uk), AQA (www.aqa.org.uk), and Edexcel (www.edexcel.com). All examinations in GCSE English include an element of media literacy and are offered by the same Awarding Bodies, and as English is compulsory at this age, the majority of young people do get some media education as part of these courses. Candidate numbers and results for Media Studies and for English can be seen at www

.jcq.org.uk/national_results/index.cfm. The actual teaching and learning that leads to these qualifications is under the control of the schools, and can vary in terms of quality, scope, and student satisfaction. Official but nonstatutory advice to teachers of literacy, citizenship, and personal social and health education in both primary and secondary schools tends to include suggestions for media education–type teaching.

II. Notable Media Literacy Organizations

British Film Institute Education Department— www.bfi.org.uk/education

BFI Education and Learning exists to reach out to audiences new to specialist, independent, archive and art film, and other forms of moving image media throughout the UK. Its five areas of activity are to educate audiences, facilitate engagement with BFI programs, advocate for the moving image in education, innovate by developing new ways of learning about film, and collaborate with partners nationally and internationally. The BFI's remit is UK-wide, not just in England.

The BFI has existed since 1933 and since 1950 has pioneered and often led developments in education about film and television. From 1983 until 2007, it was a major publisher of teaching resources for media education; from the 1950s to the 1980s, it pioneered the development of critical theory about moving image media; from the 1970s until 2007, it was a leading publisher of books about film, television, and media education and also a national leader in teacher training for media education. In collaboration with UNESCO and with CLEMI in France, the BFI organized the first global media education conference in Toulouse in 1990. In the 1970s, it helped to fund the first academic posts in film; in the 1980s, it was instrumental in establishing the first examination courses in Film Studies and Media Studies; in the 1990s, it played a key role in advocacy for media education as part of the National Curriculum.

The BFI is a national, nonprofit cultural body with a Royal Charter, funded by the government (Department of Culture, Media and Sport) through the UK Film Council.

Centre for Excellence in Media Practice—www.cemp.ac.uk

Based at the University of Bournemouth, offering postgraduate courses catering for media professionals and those working in media education. The

Centre also aims to influence media education research, through projects, publications and conferences. Runs an annual Media Education Summit for researchers and teachers in media education.

Centre for the Study of Children, Youth and Media— www.cscym.zerolab.info

Research center based at the University of London Institute of Education, the UK's leading graduate school of education and one of the major world centers of educational inquiry. Directed by David Buckingham, it undertakes funded research projects and consultancies, holds conferences and public seminars, organizes networks of researchers and practitioners, contributes to the Institute's MA Media program, supervises doctoral research students, and works with other institutions, nationally and internationally. The Centre's research themes are Film and Television, Games, Educational Media, Cultural Identities, Media Production, Gender, New Media and Media Education. Since 2001, the Centre has played a key role in developing knowledge and ideas about media education. Its research has been funded by (among others) the Economic and Social Research Council, the Arts and Humanities Research Board, the European Commission, the Arts Council of England, the EduServ Foundation, the Broadcasting Standards Commission, and the Spencer, Gulbenkian, and Nuffield Foundations.

English and Media Centre—www.englishandmedia.co.uk

A not-for-profit trust that provides publications and professional development on all aspects of English teaching for teachers and students of literature, language, and media in the UK and abroad. It serves the needs of secondary and FE teachers and students of English and Media Studies in the UK through a variety of professional development courses, more than 70 publications for the classroom, quarterly magazines for A Level students, an online library of quality teaching resources and pilot publications, consultancy, and advisory work. It has existed since the 1970s and has built a national reputation as a provider of high-quality training and resources at the cutting edge of media education.

Film Education—www.filmeducation.org

Founded in 1984 on the proposition that film is a powerful educational tool. Funded mainly by industry distributors and exhibitors, it provides curriculum-based learning materials, produces teacher training programs, and runs free screenings and events for schools. This includes National Schools Film Week, a nationwide festival that was attended by 400,000 young people in 2008.

Film Education produces a number of free teaching resources (originally print based, then CD and DVD, now mainly online) based on current, largely mainstream feature films. It has energetically promoted teaching about and with film in many school subject areas and maintains a strong public profile and a loyal community of users nationwide, as well as a large and active Web site.

First Light Movies—www.firstlightonline.co.uk
This organization was founded in 2001 by the UK Film Council to fund films made by children and young people in collaboration with media professionals.

Media Education Association (MEA)—www.themea.org
Subject association for those teaching about media at all levels of the education system. Founded in 2007, MEA has recently restructured itself as a free online community providing a "peer-review" service to media teachers through the "social bookmarking" function on its Web site which enables users to both post and review materials, classroom resources, links, and critical writing for rating and comment by others. MEA is the only independent organization in England dedicated solely to the development and promotion of education about all forms of media. It has also begun to offer annual conferences, with partners, to bring together media teachers and media education researchers at all levels of the education system.

Media Smart—www.mediasmart.org.uk
Launched in November 2002, Media Smart is a nonprofit media literacy program for schoolchildren aged 6 to 11 years old focused on advertising and funded by the advertising business in the UK. It develops and provides, free of charge and on request, educational materials to primary schools that are aimed at teaching children to think critically about advertising in the context of their daily lives.

The materials use real examples of advertising to help teach core media literacy skills. It retains an Expert Group of leading academics and educationalists in the field of media literacy who help with writing, reviewing, and approving their teaching materials, and has modified successive editions of its materials to bring them into line with the experts' advice.

National Media Museum—www.nationalmediamuseum.org.uk
This large city-center museum in Bradford, Yorkshire, is dedicated to photography, television, animation, film, radio, exhibiting materials, and artifacts relating to these media and to providing a program of educational events,

teacher training, screenings, and publications. The museum is part of the NMSI Museums Group (National Museum of Science and Industry).

Ofcom — http://stakeholders.ofcom.org.uk/market-data-research/media-literacy

Ofcom is the UK's media regulator, with responsibility for the TV and radio sectors, fixed-line telecoms and mobiles, plus the airwaves over which wireless devices operate. Under the Communications Act 2003, which set Ofcom up, it has a duty to work with others to promote media literacy. It has fulfilled this remit mainly through research, carrying out a number of audits of media use by different social sectors, commissioning reviews and studies from leading academics, and also by providing small amounts of funding to other media education organizations. It has also played a key advocacy role in trying to bring together the disparate agencies in the UK who have an interest, or potential interest, in media education.

III. Notable Individuals in National Media Literacy Programs

Cary Bazalgette

Freelance writer, researcher, and teacher trainer; chair of Media Education Association

www.carybazalgette.net

Bazalgette worked at the British Film Institute from 1979 to 2007, having previously been a teacher of English and filmmaking in London secondary schools. She has written and edited a number of pioneering classroom resources for media education and has published and spoken widely on this topic in the UK and in 25 countries around the world. She was head of BFI Education from 1999 through 2006, leading the BFI's commitment to developing new approaches to teaching and learning about the moving image media (film and TV), particularly for the 3- to 14-year age group, and helping to gain a higher profile for this area of education at policy level, nationally and internationally. After 18 months as the BFI's education policy adviser, she now works as a freelance researcher, writer, teacher trainer, and consultant specializing in media literacy and in children's media.

Robin Blake

Ofcom Senior Policy Executive, Media Literacy

Robin.blake@ofcom.org.uk

Formerly a teacher of media in further education and then worked at the Independent Television Commission, Blake has played a key, if "behind-the-scenes," role in Ofcom's media literacy team, helping to build consensus on media literacy, commissioning research, and bringing different agencies and individuals together.

David Buckingham
Director of the Centre for the Study of Children, Youth and Media
d.buckingham@ioe.ac.uk

His research focuses on children's and young people's interactions with electronic media, and on media education. He has acted as a consultant for UNESCO, the United Nations, the BBC, and Ofcom (the UK media regulator). He has directed more than 20 externally funded research projects and has been a visiting scholar at the University of Pennsylvania and New York University, and the Norwegian Centre for Child Research, where he is codirecting a major funded project on children and consumer culture. He contributed to the UK government's Byron Review on children and new technologies and recently led an independent assessment of the impact of the commercial world on children's well-being for the DCSF and DCMS. Professor Buckingham is the author, co-author, or editor of 22 books and more than 180 articles and book chapters.

Andrew Burn
Deputy Director of the Centre for the Study of Children, Youth and Media
a.burn@ioe.ac.uk

Burn taught English, drama, and media studies in comprehensive schools for more than 20 years. He was head of English and an assistant principal at Parkside Community College in Cambridge, where his main role was to direct the school's media arts specialism as the first Media Arts College in England. He has since played a major role in the development of media education and approaches to media literacy in the UK. He is involved in international developments in this field and is a member of the European Commission's media literacy expert group. He has also been involved in media literacy policy in the UK, contributing to OFCOM's media literacy initiative and to the work of the recent Byron Review of the impact of the Internet and computer games on children. He has published more than 60 articles, book chapters, and books on many aspects of the media, including media literacy, creativity, young people's use of digital video, the semiotics of computer games, and the design of computer games by young people.

James Durran
Advanced Skills Teacher at the Parkside Federation in Cambridge
http://www.parksidemedia.net/parkside_media/Training.htm

Formerly head of English, Media, and Drama at Parkside Community College, Durran has developed innovative approaches to teaching the moving image, especially to younger students, and has pioneered media arts projects with primary schools. Durran is involved nationally in developing and disseminating excellent practice in the teaching of both English and media, including consultancy work for the BFI, the DfES, QCA, the BBC, Immersive Education, and Teachers' TV. He delivers training and professional development across the UK for schools, advisers and consultants, LEAs, and professional associations.

Pete Fraser
Chief Examiner for OCR A Level Media Studies
http://petesmediablog.blogspot.com/
Formerly head of Media at Long Road Sixth Form College, Cambridge (one of England's largest centers for media teaching to 16- to 18-year-olds), Fraser has been an influential figure for generations of teachers and young people. He is now tutor on MA Creative and Media at Bournemouth University as well as chief examiner for OCR.

David Gauntlett
Professor of Media and Communications at the Communication and Media Research Institute (CAMRI), University of Westminster
http://www.theory.org.uk/david
Gauntlett is the author of several books on media and identities and the everyday creative use of digital media. These include *Moving Experiences* (1995, 2nd ed. 2005), *Video Critical* (1997), *TV Living* (with Annette Hill, 1999), *Media, Gender and Identity* (2002, 2nd ed. 2008), *Creative Explorations: New Approaches to Identities and Audiences* (2007) and *Making Is Connecting* (2011). He also edited two editions of the book *Web Studies* (2000, 2004). He produces the popular Web site about media and identities, Theory.org.uk, and has pioneered the use of creative and visual research methods, for which he has created the hub at ArtLab.org.uk He has conducted collaborative research with a number of the world's leading creative organizations, including the BBC, Lego, and Tate.

Richard Gent
Director, MediaEdusites
www.media.edusites.co.uk
Gent, a former teacher, is the creator of an increasingly influential Web site that offers a study and reference bank to paying subscribers, for all areas

and topics associated with GCSE and A Level media studies. The Web site unpacks media concepts, theories, and current debates and discussions and provides clear and easily followed advice on the various aspects of practical work such as creating an animation, making documentaries, producing a news item, creating music and drama videos, as well as camera and audio skills and techniques, including the whole area of print and photography design, analysis, and production.

Jenny Grahame

English and Media Centre

www.englishandmedia.co.uk

For many years Grahame has provided the English and Media Centre's editorial, publication, and training services in media education, particularly for teachers of the 11- to 16-year age range. She has also played a key role in many developments in media education in England and has acted as a consultant for Media Smart and for the Qualifications and Curriculum Authority. She has been a highly influential and much-admired teacher trainer and has thus influenced teaching and learning for generations of schoolchildren.

Julian McDougall

Reader in Media and Education and Head of Creative Arts, Newman University College, Birmingham

J.Mcdougall@newman.ac.uk

McDougall teaches media, education studies, PGCE English, and aspects of citizenship. His published research relates to media education, most recently investigating new ways of researching audiences for Grand Theft Auto and *The Wire*. He is the author of *The Media Teacher's Book* (Hodder) and *Studying Videogames* (Auteur), a range of textbooks for A Level media students, and *After the Media* (Routledge). He is a visiting fellow at the Centre of Excellence for Media Practice, Bournemouth University, editor of the Media Education Research Journal, principal examiner for A Level Media Studies (OCR), and executive committee member of the Media Education Association.

Jackie Marsh

Professor of Education, Head of The School of Education and Head of The Department of Educational Studies, University of Sheffield; j.a.marsh @Sheffield.ac.uk

Marsh has conducted research projects that have explored children's access to new technologies and their emergent digital literacy skills, knowledge, and understanding. She has conducted a number of research projects that have explored how creative and innovative teachers have responded to the challenges of the new media age. She has evaluated a number of national projects that have aimed to develop teachers' expertise in the teaching and learning of digital and media literacy. Key publications include *Digital Beginnings, Young Children's Use of Popular Culture, Media and New Technologies*, funded by BBC Worldwide/Esmee Fairbairn Foundation (with Brooks, Roberts, Ritchie, and Hughes), 2004–2005; Willett, R., Robinson, M., and Marsh, J. (Eds.) (2009). *Play, Creativity and Digital Cultures.* New York, London: Routledge; Marsh, J., & Hallet, E. (Eds.). (2008). *Desirable Literacies: Approaches to Language and Literacy in the Early Years* (2nd ed.), London: Sage; and Bearne, E., & Marsh, J. (Eds.). (2007) *Literacy and Social Inclusion: Closing the Gap.* Stoke-on-Trent: Trentham Books.

Guy Merchant

Principal Lecturer, Cert Ed, BEd Hons, MA, Sheffield Hallam University, and professor of literacy in education and coordinator of the Language and Literacy Research Group
g.h.merchant@shu.ac.uk

Merchant specializes in research into digital literacy in formal and informal educational settings. He is research convenor for the United Kingdom Literacy Association (UKLA) and a member of the association's Executive Committee and National Council. He was a core-group member of the ESRC-funded seminar series Children's Literacy and Popular Culture (2002–2004) and a core-group member of the ESRC-funded seminar series "Play, Creativity and Digital Culture" (2005–2007). Guy contributed to QCA's working group on multimodality and is a critical friend to UKLA's international project Critical Literacy. He is a founding editor of the *Journal of Early Childhood Literacy* and a member of the Editorial Advisory Board of Literacy.

Sarah Mumford

Learning Manager at National Media Museum, Bradford
www.nationalmediamuseum.org.uk

Mumford was formerly head of Education at Eureka! The Museum for Children, advisory teacher for Photography & Media Education in Wakefield and advisory teacher for Media Education in Bradford. She has taught many teachers and children in formal education and in informal learning contexts and has played a role in advocacy for media education, especially at the primary school level.

Mark Reid

Head of Education at the British Film Institute

mark.reid@bfi.org.uk

Reid previously taught English, media, and film for students aged 14–19 and has worked at the BFI since 1998. He undertook the BFI's master-level teacher training provision and co-led the "Reframing Literacy" initiative, which demonstrated the importance of moving image education in primary schools. Reid has written a number of influential classroom resources and provided many training sessions for a wide range of education professionals across the UK. He has played a key role in the UK Film Council's Leadership Group, which has forged alliances between leading film education organizations and built a common agenda for the development of moving image education in England.

Roy Stafford

Freelance

www.itpworld.wordpress.com

Formerly a teacher of media in further education, Stafford has also worked for many years as a freelance writer, educator, and teacher trainer. He has been a tireless activist in the development of media education over many years. He is coauthor (with Gill Branston) of *The Media Student's Book* (Routledge 1996; now in its 5th edition), played a key role in setting up the Media Education Association, and for many years edited a small but influential journal for media teachers, *in the picture*. He now blogs on world cinema as "venicelion" in The Case for Global Film blog.

Ian Wall

Director of Film Education

www.filmeducation.org

Before founding Film Education in 1985, Ian taught English and media at Holland Park School in London where he was a head of department. He has since worked on a wide range of projects, including educational resources on hundreds of feature films. Ian is the winner of two BAFTAs and speaks on issues relating to education, media literacy, and film all over the world. With Mark Reid, he has played a key role in the UK Film Council's Leadership Group, which has forged alliances between leading film education organizations and built a common agenda for the development of moving image education in England.

Finland

Prepared by Prof. Dr. Reijo Kupiainen and Dr. Sara Sintonen

I. Overview

Finland is a technologically rich country where children and young people are active users of various media, the Internet, and social networking sites. The media environment has changed rapidly and media literacy has become a continuously more important topic in the education and communication policy in Finland. For example, the Ministry on Education has launched different kinds of projects to enhance media literacy in small children and young people.

In the general school curriculum, media literacy is not a school subject but is integrated into one cross-curricular theme that is connected to many subjects. Hence, the media literacy education responsibility has been divided among all teachers, all subjects, and as part of the entire school culture, but the largest responsibility is shouldered by Finnish language teachers and visual arts teachers who have media literacy education targets set in their respective subject curricula. In practice, the implementing of media literacy education is unevenly distributed in schools. The emphasis on media literacy education varies around the country.

Outside the school, various nongovernmental organizations and public libraries are strongly enhancing citizens' media literacy skills, information retrieval skills, and reading habits necessary in a changing media environment. Important objectives are to promote critical competencies, active citizenship, and encourage the citizens' own media production and creative capacities.

National Media Literacy Programs

1. The National Media Education Portal at www.mediaeducation.fi The portal brings together actors in the field of media literacy education and offers information and learning materials for educators, librarians, social services and health care workers, and parents.

2. The Media Muffin project (2006–2007) focused on the development of media literacy of small children under eight years old.
3. Media Education in Public Libraries aimed at improving the media literacy education of library professionals.
4. Media education models in the Sámi language and for the Sámi culture.

II. Notable Media Literacy Organizations

Finnish Society on Media Education
http://www.mediaeducation.fi/seura
mediakasvatus@mediakasvatus.fi, +358 50 594 2275
The aim of the society is to support and develop the field of research and practices concerning media literacy education, contribute to the public debate, and provide opportunities to share media literacy education experiences online and offline. It is an umbrella organization for media literacy education in Finland founded in 2005.

a. The society maintains a national media literacy education portal on the Internet: www.mediaeducation.fi
b. The network within the society comprises hundreds of companies, associations, unions, cultural organizations, and private individuals from various vocational branches from all over the country.
c. The society organizes events, publishes materials, implements research and development projects, proposes initiatives to further media literacy education, and develops international relations between representatives of the field.
d. It is a partner organization of the media literacy education networks such as NORDICOM and UN-Alliance of Civilizations Media Literacy Education Clearinghouse.

III. Notable Individuals

Sol-Britt Arnolds-Granlund, PhD
Senior Researcher, Åbo Akademi University
sol-britt.arnolds-granlund@abo.fi
(+358) 324-7347
http://www.vasa.abo.fi/mediepeda

Sirkku Kotilainen, PhD
Professor of Media Education, University of Tampere
sirkku.kotilainen@uta.fi
(+358) 45-1125-858

Chair of the Finnish Society on Media Education (2005–2007). Since 1995, acting as developer of media literacy education and the field of academic research.

Reijo Kupiainen, PhD

Researcher, University of Tampere; professor of the Theory of Visual Culture, Aalto University
reijo.kupiainen@uta.fi
reijo.kupiainen@aalto.fi
(+358) 44-090-2190
kupiainen.wordpress.com
Chair of the Finnish Society on Media Education (2009–2010). Studies in the field of media literacy of young people and changing media environment.

Sara Sintonen, PhD

University Lecturer, University of Helsinki; sara.sintonen@helsinki.fi, + 358 9 191 29716
Chair of the Finnish Society on Media Education (2008).

Tapio Varis, PhD

Professor of Vocational Education at the University of Tampere
tapio.varis@uta.fi
http://www.uta.fi/~titava
(+358) 50-567-9833
UNESCO chair in global e-learning, member of a Digital and Media Literacy Expert Group of the European Commission, principal researcher of the EU Study on Media Literacy Assessment (2009).

Greece

Prepared by Hellenic Audiovisual Institute (IOM)

I. Overview

Status of Media Literacy in Greece

The Hellenic Audiovisual Institute (IOM) is the national applied research organization in the field of audiovisual communication in Greece, established in 1994. It is a legal entity of Private Law, supervised by the Ministry of Interior, Decentralization and E-government. IOM is thoroughly engaged in carrying out methodical research projects concerning, mainly, the audiovisual media: radio, television, cinema, multimedia, and new technologies.

The Institute's research work has so far covered a wide spectrum of subjects, such as the Greek Media's financial trends, the political advertising campaigns during elections at both national and European levels for the past decade, the bibliography on the broader area of communication, the research on the Greek audiovisual sector, etc.

Among its main strands of action is that of *media literacy education*, according to its Presidential Decree (art. 15, par.1, Act 3444/2006) with a special care to children and youth. On a European level, the Hellenic Audiovisual Institute is the official Greek representative of the *EU Media Literacy and Education Expert Group*, a group of individual experts from different competences and backgrounds from the member states, that discuss current trends and future policy initiatives on EU media literacy.

With reference to the important issue of media and children, IOM, at the 3rd World Summit on Media for Children in Thessaloniki (2001), took the initiative for the realization of the international declaration "Media and Children, Commitment for the Future." Furthermore, the Institute has organized events such as "The Protection of Minors in Broadcast Media" and "The Future of the Greek Audiovisual Production for Children"; it also cooperates with NORDICOM for the publication of relevant books, such as the "Outlooks on Children and Media."

IOM also constitutes the *national representative and coordinator* of Greece's positions on *European procedures and programs* for the support of the audiovisual industry, such as the MEDIA Programme and the pan-European organization European Audiovisual Observatory.

Additionally, recognizing the need for skills and expertise of people working in the audiovisual industry, the Institute contributes to training in mass media through seminars, educational workshops, handbooks, and meetings with a view to familiarize the participants (media professionals, students, researchers) with the new information technologies and the digital scene. Recent meetings have covered the issues of TV broadcasters' obligation to invest in cinematographic production, the new digital media technologies, the media stereotypes and minorities representations, and the boundaries between public and private in the media.

The IOM also provides scientific support and acts as a link to strengthen the ties between policy decision-making centers, universities, and research bodies, public and private program production, and distribution structures as well as the audiovisual industry creative forces in Greece. Within this context, the Institute issues a fortnightly newsletter with the latest news on the Greek and international media scene to cater to the need for more accurate and up-to-date information on audiovisual and print media.

The total work of the Institute is supported by the first Public Centre of Documentation and Library Services for the disciplines of communication and information, a resource fully accessible to journalists, researchers, government officials, experts, students, and others.

Finally, according to the recent Act 109/2010, all providers of Greek audiovisual media services are requested to provide the Institute with data on the obligation to promote European films and projects.

II. Notable Media Literacy Organizations

Alliance of Civilizations Media Literacy Education Clearinghouse
www.iljm.net

British Film Institute
www.bfi.org.uk

Eurimages
Council of Europe/European Audiovisual Observatory
www.coe.int

European Broadcasting Union
www.ebu.ch

Hellenic Audiovisual Institute IOM
www.iom.org.gr

International Federation of Television Archives
www.fiatifta.org

III. Notable Individuals in National Media Literacy Programs

IOM Board of Directors

President/Director: Rudolph Moronis, Journalist

Members: Stelios Papathanassopoulos, professor in the Department of Communication and Mass Media at the National and Kapodistrian University of Athens; Alexandros Priftis, journalist

Hong Kong

Prepared by Alice Lee

I. Overview

The Status of Media Literacy in Hong Kong

Media education has advanced rapidly in Hong Kong as a social movement after 1997. People in Hong Kong have great concern about their media environment. The development takes the form of a *networking model*. It is a bottom-up movement, and various organizations have taken the initiative to launch their own media education programs. These organizations include youth groups, media organizations, religious organizations, educational institutions, schools, and universities. In 2000, the Hong Kong Association of Media Education (HKAME) was established. Since that time, issue-based inquiry of the media has become an elective component of the new school subject, liberal studies.

The practice of media education in Hong Kong has great diversity. Different organizations adopt different approaches, including (1) innoculative approach, (2) critical analytical approach, (3) social participatory approach, (4) media production approach, and (5) media fun approach.

Since 2006, the development of media education in Hong Kong has moved from Media Education 1.0 to 2.0. In the Web 2.0 age, the second stage of media education in Hong Kong has the following goals: (1) cultivate media prosumers with the aim of equipping them with critical, reflective, and positive thinking skills; (2) nurture the Generation Y young people so that they know how to make good use of the new media; (3) conduct media education research and communication research to inform media education practice; and (4) encourage penetration of media education into the formal school curriculum, particularly liberal studies. In general, the media education movement in Hong Kong has the mission of nurturing informed, critical, responsible, and constructive citizens.

Hong Kong Media Literacy Programs

HKAME Media Education Program

This project was launched by the Hong Kong Association of Media Education in 2000. The aim of the project is to promote the media education movement.

Children Media Education

The Hong Kong Christian Service holds various media education projects every year for primary school students.

Point@Media

Radio Television Hong Kong has a Web site on media education. It also launches a territory-wide media production competition every year. The competition is integrated with a series of media education activities.

II. Notable Media Literacy Organizations

Breakthrough

http://www.breakthrough.org.hk

breakthrough@breakthrough.org.hk

(852) 24086373

Breakthrough is a youth organization which received a fund of HK$6 million from the government to conduct the Media and Information Literacy Education (MILE) project in the early 2000s. Breakthrough has developed a large amount of media literacy curriculum materials.

Hong Kong Association of Media Education (HKAME)

www.hkame.org; cheungck@hkucc.hku.hk

alicelee@hkbu.edu.hk

(852) 28578365

Established in 2000, the mission of HKAME is to promote and develop media education in Hong Kong. It also takes up the responsibility of liaising media education organizations locally and internationally. The Education Bureau of the HKSAR government commissioned the HKAME to run a series of in-service teacher training sessions for secondary school teachers. The association also lobbied the Education Bureau to include media education into the school curriculum.

Hong Kong Christian Service (HKCS)

http://www.hkcs.org/edcb/media/media-e.html

anniewong@hkcs.org

(852) 27316262

A project officer of HKCS is assigned to plan and organize media literacy program activities for primary school students. HKCS publishes the bimonthly *Media Express*, a media literacy newsletter. It has also published three books on media education.

Hong Kong Education City

www.hkedcity.net
info@hkedcity.net
(852) 26241000

This government-funded Web site on educational resources supports various kinds of media education programs.

Ming Pao Newspapers Limited

http://studentreporter.mingpao.com
s_reporter@mingpao.com
(852) 25953098

This organization conducts student reporter programs and media literacy training workshops.

Radio Television Hong Kong (RTHK)

http://mediaed.etvonline.tv
channa@rthk.org.hk
(852) 23393191

Radio Television Hong Kong, a government broadcast station, produced two media education television programs that include more than 20 episodes. The programs were broadcast in schools as well as on commercial television stations. RTHK runs a media education Web site, Point@Media.

The Society for Truth and Light

http://www.truth-light.org.hk
info@truth-light.org.hk
(852) 27684204

The Society for Truth and Light, a religious organization with a mission of improving the media environment in Hong Kong, has produced a number of media education teaching kits. It regularly conducts media-monitoring programs and organizes media education workshops.

Yellow Bus

http://www.yellowbus.com.hk
Helena@seedland.hk
(852) 35833131

Yellow Bus is a children's magazine devoted to media education.

III. Notable Individuals in Hong Kong Media Literacy Programs

Dr. Chitat Chan
Instructor, Department of Applied Social Sciences, Hong Kong Polytechnic University
(852) 34008515
chitat.chan@inet.polyu.edu.hk
   Dr. Chan promotes media literacy through liberal studies.

Natalie Chan
Head, eTVonline (Point@Media), Radio Television Hong Kong
(852) 23393191
channa@rthk.org.hk
   Ms. Chan leads the Point@Media media education program at RTHK

Dr. Selina Chan
Lecturer, Department of Printing and Digital Media, Hong Kong Institute of Vocational Education
(852) 27279635
chanselina@vtc.edu.hk
   Dr. Chan conducts media literacy training through media production.

Dr. C. K. Cheung
Chairman, Hong Kong Association of Media Education; assistant professor, Department of Curriculum Studies, The University of Hong Kong
(852) 28578365
cheungck@hkucc.hku.hk
   Dr. Cheung established HKAME and runs the association.

Hon Kong Chiu
Teacher, Buddhist Ho Nam Kam College
(852) 93412770
honkchiu@netvigator.com
   Mr. Chiu is a media education advocate and a key member of HKAME.

Chi Sum Choi
General Secretary
The Society for Truth and Light
(852) 27684204
choisum@truth-light.org.hk
   Mr. Choi leads his organization, which focuses on media literacy training.

Dr. Donna Chu
Assistant Professor, The Chinese University of Hong Kong
(852) 26961908
donnachu@hkbu.edu.hk
   Dr. Chu helps with teacher training programs and conducts media literacy research.

Helena Hui
Editor-in-Chief, *Yellow Bus*
(852) 35833131
helena@seedland.hk
   Ms. Hui promotes media education for young children and parents.

Dr. Alice Lee
Vice chairperson, Hong Kong Association of Media Education; Associate Professor, Department of Journalism, Hong Kong Baptist University
(852) 34117488
alicelee@hkbu.edu.hk
   Dr. Lee established HKAME and runs the association.

Wing-fai Lee
Chairman, Hong Kong Media Education Resources Web
(852) 90293734
leewingfai@hkmediaed.net
   Mr. Lee promotes media education in schools.

Eileen Mok
Teacher, Logos Academy
(852) 98630337
eileenmok2003@yahoo.com.hk
   Ms. Mok contributes to the development of media education curriculum textbooks.

Dominica Siu
Media Educator, Hong Kong Catholic Social Communications Office
(852) 90294792
dominicasiu@yahoo.com
   Ms. Siu adopts the media production approach to media education.

Annie Wong
Project Officer (Media Education), Hong Kong Christian Service
(852) 27316262
anniewong@hkcs.org
   Ms. Wong contributes to the promotion of media education for children.

India

Prepared by Dr. Keval J. Kumar

I. Overview

Status of Media Literacy in India

Media studies has been recognized as a subject in the higher secondary school curriculum. More than 20 schools of the Central Board of Secondary Education (CBSE) offer media studies as an optional subject. The National Council of Educational Research and Training (NCERT), New Delhi, has drawn up the curriculum for the course in media studies and also prepared textbooks for the same. The chief adviser to the NCERT on Media Studies is Professor Dr. Keval J. Kumar.

Besides this national program, several private initiatives by nongovernmental and Christian media organizations teach media education to schoolchildren outside the school curriculum.

National Media Literacy Programs

The CBSE/NCERT program in Media Studies is a national program.

II. Notable Media Literacy Organizations

There are currently no national media literacy organizations in India.

III. Notable Individuals in National Media Literacy Programs

Dr. Keval J. Kumar

Chief Adviser on Media Studies, NCERT, New Delhi; Director, Resource Centre for Media Education and Research
Chintamani, Kale Path, Bhandarkar Road, PUNE-411004, India.
kevalkumar@hotmail.com
(+91) 9822829085.

Dr. Kumar has published the following books on media education/literacy:

Media Education, Communication and Public Policy—An Indian Perspective (Bombay: Himalaya Publications)
Mass Communication in India, 4th ed. (Bombay: Jaico Books, 2010)

Dr. Kumar has presented research papers on media mducation at international conferences in Paris, Stockholm, Barcelona, Toulouse, New Delhi, Sao Paulo, Cairo, and London; has published several research articles/papers in academic journals on media and communication; and has been guiding students in their master's theses and PhD dissertations on media literacy since 1990. Dr. Kumar was chair of the Media Education Research Section, International Association of Media and Communication Research (IAMCR) from 1998 to 2005.

Dr. Peter Gonsalves

Dr. Gonsalves wrote a workbook on media education that is widely used in Indian high schools: *Exercises in Media Education*. The foreword to the workbook was contributed by Dr. Keval J. Kumar.

Dr. Anubhuti Yadav

Coordinator, Media Studies
National Council of Educational Research and Training (NCERT)
Sri Aurobindo Marg, New Delhi-110016

Dr. Yadav has made an invaluable contribution to the launch of the course in media studies in CBSE schools. She coordinated the writing and publication of two textbooks and also the organization of training for more than 200 schoolteachers interested in teaching the course. For details on the course, see www.ncert.nic.in

Ireland

Prepared by Brian O'Neill

I. Overview

Status of Media Literacy in Ireland

Media literacy education in Ireland, despite being underresourced and relatively new to the public policy arena, builds on a long tradition and a solid foundation of critical engagement, creative activity, and practical implementation. From a traditional position of protectionism in Irish cultural and educational policy, media literacy has rapidly moved to embrace new opportunities for greater participation and creative endeavour.

Many of the first institutions active in media literacy promotion were established by the Catholic Church in the middle of the 20th century: the National Film Institute (1945) and the Catholic Communications Centre (1968) were established by the conservative Archbishop of Dublin, John Charles McQuaid, to ensure that Catholic social teaching would prevail in use of modern media. Educational philosophies, insofar as they dealt with media literacy matters, were thoroughly protectionist in approach, seeking to inoculate against "the flood of information stimuli and exhortations conveyed by sound and image by which the pupil is assailed outside the school through posters, cinema, television, strip cartoons, radio and popular songs" (Primary Curriculum Handbook, 1971).

Media literacy gained a strong foothold in Ireland in the 1980s with the introduction of new elements into curriculum, the establishment of an education department within the Irish Film Institution, and exposure to many international developments (from the UK) in media studies and media education. Media literacy is now formally part of the English language curriculum and a component of the national primary curriculum. In addition, digital literacy skills receive a high priority in schools with investment in training and resources to ensure schools are at the forefront of Information Society development. Practical skills feature in many schools, and a Department of Education–sponsored initiative to introduce filmmaking for primary school children (the project called *Fís*, meaning "vision" in the Irish language) has proved extremely successful and popular.

The most important recent development in media literacy has been its inclusion in the terms of the Broadcasting Act 2009, giving the regulator, the

Broadcasting Authority of Ireland (BAI), the ancillary function of promoting media literacy. In keeping with European trends in which media literacy has been seen as an essential component of a participatory and democratic culture, Ireland is seeking to promote a greater understanding of media literacy issues through a multistakeholder approach of encouraging industry, national broadcasting, community media, civil society organizations, and education to work together. The community media movement has been particularly successful in this regard, offering accredited training programs and media opportunities for citizens in both radio and television. The BAI has also included media literacy as a category in its production funding scheme, Sound and Vision, enabling producers to target media literacy education as a recognized topic of broadcast content. Under the Audiovisual Media Services Directive, the European Commission will commence reporting on levels of media literacy across Europe from 2011. Preliminary data suggest Ireland will be in the middle tier of European countries for media literacy, and reports on media literacy levels will be used to guide further interventions in the field.

National Media Literacy Programs

Primary: Media literacy is incorporated in the Social Personal and Health Education strand of the national primary curriculum.

Secondary: Media literacy is a component of Cultural Literacy in the English curriculum Junior Certificate level, and as a film studies option at the senior level within English. A transition year program also offers schools extensive scope for introducing elective media studies elements.

II. Notable Media Literacy Organizations

Broadcasting Authority of Ireland
www.bai.ie

The BAI is the independent regulator for radio and television in Ireland. Established under the Broadcasting Act 2009, it has the ancillary function of promoting media literacy. It operates the Sound and Vision production-funding scheme, which offers media literacy as one of its program categories.

Irish Film Institute
http://www.ifi.ie

The Irish Film Institute traces its origins back to 1945 when it was established as the National Film Institute to promote film appreciation in Ireland. The Education Department (IFI Education) of the Irish Film Institute provides the opportunity for appreciation and critical interaction with film by a wide constituency both within and outside the formal education sector. It offers a range of evening courses open to the general public as well as courses and events designed specifically for specialized interest groups.

National Centre for Technology in Education (NCTE)

http://www.ncte.ie

The National Centre for Technology in Education is an Irish government agency established to provide advice, support, and information on the use of information and communications technology (ICT) in education.

Fís—Digital Media for All

http://www.fis.ie

FÍS—Film in Schools—is a resources and professional development program for teachers and a film festival for young filmmakers in primary classes. The program encourages teachers to incorporate and integrate film into the curriculum across all the subject areas.

III. Notable Individuals in National Media Literacy Programs

Brian O'Neill

Head of Research, College of Arts & Tourism, Dublin Institute of Technology

brian.oneill@dit.ie

O'Neill is a researcher on media literacy, media policy, and information society issues. He is a member of EU Kids Online II and of the COST Action ISO 906 Transforming Audiences, Transforming Societies. He was coauthor of the report for the Broadcasting Commission of Ireland, *Media Literacy and the Public Sphere: A Contextual Study for Public Media Literacy Promotion in Ireland.*

IV. References and Further Reading

Barnes, C., Flanagan, B., et al. (2007). *Critical Media Literacy in Ireland.* Dublin: The Radharc Trust.

Howley, H., & O'Neill, B. (2002). "Teaching the Media in Ireland." In Hart, A., & Suss, D. (Eds.). *Media Education in 12 European Countries: A Comparative Study of Teaching Media in Mother Tongue Education in Secondary Schools.* Zurich: Swiss Federal Institute of Technology

Kerr, A., & University of Ulster Centre for Media Research. (2006). *Media Literacy in Northern Ireland.* Coleraine: School Media & Performing Arts at the University of Ulster.

O'Neill, B. (2000). "Media Education in Ireland: An Overview." *Irish Communications Review 8*, 57–64.

O'Neill, B., & Barnes, C. (2008). *Media Literacy and the Public Sphere: A Contextual Study for Public Media Literacy Promotion in Ireland.* Dublin: Broadcasting Commission of Ireland.

Titley, G., & Merry, P. (2002). *Media Literacy and Image Education in Ireland, the Netherlands and the UK.* Brussels: European Commission Directorate General for Media and Culture

Universitat Autònoma de Barcelona. (2007). *Media Literacy Profile Ireland.* Brussels: Commission of the European Communities.

Israel

Prepared by Dr. Mira Feuerstein,
Oranim Academic Educational College, Israel
mirafo@netvision.net.il

I. Overview

Education for media literacy (ML) entered the Israeli education system in the early 1980s as part of public and academic discourse about the place of the media in Israeli democracy. In the Ministry of Education and Culture, a consensus evolved recognizing its importance, and the Department of Curricula developed several national programs and learning materials that are implemented at the various school levels within media studies (see box). During the 1990s, in-service courses were added for teachers, parents, and kindergarten teachers in formal education and for facilitators and youth instructors in the informal education sector. Books and learning materials were written, and special programs were introduced locally. Communications centers were also established in schools that wished to keep up with the times (Gordon, 1989), and mention should be made of the contribution of educational television, which developed critical TV viewing programs for teachers and mentors in the context of the programs broadcast by EDTV.[1] As a result, thousands of students from early childhood through 12th grade began media studies based on the key principles and concepts of media education (ME).[2]

From a historical viewpoint, Media Literacy Education (MLE) unified a coalition of bodies from across the political-ideological rifts of Israeli society and developed a unique consensus around four main issues (Lemish, 2002; Lemish & Lemish, 1997).[3]

1. This was done with the assistance of the EDTV research department, headed by Dr. Hava Tidhar.

2. Based on the broadly agreed-on basic principles of media education (see Anderson, 1983; Aufderheide, 1993, 1997; Bazalgette, 1989; Buckingham, 1993; Hobbs, 1998; Masterman, 1985; NAMLE, 2007; Tyner, 1998; etc.).

3. Professor Dafna Lemish was a member of Ministry of Education committees and played an active role in the development of education for media literacy in Israel.

1. *ML as ethnic identity.* The paternalistic aspiration to oppose the Americanization of Israeli culture and the attempt to preserve the unique Israeli-Jewish culture strengthened awareness of the importance of education for media literacy.
2. *ML as a political issue.* Groups from the right and the left joined forces from an awareness of the importance of "demystifying" TV news, and of developing critical faculties about the process of producing and creating the news.
3. *ML as an ethical issue.* In the struggle against the trend to objectify the woman's body, feminist organizations joined forces with the ultra-orthodox to promote education for critical consumption of the media that would also serve as a lever for social change in several contexts (such as media representation of women, violence, sexuality, drugs).
4. *ML as a current affairs issue.* To understand the media representation of events and swings in current affairs in Israel, the audience needed *critical media literacy* (CML) skills. This led to a growing demand from teachers to develop the learners' ability to critically evaluate media coverage and to help them develop social awareness and active involvement as citizens in a democracy.

This complex background explains the influence of cultural and political contexts on ML curricula as well as the support shown by various interest groups for ML initiatives as they sought to legitimize existing power structures or prevent social change. Each organization had its own agenda: the feminists sought to promote their struggle for egalitarianism for women in Israeli society, and the religious wanted to institute religious laws in the country and return the woman to her traditional place in the home.

These issues also highlight the development of the Israeli variation on the basic principles of the field (see note 2). "The critical orientation of Israeli goals can be attributed to the need identified by committee members to promote citizen empowerment and progressive forms of social change. . . . [M]edia literacy is offered as a cure—or as a consciousness comforter—for every social ill" (Lemish & Lemish, 1997: 222).

Israel's national ML curricula consist a series of communication competencies, including the ability to access, analyze, evaluate, and communicate information in a variety of forms, for the purpose of empowering students to be both critical thinkers and creative producers of an increasingly wide range of messages using image and language.

The Ministry of Education committees (composed of mass media scholars, Ministry representatives and educators) addressed the content matter, aims, and relevant subjects of each program according to pupils' ages, in the context of print and broadcast media. In their view, curricula should be organized at each stage to enrich students' knowledge of three aspects: the interrelationship of media, culture, and society; theories and concepts for analyzing the media; and developing and practicing the use of CML skills (Lemish & Lemish, 1997: 222). Initially, the focus was on television, which at that time was the most popular medium among children and adolescents. Therefore, the emphasis was on fostering television literacy and mastering the visual, textual, and experiential of its audiovisual language. Feedback was reflected by two studies: The first examined the efficacy of TV literacy learning among low- and middle-class kindergarten children in Tel Aviv. It found that having specially trained kindergarten teachers expose children to the program enhanced the young viewers' ability to decode TV content regardless of socioeconomic status (Tidhar, 1996). The second found that 10- to 12-year-olds demonstrated critical thinking about the content of TV programs and commercials in newspapers, even two months after completion of a systematic program of ML (Feuerstein, 2002, 2010).

Two main motifs characterized the aims of the national curricula (Lemish, 2002): the first, an emphasis on the evaluation and criticism of products, processes, artistic values, and influences; the second, urging teachers to motivate their pupils to apply the knowledge, criticism, and creativity they learned.

Despite the awareness of and positive interest in implementing MLE among members of the various committees, differences of opinions arose about programs' content and messages, that were driving the field in various directions. Three main dilemmas appeared (Lemish, 2002): Should ML be taught as a separate subject or as part of an interdisciplinary subject? Should media experts develop and supervise a national program or should educators be able to develop local programs to meet the special needs of their pupils? Should the material be taught by teachers with no deep background in mass media or by professional media personnel with no deep educational background?

This division of opinions led to the development of three main models of teaching in the education field:

1. *The patchwork model.* A program that patches together isolated segments of ML activities and materials, which was built and implemented by the cooperative efforts of media professionals and educators
2. *The autocratic/technocratic model.* Programs built by individuals with economic or ideological interests who are in positions of power in the

supervisory and educational system, who choose the learning materials, not always according to professional considerations and often for economic reasons
3. *The extra school agency model.* Programs, learning materials, in-service courses, and teaching services that are purchased from commercial companies and have not necessarily been approved by the Ministry of Education (Lemish, 2002).

It can be assumed that the dilemmas and models explain many of the difficulties in implementing the ML curricula guidelines which meet regular educational standards of media studies and practice. To this should be added the rapid turnover rate among ministers of education. This meant that they did not have the time to design and implement a given policy over time nor to allocate the required budgets for teaching hours and materials and developing up-to-date materials.

In short, the primary intention of the National Curriculum Committee to develop a spiral curriculum is still unfulfilled. In kindergartens and elementary schools, MLE must rely on individual and isolated initiatives of kindergarten teachers and educators, and is also dependent on the priorities and goodwill of municipal directors and school principals while facing limited budgets.

In such a situation, commercial bodies and media personnel have infiltrated the education field, offering teachers alternative programs and materials, including prepared lesson plans, which do not always coincide with the national educational conception of ML curricula. At times these outside forces actually distort the conception.

A better picture has emerged in recent years in junior and senior high schools where the ML specialization has gained recognition as a legitimate branch of media studies (with accredited matriculation exams). As a result, teacher colleges have initiated pre-service and in-service courses in MLE, and universities have developed many academic programs under the umbrella of mass media studies with different emphases, depending on the orientation of each program (see part II below).

ML principles were also expanded to deal with new digital media texts and with the accelerated changes in the multichannel communications map in Israel. Under the guidance of the director of Science and Technology Education in the Ministry of Education and Culture, a media site called "Doing Media" was established for teachers and pupils in junior and senior high school. The site afforded them access to academic articles, auxiliary materials, lesson plans, recent research, and experience in online tasks according to the matriculation curriculum.

Finally, the initiative of the media regulator—the Second Authority of Radio and Television—in conjunction with the education system and academia, through research grants and courses for teachers, has made a valuable contribution. By expanding this cooperation, it may become a powerful lever for MLE. Considering the centrality of the media in today's youth society and culture, and Israeli's complex social reality, the broadcasting bodies must also bear responsibility for improving the quality of Israeli communications. In other words, they must join the educational endeavor for ML for the youngsters who constitute the country's future citizens and for the ecology of Israel's democratic society.

II. Notable Media Literacy Organizations

The Ministry of Education and Culture—The Media Studies Inspectorate

Ms. Dorit Balin, National Supervisor for Academic Studies in Cinema and Media

http://cms.education.gov.il/EducationCMS/Units/Mazkirut_Pedagogit/Tikshoret/ChativatBeynayim/

Mr. Yossi Bar-David, National Supervisor for Teaching Media in the Technological Track from the Technological Education Division

http://www.amalnet.k12.il.sites/commu

The Oranim Academic Educational College, Kiryat Tivon

Dr. Mira Fuerstein

http://www.oranim.ac.il/sites/heb/academic-units/social-sciences-faculty/hugim/communication-class/Pages/default.aspx

The Media Department at the Oranim Academic Educational College trains junior high school communications teachers according to a program based on the activist concept of MLE. This is based on the importance of fostering a critical and active approach to the media in action. The program is intended to train educators as effective agents and teachers of media, who know how to use media intelligently, and to effectively promote changes in their society and community as citizens in a democracy.

Oranim is the only college in Israel to conduct a social activist media course that enables students to create social messages through the media to promote issues and matters of importance to their community. MLE serves as a conceptual framework that also guides a number of other courses, such

> ### *The Main Programs Developed by the Ministry of Education and Culture*
>
> - Mass Media: An elective program for secular, religious and Arab high schools (Jerusalem: Ministry of Education and Culture, Curriculum Department, 1993)
> - Education for Viewing Television and Cinema (Jerusalem: Ministry of Education and Culture, Curriculum Department, 1993)
> - Media and Society—curriculum for grades 10–12 (Jerusalem: Ministry of Education, Science & Technology Authority, Amal Technical Supervisor, E.Berger, A. Bernstein & D. Arev, 2001)
> - Education for Evaluative and Critical Viewing of Television and Cinema (Jerusalem: Ministry of Education, Culture and Sport, Curriculum Department, 1995)
> - Between Reality and Imagination: Activity booklet for grades 4 and 5, in secular and Arab elementary schools (Lemish, 1991)

as Children, TV and Education—Education for Critical Consumption of TV; Children and Adolescents in the New Media Environment; Digital Natives—Discourse and Identities in the Online Culture of Children and Adolescents (seminar); and Didactics of Teaching the Media. This year a new course was instituted in cooperation with the Netanya Academic College's School of Communications and funded by the European Union: CML in the Coverage of the Israeli-Palestinian Conflict (coordinated by Dr. Mira Feuerstein).

The college's Media Studies Department also holds study days and conventions on value-oriented issues connected with media consumption of children and youths. In March 2011, the second national conference on MLE was held with the participation of representatives of the national inspectorate for media studies, researchers, educators, media teachers, students, and pupils in the media departments.

Oranim College is also the Israeli representative and partner of the Alliance of Civilizations Clearinghouse on MLE: http://www.aocmedialiteracy.or

Other Bodies and Institutions That Include ML in Their Curricula

- Haifa University will open its specialization in MLE as part of its MA studies in the Communications Department, in 2012: http://hevra.haifa.ac.il/~comm/en/ma_studies.php

- The David Yellin Academic College, Jerusalem, offers a teacher-training track for communications teachers in elementary and junior high school, including a compulsory MLE course: http://www.dyellin.ac.il/index .php/unitacademic/teacherscertificatebed/circle/communications
- Gordon College, Haifa, has a bachelor's program in Communications and Education which trains communications teachers for elementary school: http://www.gordon.ac.il/template/default.asp?PageId=107&cat Id=35&maincat=1
- Seminar Hakibbutzim College and the College for Education, Technology and the Arts, Tel Aviv, offers a multidisciplinary program to train high school teachers for communications and cinema: http://www .smkb.ac.il/media-film
- Orot Israel Academic College of Education, Elkana, offers a specialization track in teaching elementary school communications: http://www .orot.ac.il/orot/InfoPageCourseOfStudy/Communication/Home/ default.aspx
- Research Department of the Second Authority for Radio and TV, Jerusalem: http://www.rashut2.org.il/info_report.asp. For several years the department has annually awarded research grants in memory of former minister of Education and Culture, the late Zvulun Hammer, for studies pertaining to education, children, and the media. The aim is to contribute directly and indirectly to the authority's policy and work. It gives preference to work that expands the basis of research knowledge in the areas of broadcasting and its influence on Israeli society and culture. In summer 2009, the authority also opened a short in-service course to inculcate teachers with the didactic tools needed for teaching ML.

References

Anderson, J. A. (1983). "Television Literacy and the Critical Viewer." In J. Bryant & D. R. Anderson (Eds.), *Children's Understanding of Television*: *Research on Attention and Comprehension*. New York: Academic Press.

Aufderheide, P. (Ed.). (1993). *Media Literacy: A Report of the National Leadership Conference on Media Literacy*. Aspen, CO: Aspen Institute.

Aufderheide, P. (1997). "Media Literacy: From a Report of the National Leadership Conference." In R. Kubey (Ed.), *Media Literacy in the Information Age: Current Perspectives, Information Behavior* (pp. 79–88). New Brunswick, NJ: Transaction.

Bazalgette, C. (Ed.). (1989). *Primary Media Education: A Curriculum Statement*. London: British Film Institute.

Bazalgette, C. (2001). "Making Movies Matter, or Whatever Happened to the Sabretooth, Curriculum?" *Journal of Art & Design Education 20*, 263–274.

Buckingham, D. (1993). *Children Talking Television: The Making of Television Literacy*. London: Falmer.

Feuerstein, M. (2002). "Media Literacy in Support of Critical Thinking." Unpublished PhD dissertation, University of Liverpool, England.

Feuerstein, M. (2010). *Media Literacy in Support of Critical Thinking—Children's Critical Thinking in Multimedia Society*. UK: VDN-Verlag Dr. Muller.

Gordon, D. (1989). *School as Media Center*. Ber-Sheva, Israel: Ben-Gurion University.

Hobbs, R. (1998). "The Seven Great Debates in the Media Literacy Movement." *Journal of Communication 48*, 16–32.

Lemish, D. (2002). *Growing-up with Television: The Little Screen in the Lives of Children and Youth* [in Hebrew]. Tel-Aviv: The Open University.

Lemish, D., & Lemish, P. (1997). "A Much Debated Consensus: Media Literacy in Israel." In R. Kubey (Ed.), *Media Literacy in the Information Age: Current Perspectives, Information Behavior* (pp. 213–228). New Brunswick, NJ: Transaction.

Masterman, L. (1985). *Teaching the Media*. London: Routledge.

NAMLE: National Association of Media Literacy Education (2007). Retrieved from http://namle.net

Tidhar, C. E. (1996). "Enhancing Television Literacy Skills among Pre-School Children through an Intervention Program in the Kindergarten." *Journal of Educational Media 22*, 97–110.

Tyner, K. (1998). *Literacy in a Digital World: Teaching and Learning in the Age of Information*. Mahwah, NJ: Erlbaum.

Malta

Prepared by Reverend Joseph Borg and Dr. Mary Anne Lauri

I. Overview

Status of Media Literacy in Malta

Media education was first taught in a systematic way in church schools in the beginning of the 1980s. Media education was also taught in other schools as part of the curricula of other subjects by teachers interested in the area. In 1999, the government of Malta published the National Minimum Curriculum (Ministry of Education, 1999). This included media education as one of the objectives of a holistic education that should be taught in all state, independent, and church schools.

State schools integrate limited components of media education mainly in social studies and personal and social development at the primary and secondary levels. Important aspects of media education are given in Information and Communication Technology courses that are an integral part of the curriculum of the primary schools and secondary. On the other hand, many church schools teach media education as a separate subject. These schools are teaching the subject in Grades 4–6 of the primary level (ages 9–11), and some continue teaching the subject in Forms 1 and 2 of the secondary level (ages 12–13).

National Media Literacy Programs

The National Minimum Curriculum can be assessed from www.curriculum.gov.mt/docs/nmc_english.pdf. Objective 8 provides information about the knowledge, attitudes, and skills that students are expected to learn about media and society, media organizations, media content, media languages, and other elements of media education.

The program used in church schools is included in three workbooks used at the primary level and two textbooks used at the secondary level. The set of books used throughout the primary and secondary schools do not only give most of the knowledge component asked for in the National Minimum Curriculum but also provide students with the practical work needed to acquire the skills and develop the attitudes indicated in the same document. They thus help to empower students in three different aspects: awareness of their media use; acquisition of tools for critical appraisal of content and language; and awareness of the importance of what goes beyond the "frame" (i.e., the societal and organizational aspects). The secondary school books, written by Borg and Lauri in 2003 and 2004, are based on and reflect the developments in the Maltese mediascape as well as the basic language conventions of print, audio, audiovisual, and new media.

II. Notable Media Literacy Organizations

Not applicable.

III. Notable Individuals in National Media Literacy Programs

Father Joseph Borg

Lecturer, University of Malta
joseph.borg@um.edu.mt
Centre for Communication Technology, University of Malta, Msida, Malta
(0035) 679440481

Father Borg is the originator of media education program in church schools, beginning in the early 1980s. He is coauthor of the two textbooks used at the secondary level. He is the author of a number of academic papers on the subject and teaches media education courses at the University of Malta.

Dr. Mary Anne Lauri

Pro-Rector, University of Malta
mary-anne.lauri@um.edu.mt
Rectorate, University of Malta, Msida, Malta
(0035) 679411441

Lauri is coauthor of the two textbooks used at the secondary level and author of a number of academic papers on the subject.

Borg, J., & Lauri, M. A. (2004). *Exploring the Media Landscape. Media Education for Form Two*. Malta: Media Centre Publications.

Borg, J., & Lauri, M. A. (2003). *Media Languages. Media Education for Form One*. Malta: Media Centre Publications

Christine Gauci
Education Officer, Media Education, Ministry of Education
Christine.p.gauci@gov.mt
Department of Education, Old Seige Road, Floriana, Malta
    Ms. Gauci is the officer in charge of media education, primarily in state schools.

Nigeria

Prepared by Dr. Sam Nkana

I. Overview

The media literacy movement has, for many decades, attempted to carve a foothold in various parts of the world. According to Art Silverblatt (2001), media literacy education is now an established field of study within the international academic arena. Most industrialized nations have embraced media literacy education, and such countries as Australia, Canada, England, New Zealand, Chile, India, Scotland, South Africa, France, Italy, Spain, and Jordan have made significant advances in the field (Silverblatt, 2001). Today, Third World countries are beginning to experiment with media literacy education in various settings, including the schools. My purpose is to discuss the status of media literacy education in Nigeria.

Nigeria, one-third larger than Texas and the most populous country in Africa, is situated on the Gulf of Guinea in West Africa (Nigeria: Geography, 2011). It has a population of 152,217,341, and major languages spoken are English (official), Hausa, Yoruba, Ibo, Fulani, and more than 200 others. There are about 250 ethnic groups, including Hausa and Fulani 29 percent, Yoruba 21 percent, Ibo 18 percent, Ijaw 10 percent, Ibibio 3.5 percent, and Tiv 2.5 percent (Nigeria: Languages, Ethnicity/Race, 2011).

Educational Status

Illiteracy has remained a major problem in Nigeria despite the progress made in recent years. In 1990, UNESCO (United Nations Educational, Scientific and Cultural Organization) launched the global Education for All movement to provide basic education for all children, youth, and adults (UNESCO, 2011a). "Although Nigeria has made considerable progress towards Education for All, illiteracy remains a major problem with an estimated 50 million adults who cannot read or write. Furthermore, some 8.6 million Nigerian primary-age children are out-of-school" (UNESCO, 2011b). On May 5, 2011, UNESCO director general Irina Bokova and Ruqayyatu Ahmed Rufa'I, Nigeria's minister of Education, signed a "Memorandum of Understanding establishing a self-benefiting funds-in-trust to revitalize adult and youth literacy in Nigeria." A major advancement in education is expected as a result of this investment, and both entities believe the successful implementation of the program would be a model for neighboring countries (UNESCO, 2011b).

Nigerian education is progressing, however. According to mapsofthe world.com (2011), the state supervises the education system. Nigeria has established 27 state-owned polytechnics and has made the first six years of primary school mandatory. Because reading and writing literacy are a prerequisite to media literacy education, progress in these areas should engender growth in the field of media literacy.

Media Literacy in Nigeria

Although there have been sporadic media literacy seminars in Nigeria, there is no central media literacy organization as found in the United States, Canada, the United Kingdom, and many other countries with well-established media literacy education programs. However, many educators, organizations, and agencies are developing new means to educate young people about the media. This new wave in Nigeria is in response to the rapid proliferation of media messages targeting this age group. A media literacy movement is growing in Nigeria with the goal of teaching its media consumers to access, evaluate, analyze, assess, and produce information from a variety of media.[1]

In 2006, Lee Rother, cofounder of the Association for Media Education in Quebec (AMEQ), was invited by the Nigerian Youth for Technology Organization and Martins Akpan, the co-coordinator of Teens Resource Center and producer of a community cable program titled TEENWORLD on MCTV, to share his media literacy experience with primary and secondary students and their teachers in western Nigeria. The trip was funded by CHUM TV, the Canadian Association for Media Education Organizations (CAMEO), headed by a well-known media education pioneer and host of *Scanning the Movies*, John Pungente, SJ and Sir Laurier School board administration, and many others.[2] Two years later the Youth Media & Communication Initiative (YMCI), British Council, Nigeria, and the National Film & Video Censors Board (NFVCB) organized the "1st Africa Media Literacy Conference

1. The most common definition of media literacy in the United States is "the ability to access, evaluate, analyze, and produce media in all forms" (Aufderheide, 2003).

2. *Youth Media in Nigeria* outlines Dr. Lee Rother's experiences in western Nigeria as he shared media literacy information with Nigerian youth and their teachers. More information on his visit can be downloaded at http://www.educationbeyondborders.org/profile/LeeRotherPhD

held July 30 & 31, 2008, in Abuja, Nigeria's capital city" (Nigerian Village Square, 2008).

A Media Institute for Children and Youth in Nigeria

The Center for Media Literacy is a project of the Youth Media & Communication Initiative (YMCI), an international nonprofit media organization dedicated to children and media. YMCI is registered in Nigeria, the United Kingdom, and Canada. Some of its partners include the British Council, the National Film & Video Censors Board, UNICEF, Ministry of Youth Development, and the Institute for Advancement of Journalism. The aim of YMCI "is to train children and youth, using media, as agents for . . . social change; to develop their capacity for effective communication and self-expression so that they can positively impact their schools, communities and society" (World Computer Exchange, 2010).

The Center for Media Literacy works with the Nigeria Union of Teachers (NUT) to coordinate an integrated media literacy project in schools focused on making students more empowered media consumers by not only helping them make decisions about what they listen to or watch without adult supervision but by also helping them to produce their own media (World Computer Exchange, 2010). YMCI also produces training manuals used by teachers to help their students understand and use the media and trains teachers in basic media literacy concepts and technology and assists them in developing lesson plans to introduce media education into some of their core subjects (World Computer Exchange, 2010).

The African Center for Media Literacy

The African Center for Media Literacy (ACML) is another organized media literacy program that "seeks to raise awareness among children, teachers, adults, parents and policy makers of children's rights and the value of children's participation in community and national development."[3] Its founder, Chido Onumah, is a Nigerian freelance journalist who has been involved for almost a decade in media training for professional journalists as well as promoting media literacy in Nigeria. As part of the 2011 International Youth Day, ACML organized a presentation titled "Social Media & the African Youth, Agenda for the 21st Century." More than 150 students, members

---

3. This information was derived from an interview with Chido Onumah, by Paul Mihailidis, and can be retrieved from http://www.africmil.org/publications/CIMA-Media_Literacy_Youth-Report.pdf, p. 10

of the National Youth Service Corps, representatives of government departments, NGO representatives, members of the civil society, and media professionals were in attendance" (Africmil, 2011).

II. Notable Individuals in National Media Literacy Programs

Martins Akpan and Chido Onumah are the two foremost proponents of media literacy in Nigeria. Dr. Martins Akpan, co-coordinator of Teens Resources Center and producer of a community cable program titled TEENWORLD on MCTV, can be reached at imaobongspecial@yahoo.com Chido Onumah, coordinator of the YMCI and founder of the ACML, can be reached at conumah@hotmail.com

Conclusion

Although media literacy education in Nigeria is currently confined to a few areas within the country, significant progress has been made in recent years. With support from media, literacy educators such as Lee Rother, Martins Akpan, and Chido Onumah, and with cooperation from the Nigerian government and media literacy organizations in the United States, Canada, and Europe, media literacy in Nigeria is becoming a reality.

However, although the idea of promoting media literacy is a noble one, the country must continue to reduce its rate of illiteracy. UNESCO has provided much support in this domain, and this partnership must continue to make media literacy achievable. Educators must have adequate training to teach media literacy. Resources must be made available to schools, the private sector, and communities to make the dream of media literacy education come true. A framework for measuring media literacy outcomes must be established. There is hope for Nigeria to excel in the field of media literacy, but it must intensify its efforts to find new initiatives and support that would amalgamate what is already in motion.

References

Africmil. (2011). "Abuja Declaration on Social Media & the African Youth: 2011 International Youth Day." *Youthlink: Journal of the African Centre for Media & Information Literacy*. Retrieved from http://www.africmil.org/publications/ Abuja%20Declaration%20on%20Social%20Media%

Aufderheide, P. (2003). *Aspen Media Literacy Conference Report—Part 2: Proceedings and Next Steps*. Queenstown, MD: Aspen Institute. Retrieved from http:// www.medialit.org/reading_room/article356.html

Maps of the World. (2011). *Education in Nigeria*. Retrieved from http://www.maps ofworld.com/nigeria/education/

Nigeria: Geography. (2011). Retrieved from *Infoplease—All the Knowledge You Need*: http://www.infoplease.com/ipa/A0107847.html?pageno=1

Nigeria: Languages, Ethnicity/Race. (2011). Retrieved from *Infoplease—All the Knowledge You Need*: http://www.infoplease.com/ipa/A0107847.html?pageno=7

Nigerian Village Square. (2008). *The Benefits of Media Literacy*. Retrieved from http://www.nigeriavillagesquare.com/articles/chido-onumah/the-benefits-of -media-literacy-2.html

Silverblatt, A. (2001). *Media Literacy: Keys to Interpreting Media Messages*. Westport, CT: Praeger.

United Nations Educational, Scientific and Cultural Organization. (2011a). *Education: History*. (2011). Retrieved from http://www.unesco.org/new/en/education/ themes/leading-the-international-agenda/education-for-all/the-efa-movement

World Computer Exchange. (2010). *The Center for Media Literacy*. Retrieved from http:// www.worldcomputerexchange.org/media-institute-children-and-youth-nigeria

Russia

Prepared by Professor Dr. Alexander Fedorov

I. Overview

Status of Media Literacy Within Russia

The first weak attempts of media literacy in Russia (film and press education in schools and culture centers) were in the 1910s, but the 1920s through 1950s was an example of strict ideological (Communist) control in Russia. The social and cultural situation in Russia in the 1960s and 1970s provided grounds for a great interest in cinema among schoolchildren and teachers. At the time, video and PCs were only dreamt of in science fiction novels. Films were seldom shown on TV (in fact, there was only one and, later, two TV channels). Therefore, cinemas were crowded (statistics showed that, on average, a person went to the cinema about 18 times a year), and schoolchildren went to the movies much more often than adults. For many Russians, the screen was the only window into the world that could cut through the still-thick "iron curtain." Ideological pressure was strong in Russia 1960s and 1970s, but not so deadly strong as under Stalin's regime. And post-Stalinist times were the period of a new wave of movement for media literacy in an aesthetic paradigm.

Curricula for film education for schools and pedagogical institutes were written in the 1960s and 1970s. These programs were significantly different from programs for many other subjects; their authors avoided a strict regulation and a dogmatic approach. It was emphasized in these curricula that communication with art should be enjoyable. The objective of cinema pedagogy was to widen the spiritual and cultural world of schoolchildren and to develop their personalities. Classes of media educators could be described as a dialogue. An old "teacher-centered" scheme, in which a teacher is a source of knowledge and a pupil is its receiver, was broken. Both pupils and teachers got a bigger field for creativity, improvisation, and game activities. Games are treated as kind of a reality model.

In the early 1980s, there was a big experiment of introducing film education into the primary and middle school curriculum in some Moscow schools. Similar experiments on media education (on the press, cinema, and TV materials) were conducted in summer children centers such as Ocean and Orlyonok. As for the universities, lectures and practical classes for future teachers were held. Some Institutes of Teachers' Professional Development (in Moscow, Kurgan, Tver, and Taganrog) also made a contribution to media education. Seminars and workshops on teaching cinema were conducted. Some universities integrated media education into courses of the aesthetic education.

By the end of the 1980s, the vigorous development of video began to change the work of clubs and amateur children's studios. VCRs and video cameras were used more and more often for making and showing films. School TV studios were emerging. In 1990, the Association of Young Journalists was established. In 1998, the Council for Film Education was transformed into the Association for Film and Media Education.

At the same time, as already mentioned, media education in Russia encountered numerous difficulties (ideological, financial, technical, etc.). From the 1920s through 1980s, the political and censorship control and poor technical equipment in schools and higher educational institutions hindered media education movement. In the 1990s, media teachers were granted freedom and independence to develop programs and their practical implementation, but they lacked financial and technical support. Many Russian schools and colleges in the 1990s didn't have enough money for teachers' salary, not to mention audiovisual equipment. Moreover, still only a few universities (e.g., Taganrog State Pedagogical Institute) were preparing future teachers for the media education of pupils.

By the 2000s, the number of secondary and higher-education Russian institutions training professionals in media had grown significantly. In addition to VGIK (Russian State Institute of Cinematography), the School for Script Writers and Film Directors, and the Russian Institute of Professional Development in the Field of Film, today there are St. Petersburg State University of Film and Television; Film-Video Colleges in Sergeev Posad and St. Petersburg; and film/television colleges in Irkutsk, Sovetsk, and Rostov-on-Don. Professional media education is included into the curriculum of St. Petersburg State Academy of Culture, St. Petersburg Academy of Theatre Art, Institute of Professional Development of TV & Radio Specialists (Moscow), Independent School of Cinema and Television (Moscow), Grymov's School of Advertising, Institute of Modern Art (Moscow), New Humanities University (Moscow), and several schools of animation.

In February 2000, Alexander Fedorov and colleagues created the Russian bilingual (Russian-English) Internet site on media education: http://www.medialiteracy.boom.ru (later http://www.edu.of.ru/mediaeducation and http://edu.of.ru/medialibrary).

Perhaps the most important event in media education development in Russia was the registration of the new specialization (minor) for pedagogical universities—Media Education (N 03.13.30) in 2002. Since then, this specialization has included the education process in Anton Chehkov Taganrog State Pedagogical Institute (head of this media educational project is Professor A. Fedorov; media educators are I. Chelysheva, E. Murukina, N. Ryzhykh, V. Kolesnichenko, D. Grigorova, among others).

The media educators team (headed by Alexander Fedorov) from Anton Chehkov Taganrog State Pedagogical Institute has published some 50 monographs since 1994, as well as textbooks and more than 600 articles about media education and media literacy. This team also received research grants for research on media education topics from many Russian and foreign foundations, including the Foundation of the President of the Russian Federation, Russian Foundation for Humanities, Foundation of Russian Ministry of Education, Kennan Institute (United States), IREX (United States), MacArthur Foundation (United States), Open Society Institute (Soros Foundation, United States), DAAD (Germany), Fulbright Foundation (United States), and others.

In 2004, UNESCO and South Urals Media Education Center conducted the interregional roundtable discussion "Media Education: Problems and Prospects" in Chelyabinsk. The participants discussed the concept and notions of media education and educational standards in this area and mapped out the ways of concerted efforts to be made by national and regional mass media in the coverage of media education problems. According to the participants, media education is a way of shaping national information and education policies and promoting information literacy, media culture of personality, and civil society. Media education problems were considered in the reports. Media education was proclaimed as one of ways of the development of a national information and educational policy, social integration, and media literacy.

The final document of the roundtable included suggestions to introduce a major specialty, media education, with a qualification of "media educator" for universities of Russia; to develop the plan of effective realization of media education in various regions of the Russian Federation; to create a databank about forms and methods of media education activities with the purpose of the analysis and generalization of experience; to publish an *Encyclopedia of Media and Media Education*; and to support the regular release of the *Media Education Journal*.

Media education literacy in Russia is not a required subject (with the exception of some secondary schools used as an experimental field and media-orientated universities and faculties). Thus, there is no national curriculum for media literacy in schools and no official standards or guidelines.

Many Russian teachers still confuse media education with using media as a technical aid. Media language is seldom a topic in its own right. Only a few school principals encourage the integration of media education or support teachers' initiative. In some Russian schools, however, media literacy education is integrated across the curriculum into Informatics (ICT, or Internet and computer application lessons), language and literature, arts, or science. Another variant is an optional autonomous media education course.

There are many local media education literacy programs in Russia for schools, universities, and culture centers. Students are expected to learn about media agencies, media languages, media audiences, media representations, media technologies, and other key aspects of media education and the history of media culture. The full texts of these programs are published on the Web at Russian Open Media Education Library: http://edu.of.ru/medialibrary

National Media Literacy Programs

- Educational program for high schools elective course: Media Education, Media Literacy, Media Competence
- Educational program for high schools elective course: Basics of Media Literacy Education
- Training Program elective course for high schools: Development of Critical Thinking in the Process of Media Education
- High school elective course: History of Media Culture
- Theories of Media and Media Literacy Education program (university level).
- History of Media Literacy Education program (university level)
- The History of Media Education in Russia program (university level)
- Media Education and Media in foreign countries program (university level)
- Fundamentals of Media Competence program (university level)
- Technology of Media Education in schools and universities program (university level)

II. Notable Media Literacy Organizations

Russian Association for Film and Media Education
http://edu.of.ru/mediaeducation
http://edu.of.ru/medialibrary

http://www.medialiteracy.boom.ru

http://www.mediaeducation.boom.ru

Scope of organization or program: Today there are about 300 members of the Russian Association for Film & Media Education, including primary- and secondary-level schoolteachers; high school, university, college, and lyceum teachers and professors; leaders of film clubs; journalists, etc. The Russian Association for Film & Media Education includes also members of the Laboratories of Screen Arts and Media Education (Russian Academy of Education, Moscow). The main directions of the Association's work are integration of media literacy courses in school and universities, development of school and university curricula, teacher training programs, conferences and seminars, publications, research, and maintaining Web resources on media education.

Location: This all-Russian organization has a central office in Moscow.

E-mail: mediashkola@rambler.ru

Targeted audience for this program: students (in school and universities), parents, teachers, university educators, film clubs audience, journalists, etc.

YNPRESS Agency (Young Press Agency)

http://www.ynpress.com

Scope of organization or program: the main directions of the YNPRESS Agency's work are development of the young student journalists' circle in schools and universities and in the local societies in the Russian regions; integration of media (press) literacy courses in school and universities; development of students and teacher training programs, conferences and seminars, and publications; and maintaining Web resources.

Location: This all-Russian organization has a central office in Moscow.

Targeted audience for this program: students (in school and universities), teachers, university educators, young people, journalists.

Anton Chekhov State Pedagogical Institute

http://www.tgpi.ru

Scope of organization or program: this is the first Russian pedagogical university with specialization for pedagogical universities—Media Education (N 03.13.30). Since 2002, this specialization includes an education program at Anton Chehkov Taganrog State Pedagogical Institute (head of this media educational project is professor A. Fedorov; media educators: I. Chelysheva, E. Murukina, N. Ryzhykh, V. Kolesnichenko, D. Grigorova, and others). The main directions of media education specialization work are integration of media literacy courses, development of school and university curricula, teacher training programs, conferences and seminars, publications, research, and maintaining Web resources on media literacy education.

Location: Taganrog, Russia.

Targeted audience for this program: university students (including PhD students), teachers, university educators.

III. Notable Individuals in National Media Literacy Programs

Professor Dr. Alexander Fedorov

President of Russian Association for Film and Media Education, editor of *Media Education Journal* (Russia), pro-rector of Anton Chekhov Taganrog State Pedagogical Institute (Russia).

1954alex@mail.ru and mediashkola@rambler.ru

(8634) 601753

Taganrog State Pedagogical Institute, ul. Iniciativnaya, 48, Taganrog, 347936, Russia

Professor Dr. Alexander Fedorov holds an MA degree from Russian Institute of Cinematography (VGIK, 1983) and a PhD (1986) and an EdD (1993) with an emphasis in media education from the Russian Academy of Education (Moscow).

Since completing his degrees, he has been a guest professor and visiting senior research scholar at Central European University (Budapest, Hungary, 1998, 2006), Kassel University (Germany, 2000, grant DAAD), Humboldt University (Berlin, Germany, 2005, grant DAAD), Maison des sciences de l'homme (Paris, France, 2002, 2009, grants MSH), Kennan Institute (The Woodrow Wilson Center, Washington, DC, 2003), Mainz University (2010).

Fedorov received scientific grants/fellowships from Federal Target Program of the Russian Ministry of Education and Science (2010–2012), Program of the Russian Ministry of Education and Science "Development of Science University Potential" (2006–2008), Russian President Program for Leading Scientific Schools (2003–2005), MacArthur Foundation (United States, 1997, 2003–2004), Russian Foundation for Humanities (1999–2010); President of Russian Federation Cultural Foundation (2002), The Russian Ministry of Education The Program "Russian Universities" (2002); Soros Foundation (United States): (1) Research Support Scheme (2000–2002); (2) Program "Civil Society" (1998–1999); (3) HESP-CDC—Course Development Competition (1998); Education Program for the best text of university lectures (1997); Switzerland Scientific Foundation (2000); and Russian Ministry of Education: research in humanities area (1997–2000).

He has been a speaker at numerous international media and media education/literacy conferences: World United Nation Forum "Alliance of Civilizations" (Media Literacy Section, Madrid, 2008), Council of Europe Conference "Media Literacy" (Graz, December 2007), International Media Literacy Conference (Prague, April 2007), UNESCO Media Education Conference (Paris, June, 2007), Information Technologies International Conference (Moscow, May, 2007), International Conference E-Citizen (Moscow, February 2006), UNESCO Conference on the Information Society (St. Petersburg, May, 2005), Conference of Association for Media and Technology in Education, Concordia University (Montreal, Canada, May, 2003), National Media Education Conference "Literacy & Liberty" (AMLA: Alliance for Media Literate America; Baltimore, Maryland, June, 2003), World Congress "Toys, Games and Media," University of London, Institute of Education (London, August 2002), The Council of Europe: Hearing on Internet Literacy (Strasbourg, France, March 2002), 3rd World Summit on Media for Children (Thessaloniki, Greece, March 2001), International Council for Educational Media ICEM-CIME Conference "Pedagogy and Media" (Geneva, Switzerland, November 2000), World Summit 2000: Children, Youth and the Media—Beyond the Millennium (Toronto, Canada, May 2000), AGORA European Children's' Television Center Summit (Thessaloniki, Greece, June, 1999), Educating for the Media and the Digital Age: UNESCO International Conference (Vienna, Austria, UNESCO, April 1999), World Media Education/Literacy Summit (Sao-Paulo, Brazil, May 1998), Media & Science Forum (Montreal, Canada, October 1997), Youth and the Media, Tomorrow: UNESCO International Conference (Paris, UNESCO, April 1997), and many others. He is the author of 500 articles and 30 books about media culture, media education, and literacy.

Professor Dr. Alexander Sharikov

Professor of National Research University, The Higher School of Economics (Russia), member of Russian Association for Film and Media Education. sharikov@mail.ru
National Research University, The Higher School of Economics, Myasnitskaya, 20, 1010200, Moscow, Russia.

Professor Dr. Alexander Sharikov graduated from Moscow State Pedagogical Institute (1973); PhD (1989), member of the Association of Film & Media education (Russia), GEAR (Group of European Audience Recearch), EAAME (European Association of Audiovisual Media Education), NTC (National Telemedium Council, US), Russian Society of Sociologists, International Union of Journalists, and others. After finishing graduate school, he worked as a researcher in the laboratory of Screen Arts, Russian Academy of Education. From 1990 to 1992, Sharikov headed the laboratory of interactive tutorials complexes, Institute of Learning, Russian Academy of Education. He taught/read the series of lectures in the universities (Moscow State University, Russian Academy of Civil Service, State University of Management, etc.). With the first half of 1990 to December 2002, led by the sociological service of the Russian Broadcasting Company (RTR). Then (until February 2005) he headed the department of sociology of regional TV Video International Analytical Center (Moscow).

He is the author of more than 100 scientific publications on various aspects of mass media, including books, encyclopedia articles, articles in academic journals, and other published articles.

He was invited as an expert on electronic media audience and media education by organizations such as UNESCO, UNICEF, the Council of Europe, the European Audiovisual Observatory, the Office of the President of the Russian Federation, Russian State Duma, Federation Council, and others in 2000, and delivered a series of lectures in Sorbonne (Paris).

He also has experience in journalism in the press and on radio. In particular, in 1992, he led the category "Children and the Media" in the psychological-pedagogical journal *Master*, and in 1995–1997 led the author's program *The Spectrum of Opinions* on Radio Russia. He has contributed numerous articles to newspapers and professional journals on the subjects of television, radio, and media education.

Sharikov has published in numerous academic anthologies on media and media education in Russian (*Master*, *World of Russia*, *Elementary School*, *Education*, *Psychological Journal*, *Family and School*, *Sociological Research/Socis*, *Media Education*, etc.) and foreign journals (*Screen*, etc.). He has participated in many international conferences on issues of media and media education (France, Spain, Germany, United Kingdom, etc.).

Professor Dr. Oleg Baranov

Professor of Tver State University (Russia), member of Russian Association for Film and Media Education.
mediashkola@rambler.ru
Tver State University, Tver, Russia

Professor Dr. Oleg Baranov was the permanent head of the film club at a boarding school from 1957 to 1971; he received his PhD in 1968. He worked at the same school as a teacher in charge of the department and was later dean of the faculty at Tver State Pedagogical University. Currently, he teaches in Tver school number 14 (where he is the deputy director for scientific work and has a large-scale experiment on aesthetic media education) and at the Tver State University. He is the author of works on film education for students in school and youth cinema clubs, as well as training aids for pedagogical institutes.

He has published more than 70 works, including a book on film education.

Professor Oleg Baranov has presented on film and aesthetic education for more than 40 scientific conferences.

Dr. Irina Chelysheva

Head of the Sociocultural Department of Anton Chekhov Taganrog State Pedagogical Institute (Russia), member of Russian Association for Film and Media Education
ichelysheva@mail.ru
(8634) 601753
Taganrog State Pedagogical Institute, ul. Iniciativnaya, 48, Taganrog, 347936, Russia

Dr. Chelysheva graduated from the Anton Chekhov Taganrog State Pedagogical Institute (Russia, 1987); PhD (2002); associate professor (2006). For many years, she worked as a schoolteacher. Since 1999, she teaches at the Faculty of Social Pedagogy of Anton Chekhov Taganrog State Pedagogical Institute.

She was the head of Media Education Project Grants of Russian Foundation for the Humanities (2008, 2011), Central European University (Budapest, 2009–2010). She was a member of research teams for grants of the Russian State Research Foundation (2001–2012), Program "Universities of Russia" (2002–2003), the Presidential Program "Leading Scientific Schools of Russian Federation" (2003–2005), the "Centers for Advanced Studies in the Social Sciences" (2004–2005), the Development of Scientific Potential of Higher Education program (2006–2008), Ministry of Education and Science of the Russian Federation, the media education project for the Federal Target Program "Research and Educational Research Frames" (2010–2012). She received third place in the all-Russia competition, Best Book on Communication Science and Education (Media Education category, 2008). The main theme of her research and teaching topics is the history, theory, and methods of media education in Russia. She is the author of several publications on media education in scientific collections and educational programs for schools. She has published in the following journals: *Further Education, Higher Education in Russia, Art and Education, Journalism and Media Market, Media Education,* and *Innovations in Education, Distance and Virtual Learning*).

Dr. Chelyshevas has presented at media education conferences (including conferences in Hungary, Poland, and Estonia).

Dr. Anastasia Levitskaya

Associate Professor of Taganrog Institute of Management and Economics (Russia), PhD (2001), member of the Russian Association of Film and Media Education.
nana77@mail.ru
Taganrog Institute of Management and Economics, Petrovskaya, 45, Taganrog, 347900, Russia

Dr. Levitskaya studied in the United States with support from an FSA (Freedom Support Act, 1994/95) grant. She graduated from the Faculty of Foreign Languages of Anton Chekhov Taganrog State Pedagogical Institute (1999). Since 2004, she has been an associate professor of Taganrog Institute of Management and Economics.

Levitskaya has received research grants from Fulbright (2003), the Russian Humanitarian Foundation (2011), the Centers for Advanced Studies in Social Sciences (2003–2005), and DAAD (2006). She received second place in the all-Russia competition, Best Book on Communication Science and Education (Media Education category).

She is the member of research teams for grants of the Russian State Research Foundation (2001–2012), Program "Universities of Russia" (2002–2003), the Presidential Program "Leading Scientific Schools of the Russian Federation" (2003–2005), the target program "Development of Scientific Potential of Higher School" (2006–2008), Ministry of Education and Science of the Russian Federation, "the Federal Target Program," and the Scientific and Pedagogical Personnel program (2010–2012).

She has published on media education since 1995 in journals such as *Alma Mater. Bulletin of Higher Education*; *Bulletin of the Russian Humanitarian Foundation*; *Distance and Virtual Learning*; *Innovation in Education*; *Art and Education*; *Media Education*; *Education, Family and School* (United States and Canada), *Bradley Herald* (United States), *Media i Skolen* (Norway), etc.

The main theme of her publications is an analysis of media education in English-speaking countries, advertising, mass communication, and teaching English in high schools .

In autumn 2000, with support from Freedom Support Act Future Leaders Grant Program (United States) for FSA/FLEX Alumni she organized a seminar on media education for students of Pedagogical Institute. In 2003–2004, she was engaged in research activities at the University of Central Florida (Orlando); in 2006, at Humboldt University (Berlin, Germany); and in 2009–2010, the Central European University (Budapest). She has participated in various research and teaching conferences (London, 2002; Orlando, 2003, etc.).

Dr. Elena Bondarenko

Head of the Laboratory of Media Education, Russian Academy of Media Education, member of the Russian Association of Film and Media Education.
letty3@yandex.ru
Laboratory of media education, Russian Academy of Media Education, Pogodinskaya, 8, Moscow, Russia

Dr. Bondarenko graduated from the Russian Institute of Cinematography (1985); PhD (1987). She worked as a researcher in the Laboratory of Screen Arts Education, Russian Academy of Education. Since 2004, she has been the head of the Laboratory of Technical Training and Media Education of the Russian Academy of Education.

She is the winner of research grants from the Russian Humanitarian Science Foundation (2000–2002, 2004–2006), the Humanities in Russia program, and Open Society (1994). She was an organizer and training group leader at the Media 95 (Russia, United Kingdom) and the Media Education and the Problem of Educational Television (1996) seminars.

She has participated in conferences of the Russian Association of Film & Media Education and has been a guest lecturer at the Russian scientific school "Media Education and Media Competence" program (Taganrog, 2009). Currently her main research focus is the formation of media competence of adolescents. She is the author of numerous articles, manuals, and programs on film and media education. She has been published in the journals *Specialist*, *Education*, *Standards and Monitoring in Education*, among others.

Professor Dr. Alexander Korochensky

Dean of Faculty of Journalism, Belgorod State University (Russia); member of Russian Association for film and Media Education
prensa@yandex.ru
Faculty of Journalism, Belgorod State University (Russia), Belgorod, Russia

Professor Dr. Alexander Korochensky graduated from Rostov-on-Don State University (1977); PhD (2004). He is a professor and a member of the Russian Association of Film and Media Education and the Russian Union of Journalists.

Korochensky conducted research work and taught at several universities in the United States, Poland, Cuba, Egypt, and Finland. He has also led the school for young journalists.

Currently he teaches courses including the History of Foreign Journalism, Outstanding Foreign Journalists, Fundamentals of the Foreign Journalist, and "Media Criticism," among others. He is one of the founders of a Web site for media criticism and media education. He has published in numerous scientific journals and the Russian press (*Higher Education in Russia, Media Education*, etc.). He has also participated in many Russian and international conferences.

Thailand

Prepared and Translated into English by Yupa Saisanan Na Ayudhya

I. Overview

Introduction

Known as the Kingdom of Siam until 1932, Thailand is the only Southeast Asian nation that has never been colonized by the West. Historically, the kingdom was ruled by kings from different dynasties who had absolute powers and served as paternalistic figures for the people of the country.

Thailand survived Western imperialism during the 18th century. In that period, visionary kings helped modernize the country socially, economically, and politically. In 1932, a group of civil servants and army officers led a political reform and established a constitutional monarchy. Since then, there have been two more kings. The current king (King Bhumiphol) is the longest-reigning king in the world. He celebrated his 60th year on the throne in 2008 and is the most respected and trusted ruler in the Thai kingdom today.

"The media in Thailand is not as free as they are in the Western world. It is believed that over time the Constitution of 1997 will provide the legal framework for reform at all levels of the government and full civil rights protection. Until that time, the voice of Thailand's revered King Bhumibol remains the nation's final guarantor for civil rights" ("Press Reference Summary," http://www.pressreference.com/Sw-Ur/Thailand.html#b). Those are the words from an online resource that reports on freedom of the press and media landscape of countries around the world. Thailand has, however, managed to take a leading role in the area in media literacy movement and in media literacy education in Asia.

Because UNESCO Communications and Information Asia Pacific headquarters is located in Bangkok, Thailand has played a key role in spearheading the media and information literacy movement in Asia Pacific. Thailand hosted the First Media Literacy Conference on January 27–28, 2011. The conference was a joint effort of UNESCO, Bangkok, and leading NGOs that have been working in media literacy initiatives (such as Child Media

Program, Thai Health Promotion Foundation, Thai PBS, Media Monitors, and universities).

This focus is a major step toward a more democratic society. The primary objective of this conference is to produce policy recommendations on media literacy in Thailand that will then be proposed to the government, businesses, and social sectors. The secondary objective is to secure as many key actors' buy-ins as possible.

The turnout was beyond expectation, and the commitments were astonishing. This event marks an auspicious occasion for a new chapter in Thailand media history toward a knowledge society. It also serves as a concrete platform for media literacy communications to all levels of Thai society in the future.

The conference ended with an announcement of the official launch of The Media Literacy Network of Thailand (MLNT). A news release from UNESCO Bangkok confirms MLNT's missions as follows:

1. Support the educational policy to implement media literacy into curriculums in all educational levels and in the formal and nonformal education system.
2. Encourage the media organization to play a role in promoting media literacy among the public that will enhance the participation of the mainstream and nonmainstream on this issue
3. Use new media and social marketing strategy as a tool to raise awareness of the people on media literacy to create participatory and creative media literacy society.
4. Set up the strategic network development that will create highest impact through the participation of all stakeholders including business, public, and academic. (SeongHoon Yoo, UNESCO Bangkok)

Defining Media Literacy in Thailand

UNESCO Bangkok is playing a central organizing role in advancing media literacy agenda in Thailand and in Asia. Thailand has adopted the concept of "Media and Information Literacy" as defined by UNESCO. The mission of UNESCO carries the theme of "Empowerment of people through information and media literacy is an important prerequisite for fostering equitable access to information and knowledge, and building inclusive knowledge societies" (UNESCO).

UNESCO news released from Thailand's "First Media Literacy Conference" also confirms that media literacy is a critical thinking skill which will equip and enable individuals to analyze, interpret, and evaluate media messages and information and to make informed decisions in the 21th century.

II. Notable Media Literacy Organizations

Child Media Program (CMP)

http://childmedia.net

Child Media Program (CMP) or Sor Sor Yor (in Thai) is a leading NGO in Thailand committed to promote the production and dissemination of quality and ethical media targeting youth, families, and general public. CMP thrives to achieve this ultimate goal by working in collaboration with public and private sector, media corporations, production companies, local communities, families, and young children.

According to the latest information provided on CMP Web site, the following are its working objectives:

- Access to quality media in all channels
- Develop best practices of quality media for youth
- Work with youth media to create and produce quality media for society
- Generate awareness of the importance of media literacy
- Encourage media and information literacy education and advance this as a national development agenda ("About Child Media")

CMP implemented a three-year (2007–2009) comprehensive program to achieve the above objectives. Some of CMP's greatest achievements are as follows

1. Access to quality media (both mainstream and new media) helps to enhance active participation, contribution, and development of local communities at large, for example:
   a. ETV stations targeting young children and their families
   b. Local cable TV and Internet TV as additional means to reach this particular target group
   c. Radio networks for children in rural areas
   d. Increase distribution of children books
   e. Use of folk arts to create relevance
2. Develop best practices for quality media program by supporting projects and activities with quality contents, for example:
   a. Broadcasting programs and prints

    b. Multimedia programs and animation creation and production

    c. Production fund raising

    d. Legislation lobbying

3. Collaborative effort with youth media by creating a network of all stakeholders

    a. Youth Media Professionals Association

    b. Media seminars and workshops for children

    c. Curriculum development for teaching media literacy courses for children

    d. Award for excellency in production/creation of quality media for children

    e. Tax policy and time of day for kid programming

4. Generate awareness of an increasing importance for young children and their families to be media literate by creating a media literacy social network such as Media Monitors

    a. Media education for consumers

    b. Media Literacy Network for children, their families, and their societies

5. Media and information literacy as a national development agenda, for example:

    a. Fund for original creative work in child media

    b. Scholarships for green journalism studies

    c. Revive reading in community centers and libraries

In addition to these activities, CMP also sponsored the first study on "Media Literacy Education in Higher Education in Thailand" in 2011.

The survey was conducted by Assistant Professor Dr. Warach Karujit and Jhatjhavee Kongdee of the School of Communication Arts, Sripratum University during January–May 2011. There are two parts in this survey. Part One is a dipstick research initiative to measure availability of media literacy education in Thailand. Part Two is a qualitative research in which the researchers conduct in-depth interviews with two instructors from two universities who have been teaching a course in "Introduction to Media Literacy."

This is preliminary research designed to collect information on media literacy courses provided by both public and private universities nationwide in Thailand. These courses must use the term *media literacy* in the titles (discipline-based courses) but do not exclude the mention of *media literacy-related terminology* both in the titles and in the descriptions of the courses being examined (interdisciplinary-based courses).

It is apparent that media literacy education in Thailand is still at its infant stage. The survey confirms that only 5.1 percent of public universities and 7.1 percent of private universities which offer degrees in Communication Arts also offer "media literacy" courses.

Teaching of media literacy from an interdisciplinary perspective does exist. By examining the mentioned "media literacy-related terminology," the survey reveals a higher percentage (60.7 percent) of universities that offer courses of this nature. This percentage only reflects universities in the survey that offer degrees in communication arts.

However, some of these universities also offer media literacy–related courses in other schools such as School of Education and School of Journalism. Thus, these percentages will naturally increase (91.1 percent) because there are more inclusions than exclusions.

An in-depth interview of two instructors also confirms that there is an increasing interest in the topic, witnessed by increasing enrollments every academic year. However, they lack support from school administers to open additional sessions. Moreover, they lack course materials and relevant texts to achieve the course learning outcomes.

Thai Health Promotion Foundation(THPF)

http://www.thaihealth.or.th

Thai Health Promotion Foundation (THPF), or Sor Sor Sor (in Thai), has been the key financial supporter/partner for media literacy initiatives in Thailand. THPF is a governmental organization founded by the 2001 Wellness Act for Thais and is funded by 2 percent of yearly excise tax collected by the Ministry of Commerce.

THPF's vision is "Sustainable Health for Thai Citizens" ("About Thai Health" http://en.thaihealth.or.th). "Sustainable Health" is defined as a type of holistic health (physical, emotional, and mental well-being) of an individual who leads a quality and healthy lifestyle.

A three-pronged approach is applied to achieve the foundation's vision of sustainable health for all. Primarily, THPF is committed to create a *Knowledge Society* by providing research grants for studies in the field of health and wellness. Next, *Social Movement* is employed to generate excitement of this new concept of well-being and to invite new ideas to promote sustainable health among alliances and the general public.

The last piece is *Political Mobilization*. As a final piece and an effort to support application of quality and ethical media, outdated media rules and regulations are being reviewed to reflect this national agenda.

The World Health Organization (WHO) has praised THPF as an outstanding organization that works in health promotion using realistic plans and sustainable and innovative funding and that should be modeled by other lower- and middle-income countries in the region and in the world.

Notable accomplishments in the field of media literacy are as follows:

1. Implementation of a TV Rating System for appropriate age levels to be used in television programming in Thailand (2008)
2. Creation of a National Public Television and Broadcasting Organization in Thailand (Thai PBS, 2008)
3. A Cyber Crime Law (2010)

Thai PBS

http://www.thaipbs.or.th

Thai PBS, or Sor Sor Tor (in Thai), is the first public media (not for profit) in Thailand's history. Previously, broadcasting media were mainly under supervision of the central government, or under control of some army officials and society elites.

Thai PBS marks an important chapter toward a more democratic society whereby people have access to unbiased news and information and are capable of making well-informed decisions by themselves.

Thai PBS pledges to produce balanced and unbiased contents by representing cultural diversities and ethical journalism.

Some notable accomplishments are as follows:

1. The *Citizen Journalist* program is the first of its kind in Thailand media history where a story is told by people in first-person. They have a chance to tell their own story from their own perspective. It makes the story more compelling and relevant to the audience in general who have only been exposed to manufactured news stories. Thai PBS has invested time and funding to train more media-literate people using programs such as "Thai PBS Training for Thai Trainers"
2. The 2012 Asia Media Summit (AMS) was held in Bangkok on May 29–30, 2012. Thai PBS hosted this summit in collaboration with UNESCO, C&I office in Bangkok. The theme of this event was designed to be a follow-up on the First Media Literacy Conference of January 2011. However, the summit also extended and expanded media literacy dialogue all throughout the Asia Pacific region.

According to its Agenda, the summit examined issues, offered best practices, and identified building blocks to enable media to harness a strong public trust and create impact in today's society. "In the Asia Pacific, has media served as a positive force or stumbling block to development? Is its capacity to serve the ends of development limited by its structure, regulation, and culture? How can media engage more to serve the ends of development without risking professional and ethical standard as well as sustainability? Is public service broadcasting still a viable alternative to serve the public's needs and interests? How can social media improve media sustainability in the context of development?" (Asia Media Summit, Agenda http://www.apfedshowcase. net/node/164).

III. Notable Individuals in National Media Literacy Programs

UNESCO, C&I Office, Bangkok
http://www.unescobkk.org
Dr. Susan Ornager
Adviser for CI in Asia
s.ornager@unesco.org
Dararat Weerapong
Communication Specialist
d.weerapong@unesco.org

Child Media Programme (CMP)
http://childmedia.net
Khemporn Wirronrapun
Managing Director
dogkem47@yahoo.com

Thai Health Promotion Foundation (THPF)
http://www.thaihealth.or.th/
Dr. Krissada Ruengareerat, Executive Director

Thai PBS
http://www.thaipbs.or.th/
Anothai Udomsilp
Director of Institution Development, anothaiu@thaipbs.or.th

The Research Center for Communication and Development and Knowledge Management, Sukhothai Open Univeristy
http://www.ccdkm.org/
Dr. Kamonrat Intaratat
Director kamolratchim@hotmail.com

Yupa Saisanan Na Ayudhya
Webster University
470 East Lockwood Avenue
St. Louis, MO 63119
yupas91@webster.edu

Turkey

Prepared by Duygu Korhan Ulkumen

I. Overview

The Media Literacy Education Project started in 2007 in Turkey as a result of the cooperation between the Ministry of Education and the Supreme Board of Radio and Television (RTUK). Conferences and press meetings were organized to inform the public about the issue. Academics from several notable universities came together to conduct research related to the subject and prepared the media literacy curriculum to be chosen only once as an elective course for Grades 6, 7, and 8. The program was tested in pilot schools from Adana, Ankara, Erzurum, Istanbul, and Izmir. Teachers, working at the pilot schools, were educated by the Ministry of Education. Up to now, out of 4.5 million students studying in the sixth, seventh, and eighth grades, approximately 330,000 students have chosen this subject as an elective course.

The aims of the program, as stated by the Ministry of Education, can be listed as follows: fostering learning by eliciting interest, encouraging students to make observations and develop a critical eye, protecting them from the negative influence of the media and providing students with the responsibility to communicate with the environment. Thus, students will be able to look at media texts from different points of view, also access, analyze, evaluate, criticize and communicate the messages sent from the media. As a result, they will take part in society as a more active and constructive individual.

Although the program started being taught in pilot schools in 2007, it lost its momentum as a result of the decrease in the training programs and seminars for teachers. New schools show low interest in the program, and most of the pilot schools stopped following the curriculum because they are not qualified to teach the subject and do not have enough technological resources.

II. Notable Individuals in National Media Literacy Programs

Duygu Korhan Ulkumen

English Teacher, Uskudar American SEV
duygu_korhan@yahoo.com
Ozel Uskudar SEV Ilkogretim Okulu, Istanbul
+90 532 665 02 01

Author of the book *Media Literacy Programs in Australia, Canada, Britain and Turkey*. The aim of the research was to find the problematic aspects in the Turkish curriculum and offer proposals for change.

Professor Dr. Meral Uysal

Professor, Ankara University
muysal@education.ankara.edu.tr
Ankara Universitesi, Egitim Bilimleri Fakultesi, Ankara
+90 312 3633350/5013
Member of the Media Literacy Program Consultation Committee

Professor Dr. Mine Gencel Bek

Professor, Ankara University, Ankara
Ankara Universitesi Iletisim Fakultesi, Room: 312 06590 Cebeci, Ankara, Turkey
+90 312 319 77 14 / 262

Coauthor of the book *A Critical Evaluation of Media Literacy in Turkey and Suggestions for Developing Critical Media Literacy for Democratic Social Transformation and Citizenship*, published in Turkish.

Professor Dr. Mutlu Binark

Professor, Baskent University, Ankara
binark@baskent.edu.tr
Başkent Universitesi Iletisim Fakultesi, Ankara, Turkey
+90(312)2341010/2077

Co-author of the book *A Critical Evaluation of Media Literacy in Turkey and Suggestions for Developing Critical Media Literacy for Democratic Social Transformation and Citizenship* published in Turkish.

Assistant Professor Meliha Nurdan Öncel TasCkıran

Assistant Professor, Kocaeli University, Kocaeli

nurdan@kocaeli.edu.tr

Kocaeli Universitesi

İletisim Fakultesi

Kocaeli, Turkey

Author of the books *Introduction to Media Literacy* and *Media Literacy Press 1*, published in Turkish.

Ukraine

Prepared by Professor Dr. Alexander Fedorov

I. Overview

The development of media education literacy in Russia and Ukraine during the Soviet period practically coincide, and emerged in an integrated form as part of compulsory subjects as literature, history, Russian, Ukrainian, and other languages.

Media education classes (mainly on film and the press) were optional and dependent on teachers' enthusiasm about theory and methodology of both the dominant aesthetic and practical approaches. From the 1960s through the 1980s, Kiev was the most active environment for Ukrainian media educators with film discussion clubs, electives and required courses (aesthetic approach), and amateur film/photo/video studios, as well as school and university amateur newspapers and magazines (practical approach). In 1997, the *Ukrainian Pedagogical Dictionary* was published in Kiev. This interpretation of the term *media education*, in fact, repeats a similar definition from the *Russian Pedagogical Encyclopedia* (1993): the direction in pedagogy, acting for the study of schoolchildren and students and the laws of mass communication (press, television, radio, film, video, etc.). The main objectives of media education are to prepare a new generation for life in the modern information world and the perception of different information, to teach the audience to understand that information world, and to realize the consequences of its impact on the psyche. On the whole, the first half of the 1990s was not productive for Ukrainian media educators. Political and economic problems made it impossible to concentrate on the "secondary" lines of media education pedagogy, although some notable conferences and festivals were held (e.g., the National Association for Film and Media Education of Ukraine under the leadership of its president, Professor Dr. Oksana Musienko).

A new page in Ukrainian media education movement began in 1999, when the Lviv National University Institute of Ecology created the media ecology department under the direction of Professor Dr. Boros Potyatinik, who

941

cooperated with the U.S. media education associations and took a course to develop new approaches to media literacy education. Professor Dr. Potyatinik's team developed the "safety-defensive" approach against the negative impact of the media. Professor Dr. Potyatinik believed that "media education [in the] scientific and educational sphere aims to assist the individual in shaping the psychological protection from manipulation or exploitation by the media and develop/cultivate an information culture."

However, Web site materials and numerous roundtables and conferences, held under its auspices, show that the basic media literacy education also discusses such concepts as the semiotic, cultural studies, sociocultural concerns, and critical thinking. The Ukrainian version of media education, according to the Lviv-based approach, brought together not only educators but also psychologists, journalists, lawyers, and priests. The most complete view of the Lviv school of media ecology, media criticism, and media education is presented in the monograph by Boris Potyatinik, *Media: The Keys to Understanding* (2004). In particular, there is considerable attention paid not only to theories of media but also the problem of media violence and the consequences of its impact on underage audiences.

At the beginning of the 21st century, through the efforts of Professor Dr. Ganna Onkovich, the Institute for Higher Education Academy of Pedagogical Sciences of Ukraine declared itself a group of media educators. In his writings, Ganna Onkovich rightly notes that it is not necessary to limit the audience of media education [to] students only. Media literacy is also needed for adults. In addition, Ganna Onkovich reasonably draws attention to the need for independent media education. Onkovich places ideas of media didactic at the forefront of its theoretical concepts.

Head of the Laboratory of Psychology of Mass Communication and Media Education Institute of Social and Political Psychology of the Academy of Pedagogical Sciences of Ukraine, Dr. Lubov Naydonova developed a model of media culture, consisting of four interrelated parts: the *reaction* (search for information, reading/scanning, identification/recognition of media texts), *actualization* (assimilation, integration of new knowledge related to the media), *generation* (incubation, the creative conversion, the transformation of media knowledge and skills), and *use* (transfer of information, innovation, research in the field of media).

Following the ideas of the British scientist Len Masterman, Ukrainian scientists in recent years are closely associated with the development of media education and critical thinking. At the same time, recognizing the importance of an autonomous professional and mass media education, Ukrainian media educators increasingly explore the possibilities of an integrated media education—in particular, linguistic material—in the preparation of public relations specialists and similar fields.

However, the current Ukrainian media educators are alien to the national education system. They carefully analyze the Russian, German, French, American, British, and Canadian media education experience. In particular, the first translations of the work of Russian authors (Professor Dr. Alexander Fedorov) into the Ukrainian language were important.

Unfortunately, as far as research, Ukrainian media educators have received virtually no grant support from the Ministry of Education of Ukraine and Ukrainian state research funds, nor does the Ukrainian movement in media education have strong support from foreign funds. Lists of Ukrainian teachers' theses published from 1992 to 2011 as well as monographs and textbooks on media education topics are not very impressive because of this lack of support.

Media education literacy in Ukraine is not a required subject (with the exception of some secondary schools where it is an experimental field and in media-orientated universities and faculties). But Ukraine has an official national program for media literacy education in schools (the Academy of Pedagogical Sciences of Ukraine, 2011), and is attempting to develop media literacy standards or guidelines.

National Media Literacy Programs

There is now a national educational program for high schools called Media Education Literacy (2011). Some local media education literacy programs exist as well, created by Professor Dr. Ganna Onkovich, Professor Dr. Boris Potyatinik, and others.

II. Notable Media Literacy Organizations

Ukrainian Association for Film and Media Education

The members of this association are primary and secondary schoolteachers; high school, university, college, and lyceum teachers and professors; leaders of film clubs; journalists, etc. The main focus of the association's work is integration of film education and media literacy courses in school and universities, development of school and university curriculums, teacher training programs, conferences and seminars, publications, and research.

Location: All-Ukrainian organization with the central office in Kiev, Ukraine.

Targeted audience for this program: students (in school and universities), parents, teachers, university educators, journalists, etc.

Department of Media Ecology at Lviv National University

http://www.franko.lviv.ua/mediaeco/index.htm

The main focus of this program is integration of media literacy courses in school and universities, development of school and university curriculums, teacher training programs, conferences and seminars, publications, research, and maintaining Web resources on media education.

Location: Lviv, Ukraine

Targeted audience for this program: students (in school and universities), parents, teachers, university educators, journalists, etc.

Academy of Ukrainian Press

http://www.aup.com.ua

The main directions of media literacy education program of Academy of Ukrainian Press are integration of media literacy courses in school and universities, development of school and university curriculums; teacher training programs, conferences and seminars, publications, and research.

Location: Kiev, Ukraine

Targeted audience for this program: students (in school and universities), teachers, university educators, journalists, etc.

III. Notable Individuals in National Media Literacy Programs

Professor Dr. Ganna Onkovich

Head, Department of Theory and Methodology of Humanities Institute of Higher Education of the National Academy of Pedagogical Sciences of Ukraine (Kiev)

National Academy of Pedagogical Sciences of Ukraine (Kiev)

Ul Artema, 52a, Kiev, 04053, Ukraine

onkovich@gmail.com

Onkan@ukr.net,

Professor Dr. Ganna Onkovich is a well-known Ukrainian media educator and researcher in the field of media education who explores issues in media didactics (mainly on the material press) and directs graduate students. Onkovich is the author of numerous publications on the subject of media education and has participated in several international scientific conferences on the subject of media culture, journalism, and media education.

Professor Dr. Oksana Musienko

President of Association of Film and Media of Ukraine

Head of the Film Studies Department of Kyiv National University of Theater, Film and Television, National University of Theater, Film and Television, ul.Yaroslav val, 40, Kiev, Ukraine
http://academia.gov.ua/sites/Musiyenko/Musiyenko.htm
http://knutkt.kiev.ua/index.php?option=com_content&view=article&id=69&Itemid=69

Professor Dr. Oksana Musienko, Honored Artist of Ukraine, member of the Academy of Sciences of Ukraine, head of the Film Studies Department of Kiev National University of Theater, Film and Television, president of Association of Film and Media of Ukraine, member of the Union of Cinematographers of Ukraine. Laureate of the Union of Cinematographers of Ukraine, member of the Board of the Association of Film Critics of Ukraine, member of the expert committee of the Ministry of Culture and the Arts. Musienko graduated from Kiev University (1960). Since 1971, she has been teaching at the Kiev Institute, University of Theater, Film and Television. She is the author of several scientific papers and monographs on the subjects of cinema, media culture, and media education. She has participated in numerous national and international scientific conferences.

Professor Dr. Valery Ivanov

President of Academy of Ukrainian Press
Head of department and professor of Kiev National University
Academy of Ukrainian Press
26 Boulevard Lesi Ukrainky
Offices 705, 706
01133 Kyiv
http://www.aup.com.ua/
info@aup.com.ua

Professor Dr. Valery Ivanov is president of Academy of Ukrainian Press, head of department, and a professor at Kiev National University. He is the author of many books and articles about mass media theory and practice and an organizer of media education literacy seminars for Ukrainian teachers and educators.

Professor Dr. Lubov Naydenova

Deputy Director for Research of the Institute of Social Psychology
National Academy of Pedagogical Sciences of Ukraine,
National Academy of Pedagogical Sciences of Ukraine (Kiev),
Ul Artema, 52a, Kiev, 04053, Ukraine
mediasicolo@gmail.com

Professor Dr. Lubov Naydenova is deputy director for Research of the Institute of Social Psychology the National Academy of Pedagogical Sciences of Ukraine and head of psychology laboratory on adverse communication and media education. Naydenova is the author of several works on the subject of media education and has participated in scientific conferences on media culture and media literacy.

Professor Dr. Boris Potyatinik

Professor, Lviv University, and media educator
boryslav@iatp.org.ua,
boryslav@yahoo.com,
ekomedia@franko.lviv.ua

Professor Dr. Boris Potyatinik is a professor at Lviv University. From 1999 to 2009, he was director of the Media Ecology Department (Lviv, Ukraine). He is a researcher of media culture and amedia educator, as well as the author of several works on media education. He has participated in numerous scientific conferences.

THREAD 6

Media Literacy Resources (Web sites, Books, Videos, Articles)

The online environment provides a rich and fluid resource for media literacy information, case studies, educational materials, research, and discussion. Web sites, wikis, e-newsletters, blogs, Facebook pages, and Twitter threads devoted to relevant topics are developed and updated frequently, offering insights into the most current issues. Search engines and YouTube are excellent tools for navigating the most current resource materials available via the Internet.

The following alphabetical list of online resources, developed in January 2012, touches on the vast assortment of ever-changing materials and information available online via a variety of individuals, academics, organizations, and educational institutions. Inclusion here of these resources should not be construed as an endorsement but as a helpful starting place for those who are interested in learning more about media literacy and in finding materials for teaching others about the role of media in society.

Given the quick-paced evolution of the field of media communications, the threads focusing on media literacy Web sites, organizations, books, and digital materials are outdated almost as soon as the book is published. However, it is hoped that this information can serve as the basis of future research on these topics. Indeed, the author hopes that there might be ways to maintain currency of this thread into the future.

- **Action Coalition for Media Education (ACME)** (http://www.acme coalition.org). ACME emphasizes its independence from "any funding from Big Media" and describes itself as "an emerging global coalition run by and for media educators. . . . " ACME provides workshops, training, and institutes for children and adults, supports media reform and promotes "democratizing our media system through education and activism."
- **Center for Digital Democracy (CDD)** (http://www.democraticmedia .org). Consumer protection and privacy organization, "CDD has been at the forefront of research, public education, and advocacy on protecting consumers in the digital age. . . . CDD's public education programs are focused on informing consumers, policy makers, and the press about contemporary digital marketing issues, including its impact on public health, children and youth, and financial services."
- **Center for Media and Public Affairs (CMPA)** (http://cmpa.com/). At George Mason University; describes itself as "a nonpartisan research and educational organization which conducts scientific studies of news and entertainment media. CMPA's goal is to provide an empirical basis

for ongoing debates over media coverage and impact through well-documented, timely, and readable studies."

- **Center for Media Literacy** (http://www.medialit.org). Mission: "to help children and adults prepare for living and learning in a global media culture by translating media literacy research and theory into practical information, training and educational tools for teachers and youth leaders, parents and caregivers of children." Provides leadership, networking, and educational resources online. Reading room offers background articles.
- **Center for Social Media** (http://www.centerforsocialmedia.org). Sponsored by American University's School of Communications; analyzes media and tracks the evolution of documentary film and video.
- **Citizens for Media Literacy** (www.main.nc.us/cml). North Carolina-based organization links media literacy with citizenship.
- **County Fair/Media Matters for America** (http://mediamatters.org/blog). "Media blog featuring links to progressive media criticism from around the Web as well as original commentary, breaking news and rapid response updates to major media events from *Media Matters* senior fellows and other staff."
- **The Education Shop** (http://www.theeducationshop.com.au). Provides materials for teachers and students.
- **FAIR** (http://www.fair.org). National media watch group covers media bias and censorship. Advocates "greater diversity in the press" and "scrutinizes media practices." FAIR believes that structural reform is ultimately needed to break up the dominant media conglomerates, establish independent public broadcasting and promote strong non-profit sources of information.
- **Gateway Media Literacy Partners** (http://www.gmlpstl.org). Non-profit organization in the St. Louis region dedicated to promoting media literacy.
- **Journal of Media Literacy Education Blog** (http://jmle.org/blog). Includes articles from the journal and opportunity to comment on them.
- **Know Your Meme** (http://knowyourmeme.com). Researches and documents Internet memes and viral phenomena.
- **Media Awareness Network** (http://www.media-awareness.ca). MNet is a Canadian nonprofit organization that promotes media literacy and digital literacy; produces education and awareness programs and resources.
- **Media Education Foundation** (http://www.mediaed.org). Produces and distributes documentary films and educational resources "to inspire

critical thinking about the social, political, and cultural impact of American mass media."

- **Media Education Lab** (http://www.mediaeducationlab.com). At the University of Rhode Island; "advances media literacy education through research and community service." Emphasis on interdisciplinary scholarship.

- **Media Literacy.Com** (http://www.medialiteracy.com). Web-based portal for online media literacy education. Check out the portal's "Site of the Week Archive" page for selected links to online resources: http://www.medialiteracy.com/media-literacy-education-site-of-the-week-archive.htm

- **Media Literacy Clearinghouse** (http://www.frankwbaker.com). Developed by Frank Baker, nationally known media educator; assists K–12 educators by providing extensive hints, ideas, and topics related to teaching media literacy.

- **Media Literacy Project** (http://medialiteracyproject.org). Provides educational media literacy resources including multimedia presentations at conferences, workshops, and classrooms; offers media literacy curricula and action guides.

- **Media Matters for America** (http://mediamatters.org). Offers "progressive" viewpoint on media criticism: "A Web-based, not-for-profit, 501(c)(3) progressive research and information center dedicated to comprehensively monitoring, analyzing, and correcting conservative misinformation in the U.S. media."

- **The Media Research Center** (http://www.mrc.org/public/default.aspx). Offers "conservative" viewpoint on media criticism: "501(C)3 organization whose mission is to educate the public and media on bias in the media. . . . As 'America's Media Watchdog,' the MRC seeks to bring balance to the news media. Leaders of America's conservative movement have long believed that within the national news media a strident liberal bias existed that influenced the public's understanding of critical issues."

- **The Media Spot** (http://themediaspot.org). Promotes media literacy through the integration of digital media, the Internet, and other emerging technologies into existing curricula. Brings digital media production to educational settings. Provides resource for students and educators to tap into the larger media literacy movement.

- **MediaEdu** (http://media.edusites.co.uk). Provides resources for media studies teachers and students.

- **MissRepresentation.org** (http://www.missrepresentation.org). Web site spin-off of the film *Miss Representation*, which "exposes how

American youth are being sold the concept that women and girls'
value lies in their youth, beauty and sexuality." MissRepresentation.org
describes itself as "a call-to-action campaign that seeks to empower
women and girls to challenge limiting labels in order to realize their
potential."

- **Mountain Area Information Network** (http://main.nc.us). "MAIN is
a nonprofit community network using integrated media technologies
to expand the local public sphere and to support: participatory democracy, citizen access to media, independent journalism, local cultural and
artistic expression, locally-owned businesses, social and economic justice and environmental stewardship."

- **My Pop Studio** (http://www.mypopstudio.com). Offers creative play
opportunities to promote literacy about television, music, magazines,
and online media.

- **NAMLE (National Association for Media Literacy Education)**
(http://www.namle.net). Membership organization whose mission is
"to expand and improve the practice of media literacy education in the
United States." NAMLE brings together "media literacy practitioners,
educators, scholars, students, health care professionals, K-12 teachers,
community activists and media business professionals . . . to act as a key
force in bringing high quality media literacy education to all." Offers
catalog of media literacy teaching resources and the online *Journal of
Media Literacy Education.*

- **NAMLE Graduate Student Caucus Web site** (http://www.chrisboul-
ton.org/caucus/index.html). Online community for emerging media literacy scholars.

- **National Telemedia Council** (http://www.nationaltelemediacouncil
.org). National organization that promotes concept of media literacy;
publishes *Journal of Media Literacy.*

- **The News Literacy Project** (http://www.thenewsliteracyproject.org).
National educational program using journalists to help students think
more critically about information and become news literate. "The
project also aspires to elevate the mission of news literacy nationally
through classroom programs, digital media, public events and the news
media itself."

- **Newseum** (http://www.newseum.org/digital-classroom/default.aspx).
National news literacy Web site; provides digital media content in a
curriculum-based structure for K–12 and college classes. Content covers First Amendment issues.

- **PBS Kids Don't Buy It** (http://pbskids.org/dontbuyit). Includes educational games for kids and guides on media literacy for parents and teachers.
- **PBS MediaShift** (http://www.pbs.org/mediashift). Tracks "how social media, weblogs, podcasting, citizen journalism, wikis, news aggregators and online video are changing our media world." Includes commentary and reporting. "Not only is this a story of technology, but a story of changing mindset for journalists who must adjust to the increasing power of the 'people formerly known as the audience.'" Includes related group blog IdeaLab: http://www.pbs.org/idealab/
- **PBS Teachers Digital Media Literacy Resources** (http://www.pbs .org/teachers/digital-media-literacy/pbs-resources). Includes access to dozens of excellent PBS Web sites and TV programs dealing with both traditional and digital media literacy.
- **Pew Research Center's Internet & American Life Project** (www .pewinternet.org). Provides free data and analysis on the social impact of the Internet.
- **Poynter Institute** (http://www.poynter.org). Provides insights into issues related to news reporting. "School dedicated to teaching and inspiring journalists and media leaders. It promotes excellence and integrity in the practice of craft and in the practical leadership of successful businesses. It stands for a journalism that informs citizens and enlightens public discourse. It carries forward Nelson Poynter's belief in the value of independent journalism in the public interest."
- **Project Censored** (http://www.projectcensored.org). Student-faculty media research group; investigates news censorship. Includes annual lists of "Top Censored" news stories.
- **Project Look Sharp** (http://www.ithaca.edu/looksharp). Media literacy initiative of Ithaca College; provides materials for integration of media literacy into the classroom.
- **Project New Media Literacies** (http://newmedialiteracies.org). Project of the USC Annenberg School of Communications offering resources for teachers.
- **Project New Media Literacies Community Site** (http://projectnml .ning.com). Social network from Project New Media Literacies.
- **Reality Bites Back** (http://www.realitybitesbackbook.com/blog). Media literacy author and speaker Jennifer L. Posner's blog.
- **Robin Williams** (http://www.robwilliamsmedia.com). Web site of Rob Williams, essayist and speaker on media studies and media literacy.

- **SWAMP** (http://www.swamp.org). Texas-based Southwest Alternate Media Project (SWAMP) "promotes the creation and appreciation of film, video, and new media as art forms of a multicultural community."
- **Teaching Media Literacy** (http://teachingmedialiteracy.pbworks.com). University of Minnesota media literacy wiki.
- **Voices of Media Literacy** (on the Center for Media Literacy Web site at http://www.medialit.org/voices-media-literacy-international-pioneers-speak). Features collected interviews conducted in 2010–2011 with 20 media literacy pioneers representing the United Kingdom, Canada, Australia, and the United States "Their views not only shed light on the development of media literacy, but also on where they see the field evolving and their hopes for the future."
- **Webster University Media Literacy Site** (http://webster.edu/media literacy). Provides information on media literacy studies, careers, and research. Includes selected student and faculty research papers.
- **Women in Media & News (WIMN)** (http://www.wimnonline.org). National media analysis, education, and advocacy group.

Print and Electronic Media

Rapidly changing technology continues to dramatically affect how media is produced, distributed, and consumed throughout the world. As a result, books, textbooks, scholarly journals, periodicals, documentaries, and films proliferate to meet the latest challenges of learning and teaching media literacy for the 21st century.

The following lists, developed in January 2012, provide a small glimpse of available media literacy–related publications, films, and videos out of the hundreds available. Many organizations offer lists of current recommended titles on their Web site reading rooms, etc. One excellent resource is NAMLE (the National Association for Media Literacy Education) marketplace, which offers an updatable online list of selected media literacy books at http://namle.net/marketplace.

These lists offer a sample of the wide array of relevant print and electronic media available. Inclusion of these resources should not be construed as an endorsement but as a helpful starting place for those who are interested in learning more about media literacy or in finding materials for teaching others about the role of media in society.

TV Programs, Documentaries, and Podcasts
- **The Colbert Report** (http://www.colbertnation.com). Similar to *The Daily Show* in its satirical approach; focuses on political issues.

- **CounterSpin** (http://www.fair.org/index.php?page=5). Radio show/podcasts from FAIR.org "provides a critical examination of the major stories every week, and exposes what the mainstream media might have missed in their own coverage. . . . CounterSpin exposes and highlights biased and inaccurate news; censored stories; sexism, racism and homophobia in the news; the power of corporate influence; gaffes and goofs by leading TV pundits; TV news; narrow political spectrum; attacks on free speech; and more."
- **The Daily Show with Jon Stewart** (http://www.thedailyshow.com). Comedic approach to "fake news" and satirical commentary. Offers many segments relevant to media criticism.
- **IFC Media Project** (www.IFC.com), an American TV series that examines American news media. Episodes from the series currently may be viewed online on the IFC.com Web site.
- **Media Education Foundation** (http://www.mediaed.org/cgi-bin/commerce.cgi?display=user1). Online video store offers a variety of videos on media, culture and society.
- **PBS Frontline** (http://www.pbs.org/wgbh/pages/frontline/view). Includes numerous excellent online videos relevant to media literacy, with new topics added frequently. Sample: "News War," "Merchants of Cool," "The Persuaders," "Digital Nation."
- **TED: Ideas Worth Spreading** (http://www.ted.com). Nonprofit organization offering numerous excellent talks relevant to media literacy.

Periodicals, Professional Journals, and Scholarly Publications
- *American Journalism Review* (http:/www.ajr.org). National magazine that covers all aspects of print, television, radio, and online media. "AJR analyzes ethical dilemmas in the field and monitors the impact of technology on how journalism is practiced and on the final product." Published by the University of Maryland Foundation.
- *Columbia Journalism Review* (http://www.cjr.org). Media criticism publication of the Columbia University Graduate School of Journalism. Includes updated "Who Owns What" listing.
- *Gateway Journalism Review* (http://www.sjreview.org). Publication of Southern Illinois University Carbondale School of Journalism; media criticism articles published online and in print, covers Midwest.
- *International Journal of Learning and Media* (http://ijlm.net). Online journal and forum, subscription-based, explores relationship between media and learning.

- *Journal of Media Literacy* (http://journalofmedialiteracy.org/). Official publication of National Telemedia Council.
- *Journal of Media Literacy Education* (http://www.jmle.org). Peer-reviewed online journal.

Books and Textbooks

Baker, Frank. (2009). *Political Campaigns and Political Advertising: A Media Literacy Guide.* Santa Barbara, CA: Greenwood Press.

Baran, Stanley J., & Davis, D. K. (2012). *Mass Communication Theory: Foundations, Ferment, and Future* (6th ed.). Boston: Wadsworth.

Beach, Richard. (2007). *Teachingmedialiteracy.com: A Web-Linked Guide to Resources and Activities.* New York: Teachers College Press.

Berkowitz, Daniel A. (Ed.). (2011). *Cultural Meanings of News: A Text-Reader.* Los Angeles: Sage,.

Buckingham, D. (2003). *Media Education: Literacy, Learning and Contemporary Culture.* Cambridge, MA: Polity Press.

Buckingham, D. (2007). *Beyond Technology: Children's Learning in the Age of Digital Media.* Cambridge, MA: Polity Press.

Carey, James W. (1992). *Communication as Culture: Essays on Media and Society* (Reprint). New York: Routledge.

Considine, David M., & Haley, G. E. (1999). *Visual Messages: Integrating Imagery into Instruction. A Media Literacy Resource for Teachers* (2nd ed.). Englewood, CO: Teacher Ideas Press.

Croteau, David, Hoynes, W. & Milan, S. (2012). *Media/Society: Industries, Images and Audiences* (4th ed.). Los Angeles: SAGE.

Fisherkeller, J. (Ed.). (2011). *International Perspectives on Youth Media: Cultures of Production and Education.* New York: Peter Lang.

Fuller, Jack. (2010). *What Is Happening to News: The Information Explosion and the Crisis in Journalism.* Chicago: The University of Chicago Press.

Goodman, Steven. (2003). *Teaching Youth Media: A Critical Guide to Literacy, Video Production & Social Change.* New York: Teachers College Press.

Hobbs, Renee. (2011). *Digital and Media Literacy: Connecting Culture and Classroom.* Thousand Oaks, CA: Corwin.

Holtzman, Linda. (2000). *Media Messages: What Film, Television and Popular Music Teach Us about Race, Class, Gender and Sexual Orientation.* Armonk, NY: ME Sharpe.

Jenkins, Henry. (2006). *Fans, Bloggers and Gamers: Exploring Participatory Culture.* New York: New York University Press.

Jenkins, Henry. (2008). *Convergence Culture: Where Old and New Media Collide.* New York: New York University Press.

Jowett, Garth S. , & O'Donnell, V. (2012). *Propaganda & Persuasion* (5th ed.). Los Angeles: SAGE

Kilbourne, Jean. (2000). *Can't Buy My Love: How Advertising Changes the Way We Think and Feel.* Touchstone.

Klein, Naomi. (2000). *No Logo: Taking Aim at the Brand Bullies.* New York: Picador.

Lankshear, C., & Knobel, M. (Eds.). (2008). *Digital Literacies: Concepts, Policies and Practices.* New York: Peter Lang.

Livingstone, S. (2009). *Children and the Internet: Great Expectations and Challenging Realities.* Cambridge: Polity.

Masterman, Len. (1990). *Teaching the Media* (Reprint). New York: Routledge.

McLuhan, Marshall. (1994). *Understanding Media: The Extensions of Man.* (1st ed.) Cambridge, MA: MIT Press.

McLuhan, Marshall. (2011). *The Gutenberg Galaxy* (Centennial ed.). Toronto: University of Toronto Press.

Pozner, Jennifer. (2010). *Reality Bites Back: The Troubling Truth about Guilty Pleasure TV.* Seal Press.

Rapaille, Clotaire. (2006). *The Culture Code: An Ingenious Way to Understand Why People Around the World Live and Buy as They Do.* New York: Broadway Books.

Scheibe, C., & Rogow, F. (2010). *The Teacher's Guide to Media Literacy: Critical Thinking in a Multimedia World.* Thousand Oaks, CA: Corwin, 2011.

Silverblatt, Art. (2008). *Media Literacy: Keys to Interpreting Media Messages* (3rd ed.). Westport, CT: Praeger.

Silverblatt, Art. (2007). *Genre Studies in Mass Media: A Handbook.* Armonk, NY: M.E. Sharpe.

Tyner, Kathleen (Ed.). (1998). *Literacy in a Digital World.* New York: Erlbaum/Routledge.

Tyner, Kathleen. (2009). *Media Literacy: New Agendas in Communication.* New York: Routledge.

Index

About the Editor

Art Silverblatt, PhD, is Professor of Communications and Journalism at Webster University, St. Louis, Missouri. He earned his doctorate in 1980 from Michigan State University. He is the author of numerous books and articles, including *Media Literacy: Keys to Interpreting Media Messages* (Praeger, 1995, 2001, 2007), *The Dictionary of Media Literacy* (Greenwood Press, 1997), *Approaches to the Study of Media Literacy* (M.E. Sharpe, 1999, 2008), *International Communications: A Media Literacy Approach* (M.E. Sharpe, May 2004), *Approaches to Genre Study* (M.E. Sharpe, 2006), and *Handbook of Media Literacy* (ABC-CLIO, 2012). He is currently Vice President of the Gateway Media Literacy Partners (GMLP), a regional media literacy consortium.